THE "I" IN THE STORM

THE "I" IN THE STORM

A Study of Romans 7

by

Michael Paul Middendorf

Concordia Academic Press

A Division of

Concordia Publishing House

Saint Louis, Missouri

Unless otherwise noted, Scripture quotations are translations by the author.

The LaserHEBREW™ and LaserGREEK™ fonts used in this publication are available from Linguist's Software, Inc., P.O. Box 580, Edmonds, WA 98020-0580, telephone (206) 775-1130. E-Mail 75507 @compuserve.com

Copyright © 1997 Concordia Academic Press
3558 S. Jefferson Avenue, Saint Louis, MO 63118-3968
Manufactured in the United States of America

Library of Congress Cataloging-in-Publication Data

Middendorf, Michael Paul, 1959-
    The "I" in the storm: a study of Romans 7 / by Michael Paul Middendorf.
       p.   cm.
    ISBN 0-570-04261-5
    1. Bible. N. T. Romans VII—Criticism, interpretation, etc. 2. Bible. N. T. Romans VII—Theology. 3. Paul, the Apostle, Saint.
1. Title
BS2665.2.M5 1997
227 '. 106—dc21   97–27932

Acknowledgments

First of all, I wish to express gratitude to my advisor, Dr. James Voelz, for his many keen insights into this topic, as well as hermeneutic issues in general. I am also indebted to my readers, Dr. J. A. O. Preus, III, and Prof. Francis Rossow, and to all of the faculty members of Concordia Seminary, St. Louis. Thanks also to Concordia Publishing House and Dr. Dale Griffin for being gracious enough to pursue publishing this work. It is dedicated to my father, who "loved you into Greek," and my wife, Lana. Without her love, support, and labors in the classroom, it would not have been possible.

This work is a modified version of my 1990 thesis for a Doctor of Theology degree from Concordia Seminary, St. Louis, Missouri. Aside from some updating and condensing, the text is essentially the same. However, the material in the footnotes is shortened significantly and one appendix discussing textual criticism of Romans 7:24-25 is omitted.

Contents

Introduction

While describing the letters of "our beloved brother Paul," the third chapter of 2 Peter notes that some things in them are "hard to understand" (δυσνόητα; vv. 15-16). One of the passages in Paul's epistles which has proven most difficult to comprehend is the seventh chapter of Romans. According to Anders Nygren, this chapter "is perhaps the most discussed and fought over part of Romans. It presents us with one of the greatest problems in the New Testament."[1] These thoughts are echoed by John A. T. Robinson, who concisely summarizes the major issues of dispute as follows:

> More ink, I suppose, has been spilled over this passage of Romans than any other. Quite apart from the details of exegesis . . . two questions have agitated interpreters: (a) Does the use of the first person singular indicate genuine autobiography—or is it simply cast in the first person for vividness? and (b) Does it refer to the Christian or to the pre-Christian state—is the use of the present from verse 14 onwards again merely for vividness?[2]

The identification of the "I" in Romans 7 and a correct appraisal of the spiritual status of the "I" in verses 14-25 are not inconsequential questions over which one might simply "express resignation."[3] On the contrary, it is precisely because of such questions that Romans 7 has

---

[1] Anders Nygren, *Commentary on Romans,* tr. C. Rasmusssen (Philadelphia: Muhlenberg Press, 1949), 284.

[2] John A. T. Robinson, *Wrestling with Romans* (Philadelphia: The Westminster Press, 1979), 82. See also Jan Lambrecht, *The Wretched "I" and Its Liberation: Paul in Romans 7 and 8,* Louvain Theological & Pastoral Monographs, 14 (Grand Rapids: Eerdmans, 1992), 42; C. K. Barrett, *A Commentary on the Epistle to the Romans,* Black's New Testament Commentaries (London: Adam and Charles Black, 1962), 140

[3] As Ernst Käsemann, *Commentary on Romans,* tr. and ed. by G. Bromiley (Grand Rapids: Eerdmans Publishing, 1980), 196, suggests; citing U. Luz, *Geschichtverständnis des Paulus,* BEVT 49 (Munich: Christian Kaiser, 1968), 163. Käsemann, 196, properly concludes, "But this would mean dropping any understanding of a text which is obviously of supreme importance for Paul himself."

appropriately been called "one of the few really pivotal passages in Paul's theology; . . . our understanding of it will in large measure determine our understanding of Paul's theology as a whole."[4]

The purpose here is not merely "to spill more ink." Rather, it is to address approaches to and facets of these issues which have not yet been adequately considered or appreciated.[5] This study proposes to answer the questions surrounding the identity, the spiritual condition, and the purpose of the "I" in Romans 7 by utilizing a modern linguistic approach. Chapter Two will focus on the *semantic* content of the words in Romans 7 with an exegetical study. Distinct from semantics is the key question of *referent*. The referent of the "I" will be determined in Chapters Three and Four by an analysis of Paul's overall use of the first person singular and on the basis of Pauline theology. The *pragmatic* purpose or function of the "I" statements will be assessed in Chapter Five.

In order to provide the necessary background for this study, Chapter One will enumerate the various identifications of the "I" in Romans 7 which have been proposed. Both the complexity and the significance of the questions under consideration here are evidenced by the sheer number of answers which have been given to them. As a result, it will not be possible to conduct a complete historical survey.[6]

---

[4]James Dunn, "Rom. 7,14-25 in the Theology of Paul," *Theologische Zeitschrift* 31 (1975):257. He adds that this passage is particularly significant for our understanding of Paul's anthropology and soteriology.

[5]Despite the plethora of studies on Romans 7, many problems still remain to be resolved. For example, in his discussion of "The Complaint of the Enslaved (7:14-25)" and particularly regarding the "I" as depicted in verses 16 and 23, Käsemann concludes, 207, "It is astounding that the problem has not been sharply pinned down." His statement applies equally well to a variety of issues which surround the interpretation of this chapter.

[6]Werner Kümmel, *Römer 7 und die Bekehrung des Paulus* (Leipzig: Hinrichs, 1929); reprinted in *Römer 7 und das Bild des Menschen im Neuen Testament: Zwei Studien*, Theologische Bücherei, Neues Testament Band 53 (Munich: Christian Kaiser Verlag, 1974), 3, similarly concludes, "That total completeness is impossible, no expert in the area will deny" ("*Daß restlose Vollstandigkeit unmöglich ist, wird kein Kenner der Sachlage bestreiten*"). Maurice Goguel, *The Birth of Christianity*, tr. H. Snape (New York: Macmillan, 1954), 213, n. 5, states, "Chapter vii of the epistle to the Romans has been the subject of so many different interpretations that it is quite impossible to enumerate them." However, it is not proper to proceed, as he does, by limiting "myself to describing the one which I think should be adopted."

The overview provided here will concentrate upon the answers which have been given in contemporary scholarship.[7] Within this sphere the landmark study is Werner Kümmel's *Römer 7 und die Bekehrung des Paulus* published in 1929.[8] His basic conclusion is that the "I" in Romans 7:7-25 is a rhetorical figure of speech used to depict the non-Christian under the Law "whose condition is portrayed in the style of the first person and seen with the eyes of the Christian."[9] The impact of Kümmel's "epoch-making study" cannot be over-exaggerated.[10] Although not yet translated into

---

[7]For a review of the major interpretations advanced prior to this century, see the Appendix, "A Survey of Interpretations of the 'I' in Romans 7 in Sources Prior to 1900," below.

[8]The basic tenets of Kümmel's position were suggested earlier by William Wrede, *Paul*, tr. E. Lummis (Lexington, KY: American Theological Library Association Committee on Reprinting, 1962), 92-97, 144-47; on this point see Matthew Black, *Romans*, New Century Bible (London: Oliphants, 1973), 101; Stephen Westerholm, *Israel's Law and the Church's Faith* (Grand Rapids: Eerdmans Publishing, 1988), 16-22.

[9]Kümmel, *Das Bild des Menschen im Neuen Testament* (Zürich: Zwingli-Verlag, 1948); also reprinted in *Römer 7 und das Bild des Menschen im Neuen Testament: Zwei Studien*, Theologische Bücherei, Neues Testament Band 53 (Munich: Christian Kaiser Verlag, 1974), 186, "*und Röm. 7,14ff. auf den Nichtchristen bezogen, dessen Zustand in der Stilform des Ich geschildert und mit den Augen des Christen gesehen werde.*" Here Kümmel is speaking specifically of verses 14-25, but, as will be seen, he reaches the same conclusion in verses 7-13; see idem, *Römer 7 und die Bekehrung des Paulus*, 118,134. [Hereafter, his two separate studies will be denoted *Römer 7* and *Das Bild des Menschen*].

[10]Krister Stendahl, "The Apostle Paul and the Introspective Conscience of the West," *Harvard Theological Review*, 56 (1963):211, n. 19. Timo Laato, *Paul and Judaism* (Atlanta: Scholars Press, 1995), 110, states in reference to Kümmel's view, "Exegetes are almost unanimous. . . . They rightly uphold an interpretation of that kind as opinio communis." According to Günther Bornkamm, "Sin, Law and Death: An Exegetical Study of Romans 7," in *Early Christian Experience*, The New Testament Library, tr. P. Hammer (London: SCM Press, 1969), 89, "This understanding, already demanded by the context, has been carefully established and developed at all points by W. G. Kummel, and now only a few exegetes dispute it." Käsemann, 192, states that the correctness of the rhetorical interpretation "is generally agreed since Kümmel's monograph." Douglas Moo, "Israel and Paul in Romans 7:7-12," *New Testament Studies* 32 (1986):122, concedes that the interpretation of the ἐγώ as "a rhetorical figure . . . has been widely held since Kümmel's monograph." See also Ernst Gaugler, *Der Brief an die Römer*, vol. 1, Prophezei: Schweizerisches Bibelwerk für die Gemeinde (Zürich: Zwingli-Verlag, 1945), 1:240-41; Rudolf Schnackenburg, "Römer 7 im Zusammenhang des Römerbriefes," in *Jesus und Paulus*, ed. E. Ellis and E. Grässer (Göttingen: Vandenhoeck & Ruprecht, 1975), 239. Kümmel himself, *Das Bild des Menschen*, 186, asserts, "This view which I earlier propounded has found all sorts of agreement" ("*Diese von mir früher neu*

English, his interpretation "has come to be regarded as all but definitive"[11] and Gerd Theissen can now speak of it as "the classical solution to the problem."[12] Rudolf Bultmann, who adopted, further "developed and championed" Kümmel's interpretation,[13] concludes, "It seems to me that these questions [concerning the 'I' in Romans 7] have been adequately discussed and that there can be no doubt about the answer."[14] The sharpest evidence of Kümmel's influence is revealed in this statement by P. Demann:

> The traumatic condition which interpreters have desired to see in Rom. 7 and which has been linked with the painful failure of Paul in the observation of the law, is now relegated to the museum of exegetical absurdities.[15]

Due to the influence of Kümmel's monograph, his conclusions will be a major focus throughout this study.

The second chapter of this work will comprise an exegetical study of Romans 7 within its total context. It has been asserted that "dispute about a tense, a phrase, a half-verse in Rom. 7 means in fact dispute about the whole character of Paul's gospel."[16] In view of this, careful attention to each of these *semantic* matters is certainly warranted. An exegetical study is further deemed necessary because the text itself, rather than one's own theological presuppositions, must be allowed to

---

begründete Anschauung hat mancherlei Zustimmung gefunden"); he proceeds, 186-87, n. 59, to cite over 15 scholars who have supported his conclusion.

[11]Westerholm, 53.

[12]Gerd Theissen, *Psychological Aspects of Pauline Theology*, tr. J. Galvin (Philadelphia: Fortress Press, 1987), 234; even though Theissen himself supports a psychological interpretation, he concludes, 177, that in *Römer 7*, "Kümmel prepared an end to all efforts at psychological interpretation."

[13]So John Espy, "Paul's 'Robust Conscience' Re-Examined," *New Testament Studies* 31 (1985):161.

[14]Rudolf Bultmann, "Romans 7 and Paul's Anthropology," in *The Old and New Man in the Letters of Paul*, tr. K. Crim (Richmond, VA: John Knox Press, 1967), 33.

[15]P. Demann, "Moïse et la loi dans las Pensée de saint Paul," in *Moïse, l'homme de l'alliance* (1953), 229; cited from Franz Leenhardt, *The Epistle to the Romans*, tr. H. Knight (London: Lutterworth Press, 1961), 181, n. *.

[16]Dunn, "Rom. 7,14-25 in the Theology of Paul," 257.

dictate the proper resolution to the problems surrounding Paul's use of the first person singular in this chapter. Also, the debate concerning the identification of the "I" in 7:7-25 and the spiritual condition of that "I" in verses 14-25 must be considered within the overall structure of Paul's letter to the Romans.[17]

On the basis of this textual study, more specific attention will be directed toward the "I" in Romans 7. Chapter Three will seek to determine the identity or *referent* of the "I." Can Paul be the ἐγώ in Romans 7, or is the manner in which he depicts the "I" there inconsistent with the way in which he describes his own life elsewhere? If this appears to be the case, is it possible to reconcile and make sense of these varied "portrayals"? If not, is the "I" someone other than Paul, or is Kümmel correct in directing us toward a rhetorical interpretation? An investigation of the various ways in which Paul employs the first person singular in other contexts will help to answer the question so crucial to Romans 7. When Paul utilizes the first person singular in verses 7-25, to whom does he refer?

The other major contested issue surrounding Romans 7 concerns the spiritual state of the "I" in verses 14-25. This matter will be explored in Chapter Four. Is the "I" in verses 14-25 a believer, or is one led, and even forced, to conclude that Paul is characterizing the existence of a non-Christian? The answer to this question must be based upon the exegesis of Romans 7 as considered within the overall context of Paul's understanding of non-Christian existence and the Christian life.[18]

Paul very commonly uses the first person singular throughout his letters. Chapter Five will utilize the field of *pragmatics* to analyze the wide variety of functions his "I" statements are able to perform. It will then assert that Paul's *pragmatic* purpose in writing Romans 7 is to convey a crucial aspect of his theology.

---

[17]The importance of this is revealed by Käsemann, 192, who points out that one indication of the problematic nature of verses 7-25 is that they are "nearly always regarded as an excursus." He properly responds, 210, "Paul does not grant himself the luxury of digressions."

[18]This has been hinted at cursorily by various commentators, but none has proceeded to explore Paul's letters thoroughly with this specific question in mind. See, for example, Nygren, *Commentary on Romans*, 289-90; Kümmel, *Römer 7*, 135.

The goal of the method adopted here is to approach in a new way the deep division of interpretations surrounding Romans 7, "a division which has persisted from the earliest centuries until today."[19] It is also hoped that the effort needed to resolve these issues "does not make us lose sight. . . . of the significance of these Pauline passages for modern Christians."[20] These are truly desirable goals since, as Chapter Five will show, Paul's purpose in writing Romans 7 is to convey a crucial aspect of his theology.

---

[19]Dunn, "Rom. 7,14-25 in the Theology of Paul," 257.

[20]Lambrecht, *The Wretched "I" and Its Liberation*, 11.

Chapter One

Contemporary[1] Interpretations of the "I" in Romans 7:7-25

Romans 7:7-11

In his discussion in Romans 7:7-11 Paul utilizes the first person singular five times as a pronoun and three times as the subject of various verbs. He writes:

> (7) Therefore what will we say, the Law [is] sin? May it never be! But I would not have known sin except through the Law. For I also had not known desire except the Law was saying, "You shall not desire." (8) But sin, seizing the opportunity, through the commandment worked out every desire in me. For without the Law sin was dead. (9) And I was formerly living without the Law, but when the commandment came, sin came to life (10) and I died. The commandment which was for life, this very one has been found to result in death for me. (11) For sin, seizing its opportunity through the commandment, deceived me and through it killed [me].[2]

Who is this "I"? Attempts at identifying the "I" in these verses have resulted in the following interpretations:

Paul

Proponents

The most "natural way to understand" the first person singular is in an individual, personal, and autobiographical sense.[3] The "I" is Paul

---

[1]For a review of the major interpretations advanced prior to this century, see the Appendix, "A Survey of Interpretations of the 'I' in Romans 7 in Sources Prior to 1900," below.

[2]The translations given throughout this book are the author's own.

[3]J. I. Packer, "The 'Wretched Man' in Romans 7," in *Studia Evangelica*, vol. 2, ed.

himself. If Paul is recounting his own experience, what stage in his life is being described? The past tense, as well as the content of these verses, would seem to indicate that they depict events which occurred prior to Paul's conversion.[4] As Martin Franzmann suggests, "Paul is speaking of his Jewish past."[5]

A number of scholars have attempted to narrow down the time more specifically by focusing on verses 9-10a which state: "And I was formerly living without the Law, but when the commandment came, sin came to life and I died."[6] These words have been interpreted as a description of an actual series of events which occurred at the end of Paul's childhood when he entered adolescence or adulthood.

If Paul's former life "without the Law" (v. 9) is understood in a literal sense, this phrase is applied to the time prior to Paul's *bar mitzvah* which occurred around the age of 12 or 13.[7] C. K. Barrett

---

F. Cross (Berlin: Akademie-Verlag, 1964), 622. Recognized also by Werner Kümmel, *Römer 7 und die Bekehrung des Paulus* (Leipzig: Hinrichs, 1929); reprinted in *Römer 7 und das Bild des Menschen im Neuen Testament: Zwei Studien*, Theologische Bücherei, Neues Testament Band 53 (Munich: Christian Kaiser, 1974), 76. [Hereafter, *Römer 7*.]. C. E. B. Cranfield, *A Critical and Exegetical Commentary on the Epistle to the Romans*, 2 vols., The International Critical Commentary, vol. 32, 6th ed. (Edinburgh: T. & T. Clark, 1975,1979), 1:342, describes this view as "strictly autobiographical."

[4]The death worked by sin through the Law's commandment in verses 7-11 especially points to this, as recognized by Kümmel, *Römer 7*, 76-77. Later, 79, he argues that Paul made a sharp division between his existence before and after his conversion. He speaks of the latter as "a new creation" (2 Cor. 5:17; see also 2 Cor. 4:6).

[5]Martin Franzmann, *Concordia Commentary: Romans* (St. Louis: Concordia Publishing House, 1968), 125-26. He goes on to add, 129, "He is looking back to his youth perhaps." See also C. H. Dodd, *The Epistle of Paul to the Romans*, The Moffatt New Testament Commentary (London: Fontana Books, 1959), 126.

[6]Gerd Theissen, *Psychological Aspects of Pauline Theology*, tr. J. Galvin (Philadelphia: Fortress Press, 1987), 251, recognizes that verse 9 presents "a chief argument against the thesis that Romans 7 has a personal background."

[7]The *bar mitzvah* occurs around the age of 12 when a Jewish youth pledges himself to be "a son of the commandment." See the discussion by W. D. Davies, *Paul and Rabbinic Judaism*, 4th ed. (Philadelphia: Fortress Press, 1980), 24-25; Adolf Deissmann, *St. Paul*, tr. L. Strachan (New York: Hodder and Stoughton, 1922), 92; Ernest Best, *The Letter of Paul to the Romans*, The Cambridge Bible Commentary (Cambridge: At the University Press), 81. Aboth 5:21 in the Mishnah contains the following citation of Rabbi Judah ben Teman, "At five years old [one is fit] for the Scriptures, at ten years for the Mishnah, at thirteen for [the fulfilling of] the commandments, at fifteen for the Talmud," cited from *The Mishnah*, ed. H. Danby (Oxford: Oxford University Press, 1972), 458;

describes the transition portrayed in verses 9-10 as

> the moment when the Jewish boy became a "Son of the Commandment," and assumed responsibility before the law. With this new legal responsibility sin took its place in the boy's experience.[8]

Robert Gundry agrees that a recollection of Paul's *bar mitzvah* leads him to make reference to himself. But Gundry proceeds to interpret the "desire" in verses 7-8 primarily in terms of sexual lusts which arose in Paul about the same time.[9]

A somewhat less literal interpretation of Paul's existence "without the Law" (v. 9a) is also advocated. William Arndt suggests that this phrase speaks of the days before Paul "became fully acquainted with the Law."[10] This period is further identified in psychological terms. According to Gerd Theissen, it was the time when Paul had "an incomplete consciousness of sin."[11] William Sanday and Arthur Headlam also speak of it as the period "before the consciousness of law has taken hold upon him."[12] Verses 7-11 are then said to describe the coming of sin and the Law which brought an end to the innocence of Paul's childhood. As a result,

---

compare also Lk. 2:40-42. Deissmann, 94, further contends, "Jewish teachers, at least of a later period, seem to have assumed that a child grew to the age of nine without knowing anything of sin" (citing Tanchuma, a late commentary on the Pentateuch, on Gen. 3:22).

[8]C. K. Barrett, *A Commentary on the Epistle to the Romans*, Black's New Testament Commentaries (London: Adam & Charles Black, 1962), 143-44.

[9]Robert Gundry, "The Moral Frustration of Paul Before His Conversion: Sexual Lust in Romans 7:7-25," in *Pauline Studies*, eds. D. Hagner and M. Harris (Exeter: Paternoster Press, 1980), 232.

[10]William F. Arndt, "Romans," n.d., Concordia Seminary Library, St. Louis, MO, 47. He further states, 46, "The time the apostle is speaking of here was a time when he either had not learned the written law at all, or had not fully grasped its meaning. He is referring to his younger days."

[11]Theissen, 231, who also speaks of it as the time when Paul's conflict with the Law was "unconscious"; he contends, 222, "If any Pauline texts can be interpreted psychologically, it is these chapters" (Rom. 7 and 8).

[12]William Sanday and Arthur Headlam, *A Critical and Exegetical Commentary on the Epistle to the Romans*, The International Critical Commentary, vol. 32 (New York: Charles Scribner's Sons, 1902), 180.

Even in his old age there stood out clearly to his soul one experience of his childhood, concerning which he gives pathetic hints in his letter to the Romans. We might speak of it as his fall: [citing Rom. 7:9-11] . . . St. Paul does not say what the occasion was. But he indicates that this first sin wrought terrible havoc in his sensitive young soul: he felt himself deceived, it was as if he had tasted death.[13]

F. F. Bruce brings these interpretations together by stating, "In verses 7-13 Paul shows how entry into life under the law coincides with the dawn of conscience and the first awareness of sin."[14]

Scholars have also narrowed the application of verses 7-11 to Paul in another manner, by means of his vantage point or perspective. Such an interpretation recognizes that if Paul is describing his pre-Christian state, including his days as a Pharisee, the negative effects of the Law presented in Romans 7:7-11 would seem to contradict Paul's other portrayals of his positive relationship with the Law prior to his encounter on the Damascus road (for example, compare vv. 9-11 with Gal. 1:13-14; Phil. 3:4-6).[15] As a result, they argue that "Paul here describes his pre-Christian experience from his *now Christian* standpoint."[16]

Objections

A number objections have been raised against identifying the "I" as Paul. The notion that Paul, or any Jew for that matter, would have ever conceived of himself as being alive "apart from the Law" (7:9) is

---

[13]Deissmann, 93-94.

[14]F. F. Bruce, *The Letter of Paul to the Romans*, rev. ed., The Tyndale New Testament Commentaries, vol. 6 (Grand Rapids, Eerdmans Publishing, 1963), 139.

[15]For example, in Phil. 3:4 Paul recalls the confidence he formerly placed in the flesh on the basis of the Law. This "contradiction" is pointed out by Günther Bornkamm, "Sin, Law and Death: An Exegetical Study of Romans 7," in *Early Christian Experience*, The New Testament Library (London: SCM Press, 1969), 93; Ernst Käsemann, *Commentary on Romans*, tr. and ed. G. Bromiley (Grand Rapids: Eerdmans Publishing, 1980), 192.

[16]James Dunn, "Rom. 7,14-25 in the Theology of Paul," *Theologische Zeitschrift* 31 (1975): 261. So also James Denney, "Romans," in *The Expositor's Greek Testament*, vol. 2 (Grand Rapids: Eerdmans Publishing, 1897), 639; John A. T. Robinson, *Wrestling with Romans* (Philadelphia: Westminster Press, 1979), 83; Hans Conzelmann, *An Outline of the Theology of the New Testament*, tr. J. Bowden (London: SCM Press, 1969), 163.

rejected.[17] Whether or not some form of the *bar mitzvah* was practiced already in Paul's day is a disputed matter.[18] But even if it were, there is evidence which suggests that the Jews of that time considered themselves to be under the Law from birth.[19] It is also argued that "the idea of childish innocence is completely unbiblical" and foreign to Judaism.[20] In response to any psychological interpretation of verses 9-10, Richard Longenecker contends,

> Paul's use of 'life' and 'death,' while not designating physical life and death, certainly cannot easily be weakened to mean only untroubled childhood and a consciousness of guilt.[21]

As a result, Werner Kümmel concludes that the text of verses 7-11 will not allow any application of the events there depicted to Paul's own life.[22] Kümmel also points out that Paul's main concern in

---

[17]According to Kümmel, *Römer 7*, 81, this is "unthinkable" (*"undenkbar"*); also Franz Leenhardt, *The Epistle to the Romans*, tr. H. Knight (London: Lutterworth Press, 1961), 187; Cranfield, 1:343; Bornkamm, "Sin, Law and Death," 93; and Conzelmann, 233.

[18]Kümmel, *Römer 7*, 84, argues that the institution of the *bar mitzvah* "is a creation of the Middle Ages" (*"ist eine Schöpfung des Mittelalters"*). He also points out, 82, that the term itself occurs only once in the entire Talmud ("Baba mezia 96a unten"); for this reference, see *The Babylonian Talmud: Seder Nezikin*, tr. and ed. I. Epstein (London: Soncino Press, 1935), 556.

[19]Kümmel, *Römer 7*, 81, concludes, "According to a Jewish conception, then, the child knew and learned the Law from earliest childhood on" (*"Denn nach jüdischer Vorstellung kennt und lernt das Kind von frühester Kindheit an das Gesetz"*). He, 81-82, cites for support 2 Tim. 3:15; Philo, *De Legatione ad Gaium*, 16.115; 31.210; and Josephus, *Contra Apion*, 2.178. For these references, see *Philo*, tr. F. Colson, 10 vols., The Loeb Classical Library (Cambridge, MA: Harvard University Press, 1962), 10:59-57,108-9; *The Works of Josephus*, tr. William Whitson, rev. ed. (Peabody, MA: Hendrickson Publishers, 1987), 805; see also Cranfield, 1:343.

[20]Käsemann, 193; he concludes that any such conception is "part of our modern theology"; also Barclay Newman, "Once Again—The Question of 'I' in Romans 7:7-25 *The Bible Translator 34* (1983):134; Kümmel, *Römer 7*, 81-83.

[21]Richard Longenecker, *Paul* (New York: Harper and Row, 1964), 91.

[22]Kümmel, *Römer 7*, 84, states, "Whether Paul speaks only of himself or himself as [a] type, at any rate he speaks of himself, and that it appears to me the text does not allow" (*"Denn ob Paulus von sich allein oder von sich als Typus redet, jedenfalls redet er von sich, und das scheint mir der Text nicht zuzulassen"*).

Romans 7 is to defend the Law.[23] He contends that such a far-reaching apologetic purpose could not be accomplished if Paul is only speaking of his own experience.[24] Therefore "the portrayal cannot be merely personal."[25]

Adam

Proponents

Another effort at a personal interpretation identifies the "I" in verses 7-11 as Adam. This is based upon the prevalence of motifs, imagery, and language from Genesis 2-3 in this section.[26] J. Christiaan Beker contends that these verses display "Paul's midrashic use of Genesis 3."[27] Indeed, when they are set forth, the points of correspondence between the initial chapters of Genesis and Romans 7:7-11 appear to be quite substantial.[28] As a result, Günther Bornkamm

---

[23]Ibid., 9-11,56,74; see also idem., *Das Bild des Menschen* (Zürich: Zwingli-Verlag, 1948), reprinted in *Römer 7 und das Bild des Menschen im Neuen Testament: Zwei Studien*, Theologische Bücherei, Neues Testament Band 53 (Munich: Christian Kaiser, 1974), 192. [Hereafter, *Das Bild des Menschen.*]

[24]Kümmel, *Römer 7*, 84, where he concludes, "Now whether Paul could assume that all Jews had the same experience most certainly appears very doubtful to me" (*"Nun scheint es mir allerdings sehr zweifelhaft, ob Paulus voraussetzen konnte, daß all Juden die gleiche Erfahrung machten"*); see also ibid., 12.

[25]Ibid., 12.

[26]This view has been championed in recent years by Stanislas Lyonnet, "'Tu Ne Convoiteras Pas' (Rom. vii. 7)," in *Neotestamentica et Patristica*, Novum Testamentum Supplements, vol. 6 (Leiden: E. J. Brill, 1962), 157-65; idem., "L'historie du Salut selon le Chapitre VII de l'Epître aux Romains," *Revue Biblica* 43 (1963):130-42. This interpretation is advocated by Leenhardt, 184-90; Longenecker, 92-96. It is accepted in part by Barrett, 143-45; Bornkamm, "Sin, Law and Death," 93-94; Dodd, 124; John Espy, "Paul's 'Robust Conscience' Re-Examined," *New Testament Studies* 31 (1985):169; Hans Hübner, *Law in Paul's Thought*, tr. J. Greig, ed. J. Riches (Edinburgh: T. & T. Clark, 1984), 70-76; and Cranfield, 1:343.

[27]J. Christiaan Beker, *Paul the Apostle* (Philadelphia: Fortress Press, 1980), 239; according to Matthew Black, *Commentary on Romans*, New Century Bible (London: Oliphants, 1973), 103, "Verse 11 is a kind of allegorizing of the story of the Fall."

[28]Compare, for example, the deception of Gen. 3:13 with Rom. 7:11; the commandment of Gen. 2:17 with 7:7-8. See Espy, 169; and Dodd, 124, who concludes that when this section of Romans 7 is compared with the narrative of Gen. 2-3, "it fits like a glove."

concludes, "The Adam of Rom. 5:12ff. speaks in the 'I' of Rom. 7:7ff."[29] It is also pointed out that Adam alone could legitimately declare, "I was formerly living without the Law, but when the commandment came, sin came to life and I died" (9-10a).[30]

Objections

A number of objections to the Adamic interpretation have been made.[31] For example, Kümmel argues that Adam cannot be involved in Romans 7 since Paul's major concern here is a defense of the Mosaic Torah.[32] As evidence for this he points out that Paul cites the Tenth Commandment as it was given to Moses on Mount Sinai (v. 7; compare Ex. 20:17).[33] This commandment is not at all present in the narrative of Genesis 2-3. Finally, while the account of the Fall in Genesis is depicted in external terms, the events in Romans 7:7-11 occur within the "I."[34]

Israel

Proponents

In view of the importance of the Mosaic Torah in Romans 7, Douglas Moo proposes that "Rom 7.7-12 has as its main focus the giving of the law to Israel."[35] If these verses are taken as a description

---

[29]Bornkamm, "Sin, Law and Death," 94.

[30]Käsemann, 196, goes so far as to state, "Methodologically the starting point should be that a story is involved in vv. 9-11 and the event depicted can refer strictly only to Adam."

[31]Kümmel, *Römer 7*, 86-87; Douglas Moo, "Israel and Paul in Romans 7:7-12," *New Testament Studies* 32 (1986):125. For a detailed attempt to refute these objections, see Lyonnet, "'Tu Ne Convoiteras Pas' (Rom. vii 7)," 157-65.

[32]Kümmel, *Römer 7*, 87.

[33]Ibid., 56,87.

[34]Theissen, 202-3; he terms this "the interiorization of the Fall." For example, there is no mention of the serpent, the tree, the fruit, Eve, and so forth in Romans 7.

[35]Moo, 123,129; see also *Theological Dictionary of the New Testament*, 10 vols, ed. G. Kittel and G. Friedrich, tr. and ed. G. Bromiley (Grand Rapids: Eerdmans Publishing, 1973), s.v. "ἐντολή" by Gottlob Schrenk, 2:550-51. [Hereafter, *TDNT*]

of the events and effects of Israel's experience at Mount Sinai, the "I" is interpreted as representing the people of Israel in a corporate or collective manner.

The interpretation of Ethelbert Stauffer is comparable. He contends that through his use of ἐγώ Paul is speaking in terms of salvation history.[36] In verses 7-8 Paul describes the time before Moses when "sin was dead" (v. 8; compare 5:12-14); in verses 9-11 the entrance of the Law into human history and its effects upon mankind are depicted.

Objections

Rudolf Bultmann responds to the suggestion that the "I" here represents Israel by pointing out that this contradicts the manner in which Paul generally characterizes the Jewish people.

> The main difficulty is that what this view would regard as the sinful nature of the Jews is not such in the rest of Paul's writings, and what is elsewhere regarded as the real sin of the Jews would not even enter the picture here![37]

Kümmel excludes this interpretation because nothing in the text explicitly indicates that the "I" is to be understood as Israel and because of the inconsistencies which arise as one attempts to relate this identification with the "I" in verses 14-25.[38] The difficulties these would pose for Paul's readers are judged to be insurmountable.

---

[36]Ethelbert Stauffer, in *TDNT*, s.v. "ἐγώ," 2:356-62. He, 357, links the use of "I" here with the "Rabbinic disputation and debate concerning the Torah" as in Galatians 2:15-21.

[37]Rudolf Bultmann, "Romans 7 and Paul's Anthropology," in *The Old and New Man in the Letters of Paul*, tr. K. Crim (Richmond, VA: John Knox Press, 1967), 34; citing Rom. 2:17-24; 3:29. See also idem., *Theology of the New Testament*, 2 vols. in 1, tr. K. Grobel (New York: Charles Scribner's Sons, 1951), 1:266-67.

[38]Kümmel, *Römer 7*, 85.

Transpersonal

Proponents

Kümmel advances a more general interpretation which proposes that Paul employs the "I" in verses 7-11 as a "figure of speech" or "rhetorical form."[39] On the basis of verses 9-10a, Kümmel suggests that Paul's readers would have questioned and then rejected any notion that Paul himself is the subject.

> But then there is left for them only one remaining solution, that the "I" is a figure of speech, that is, that Paul through the first person expresses a general thought in a lively manner.[40]

This reveals a significant aspect of Kümmel's methodology. He neither reaches nor defends his rhetorical interpretation solely upon its own merits. Rather, he arrives at it only after excluding the other possibilities which have been suggested. He writes,

> Therefore it appears to me not only the interpretation to Paul, but also to the Jewish people or humanity in Adam, fail when compared with the text of Romans 7:7-13. But if Paul does not speak of himself, then there remains no other possibility than to seek after another subject and to ask whether the "I" is not somehow a rhetorical form [used] for the carrying out of a thought.[41]

---

[39]Ibid., 87, 124, *"eine Stilform"* or *"ein rhetorische Form"*; see also 86-90 and 121-23, where he cites a number of parallels where the first person is also used by Paul in a non-autobiographical sense. In support of him, see Bornkamm, "Sin, Law and Death," 85, 89-92; Bultmann, "Romans 7 and Paul's Anthropology," 33; Leenhardt, 183-84; Käsemann, 193; Otto Michel, *Der Brief an die Römer*, Kritischer-exegetischer Kommentar über das Neue Testament, 13th ed. (Göttingen: Vandenhoeck und Ruprecht, 1966), 170-71. The latter two cite parallels from the Greek World, in Old Testament Psalms of Thanksgiving, and Hymns from the Qumran community.

[40]Kümmel, *Römer 7*, 124, *"Denn blieb aber für sie nur die Lösung übrig, daß das Ich eine Stilform sei, d. h. daß Paulus einen allgemeinen Gedanken durch die 1. Person lebendig ausdrücke."*

[41]Ibid., 87, *"So scheinen mir sowohl die Deutung auf Paulus wie auf das jüdische Volk oder die Menschheit in Adam dem Text von Röm. 7,7-13 gegenüber zu versagen. Wenn aber Paulus nicht von sich selber redet, so bleibt nichts anderes übrig, als nach einem andern Subjekt zu suchen und zu fragen, ob das Ich nicht irgendwie eine rhetorische Form zur Ausführung eines Gedankens ist."* In verses 14-25, this same

These verses are said to illustrate the use of the first person singular "to represent any third person in order to illustrate something universal in a vivid manner."[42] The "I" is not to be identified as Israel, Adam, or even Paul. Rather, it is used by Paul more generally in order to speak of mankind as a whole.[43] The entirety of verses 7-25, though written from a Christian perspective, are a presentation of the truth that sin uses the Law as a means of bringing death to man and that man under the Law cannot redeem himself from this predicament.[44] The "I" in verses 7-11 gives an objective description of the death which the Law inflicts upon those who are under it. In verses 7-8 Paul begins to make his point

> through the reference to the psychological fact that the forbidden always has a special temptation, . . . but he uses it for a portrayal of the "objective existence of the unredeemed."[45]

---

methodology persists; see ibid., 117-18. In speaking explicitly of the "historical sequence" in 7:7-12, Moo, 126, properly assesses that Kümmel's interpretation is "established *via negationis*: no single set of circumstances, it is argued, can satisfactorily account for all the details of the text, so a generalized situation is posited."

[42]F. Blass and A. Debrunner, *A Greek Grammar of the New Testament*, tr. and rev. R. Funk (Chicago: University of Chicago Press, 1961), 147[281]; though they add that this "does not appear in Greek as frequently as in other languages." Nigel Turner, *Grammatical Insights into the New Testament* (Edinburgh: T. & T. Clark, 1963), 86, on the other hand, describes this as "conventional rhetoric." Lucien Cerfaux, *The Christian in the Theology of St. Paul*, tr. Lilian Soiron (New York: Herder and Herder, 1967), 436, also states that the "use of the first person singular [in] a purely rhetorical method, . . . was well known at that time both in Greek and Latin literature and . . . had penetrated into the Jewish world."

[43]According to Kümmel, *Römer 7*, 89, Paul "employed the first person for [a] portrayal of general human experiences" (*"er benütze die erste Person zur Schilderung allgemein menschlicher Erlebnisse"*). Leenhardt, 184, similarly concludes that Paul speaks of "man in general."

[44]Kümmel, *Das Bild des Menschen*, 192; idem, *Römer 7*, 124;

[45]Idem., *Römer 7*, 124, *"Dieser Gedanke ist ausgeführt zuerst durch den Hinweis auf die psychologische Tatsache, daß das Verbotene immer einen besonderen Reiz hat, . . . aber [Paul] benutzt sie zur Schilderung des 'objektiven Seins des Unerlösten'."* According to note 2, his concluding citation is from Rudolf Bultmann, "Das Problem der Ethik bei Paulus," *Zeitschrift für die neutestamentliche Wissenschaft und die Kunde der älteren Kirche* 23 (1924):130; an English translation is "The Problem of Ethics in the Writings of Paul," in *The Old and New Man in the Letters of Paul*, 7-48.

Kümmel contends that Paul's original readers would have understood these verses in this way and concludes that this identification of the "I" avoids the difficulties present in all of the other interpretations.[46]

One indication of the impact of Kümmel's view is revealed in the statement that it "lies at the heart of Bultmann's influential existentialist analysis of Paul's theology."[47] Bultmann characterizes verses 7-11 as "a passage in which Paul so depicts the situation of man under the Torah as it has become clear to a backward look from the standpoint of Christian faith."[48] Following Bultmann, Hans Conzelmann paraphrases the words of the "I" in this manner: "Only faith shows me that without faith I was objectively in despair."[49] Karl Barth's similarly contends that these verses speak of the problem which affects all ages and peoples.[50]

Objections

The textual basis for the rhetorical or impersonal interpretation has been questioned.[51] In addition, Bornkamm challenges any purely "rhetorical" interpretation with this response:

> It is not by chance that Rom. 7 does not speak about "man"; rather, it refers to that man which can be spoken of only in the first person, more precisely, in the first person singular (not even in the first person plural!). It is in the nature of things that Paul can only say "I"—not "man"—nor even "we." An interpretation which overlooks this fact,

---

[46]Kümmel, *Römer 7*, 10-12,126.

[47]Dunn, "Rom. 7,14-25 and the Theology of Paul," 258. See Rudolf Bultmann, "Romans 7 and the Anthropology of Paul," 147-57; idem., *Theology of the New Testament*, 1:245-49.

[48]Bultmann, *Theology of the New Testament*, 1:247; Bornkamm, "Sin, Law and Death," 94, agrees; also Käsemann, 192.

[49]Conzelmann, 163.

[50]Karl Barth, *The Epistle to the Romans*, 6th ed., tr. E. Hoskyns (New York: Oxford University Press, 1933), 247-49; similarly Barrett, 140-42.

[51]See, for example, Andrew Bandstra, *The Law and the Elements of the World* (Grand Rapids: Eerdmans Publishing, n.d.), 136-38; Moo, 125-27.

however correct it might be in detail, would not do justice to the content if it tried to speak *about* it rather than *from* it.[52]

The vivid aorist tenses in verses 7-11 are also said to speak against such an unspecific or "timeless" interpretation.[53]

Combinations of the Above[54]

Many of those who support one of the previous identifications of the "I" proceed to mingle their interpretation with one or more aspects of the other positions. Some of those who support the identification of the "I" as Paul himself include in their view the suggestion that the events portrayed in verses 7-11 have a far wider application. T. W. Manson can even conclude, "Here Paul's autobiography is the biography of Everyman."[55]

Those who identify the "I" with Adam suggest that some sort of "Adam typology" is present in verses 7-11. According to Franz Leenhardt, "The apostle thought out the scene which he here constructs on the basis of the picture of Adam as at once collective and individual."[56] John Espy contends,

> The first point to be noted here is that Paul speaks on two levels, referring both to Adam and Eve and to a more contemporary party. . . . As in 5:12ff., a member of the first couple is set forth as a prototype for sins under the Law.[57]

---

[52]Bornkamm, "Sin, Law and Death," 87. See also Bandstra, 135-36; Gundry, 228-29; Moo, 130, n. 5; and Stauffer, 357.

[53]Stauffer, 357; also by Bornkamm, "Sin, Law and Death," 91; Longenecker, *Paul*, 90.

[54]Lambrecht, *The Wretched "I" and Its Liberation*, 66, keenly identifies these in a similar manner as "Composite Proposals."

[55]T. W. Manson, "Romans," in *Peake's Commentary on the Bible*, ed. M. Black (New York: Thomas Nelson and Sons, 1963), 945; so also Theissen, 178; Bandstra, 136.

[56]Leenhardt, 185; similarly Longenecker, *Paul*, 92; Barrett, 143-44; Gundry, 230-31.

[57]Espy, 169.

What is Paul's purpose in combining the events of his own life with the experience of Adam? It is proposed that Paul is affirming and confessing that he, as well as all other people, were implicated and share in the fallen nature of Adam. Since "every man recapitulates in his own personal life the fall of Adam," all people under the Law can identify themselves in the experience of the "I" in verses 7-11.[58] Jan Lambrecht finally asserts, "Through Adam Paul wants to see Israel and, more specifically, the Israelite he himself was."[59]

It may be noted here that the influence of Kümmel's interpretation has exhibited itself in two diverse tendencies. First, a number of scholars now espouse interpretations which tend to avoid the basic issue of whether the "I" refers directly to Paul or not.[60] Second, it has resulted in various attempts to combine a rhetorical or "transpersonal" interpretation with the other identifications noted above. C.E.B. Cranfield, for example, suggests the "I" is "speaking in the name of Adam" and/or being used "in a general way without intending a specific reference to any particular individual or group, to depict the situation in the absence of the law and in its presence."[61] Since, according to Kümmel, the Mosaic Law is the focus of Paul's argument, the rhetorical "I" is also said to represent the objective predicament of the Jewish people. Käsemann concludes, "It is to be maintained under all circumstances that the apostle is speaking . . . specifically of the pious Jew."[62]

If one adopts Käsemann's identification of the "I," which is based upon Kümmel's work, it is hard to imagine how the experience of the people of Israel and even Paul's own pre-Christian life could be far from any identification of the "I" as a "typical" or "pious" Jew. Yet these are two interpretations Kümmel explicitly rejects!

In conclusion, the number of identifications which have been made of the "I" in verses 7-11 is perplexing enough. However, the mixing

---

[58]Black, 101; see also Käsemann, 196; Bandstra, 136.

[59]Lambrecht, *The Wretched "I" and Its Liberation*, 83.

[60]For example, Dunn, "Rom. 7,14-25 in the Theology of Paul," 260, states that Paul is "at least describing *typical experience* of an 'I' . . ." (citing for comparison 2 Baruch 54:19); see also Gundry, 229; and Moo, 135, n. 59.

[61]Cranfield, 1:342.

[62]Käsemann, 195; see also Beker, 238; Gundry, 232.

together of these varied interpretations has only resulted in further confusion. As this survey moves on to examine the various identifications which have been made of the "I" in verses 14-25, the waters become, if anything, even more murky.

Romans 7:14-25

After Paul draws a number of extremely significant conclusions regarding the Law in Romans 7:12-13, the "I" once again becomes a prominent focus in his discussion. Paul continues,

(14) For we know that the Law is Spiritual, but *I* am fleshly, sold under sin. (15) For I do not approve of that which I accomplish; indeed, I do not practice that which I will, but that which I hate, this I do. (16) But since I am doing that which I do not will, I agree with the Law that [it is] excellent. (17) But, this being the case, it is not then *I* who am accomplishing this, but sin which is dwelling in me. (18) For I know that good is not dwelling in me, this is, in my flesh. For to will [the good] lies at hand for me, but the accomplishing of the good, no. (19) For I am not doing [the] good I will, but [the] evil I do not will, this I am practicing. (20) But if *I* am doing this which I do not will, *I* am no longer accomplishing it but the sin which is dwelling in me. (21) So then I find the Law for me the one determining to do the excellent [thing], that for me evil lies at hand. (22) I rejoice with the Law of God according to the inner man. (23) But I see another Law in my members waging war against the Law of my mind and taking me captive to the Law of sin which is in my members. (24) I am a distressed/miserable man; who will rescue me from this body of death? (25) Thanks [be] to God through Jesus Christ our Lord. So then *I* myself in my mind am enslaved to [the] Law of God, but, on the other hand, in the flesh, [I am enslaved to the] Law of sin.

At the outset, Andrew Bandstra observes,

The purely autobiographical interpretation quite clearly has the least to commend it when applied to vv. 7-13; the rhetorical and "salvation-history" interpretations give a less satisfactory account of the intense personal emotions expressed in vv. 14-25.[63]

---

[63]Bandstra, 135-36.

Nevertheless, it is difficult to argue with the "rather obvious point that the 'I' is the same as the 'I' of vv. 7-12."[64] Though often overlooked, the integral connection between the two sections cannot be over-stressed.[65] The identification which is accepted in verses 7-11 is in many ways determinative of the conclusions which will be made about the "I" in verses 14-25.[66]

The question which generally receives the most attention in verses 14-25 is whether the first person singular is being used by Paul to portray a Christian or a non-Christian. The majority of scholars contend that this "passage refers to the unregenerate man."[67] Usually this is concluded because descriptions such as "having been sold under sin" (v. 14), "practicing evil" (vv. 19,20), and, indeed, the entire characterization of the "wretched man" (v. 24) are said to employ language which Paul uses nowhere else "of the regenerate state."[68] If this view is adopted, verses 14-25 are often read as the pre-conversion experience of Paul himself.

Paul Prior to His Conversion

Proponents

At the beginning of this century, the dominant interpretation saw verses 14-25 as autobiographical of Paul's experience "before his Conversion."[69] Yet even this view is divided into two main factions

---

[64]Espy, 173; also Kümmel, *Römer 7,* 97,110. However, the implications of this statement are not always appreciated.

[65]Bornkamm, "Sin, Law and Death," 95, justifiably asserts, "It is disastrous to connect the anthropological problem of ch. 7 essentially only to 7:14ff., as usually happens."

[66]For example, Kümmel, *Römer 7,* 110, concludes "that Paul himself cannot be the subject in 7:14ff., because in 7:7-13 this is impossible" (*"daß in 7,14ff. nicht Paulus selbst Subjekt sein kann, wenn in 7,7-13 diese Deutung unmöglich ist"*); so Cranfield, 1:347.

[67]Sanday and Headlam, 184; they are joined, for example, by Bultmann, "Romans 7 and Paul's Anthropology," especially 43-45; Conzelmann, 233-35; Dodd, 125-26, 132; Käsemann, 201; Kümmel, *Römer 7,* 98-9,106,109; Leenhardt, 195-99; Robinson, *Wrestling with Romans*, 83.

[68]Sanday and Headlam, 185.

[69]Ibid., 186; also Dodd, 126; Kümmel, *Römer 7,* 141-42, n. 2, cites over 50

according to the vantage point of the "I."

On one hand, verses 7-25 have been appraised as representing Paul's pre-conversion experience *as seen by him then*. While verses 7-11 portray the innocent days of Paul's childhood, the latter verses describe "the incubus of the Law he had felt most keenly when he was a 'Pharisee of Pharisees.'"[70] Heinrich Weinel very dramatically recounts Paul's "anguish" as follows:

> In this conflict Saul lived, as Pharisee and persecutor. Heavier and heavier did the curse of the law become to him, the more he studied it and the more exactly he tried to keep the commandment. . . . It was just his vehement, proud and fiery temperament that longed after good so passionately, just this rushed headlong into manifold sins that separated him farther and farther from God. What struggles must have raged through his conscience, until, at last, he breaks out in a despairing cry (7:18-20).[71]

W. D. Davies contends that through most of Romans 7 "Paul reflects and possibly has in mind the doctrine of the Two Impulses."[72]

---

adherents of this position. For example, James Stewart, *A Man in Christ* (New York: Harper and Brothers, n.d.), 99, states that Romans 7 portrays "the experience of a life still requiring to be born again." Johannes Weiss, *The History of Primitive Christianity*, 3 vols., completed by R. Knopf, tr. and ed. F. C. Grant (New York: Wilson-Erickson, 1937), 515, n. 4, writes, "What purpose could rebirth and redemption have had, if they could not even remove the unhappy condition of inner conflict and servitude?"

[70]Sanday and Headlam, 186.

[71]Heinrich Weinel, *St. Paul*, Theological Translation Library, tr. G. Bienemann, ed. W. Morrison (New York: G. P. Putnam's Sons, 1906), 74-75. This conflict is often depicted as being preparatory to Paul's conversion. Theissen, 235-36, cites extensively from Oskar Pfister, "Die Entwicklung des Apostels Paulus," *Imago* 6 (1920):277, who concludes that prior to his conversion "Paul came into contact with the Christians and their teaching as an unsatisfied man, torn by inner needs." His hatred toward Christianity was a result of their calling his attachment to the Law into question. Pfister, 279, suggests that "the persecutor found in the persecuted some great things which he could not deny."

[72]Davies, 27; others who agree that this conception is present in Romans 7 include Barclay Newman and Eugene Nida, *A Translator's Handbook on Paul's Letter to the Romans*, Helps for Translators, vol. 14 (London: United Bible Societies, 1973), 133,137; and Hans Schoeps, *Paul*, tr. H. Knight (Philadelphia: Westminster Press, 1961), 184-86.

The background for this is found at Qumran and in the Jewish rabbis who characterized the struggle between good and evil in man as a conflict between two opposing forces.[73] They called the evil impulse which directs man to all sorts of wickedness the יצר הרע.[74] However, the rabbis did not conceive of this impulse as evil in and of itself. It basically reflects "the urge to self-preservation and propagation in a man and can therefore be mastered and put to good use."[75] The way to direct and control this יצר הרע is to study and "obey the Law."[76] Though the impulse to evil cannot be destroyed until the Age to Come, repentance is available and required for those who yield to it.[77] The rabbis held that the יצר הרע was thirteen years older than the impulse to good (יצר הטוב) which arrived when a boy became a morally responsible "son of commandment."[78] Davies concludes, "Paul's description of his moral experience in [Romans 7:14-25] is probably an account of his struggle against his evil *yêtzer*."[79]

On the other hand, a number of scholars propose that verses 14-25 describe Paul's pre-conversion experience as seen by him now, and only, *in the light of his Christian faith*.[80] In Beker's words, "In Romans 7, Paul views in retrospect the objective condition of his former Jewish life."[81] This interpretation largely stems from a recognition of the

---

[73]See the discussion of C. Marvin Pate, *The End of the Age Has Come* (Grand Rapids: Eerdmans, 1995), 102-5; citing 1QS 3:13-4:26.

[74]Davies 20-21; the Scriptural source is Gen. 6:5. It is described variously as existing on the left side of man, in his kidneys, and in the heart. The impulses are directed especially toward sexual sins. Davies, 26, proposes that the יצר הרע is comparable to the φρόνημα τῆς σαρκός in Paul (8:6) and to that which Paul describes as σάρκινος/σαρκικός (7:14).

[75]Ibid., 22.

[76]Pate, 104.

[77]George F. Moore, *Judaism in the First Centuries of the Christian Era*, 2 vols. (New York: Schocken Books, 1971), 1:491,520; Schoeps, 185-88.

[78]Davies, 24-25; see also Gen. 8:21. Davies refers to Aboth 5:21 from the Mishnah and contends, 20, the יצר הטוב is represented in Paul by "πνευματικός" and "ψυχικός."

[79]Davies, 23-24.

[80]Barrett, 151; Anders Nygren, *Commentary on Romans*, tr. C. Rasmussen (Philadelphia: Muhlenberg Press, 1949), 286.

[81]Beker, *Paul the Apostle*, 241.

difficulties which passages such as Galatians 1:13-14 and Philippians 3:5-6 pose for applying Romans 7:14-25 to Paul's experience prior to his conversion.[82]

Theissen also believes Romans 7:7-24 "is a retrospective on an unredeemed state."[83] He argues, from a psychological perspective, that what is portrayed in these verses is "a progressive process of developing consciousness of a formerly unconscious conflict with the law."[84] What had been unconscious in verses 7-11 is "replaced step by step with conscious insight" (vv. 14-24).[85] Since "there are no convincing linguistic or stylistic grounds to exclude in principle the person of Paul from the *ego* ('I') of Romans 7," Theissen concludes that the experience represented is that of Paul himself.[86] But he argues that Paul's "becoming conscious" of his conflict with the Law was not preparatory to his conversion.[87] Neither was this conflict overcome simply by his becoming conscious of it. Rather, it ended "through the saving intervention of Christ."[88]

All of the previous interpreters proceed to draw a sharp contrast between Romans 7 and Romans 8 which reveals an "entirely different atmosphere."[89] The emphatic νῦν of 8:1 is said to signal Paul's conversion to Christianity, the coming of the Holy Spirit, and the beginning of the life described in Chapter 8. In Gundry's words, all of 7:7-25 moves Paul ahead toward the "availability of moral victory in Romans 8:1-17, a victory that is characteristic as well as possible."[90]

---

[82]For example, Maurice Goguel, *The Birth of Christianity*, tr. H. Snape (New York: Macmillan, 1954), 213.

[83]Theissen, 222; see also 265.

[84]Ibid., 234.

[85]Ibid., 232; this explains the transition to the present tense.

[86]Ibid., 234; similarly Beker, *Paul the Apostle*, 240-1.

[87]See Theissen's critiques of Oskar Pfister, Carl Jung, and H. Fischer on this point, 235-37.

[88]Ibid., 246.

[89]Charles Mitton, "Romans 7 Reconsidered," *Expository Times* 65 (1953-54):79; also Schoeps, 184; Theissen, 182-83. Sanday and Headlam, 186, agree since in 7:7-24 there is not "a single expression which belongs to Christianity."

[90]Gundry, 240; also Alfred Garvie, *Romans*, The Century Bible, vol. 27 (London: Caxton Publishing, n.d.), 175.

Objections

There are a number of significant objections to interpreting these verses as representative of Paul's pre-conversion experience. The major difficulty for those who interpret Romans 7:14-25 as Paul's account of his own struggles with the Law which he felt prior to his conversion is that what these verses depict is not at all consistent with the other descriptions Paul makes of his pre-conversion experience. In fact, the intense conflict of Romans 7 is said to be "altogether contrary" to the picture Paul presents of himself in Philippians 3:5-6 and Galatians 1:13-14.[91] Kümmel argues that Paul was a typical Pharisee and concludes, "Nothing forces [one] to the conclusion that the uncertainty in the ability to fulfill the Law came already to the Pharisee Paul."[92] On the contrary, these other passages indicate that the condition characterized in verses 14-25 "was not a matter of conscious reflection while [Paul] was a Pharisee."[93] As Leenhardt observes,

> The conversion of Paul was not that of a heart devoured by remorse for its acts of disobedience, but rather that of a proud soul exalting itself before God because of its obedience to the law.[94]

Specifically in response to Davies's proposal, is it possible that Paul is describing the battle between the "two impulses" which took place in him prior to his conversion? A number of scholars have answered, "No."[95] First, as Davies recognizes, there is no equivalent to the יצר הטוב in Romans 7.[96] For Paul, the impulse toward good comes

---

[91]Pointed out, for example, by Cranfield, 1:344; Bandstra, 141; Beker, *Paul the Apostle*, 217-18; Espy, 161; Kümmel, *Römer 7*, 117; Mitton, 80; Nygren, *Commentary on Romans*, 286, 290-01; Theissen, 234; see also Acts 22:3.

[92]Kümmel, *Römer 7*, 114, "*Nicht zwingt zu der Annahme, daß die Zweifel an der Erfüllbarkeit des Gesetzes schon dem Pharisäer Paulus kamen.*"

[93]Beker, *Paul the Apostle*, 241; as also argued effectively by Kümmel, *Römer 7*, 111-17.

[94]Leenhardt, 181; also Barrett, 151-52.

[95]For example, Barrett, 148; Beker, *Paul the Apostle*, 237; Bruce, *The Letter of Paul to the Romans*, 143, n. 1.

[96]Davies, 26; citing F. C. Porter, "Biblical and Semitic Studies," in *Yale Bicentennial Publications*, 134, whom Davies, 26, n. 1, evaluates as being "right in saying that Paul's conception of the Spirit has almost nothing in common with the

only from outside of man. Second, it is asserted that Paul would strongly object to any notion that the inclination to evil in man, namely, sin, is basically directed toward "self-preservation and propagation," and merely needs to be controlled and used for good.[97] Finally, Paul's method for resisting the fleshly impulse is not obedience to the Law, but dependence upon the Spirit.[98]

Any psychological interpretation must reckon with the objection that in Romans 7 Paul is engaged in a theological discussion regarding the Law which is "not the least interested in psychology."[99] Therefore Beker concludes,

> We cannot revert to speculations about Paul's psyche which lie behind the text. Speculations about Paul's encounter with the 'evil impulse' (*yetzer harah*) after his youthful innocence, or about his bar mitzvah and his subsequent frustration with the law are illegitimate and have no warrant in the text.[100]

A number of further objections have been levied against interpreting the "I" in Romans 7:14-25 as descriptive of Paul's pre-conversion experience from either his pre-Christian or Christian vantage point. The first is that Paul switches to verb forms in the present tense in verse 14 and consistently employs them throughout the rest of the chapter.[101] This change to the present tense is explained by those who advocate a pre-conversion interpretation as indicative of an "intensification" in the conflict[102] or as being dramatic. "The Apostle

---

relatively unimportant rabbinical idea of the good *yêtzer*."

[97] As Davies, 22, suggests. Barrett, 148, agrees that the two may be similar. For Paul, however, "there is an element in human nature so completely under the power of sin that . . . it corrupts all man's activity" (see, for example, Rom. 1:18-32; 2:21-24; 3:9-18).

[98] Pate, 105.

[99] Barrett, 145.

[100] Beker, *Paul the Apostle*, 237.

[101] Cranfield, 1:344; also Barth, 270.

[102] Asserted by Eduard Ellwein, "Das Rätsel von Römer VII," *Kerygma und Dogma* 1 (1955):262, *"diese Steigerung."* See also Karl Kertelge, "Exegetische Überlegungen zum Verständnis der paulinischen Anthropologie nach Römer 7," *Zeitschrift für die neutestamentliche Wissenschaft* 62 (1971): 113; and Theissen, 233.

throws himself back into the time which he is describing."[103]

A second major objection to any application of verses 14-25 to Paul's pre-conversion experience is the order of the sentences in verses 24-25. If Paul is describing his pre-conversion experience, it would seem that verse 25a announces his release from "this body of death" in declaring, "Thanks [be] to God through Jesus Christ our Lord!" Yet verse 25b immediately adds, "So then *I* myself in my mind am enslaved to [the] Law of God, but, on the other hand, in the flesh, [I am enslaved to the] Law of sin." As it stands verse 25b implies that the deliverance of 25a has left the "I" in the same condition as he stood in verse 24!

As a result of the latter objection, some adherents of the pre-conversion interpretation have attempted to rearrange verses 24-25. James Moffatt's translation, for example, places verse 25b before verse 24. He justifies this by noting that he is "restoring the second part of ver. 25 to its original and logical position."[104] Ernest Best responds, "There is no evidence in any manuscript that [the position of verse 25b] is other than where we have it."[105] If the order of the text is allowed to stand as is, Barclay Newman has suggested that verse 25b "is a brief restatement of the problem in anticipation of the full reply which follows in Chapter 8."[106]

Paul's Christian Experience

Proponents

Could Paul, in Romans 7:14-25, be describing his own present and continuing existence as a Christian?[107] In view of the switch to the

---

[103]Sanday and Headlam, 185.

[104]James Moffatt, *A New Translation of the Bible Containing the Old and New Testaments* (New York: Harper and Brothers, 1935), note on p. 194.

[105]Best, *The Letter of Paul to the Romans*, 84.

[106]Newman, 135. Similarly for Best, *The Letter of Paul to the Romans*, 84.

[107]As asserted by Espy, 172-75; Dunn, "Rom. 7,14-25 in the Theology of Paul," 258-64; Nygren, *Commentary on Romans*, 284-303; John Murray, *The Epistle to the Romans*, 2 vols. (Grand Rapids: Eerdmans Publishing, 1959,1965), 1:256-59; R. C. H. Lenski, *The Interpretation of Romans*, Commentaries on the New Testament (Minneapolis: Augsburg Publishing, 1961), 473-74; Franzmann, 134-37.

present tense in verse 14, the consistent use of the first person singular in verses 14-25, and Paul's use of both of these elements to describe his present Christian experience in other passages, this is hailed as the most natural identification of the "I" and the one which should be accepted.[108] Its adherents argue that since there are no compelling reasons which force one to abandon this interpretation,

> The emphatic "I" must refer to Paul himself as he is now; . . . if this is not understood as Paul's actual, present experience, the cry of v. 24— "Wretched man that I am! . . ."—is theatrical and inappropriate.[109]

In further support of this interpretation, it is pointed out that certain expressions in these verses could *only* be used by Paul to refer to himself as a Christian.[110] Paul describes all people before conversion as slaves of sin (6:17,18,20) and declares, "Those who are in the flesh cannot please God" (8:7). But here Paul writes that "I" will the good (15,16,19,20), delight in the Law of God (22), and serve it with my mind (25b). Those who support this interpretation conclude that, for Paul, such things are "not possible for the man not under grace."[111] Therefore Paul cannot be referring to his own pre-conversion experience or to any other non-Christian. The terms ἐγώ, νοῦς (vv. 23,25b), and ὁ ἔσω ἄνθρωπος (v. 22) must be describing the human self which is being renewed by the Holy Spirit. The "I" is a believer in Christ who is part of the new age, but who is, at the same time, still in the flesh.[112] Cranfield asserts, "A struggle as serious as that which is here described, can only take place where the Spirit of God is present and active (cf. Gal. 5.17)."[113]

---

[108]Packer, 622, again states this is "the most natural way to read" this section; also admitted by Kümmel, *Römer 7*, 90.

[109]Espy, 168.

[110]Franzmann, 136, states: "If we refer 7:14-25 to man outside Christ, we find Paul here attributing to the natural human 'mind' an assent to, and harmony with, the law of God which he expressly denies elsewhere."

[111]Espy, 168; also Murray, 1:257.

[112]Dunn, "Rom. 7,14-25 in the Theology of Paul," 262. This is the major thesis of Pate, see especially 110-13.

[113]Cranfield, 1:346.

Furthermore, it is argued that Paul speaks of the Christian life in a manner comparable to Romans 7:14-25 in Galatians 5:17 which states,

> For the flesh desires [what is] against the Spirit, and the Spirit against the flesh. For these are opposing one another, with the result that you do not do the things which you will.[114]

In Romans 8:23 Paul includes himself in declaring, "Even we ourselves groan within ourselves, waiting eagerly for our adoption as sons, the redemption of our bodies." So R. C. H. Lenski concludes that the "I" is Paul himself and that verses 14-25 are "written from the standpoint of a regenerate man, whose experience is normal."[115]

Objections

The main argument against viewing these verses as descriptive of Paul's continuing Christian experience is that they paint a very dismal picture of his Christian life.[116] Even though these objectors admit that Paul is aware of the possibility that he and other Christians might sin,[117] they contend that sin, the flesh, and the Law cannot have the power over Paul the Christian which is ascribed to them here. The portrayal of the "I" in 7:14-25 contradicts the Christian's liberation from sin and the "death to the Law" already announced by Paul (6:6-7,14-15,17-18, 22; 7:1-6). If the Christian of 7:6 is freed from the Law, how can what the "I" states in 7:14 also be true of him? In Chapter 8 Paul includes himself among Christians "who do not walk according to the flesh, but according to the Spirit" (8:4; compare also 8:2; 2 Cor. 10:3; 13:6.).

As a result, a number of scholars have concluded that, when compared with Paul's statements in 6:1-7:6 and 8:1-39, the "I" in 7:7-

---

[114]Espy, 186, n. 70; Nygren, 294, asks, "Since Paul, in Galatians, can say that about the Christian, why should it be impossible for him to say it in Romans 7:14-25?"

[115]Lenski, 475.

[116]Sanday and Headlam, 183; Kümmel, *Römer 7*, 97-104, argues that it is "impossible" ("*Unmöglichkeit*") for these verses to be describing Paul as a Christian or any other Christian.

[117]For example, Kümmel, *Römer 7*, 101; Leenhardt, 182.

25 cannot be a Christian.[118] Phrases such as "fleshly," "sold under sin," and "captive to the Law of sin" cannot apply to a believer (vv. 14,23). In fact, there is "no single expression in Chapter 7 (until the parenthesis of verse 25) which is distinctively Christian—no mention of Christ or the Spirit."[119]

An additional argument which weighs heavily against the application of 7:14-25 to Paul the Christian is the contention, "Nowhere else does Paul speak thus of the present Christian life."[120] Galatians 5:17 is rejected as a parallel because Paul there exhorts Christians to use their freedom to choose and to obey.[121] In contrast, Romans 7:14-25 depicts a situation of utter helplessness. The "I" is sold under sin and exhibits continued and uninterrupted failure and despondency.

Kümmel is representative of those scholars who contend that any identification of this "I" with Paul the Christian must be given up.

> The reader who had heard most distinctly from Paul in Chapter 6 that the Christian is free from sin (6:22) could not come to the conception that Paul here describes himself.[122]

In light of all of this, Lambrecht concludes:

> In Romans 7 Paul has depicted his pre-Christian, not his Christian, situation. We, present-day Christians, cannot agree with the Lutheran *simul iustus et peccator* (simultaneously righteous and sinner). The adage,

---

[118]See, for example, Kümmel, *Römer 7*, 126.

[119]Robinson, *Wrestling with Romans*, 84; also Leenhardt, 194; Kümmel, *Das Bild des Menschen*, 190-91, points out that the Holy Spirit, who differentiates Christians from non-Christians, is absent from Romans 7:14-25.

[120]Robinson, *Wrestling with Romans*, 85; see also 87.

[121]On this point, see Kümmel, *Römer 7*, 104-6; Leenhardt, 182-83; Mitton, 102; Michel, *Der Brief an die Römer*, 171; Bornkamm, "Sin, Law and Death," 100-1; Robinson, *Wrestling with Romans*, 87; Bruce, *The Letter of Paul to the Romans*, 144.

[122]Kümmel, *Römer 7*, 125, "*Die Leser, die in Kap. 6 von Paulus eindringlich gehört hatten, daß der Christ von der Sünde befreit ist (6, 22), konnten nicht auf den Gedanken kommen, daß Paulus sich hier selber schildere.*" He, 12, argues that the "I" is either a different subject or in a different situation than presented in Chapter 6; see also 118.

at least in the way most commentators understand it, is incorrect and, moreover, dangerous.[123]

Transpersonal

Proponents

Many of those who reject an autobiographical interpretation of the "I" in verses 7-11 accept an "impersonal" or "rhetorical" interpretation in verses 14-25. Kümmel, again by way of negation, has championed this view. He contends any attempt "to understand and to employ Romans 7:7-24 as a biographical text of Paul" must be given up for the following reasons:[124]

> 1) The difficulties involved in ascribing verses 7-13 to the life of Paul are insurmountable. 2) It is impossible for verses 14-25 to be a characterization of Paul the Pharisee. 3) The close connection between the two sections indicates that the "I" is the same throughout verses 7-25. 4) The transition to Chapter 8 excludes the interpretation that the "I" in 7:14-25 is a Christian.

Aside from the Christian views which intrude in verses 14a and 25a, "it is . . . clear that the portrayed person can only be the non-Christian, that is, the person here [is] under the Law."[125] Verses 14-25 describe the conflict within an unbelieving "I" who wills to obey God's Law, but cannot do so because sin has made the "I" its prisoner.

Who then is the "I"? For Kümmel,

> No one or everyone is [the] subject. Certainly it is better that $\tau \iota \varsigma$ be thought of as [the] subject. But then it results that the portrayal may not be presented as a portrayal of a distinct experience, but must be presented as [a] general, more or less theoretical presentation of the

---

[123]Lambrecht, *The Wretched "I" and Its Liberation*, 90.

[124]Kümmel, *Römer 7*, 117, *"Röm. 7,7-24 als biographischen Text des Paulus zu verstehen und zu verwenden . . ."*; see also 117-26. It should be noted that two of his four objections are directly related to verses 7-13.

[125]Ibid., 118, *"Es ist . . . klar, daß der geschilderte Mensch nur der Nichtchrist, d. h. hier der Mensch unter dem Gesetze sein kann"*; see also, 125.

thought that the Law must assist sin for the death of the person and that the person therefore cannot come out of the condition of inability.[126]

Paul cannot be speaking of himself or any other Christian. Neither is the "I" to be identified as anyone in particular. Rather, it is a "rhetorical fictive 'I'"[127] utilized by Paul to present the condition of man in general outside of Christ. As in verses 7-11, Paul uses the first person singular as a "figure of speech" in order to make the portrayal more vivid.[128]

Kümmel's explanation of the change in tenses is that the aorist tense is used initially

> because in 7:7-13 how the person fell to death through sin which used the Law is being described on the basis of a psychological fact. Consequently an event is being portrayed. But in 7:14-24 the essence of the Law and of mankind is used to clarify the event of 7:7ff.[129]

Paul's use of the present tense in verses 14-25 is due to "the lively contemporization of that which is portrayed."[130] These verses describe the condition which inevitably results from the events which occur in verses 7-11. Verse 24 then expresses the desire of the "I" to be released from the life ruled by sin, a desire which is satisfied in Chapter 8.[131]

---

[126]Ibid., 132, "*niemand oder jedermann ist Subjekt. Doch ist es besser, sich τις also Subjekt zu denken. Dann aber ergibt sich, daß die Schilderung nicht als Schilderung eines bestimmten Erlebnis gefaßt werden darf, sondern als allgemeine, mehr oder weniger theoretische Darstellung des Gedankens gefaßt werden muß, daß das Gesetz der Sünde zum Tode des Menschen verhelfen muß und daß der Mensch darum unter dem Gesetz nicht aus dem Zustand des Nichtkönnens herauskommt.*"

[127]Theissen, 177-78, aptly characterizes Kümmel's view in this way.

[128]Kümmel, *Römer 7*, 7, 124, 126; he uses the term "*Stilform*""

[129]Ibid., 126, "*Denn in 7,7-13 wird ausgehend von einer psychologischen Tatsache, geschildert, wie der Mensch durch Sünde, die das Gesetz benützt, dem Tode verfällt. Es ist also ein Geschehen geschildert. In 7,7-24 aber wird das Wesen des Gesetzes und des Menschen benutzt, um das Geschehen von 7,7ff. zu eklären.*"

[130]Ibid., 110, "*aus der lebhaften Vergegenwärtigung des Geschilderten.*"

[131]Ibid., 68-73,117; see also Bornkamm, "Sin, Law and Death," 100-1; Käsemann, 210.

A number of scholars have built upon or expanded Kümmel's view.[132] Bultmann, for example, agrees that in Romans 7 we have Paul's fullest expression of human existence apart from faith.[133] Paul's purpose in verses 14-25 is to show "how law and sin determine man's nature."[134] For Bultmann, the Law determines man's condition primarily by leading a person into deception and a false-striving to "become right with God by keeping the law."[135] "The object of man's intention is life, but the results of what he does is death."[136] So "then *the ultimate purpose of the Law is to lead man to death*."[137]

> But the Law does this not by leading man into subjective despair, but by bringing him into an objectively desperate situation which he does not recognize as such until the message of grace hits its mark.[138]

According to Bultmann, Paul uses verses 14-25 to reveal, from an *objective vantage point*, the impossibility of justifying oneself. This section then characterizes "the total tendency of human existence, and transcends subjectivity."[139] Hans Conzelmann puts it this way: "Paul describes in general terms the objective situation of the man outside of faith—where 'objective' means the perspective which faith has on unbelief."[140]

On the basis of Kümmel's work, other interpreters have concluded that Paul employs the "I" in Romans 7 to portray, *in subjective terms*,

---

[132]In addition to those cited below, see also Keith Nickle, "Romans 7:7-25," *Interpretation* 33 (1979):181-87; Paul Althaus, *Paulus und Luther über den Menschen*, Studien der Luther-Akademie, 14 (Gütersloh: "Der Rufer" Evangelische Verlag, 1938), 38-40.

[133]Bultmann, *Theology of the New Testament*, 1:191; Bornkamm, "Sin, Law and Death," 96, supports "the correctness of Bultmann's explanation."

[134]Bultmann, "Romans 7 and Paul's Anthropology," 41.

[135]Ibid., 35; similarly Käsemann, 201.

[136]Bultmann, "Romans 7 and Paul's Anthropology," 43. As Käsemann, 203, puts it, "What a person wants is salvation. What he creates is disaster."

[137]Bultmann, *Theology of the New Testament*, 1:267; emphasis his.

[138]Ibid., 1:266.

[139]Idem., "Romans 7 and Paul's Anthropology," 37-38.

[140]Conzelmann, 230; see also 234.

"the schizophrenia of the unredeemed person" or the divided state of the soul of man under the Law.[141] The "I" is an unbeliever who is able to will both good and evil, but who is torn asunder by his inability to accomplish the good. "At the very heart of his being is a deep schism which robs him of the power to accomplish the will of God."[142] In verses 14-25 we have "man wrenched apart under the rule of the Law."[143]

In regard to the spiritual state of the "I," those who adopt Kümmel's interpretation contend that the difference between the "I" in verses 7-11 and in verses 14-24 "is in vocabulary, not in content."[144] According to Käsemann, the past tense in verses 7-11 speaks of the Jewish people under the Law. With the present tense in verses 14-25, "the perspective is at least broadened" to include all unbelievers.[145] For Käsemann, the "I" throughout Romans 7 represents the pious person who "typifies as no one else can the nature of self-willed, rebellious, perverted, and lost creation."[146]

One dramatic sign of the impact of the rhetorical line of interpretation upon Romans 7 is *Die Gute Nachricht's* translation of the "I" in 7:7 as "*wir Menschen.*"[147] This is followed by the use of the inclusive forms "*wir*" and "*uns*" for the first person singular throughout the remainder of the chapter.[148]

---

[141]Beker, *Paul the Apostle*, 238. See also Althaus, *Paulus und Luther über den Menschen*, 37-38; on Althaus's view, see the undocumented citations made by Nygren, *Commentary on Romans*, 290-92.

[142]Leenhardt, 198; he also calls this, 197, an "eternal rent in man's being."

[143]Newman, 134; citing for comparison Galatians 2:15-16,19.

[144]Käsemann, 202; so Kümmel, *Römer 7*, 90.

[145]Käsemann, 195; also Newman, 133.

[146]Käsemann, 209.

[147]*Die Gute Nachricht*, ed. Bibelgesellschaften und Bibelwerk im deutschsprachigen Raum (Stuttgart: Deutsche Bibelgesellschaft, 1976), 352, "we human beings."

[148]Ibid., 352-53, "we" and "us"; Newman, 134, agrees that this translation "would appear to suit best the demands of the context."

Objections

Certainly, as Kümmel effectively argues, one must accept the possibility that Paul may be using a rhetorical "I" as a "figure of speech."[149] However, a number of objections have been cited against the "confident assumption" of this interpretation.[150] The first concerns the resulting place of Romans 7:14-25 within the entire Epistle. Since the main topic in the rest of Romans 5-8 concerns the Christian life, this interpretation necessitates viewing these verses as a digression.[151] Second, Kümmel's explanation of the change in tenses has been questioned. Third, if this rhetorical "I" is said to depict what is true of "man" in general, how can Paul be completely excluded? To claim that the experience described here is typical is one thing, but to contend that the "I" is rhetorically fictive and in no way a description of Paul's own experience is said to ignore the fact that

> apart from one or two [passages] which quote the objections of (real or imaginary) objectors, in the rest Paul uses 'I' as including me, not 'I' meaning anyone but me.[152]

It has also been argued,

> The existential anguish and frustration of vv. 15ff. and 24 is too real, too sharply poignant to permit any reduction of the "I" to a mere figure of style. Whatever else this is, it is surely Paul speaking from the heart of his *own experience.*[153]

In addition, two of the objections cited previously against identifying the "I" as Paul's pre-conversion experience also speak

---

[149]As Kümmel, *Römer 7*, 119,132 argues; see the examples of this use he cites from Greek and Jewish sources, 126-32.

[150]Bruce, *The Letter of Paul to the Romans*, 144; he is skeptical of the attempt to omit any autobiographical element because what Paul describes here "has been the real experience of too many Christians."

[151]Nygren, *Commentary on Romans*, 288.

[152]Dunn, "Rom. 7,14-25 in the Theology of Paul," 261.

[153]Ibid., 260; see also idem., *Romans 1-8*, Word Biblical Commentary, vol. 38a, eds. R. Martin, D. Hubbard, and G. Barker (Dallas: Word Books, 1988), 405; Dodd, 123-26; Goguel, 213-14; Cranfield, 1:344.

against Kümmel's rhetorical line of interpretation. The first of these asks how the struggle depicted in Romans 7:14-25 could occur in unregenerate man.[154] Even Kümmel recognizes a problem here when he admits,

> There can be no doubt, in my opinion, that, in Romans 7:14ff., there is ascribed to the person a natural harmony with the spiritual Law, which Paul does not recognize elsewhere.[155]

A final objection to the "rhetorical" interpretation as a whole is found in the text of Romans 7 where the order of verses 24-25 oppose it. A number of solutions have been proposed in attempts at resolving this difficulty. The attempts to rearrange these verses were discussed previously.[156] Bultmann is led to argue that 7:25b is a later gloss.[157] However, both of these alternatives lack any textual evidence.[158] Kümmel prefers to see verse 25b as a summary of the pre-Christian

---

[154]For example, Cranfield, 1:346; also recognized, by Althaus, *Paulus und Luther über den Menschen*, 35; Nygren, *Commentary on Romans*, 289.

[155]Kümmel, *Römer 7*, 135, "*Es kann m. E. kein Zweifel daran sei, daß dem Menschen in Röm. 7, 14ff. eine natürliche Übereinstimmung mit dem pneumatischen Gesetz zugesprochen wird, die Paulus sonst so nicht kennt.*" He attempts to answer this objection by asserting, 125, that Paul's Christian faith enters into and influences this description, particularly in verses 14a and 25a. In addition, he contends, 134-38, that Paul's Christian experience of the Spirit's resistance to the flesh has colored his picture of the struggle between the mind and the flesh. Kümmel, *Das Bild des Menschen*, 191, finally resolves this tension by placing the blame upon "Paul's inadequate, dualistic, form of expression" ("*die unzulängliche dualistische Ausdrucksform des Paulus*").

[156]In addition to those cited above, see Michel, 179-80; F. Müller, "Zwei Marginalien im Brief des Paulus an die Römer," *Zeitschrift* 40 (1941):249-54; Dodd, 132-33.

[157]Bultmann, "Glossen im Römerbrief," *Theologische Literaturzeitung* 72 (1947): cols. 198-99. See also Otto Kuss's discussion "Zur Geschichte der Auslegung von Röm. 7,7-25," in *Der Römerbrief*, 3 vols., (Regensburg: Verlag Friedrich Pustet, 1963), 2:461, who evaluates v. 25b as "the gloss of a reader or copyist" ("*die Glosse eines Lesers order Abschreibers*").

[158]See Best, *The Letter of Paul to the Romans*, 94; also Kümmel, *Römer 7*, 67. Bruce, *The Letter to the Romans*, 148, responds, "It is precarious to rearrange the words of Paul in the interests of a smoother logical sequence."

experience described in verses 7-24.[159] James Dunn responds that this "makes too light of v. 25a and leaves 7,25b as a pathetic anti-climax."[160]

Specifically in response to Bultmann's view, Beker points out that any "striving for righteousness" is completely absent from verses 14-24.[161] In addition, Bultmann's trans-subjective interpretation

> is based, first, on identifying the good and evil in Rom. 7:18-19 with life and death (7:10,13), i.e., identifying them not with the good and evil actions themselves but with their results, and second, on the position that the motif of illusion in Rom. 7:11 is also presupposed in 7:13-23.[162]

Theissen contends that neither of these are supported by the text.[163] Even Kümmel rejects the "objective" aspect of Bultmann's interpretation because the "I" is not completely oblivious to his situation. On the contrary, the "I" subjectively recognizes his utter helplessness and his need for a Redeemer.[164] As a result, Beker concludes that Bultmann's interpretation "does not apply."[165]

Combinations of the Above

A number of the previous interpretations of the "I" in verses 14-25 have been mingled together. One approach acknowledges that the statements of the "I" depict Paul's own experience, but the scope of the words is expanded to represent the situation of other people as well. As Newman states,

> Whether or not Paul is speaking in the first instance of himself, it seems

---

[159]Kümmel, *Römer 7*, 65-66; see also Sanday and Headlam, 184.

[160]Dunn, "Rom. 7,14-25 in the Theology of Paul," 263, n. 32.

[161]Beker, *Paul the Apostle*, 239-40.

[162]Theissen, 232, n. 22.

[163]Ibid., "Observations with regard to verbal semantics [equating the 'good' with 'life'], structure [the deception of 7:11 is revealed by v. 13], and the history of tradition [citing, for example, Althaus, *Paulus und Luther über den Menschen*, 45-47; Kuss, 2:496-72] speak against this interpretation."

[164]Kümmel, *Römer 7*, 134.

[165]Beker, *Paul the Apostle*, 239.

impossible to avoid the conclusion that he intends to include others . . . together with himself in the description of the "I".[166]

Scholars who identify the "I" with Paul's pre-conversion experience suggest that the struggles of the "I" are typical of Jewish unbelievers. According to Hans Schoeps, Paul intends verses 14-25 to be understood as "a description of the life of all Jews, including that of Saul."[167] Bandstra contends that they more specifically present "a description of the Saul on the Damascus road, and, indeed, all Jewish Christians when confronted with the crucified and risen Messiah."[168]

Other interpreters expand the application of verses 14-25 even further to include all non-Christians.[169] Weinel contends that the description of the "I" represents "an experience common to us all."[170] Gundry points to the ability of "I" to delight in the Law (7:22) as indicative of a "moral monitor" present in all people.[171] Sanday and Headlam support this by making reference to "parallels . . . from Pagan literature."[172] Yet they somewhat more cautiously conclude,

The process described comes to different men at different times and in different degrees; . . . in one it would be quick and sudden, in another the slow growth of years.[173]

Those who see the "I" in verses 14-25 as representative of Paul's Christian experience similarly extend the struggle characterized by

---

[166]Newman, 134; similarly Barrett, 152.

[167]Schoeps, 184.

[168]Bandstra, 147; see also 143.

[169]Robinson, *Wrestling with Romans*, 87, cites Romans 2:14-17 as indicating the ability of unbelievers to know, agree with, and do God's will "precisely as 7.16 and 22 depict."

[170]Weinel, 74; though he qualifies this by stating that it does not affect all of us "with such profoundness and power."

[171]Gundry, 236, citing Rom. 1:18-32; 2:14-15.

[172]Sanday and Headlam, 185. For example, they cite Ovid who writes in *Metamorphoses* 7,21: "*video meliora proboque, deteriora sequor*" ("I see the better and approve; the lower I follow"). Cerfaux, 438, concludes, "It is reasonable to compare the inner conflict which Paul describes with that of Greek psychology."

[173]Sanday and Headlam, 186.

them to other Christians.[174] The present tense is said to warrant their application as one aspect of present Christian existence.[175] According to J. I. Packer,

> Paul means the whole experience . . . to be understood, not as a private peculiarity of his own, but as a typical and representative experience, for he presents it as affording a universally valid disclosure.[176]

Anders Nygren's view is that beginning in verse 14 Paul "describes the *present status* of the Christian, and the role of the law in the Christian life."[177] He concludes that Paul here intends to portray himself *and* all other Christians as being free from the Law, and yet not righteous by it. Although the Christian does not completely fulfill the Law in the flesh, he is now free from the Law "principally in the sense that he has been justified entirely without the cooperation of the law."[178]

A recognition of the difficulties present in all of the above interpretations has resulted in an entirely different approach to the problem. John A. T. Robinson suggests that simply asking whether the "I" in verses 14-25 is a Christian or not is to ask the wrong question. The contrast in verses 14-25 is not between the "then" and the "now" of the believer but between the "I" and the Law.[179] As a result, the issue of the spiritual condition of the "I" "is a little too complicated to be solved by a single Yes or No."[180]

By following this approach, it is argued that interpreting the "I" *either* as Paul before his conversion *or* as Paul after he became a Christian makes an unwarranted temporal limitation. Michael Grant applies the statements of the "I" in Romans 7:14-25 both to Paul's pre-conversion experience and to his life after conversion to Christianity.

---

[174]For example, Black, 101.

[175]Nygren, *Commentary on Romans*, 288-89; Franzmann, 128; Packer, 626-27.

[176]Packer, 623; he speaks this of verses 7-25 as a whole.

[177]Nygren, *Commentary on Romans*, 275; also 296-97.

[178]Ibid., 302.

[179]Robinson, *Wrestling with Romans*, 88.

[180]Emil Brunner, *The Letter to the Romans*, tr. H. Kennedy (Philadelphia: Westminster Press, 1959), 62.

After citing verses 19, 21, and 24, Grant concludes, "These self-tortures continued throughout [Paul's] life."[181] Charles Mitton similarly contends that Paul is not merely describing his experience before conversion. Rather, this is

> also the similar experience into which that same man, even after his conversion, can all too easily relapse . . . if ever he begins to imagine that it is in is own strength that he stands.[182]

The "I" then reveals "that which was true of Paul's past, and may become true of the present."[183] Barth's interpretation is comparable. He proposes that in verses 14-25

> Paul describes his past, present, and future existence. He portrays a situation as real after the episode on the road to Damascus as before it. He is writing about a man, broken in two by the law, but who, according to [the] law, cannot be thus broken. Paul is thrust into a dualism which contradicts itself. He is shattered on God, without the possibility of forgetting him.[184]

A number of those who adopt this broader description of Paul's own experience, or at least his potential experience, then expand the description of the "I" in verses 14-25 to include any Christian "in so far as he falls short of claiming and using the grace offered to him in Christ."[185] In addition, the "I" is also said to portray the struggles of any unconverted person. In Emil Brunner's words,

> Whether he feels it more deeply or less, this misery, truly considered, is the condition of man outside of Christ and that of the Christian always in so far as he places himself outside Christ, in so far as he lapses.[186]

---

[181]Michael Grant, *Saint Paul* (London: Weidenfeld and Nicolson, 1976), 109.

[182]Mitton, 132.

[183]Ibid., 134.

[184]Barth, 270; see also 257-70.

[185]Garvie, 174. So also Bruce, *The Letter of Paul to the Romans*, 145, "The inability persists only so long as I fight the battle in my own strength."

[186]Brunner, 66.

The "I" is then identified both with unbelievers and with Christians who are relying upon themselves or the Law for sanctification. Mitton states,

> The description [is] of a man who is trying to live the good life, but doing it in his own strength, relying on his own resources, whether the period in his life be before his conversion to Christ or after it, in a later period of "back-sliding," when through carelessness the absolutely essential "injection" of Divine power has been neglected.[187]

Those who support this line of interpretation translate the ἐγώ εἰμί of Romans 7:25 as "I left by myself" or "entirely on my own."[188] Robinson interprets the phrase as "Paul simply *qua* man, the self in its own unaided human nature. . . . a mere man (ἐγὼ ἄνθρωπος) facing the law by himself."[189] Romans 8 then proceeds to describe the mature Christian who is truly under the influence of the Spirit. There the "I" has "passed out of the storm and cloud of [Romans] 7" and left behind his earlier life or a lower stage of his Christian life which was isolated from the Spirit.[190]

While this latter approach at identifying the "I" may look attractive to some, those who oppose it argue that it creates more problems than it solves. First, the order of verses 24-25 speaks against it. If the desired deliverance or a higher stage of Christian living has been reached in 7:25a, how is the continued state of 25b explained? Dunn also notes that it relies rather heavily upon "forcing the αὐτὸς ἐγώ [in verse 25] into the unparalleled sense, 'I left to myself.'"[191]

---

[187]Mitton, 135.

[188]Ibid., 133-34. See also Bandstra, 147, who translates, "I on my own"; both Lambrecht, *The Wretched "I" and Its Liberation*, 55, and Moffatt, 194, render the phrase as, "I left to myself"; J. B. Phillips, *Letters to Young Churches* (New York: Macmillan, 1958), 16, translates, "I in my own nature"; and the Revised Standard Version, *The Oxford Annotated Bible,* eds. H. May and B. Metzger (New York: Oxford University Press, 1973), 1369, gives "I of myself."

[189]Robinson, *Wrestling with Romans*, 89-90; he contends that 1 Cor. 3:1-3 proves that believers can also be described as "fleshly," that is, as babes or immature Christians.

[190]Mitton, 134.

[191]Dunn, "Rom. 7,14-25 in the Theology of Paul," 263, n. 32.

Second, this line of interpretation contends "that Paul could conceive of Christian experience apart from Christ or apart from the Spirit."[192] The objection to this is the assertion that for Paul "the characteristic fact of the Christian is just this, that he is never left to himself. He lives his life 'in Christ.'"[193]

Finally, it maintains that a Christian must rely on his own strength to persevere in the Christian life with the aid of injections of "Divine reinforcement."[194] This stands in contrast to the foundation of the Christian hope which is laid by Paul in Romans 5:1-5 and 8:23-27, for example.

This last approach at interpreting Romans 7:14-25 illustrates the muddling which results from each of the "combined" interpretations mentioned above. Within it the "I" can ultimately be identified *as in each and every one of the disparate interpretations noted above!* As a result, these "combined" proposals are all left to face the objections levied against every one of the interpretations they bring together.

Conclusion

This survey has illustrated the general disagreement which continues to surround Romans 7, and has also revealed some of the difficulties involved in each of the widely-varied identifications which have been made of the "I." Attempts to resolve these problems have resulted in a number of interpretations which have only further complicated matters.

Two key factors have yet to be satisfactorily resolved. First, who is the "I" in Romans 7:7-25? Any attempt to identify the "I" should grapple with the issues involved in determining why and with what force Paul employs the first person singular so extensively here. An investigation of the various ways in which Paul employs the first person singular throughout his letters should shed some light on this issue.

---

[192]Stephen Westerholm, *Israel's Law and the Church's Faith* (Grand Rapids: Eerdmans Publishing, 1988), 61. He evaluates this conclusion as "incredible."

[193]Nygren, *Commentary on Romans*, 302.

[194]See Mitton, 135.

The second unresolved factor concerns the spiritual state of the "I" in verses 14-25. Paul's description in these verses may be unique as is evidenced by the claims that he "nowhere else" speaks of believers or unbelievers as he does here. The solution to this controversy can be found by comparing the "I" statements with what Paul says about himself before and after his conversion, as well as with the more general descriptions of unbelievers and the Christian life throughout the Pauline corpus.

Both of these aspects will be addressed more thoroughly in Chapters Three and Four. If these issues are properly appraised and then integrated into the interpretation of Romans 7, a correct understanding of Paul's meaning and of his purpose in writing this chapter can be more readily perceived.

In dealing with these contested issues, the constant temptation is to allow one's theological presuppositions to determine the solution which is adopted, rather than the words of Paul himself.[195] With this in mind, this study now turns to examine the text of Romans 7. For Paul's own words must be allowed to direct us toward a resolution of the disputed questions surrounding that chapter.

---

[195]Robinson, *Wrestling with Romans*, 84, in speaking of the varied answers which have been given to the question, "*Could* Paul have said this or that as a Christian?" charges, "In each case the judgment is made as much for subjective theological reasons as by any objective canon of exegesis."

Chapter Two

Semantics: An Exegetical Study of Romans 7 within Its Context

It has been suggested that the text of Paul's letters is not the place to begin an attempt to answer questions about his theology.[1] However, if the purpose is, indeed, to determine *Paul's view* on a given subject, the content of his own words certainly is the proper starting point. This chapter, then, begins to seek solutions to the disputed issues surrounding Romans 7 by investigating the sense, meaning, or content of the signs present in the text of Romans 7 within their context. This is the field of *semantics*.

> Semantics describes the relationship between the form of signs and their content (meaning). Here the question is addressed: How should/must what is said be understood? What is that which is meant?[2]

Romans 1-4

After an extended address (1:1-7) and a description of his relationship with the Christians in Rome (1:8-11), Paul states the theme of his

---

[1] For example, F. J. Bottorff, "The Relation of Justification and Ethics in Pauline Epistles," *Scottish Journal of Theology* 26 (1973):421, contends: "Any theologian who deludes himself into believing that he may begin studying a topic purely on the basis of the Greek text is almost surely doomed to repetition of past theological mistakes."

[2] Wolfgang Schenk, *Die Philipperbriefe des Paulus* (Stuttgart: Verlag W. Kohlhammer, 1984), 19, "*Semantik beschreibt die Relation zwischen Zeichengestalt und Zeichengehalt (Bedeutung): R(Z,B). Hier wird auf die Frage geantwortet: Wie sollte/müßte das Gesagte verstanden werden? Was ist das Gemeinte?*" The foundational study in the field of semantics is James Barr, *The Semantics of Biblical Language* (London: Oxford University Press, 1961); see also Anthony Thiselton, "Semantics and New Testament Interpretation," Chapter 4 in *New Testament Interpretation*, ed. I. Marshall (Grand Rapids: Eerdmans Publishing, 1977), 75-104.

letter in 1:16-17. He proceeds to expound these verses not by focusing upon the δικαιοσύνη θεοῦ revealed in the Gospel (1:17), but by declaring that the wrath of God (ὀργὴ θεοῦ) is "revealed from heaven against all ungodliness and unrighteous men" (1:18). Paul's goal in 1:18-3:20 is to validate his charge that "Jews and Greeks are all under sin" (πάντας ὑφ' ἁμαρτίαν; 3:9). He primarily deals with the condemnation of the Gentiles in 1:18-32 and, after a section applicable to both (2:1-16), turns to direct his attack specifically at the Jews who "rely on the Law and boast in God" (2:17).

A number of statements Paul makes in 1:18-3:20 regarding the Law have important implications in Chapter 7. His description of the Jews as those who have "the form (μόρφωσιν) of the knowledge and the truth ἐν τῷ νόμῳ" (2:20) at the same time conveys Paul's definition of the Mosaic Torah.[3] He charges that those who possess the revealed Torah will be judged διὰ νόμου (2:12). Therefore, throughout Chapter 2 Paul bases his accusations against the Jews on their transgression of God's Law (διὰ τῆς παραβάσεως τοῦ νόμου in 2:23; see also vv.25,27). He even concludes that one of the Law's effects is to bring forth the knowledge or recognition of sin (ἐπίγνωσις, 3:20).

Yet those who do not possess the revealed Law are not in any way excused from God's condemnation (1:20,28). "For those who sinned without the Law will also perish without the Law" (2:12). Paul explains the reason for this. The fact that those without the Mosaic Torah "by nature do the things of the Law" (2:14) shows that τὸ ἔργον τοῦ νόμου is written in their hearts and on their conscience (2:15). These will accuse them on the day of judgment (2:16).

---

[3]"The conventional translation of 'Torah' with 'Law' is most lamentable" according to Horace Hummel, *The Word Becoming Flesh* (St. Louis: Concordia Publishing House, 1979), 62. In the total Old Testament context, the reference is assuredly to "the Word of God." The translation "Law" has come through the Greek use of νόμος to (mis)translate the Hebrew תורה ("instruction/revelation"). As a result, the term "Law," when it refers to all or part of the Torah, will be capitalized here except when it occurs otherwise in quotations from other sources. Hummel, 62, recognizes that since it is not possible to "turn back the clock," we are left with the translation "Law." However, in view of the more narrow sense of the "Torah" Paul speaks about in Romans 7, the translation "Law" serves quite adequately.

Having demonstrated that all the world is accountable to God (3:19), Paul gives a concise, yet also profound and complete, statement of the δικαιοσύνη θεοῦ (3:21-26). The righteousness of God is given freely through faith in "the redemption which is in Christ Jesus" (3:24). This righteousness excludes any boasting in one's own works of the Law, but it does not thereby negate the Law. On the contrary, it firmly establishes the Law (3:27-31).

Paul validates his teaching of the δικαιοσύνη θεοῦ διὰ πιστεώς in Chapter 4 by appealing to Scripture's account of Abraham and the testimony of David (Gen. 15-22; Ps. 32:1-2). Regarding the promise to Abraham and his descendants, Paul asserts,

> For if the heirs are from the Law, then faith has been made empty and the promise has been rendered invalid. For the Law accomplishes wrath (ὀργήν). But where there is no Law, neither is there transgression (παράβασιν; 4:14-15).

Paul does not say there is no sin without the Law (2:12-16; 3:19-20,23), but that without the revealed Law there can be no transgression of the specific commands it lays upon man. His point is that once the Law comes, the wrath of God abounds all the more (1:18; 4:15).

Romans 5

Many commentators see Chapters 5-8 as comprising the next major section of Romans.[4] For example, Anders Nygren views them as an exposition of the manner in which "He Who Through Faith is Righteous Shall Live."[5] According to C. E. B. Cranfield, this life is characterized by peace with God (ch. 5), by sanctification (ch. 6), by freedom from the Law's condemnation (ch. 7), and by the indwelling

---

[4]C. E. B. Cranfield, *A Critical and Exegetical Commentary on the Epistle to the Romans*, The International Critical Commentary, vol. 32, 6th ed., 2 vols. (Edinburgh: T. & T. Clark, 1975,1979), 1:28, entitles Chapters 5-8 "The Life Promised for Those Who Are Righteous by Faith." Similarly C. H. Dodd, *The Epistle to the Romans*, The Moffatt New Testament Commentary (London: Fontana Books, 1959), vii-viii.

[5]Anders Nygren, *Commentary on Romans*, tr. D. Rasmussen (Philadelphia: Muhlenberg Press, 1949), 187.

of God's Spirit (ch. 8).[6] Others include Chapter 5 along with 3:21-4:25.[7] While either division may allude to one's interpretation of the section, neither is determinative of it. In Chapter 5 the connections with Romans 7 become more direct and by Chapter 6 the parallels are inescapable. As a result, these two chapters need to be presented in greater detail.

The first verse of Chapter 5 marks a transition in Paul's thought which is now directed toward the present state of the justified (δικαιωθέντες οὖν ἐκ πίστεως εἰρήνην ἔχομεν; 5:1). Instead of wrath, Christians now have peace with God and access to him through Christ (5:1-2). Yet due to the believer's continued presence in this world we also endure afflictions (ταῖς θλίψεσιν; 5:3). But these tribulations do not raise doubts about our peace with God. Rather, they serve to strengthen the perseverance and character of believers as we await the glory of God with renewed hope (vv. 2-4). This hope "is not put to shame because the love of God has been poured into and remains in our hearts through the Holy Spirit given to us" (v. 5).

In verses 6-11 Paul contrasts the "then" and the "now" of the believer. While still incurably sick sinners and enemies of God, "we were reconciled to God through the death of his Son" (v. 10). The fact that individual believers have received this reconciliation (ἐλάβομεν; v. 11) assures us that "we will be saved from the wrath" of God (σωθησόμεθα; vv. 9,10).

The argument in verses 12-21 begins to explain the previously alluded to interrelationship between sin, death, and the Law in more detail (3:20; 4:15). It was sin that brought death into the world through the sin of the one man, Adam. Death then spread to all people ἐφ' ᾧ

---

[6]Cranfield, 1:28. Nygren, *Commentary on Romans*, 188, summarizes the message of Chapters 5-8 as expressing the Christian's freedom from the wrath of God, from sin, from the Law, and from death.

[7]As such it comprises the conclusion of Paul's exposition of "The Way of Righteousness" according to Frederick F. Bruce, *The Letter of Paul to the Romans*, rev. ed., The Tyndale New Testament Commentaries, vol. 6 (Grand Rapids: Eerdmans Publishing, 1977), 64; see also Werner Kümmel, *Römer 7 und die Bekehrung des Paulus* (Leipzig: Hinrichs, 1929); reprinted in *Römer 7 und das Bild des Menschen im Neuen Testament: Zwei Studien*, Theologische Bücherei, Neues Testament Band 53 (Munich: Christian Kaiser Verlag, 1974), 7 [Hereafter, *Römer 7*]; Martin Franzmann, *Concordia Commentary: Romans* (St. Louis: Concordia Publishing House, 1968), 19.

πάντες ἥμαρτον (v. 12).[8] Paul has earlier held the whole world accountable to God because all have sinned (2:12-16; 3:9,19-20,23). In verse 18 he explicitly states another dimension: "Through one transgression there resulted condemnation for all men." Judgment comes upon all people as a result of Adam's transgression, as well as because of each person's own sin.

Paul explains that in the period before the Torah was given through Moses, "sin was in the world but sin is not accounted where there is no Law" (v. 13). In this context ἐλλογέω (to "charge to someone's account") means that the sins committed between Adam and the giving of the Law at Sinai could not be charged against a person as a παράβασις of the revealed Law of God. The following verse makes this clear when Paul points out that the sins of those ἀπὸ Ἀδαμ μέχρι Μωϋσέως (v. 14) were unlike Adam's sin. Since Adam knew the divinely revealed command of God (Gen. 2:16-17), his sin was a παράβασις of the Law.

This does not, however, excuse those who lived in the era between Adam and Moses from condemnation (vv. 15,18). Rather, Paul places them in a situation analogous to that of the Gentiles who do not know the Torah (2:12-16). Even apart from the revealed Law, God's condemnation of all people of all times is just. This is proven by the fact that even when the Law was not yet present, death still reigned over all people because of sin (βασιλεύω; v. 14).

Paul's point is that Adam is the father of all those who sin and all those who, therefore, die (v. 12). His reference to the Law is not to excuse those who sinned without the Law, but to emphasize that the giving of the Law only served to enhance the reign of sin and death. Paul concludes the negative side of his argument by stating, "The Law entered in order to make transgression increase" (v. 20).

Yet Adam is also a τύπος of the one who was about to come (v. 14). Paul contrasts the tragic results of Adam's transgression with the gift of grace which has abounded to the many through Jesus Christ (v.

---

[8]This is a difficult phrase. Louis Brighton, in his lecture notes on "Romans," New Testament Exegetical Department, Course EN-420, Concordia Seminary, St. Louis, MO, Fall, 1989, reads it as ἐπὶ τούτῳ ὅτι and translates, "on the basis of which." It seems to contain both the thought that Adam's sin led to the death of all and also that their own sin resulted in the same consequence. This is supported in the verses to follow.

15). Through the instrumentality of Adam's transgression, condemnation and judgment fell upon all people and all were placed under the reign of death (vv. 14-16,18). But "how much more did the grace of God and the gift in the grace of the one man, Jesus Christ, abound for the many" (v. 15). Those who receive "the gift of righteousness will reign in life through the one man, Jesus Christ" (v. 17).

Two observations emerge: 1) For Paul it is a matter of reigning (βασιλεύω). Either sin will reign, the end of which is death, or grace will rule through righteousness in Christ whose end is eternal life. 2) The major contrast in this chapter is between the "then" and the "now" of the Christian. Yet Paul has also indicated that there are elements which have yet to be removed from this present existence before the believer's reigning with Christ will be fully realized.[9] Both of these aspects are present in the last verses of Chapter 5:

> But where sin increased [through the Law!], grace increased all the more, in order that as sin reigned in death, so also grace might reign through righteousness to the end of eternal life through Jesus Christ our Lord (20b-21).

Romans 6

A rhetorical question prompts the discussion which begins Chapter 6 (τί οὖν; 6:1). The Law entered in order to increase transgression, thereby causing sin to abound all the more. Yet this abounding sin was "over-abounded" by grace (ὑπερπερισσεύω; 5:20). One might infer that our continuing to remain in sin would cause grace to abound still more. Paul responds to any such suggestion with μὴ γένοιτο. "We who have died to sin, how can we still live in it?" (v. 2).

"We died to sin" by being baptized into Jesus Christ (v. 3) whereby we were dead and buried into Christ's death.[10] The purpose of this was "so that just as Christ was raised from the dead through the

---

[9]Note the future tense in verses 9,10,19b and 23. This is the major thesis of C. Marvin Pate, *The End of the Age Has Come* (Grand Rapids: Eerdmans, 1995), see especially 80-83, 99-121.

[10]Note the four aorist passives in verses 3-4. They signify that this event was a one-time completed action effected by God (divine passives).

glory of the Father, so we also might walk in newness (καινότητι) of life" (v. 4b). παλαιὸς ἡμῶν ἄνθρωπος[11] was crucified together with Christ in order that τὸ σῶμα τῆς ἁμαρτίας might be done away with (v. 6). Paul further explains what he means by referring to the destruction of "the body of sin." It entails that "we are no longer enslaved to sin" (v. 6). Paul concludes, "For the one who has died has been and stands justified [or acquitted] from sin" (δεδικαίωται; v. 7).[12] But does this mean that the Christian no longer sins or that sin no longer has an effect upon the Christian?

Paul makes an interesting contrast in verses 5 and 8 (as in 5:9-11). Though our identification with the death of Christ in Baptism is now complete and enduring (perfect tense of γεγόναμεν; v. 5), our complete likeness in regard to his resurrection is spoken of in the future tense (ἐσόμεθα; v. 5). At the present time, the Christian believes (πιστεύομεν) that we shall in the future live together with Christ (συζήσομεν; v. 8). This does not detract from the fact that the believer now lives in Christ, but it acknowledges that our complete likeness in regard to his resurrection is not yet fulfilled. Since Jesus has already been raised from the dead, "death no longer exercises lordship over him" (v. 9). Christians, on the other hand, are still subject to physical death.

Paul concludes this thought in verses 10-11. Christ has died to sin and, having risen from the dead, now lives to God. So we should consider ourselves to be dead to sin but alive to God in Christ Jesus. Paul does not simply state that we are free from death or sin. He rather points out that in view of our past death with Christ through Baptism we should *reckon ourselves* to be dead to sin and alive to God. Paul's

---

[11]Since "sin entered the world through one man [Adam], and death through sin" (5:12), to term what is put to death here "the Old Adam" is indeed appropriate.

[12]Here the New International Version, *The Holy Bible* (International Bible Society, 1984) translates, "Because anyone who has died has been freed from sin." Similary the Revised Standard Version, *The New Oxford Annotated Bible*, eds. H. May and B. Metzger (New York: Oxford University Press, 1973), 1367, translates, "For he who has died is freed from sin." Paul does *not* say believers are "free" (ἐλευθερόω) from sin. His sense is closer to "having been forgiven," "acquitted," or, literally, "justified"; see Walter Bauer, *A Greek-English Lexicon of the New Testament and Other Early Christian Literature*, 2nd ed., tr. W. Arndt and F. Gingrich, rev. and augmented from Bauer's 5th ed., 1958, by F. Gingrich and F. Danker (Chicago: The University of Chicago Press, 1979), 197[3a]. [Hereafter, *BAGD*]

use of λογίζομαι[13] indicates that if we examine our existence from a human point of view, we may not yet appear to be dead to sin or fully alive to God. But in the same manner in which God *accounted* the faith of "ungodly" Abraham as righteousness (4:3,5; Gen. 15:6), we can confidently *reckon* our death to sin and our life to God as real in spite of the possibility that present experience appears to contradict this.

This tension leads into a section of exhortation within which its paradoxical nature is exhibited even more clearly. "Do not continue to allow sin to rule (βασιλευέτω) in your mortal body (ἐν τῷ θνητῷ ὑμῶν σώματι) so that you obey its desires" (ἐπιθυμίαις; 6:12). In view of the preceding, this transition is very significant. Even though we Christians have died to sin and "our body of sin" has been done away with (vv. 2,6), ἐπιθυμίαι are still present in our "mortal bodies" and sin continues to pose a force which must constantly be battled. Paul urges his fellow Christians to avoid putting these desires into action. They are to fight against sin as it strives to "rule" once again.

Verse 13 adds the positive side. Paul implores his readers to yield their "members" to God. τὰ μέλη are introduced here and depicted as the "members" of a Christian which can either be used by sin as weapons or tools (ὅπλα) of unrighteousness or presented to God as tools of righteousness (see 7:23).

Paul's basis for his entire exhortation is given in verse 14: "Sin will not be lord over you,[14] for you are not under the Law but under grace." In this verse Paul gives us another glimpse into the relationship between sin and the Law.[15] He implies that there are two powers under which the Christian once lived and under whose domination he might again fall. However, the contrast Paul sets up is not between grace and

---

[13]λογίζομαι is the same verb used to express that God counted Abraham righteous (Gen. 15:6 cited in Rom. 4:4; see *BAGD*, 476[b]). In 4:5 Paul concludes that "to the one who does not work but believes in the One who justifies the ungodly, his faith is counted for righteousness."

[14]Nigel Turner, *A Grammar of New Testament Greek*, vol. 3 (Edinburgh: T. & T. Clark, 1963), 177, very significantly points out that ἁμαρτία here does not carry the idea of "no sin," but speaks of the power of sin to rule. See also F. Blass and A. Debrunner, *A Greek Grammar of the New Testament*, tr. and rev. by R. Funk (Chicago: The University of Chicago Press, 1961), 258[2]. This is implied in verses 18 and 22 as well.

[15]Most commentators identify this as the thought to which Paul returns in 7:1.

sin but stated in terms of grace and the Law. Paul thereby equates being "under the Law" with remaining under the lordship of Master Sin!

The hypothetical question of verse 15 is posed in reaction to this and introduces a topic (τί οὖν) which dominates the discussion until the end of the chapter. The hypothetical questioner of 6:1 wanted to continue in sin since that would lead grace to abound all the more. Now in verse 15 it is suggested, "Let us sin because we are not under the Law but under grace." Paul, as in 6:2, sharply responds, "μὴ γένοιτο!" He then presents an either/or scenario which is applied to the life of the believer before and after faith. The contrast between the "then" and the "now" is stated in terms of two kinds of slavery. The person is either a slave of sin which leads to death (vv. 16,17, 18,20,22) or one who "listens to"[16] God's Word which leads to righteousness (vv.16,18,22). In essence Paul declares,

> You Christians were formerly slaves of sin[17] who presented your members (μέλη) as slaves to impurity and into more and more lawlessness (vv. 17,19). The fruit of such a life was things of which you believers are now ashamed and whose end you now recognize was death (v. 21).

Paul contrasts this with what happened when "you listened from the heart to the form of teaching to which you were delivered" (v. 17). A believer has been moved from one slavery to another. "Having been freed from [slavery to] sin,[18] you were enslaved to righteousness" (v. 18; also v. 22). The result of this "slavery to God" is that Christians have fruit which is directed toward sanctification and ends with the goal of eternal life (v. 22). Verse 23 succinctly sets forth this contrast: "For the wages of sin is death, but the free gift of God is eternal life in Christ Jesus our Lord."

---

[16]The conventional translation of ὑπακούω with "obey" is appropriate at times. However, if it implies "doing the Law's commands," such an understanding of v. 16 is rejected by Paul in Romans (3:19-20; 4:4-5). In 10:16 Paul parallels ὑπακούω with πιστεύω. The Hebrew שמר ל ("to hearken to") is the background.

[17]The imperfect tense of ἦτε indicates durative action in past time and stands in sharp contrast to the present; see Blass and Debrunner, 327.

[18]The "slavery to" sin is clearly implied in both verses 18 and 22.

Romans 7

Werner Kümmel, along with many other scholars, contends that Paul's main purpose in Romans 7 is to defend the Law.[19] Since Paul's over-arching topic of concern throughout Romans 5-8 is the Christian life,[20] Anders Nygren more specifically concludes that Chapter 7 discusses the *"Christian's freedom from the law."*[21] It would appear

---

[19]*"Die Apologie des Gesetzes"* according to Kümmel, *Römer 7,* 56; see also 9,10,11. He concludes that this is especially the case after verse 7, but senses a somewhat altered focus beginning in verse 18. In regard to the general view, see also, for example, J. Christiaan Beker, *Paul the Apostle* (Philadelphia: Fortress Press, 1980), 83,105; Rudolf Bultmann, "Romans 7 and Paul's Anthropology," chap. in *The Old and New Man in the Letters of Paul*, tr. K. Crim (Richmond, VA: John Knox Press, 1967), 41; James Dunn, *Romans 1-8*, Word Biblical Commentary, vol. 38a, eds. R. Martin, D. Hubbard, and G. Barker (Dallas: Word Books, 1988), 377; Krister Stendahl, "The Apostle Paul and the Introspective Conscience of the West, *Harvard Theological Review* 56 (1963):211-12. Ernst Käsemann, *Commentary on Romans*, tr. and ed. G. Bromiley (Grand Rapids, Eerdmans Publishing, 1980), 192, considers this "a common German view" and he further proposes, 195, that these verses attempt to distinguish the intention and the function of the Law. Yet, in a manner somewhat similar to Kümmel, Käsemann contends that after 14a, "the Torah recedes completely into the background." He concludes, ibid., 192, that "the effectiveness of sin is more strongly emphasized" in the remainder of Chapter 7.

Reflecting a slightly different interpretation, Barclay Newman, "Once Again— The Question of 'I' in Romans 7:7-25," *The Bible Translator* 34 (1983):133, goes on to state that Paul's *"primary goal* in the chapter *is that of defining the role of the Law in the history of salvation."* On this approach, see also Ethelbert Stauffer, in *Theological Dictionary of the New Testament*, 10 vols., eds. G. Kittel and G. Friedrich, tr. G. Bromiley (Grand Rapids: Eerdmans Publishing, 1973), s.v. "ἐγώ," 2:358-62. [Hereafter, *TDNT.*]

[20]Nygren, *Commentary on Romans*, 287-88, concludes that on the question of the nature of the Christian life, Paul's "answer is fourfold: it means to be free from Wrath, Sin, the Law, and Death." A further distinction has been pointed out by Nils A. Dahl, "Two Notes on Romans 5," *Studia Theologica* 5 (1951):40, points out that Chapters 5 and 8 speak of the final eschatological deliverance from wrath and death, while Chapters 6-7 deal with the present forces of sin and the Law. Dunn, *Romans 1-8*, 260, affirms that 7:7-25 speaks of the same condition as both 6:1-7:6 and Chapter 8, but from a different aspect. See also John Espy, Paul's 'Robust Conscience' Re-examined, *New Testament Studies* 31 (1985):169,181.

[21]Nygren, *Commentary on Romans*, 288. Cranfield, 1:330, introduces Chapter 7 as follows: "The life promised for the man who is righteous by faith is, in the third place, described as a life characterized by freedom from the law, that is, from the law in the limited sense of the-law-as-condemning or the law's condemnation." Similarly

then that Romans 7 focuses our attention upon the Law and its function(s), possibly both before and also within the Christian life.

The significance of Romans 7 for Pauline theology cannot be over-exaggerated. For "when the issue is freedom from the law, Paul's doctrine of justification is under debate at its most offensive point."[22] As a result, while Paul strives to defend the Law in this chapter, he also "brings out the essential point that the law . . . has no saving power."[23]

However, even if there was general agreement concerning these points, controversy continues to surround the fact that in Romans 7 Paul employs "a form of words that inevitably arouses interest about the deeper background of his thought."[24] The specific "form of words" which has been the focus of so much attention is Paul's consistent use of the first person singular.[25] How this "I" is to be identified remains a matter of great dispute. A full discussion of the issue will be reserved for the third and fourth chapters of this study.

---

also Günther Bornkamm, "Sin, Law and Death," in *Early Christian Experience*, The New Testament Library, 87-104, tr. P. Hammer (London: SCM Press, 1969), 87-88.

[22]See, for example, James Dunn, "Rom. 7,14-25 in the Theology of Paul," *Theologische Zeitschrift* 31 (1975):257, who believes that "dispute about a tense, a phrase, a half-verse in Rom. 7 means in fact dispute about the whole character of Paul's gospel." See also Käsemann, 210; Nygren, *Commentary on Romans*, 266, agrees that within Chapters 5-8, the topic of Chapter 7 represents "the most important and hardest point."

[23]R. C. H. Lenski, *The Interpretation of St. Paul's Epistle to the Romans*, Commentaries on the New Testament (Minneapolis: Augsburg Publishing House, 1961), 450; he also concludes that Paul shows that the Law cannot be relied upon "as a producer of good works." See below on 8:3.

[24]Douglas Milne, "Romans 7:7-12, Paul's Pre-Conversion Experience," *The Reformed Theological Review* 43 (1984):9. Leon Morris, *The Epistle to the Romans* (Grand Rapids: Eerdmans Publishing, 1988), 269, properly keeps both of these in focus in stating that other "questions" which have arisen concerning this chapter "are not unimportant, but we should be clear that it is the place of the law that Paul is discussing. . . . The 'I' . . . is only of secondary interest."

[25]The first person singular occurs in a verb form or as a pronoun 48 times in verses 7-25. In contrast, there are two references to the first person plural (vv. 7,14), one in the second person singular (the commandment of v. 7), and none in the second person plural in those same verses. The emphatic ἐγώ occurs first in verse 9 and is used 7 or 8 times through verse 25, depending on the variant in v. 20a.

The language and structure of the first six verses of Romans 7 closely parallel the discussion regarding the Christian's relationship to sin and death in Chapter 6. For example,

Chapter 6	*Chapter 7*
ἡ ἁμαρτία (v. 1)	ὁ νόμος (v. 1)
ἀπεθάνομεν τῇ ἁμαρτίᾳ (v. 2)	ἐθανατώθητε τῷ νόμῳ (v. 4)
ἐν καινότητι ζωῆς περιπατήσωμεν (v. 4)	ἐν καινότητι πνεύματος δουλεύειν (v. 6)
Χριστὸς ἐγερθεὶς ἐκ νεκρῶν (v. 9)	τῷ ἐκ νεκρῶν ἐγερθέντι (v. 4)
ὁ γὰρ ἀποθανὼν δεδικαίωται ἀπο τῆς ἁμαρτίας (v. 7)	κατηργήθημεν ἀπο τοῦ νόμου ἀποθανόντες ἐν ᾧ κατειχόμεθα (v. 6)
ἐλευθερωθέντες ἀπὸ τῆς ἁμαρτίας (v. 18)	ἐλευθερωθέντες ἀπὸ τοῦ νόμου (v. 3)

While 6:1-11 had stressed the Christian's discontinuity with the present age of sin and death, the exhortation of 6:12-23 emphasized the believer's continuing existence within it. In view of the above parallels, one would expect the same pattern to begin again in Romans 7.

A number of previous passages have provoked the discussion in Chapter 7, but Paul returns most directly to his statement in 6:14 as he begins: "**Or are you ignorant, brothers, for I am speaking to [ones] knowing the Law, that the Law exercises lordship over a man as long as he lives?**" (v. 1).

For the first time since 1:13, Paul addresses his hearers as ἀδελφοί (also v. 4). He further identifies them as "those who know the Law" (γινώσκουσιν νόμον). This phrase is not "in any way restrictive," but includes all of the letter's recipients.[26] While Paul had previously treated the all-encompassing lordship of sin and death,[27] he now adds, "ὁ νόμος κυριεύει." He has also alluded to a connection between the Law, sin, and death (for example, 3:20; 4:15; 5:13,20), and he now turns to spell out the relationship which exists between them.[28]

Paul proceeds by presenting this illustration: **"For example, a married woman has been and remains bound by the Law to the living husband. But if the husband dies, she is completely absolved from the Law of the husband. So then, as long as the husband is living, she would be called an adulteress if she marries another man. But if the husband dies, she is free from the Law, so that she would not be an adulteress if she marries another man"** (vv. 2-3).

Legal pronouncements similar to those present here could certainly have been drawn from other systems of law or even "the idea of law in general."[29] Yet Paul's authoritative source is clearly the Mosaic Torah.

---

[26]John Murray, *The Epistle to the Romans*, 2 vols. (Grand Rapids: Eerdmans Publishing, 1959,1965), 1:240, states, "All are credited with this knowledge. . . . Gentiles as well as Jews in the church at Rome could be credited with the knowledge of the Old Testament." According to Dunn, *Romans 1-8*, 359, this passage, along with the illustration to follow, which "presupposes the legislative position of Judaism," indicates that Paul assumes a familiarity with the Old Testament on the part of his readers. This "strengthens the likelihood that the bulk of the gentile converts had previously been adherents to the Jewish synagogues." See also Lenski, 442. This expression need not imply with Alan Segal, "Romans 7 and Jewish Dietary Law," *Studies in Religion* 15 (1986): 362, that "Paul addresses himself primarily to the Jewish Christians."

[27]See especially 5:14,17,21; 6:6,9,12,14,16,22.

[28]John A. T. Robinson, *Wrestling with Romans* (Philadelphia: The Westminster Press, 1979), 80, concludes that Paul "can postpone a thorough reckoning with the law and its status no longer." See also Kümmel, *Römer 7*, 7-8,36; and Beker, *Paul the Apostle*, 83, who contends that these previous references "compel Paul to a fuller discussion. And yet that discussion cannot occur until 5:12-21 and 6:1-15 have laid the foundations. Thus Rom. 7:1-25 functions as a necessary excursus."

[29]Barclay Newman and Eugene Nida, *A Translator's Handbook on Paul's Letter to the Romans*, Helps for Translators, vol. 14 (London: United Bible Societies, 1973), 128; Käsemann, 187, similarly refers to "the legal order." William Sanday and Arthur C. Headlam, *A Critical and Exegetical Commentary on the Epistle to the Romans*, The International Critical Commentary, vol. 32 (New York: Charles Scribner's Sons, 1902), 172, attribute this to law in general since what follows is based upon "an obvious axiom of political justice—that death clears all scores."

Particularly in contrast to Roman law, the Old Testament Law provided the right of divorce only to the husband (Deut. 24:1-4) and freed the wife immediately at her husband's death.[30]

Many have assailed the propriety of Paul's analogy.[31] "But all these difficulties fall away as soon as one gives up the thought of an allegorical connection between 7:2-3 and 7:4."[32] Since "there is

---

Lenski, 441,444,451, follows this interpretation and attempts to support it by pointing to a distinction between Paul's use of νόμος with and without the article, the former denoting the Torah. Whether a distinction between the arthrous and the anarthrous use can or should be made has been debated. Questions mainly center on whether νόμος, without the article as in 7:2, can refer to the Mosaic Law. Following Origen, Sanday and Headlam, 58, set up general categories where νόμος with the article conveys the Law of Moses or a Law familiar to the readers, and the anarthrous use specifies "law in general." Yet they admit many difficulties. It is not possible to establish and maintain any such distinction. The foundational study here is Eduard Grafe, *Die paulinische Lehre vom Gesetz nach den vier Hauptbriefen* (Tübingen, J. C. B. Mohr, 1884), see especially 5-8. See also Kümmel, *Römer 7*, 55, who concludes that in this context νόμος with or without the article means the same thing, "namely the Mosaic Law." *BAGD*, 542, defines νόμος "especially as the Law of Moses" and includes the meaning of "νόμος without the article in the same sense" (citing Rom. 2:13a,b,17,25a; 3:31a,b; 5:13,20; 7:1a; also Gal. 2:19b; 5:23). W. Gutbrod, in *TDNT*, s.v. "νόμος," 4:1074, states, "It is certainly not true that νόμος is 'a' law as distinct from ὁ νόμος, 'the' Law."

[30]According to Roman law, either partner could end the marriage. In addition, when a husband died, the wife was obligated to mourn and remain unmarried for 12 months or forfeit anything which was supposed to come to her from her deceased husband. See P. E. Corbett, *The Roman Law of Marriage* (Oxford: Clarendon Press, 1930, reprint 1969), 249, as cited by Dunn, *Romans 1-8*, 359-60; see also C. K. Barrett, *A Commentary on the Epistle to the Romans*, Black's New Testament Commentaries (London: Adam and Charles Black, 1962), 135-36.

[31]Joyce Little, "Paul's Use of Analogy: A Structural Analysis of Romans 7:1-6," *Catholic Biblical Quarterly* 46 (1984):87, concludes that "viewed as analogy or allegory, this section, if not a failure, certainly limps very badly." The most extreme criticism comes from Dodd, 119-121; somewhat more mildly, Newman and Nida, 129, state, "Paul's analogy . . . is not perfect." Murray, 1:242-43, attempts to explain Paul's intention in allowing the apparent discrepancies.

[32]Kümmel, *Römer 7*, 41, "*Aber alle diese Schwierigkeiten fallen, sobald man den Gedanken an die allegorische Beziehung von 7, 2.3 und 7, 4 aufgibt*" For a survey of interpretations, see Kümmel, *Römer 7*, 39-40; Little, 86; J. C. O'Neill, *Paul's Letter to the Romans* (Baltimore: Penguin Books, 1975), 120-24.

nothing in the text to suggest allegorical intent,"[33] it is more proper to understand these verses as something of an illustration or parable with one *tertium comparationis*. In this way, Paul's point is readily understood: "The occurrence of a death effects a decisive change in respect of relationship to the law."[34]

The application Paul makes from his statement in verse 1, as illustrated in verses 2-3, is this: **"So, my brothers, *you* were also made to die to the Law through the body of Christ, so as to belong to another,[35] to the one who has been raised from the dead, so that we might bear fruit for God"** (v. 4). To those who had been under the lordship of the Law which confirmed and sealed their bondage to sin, Paul states, "ὑμεῖς ἐθανατώθητε."[36] He asserts that just as "there is a death which liberates from the lordship of sin (6:9-10,18); so there is a death which liberates from the lordship of the law."[37] In light of 6:2-11, the manner in which Paul draws this conclusion points

---

[33]Murray, 1:240; Käsemann, 187, similarly concludes, "There is not the slightest basis for the common practice . . . of allegorically importing the subject matter of vv. 4-6 already here." So also Lenski, 445.

[34]Cranfield, 1:334-35. He believes, 1:335, that "this is confirmed by the fact that verse 4 is introduced by ὥστε." Dunn, *Romans 1-8*, 369, observes that "the illustration is *not* one of the believer's transition from one state to another, but of the basic principle that death liberates from the law." Henry Alford, *The Greek New Testament*, 4 vols., 5th ed. (Cambridge: Deighton, Bell, and Co., 1865), 2:375, similarly concludes "that the Apostle is insisting on the fact, that DEATH DISSOLVES LEGAL OBLIGATION: but he is not drawing an exact parallel." See also Kümmel, *Römer 7*, 39; Dodd, 101.

[35]The metaphor of marriage used in the illustration in verse 3 is also present here. Nygren, *Commentary on Romans*, 273, points out that these words "take on a certain coloring from the illustration." Indeed, they convey the idea of an intimate relationship (1 Cor. 6:17; 2 Cor. 1:2; Eph. 5:25-33).

[36]The aorist passive tense of θανατόω emphasizes that the past death of the Christian is God's doing and not an act of the natural course of nature. Both "our passivity and the effectiveness of the action are clearly indicated," according to Murray, 1:243. Here θανατόω must be interpreted in light of being crucified and buried with Christ in 6:2-4; see also 8:13; Cranfield, 1:336; Lenski, 448-49.

[37]Dunn, *Romans 1-8*, 368; Nygren, *Commentary on Romans*, 271, "a death has intervened"; see also 6:11,22: Gal. 2:19-20.

"unmistakably" to Baptism[38] where the Christian has been made to die "διὰ τοῦ σώματος τοῦ Χριστοῦ" (7:4; see 6:3-4a).[39]

What does the resulting freedom from the Law entail? Certainly not the abrogation of the Law (3:31).[40] Paul does not say the Law has died, rather, the Christian has. As a result, the Christian is free from the Law's dominion and from the Divine wrath which it pronounces upon those who fail to fulfill its demands (see v. 6b; 1:18; 3:19-20; 4:15; Gal. 3:10). Furthermore, this freedom is directed toward a positive end, service to God (as in 6:22; 7:6).

The interrelationship between the first four verses of the chapter is clear:

> The steps of the proof are these: *The law binds a man only so long as he lives* (ver. 1), e.g., a married woman is only bound to her husband so long as he lives (vv. 2, 3), so also the Christian *being dead* with Christ and alive to Him *is freed from the law* (ver. 4).[41]

---

[38]Käsemann, 188; he cites "the aorist tense and the total context" as evidence for the fact that in Baptism, 189, "incorporation into the rule of Christ and total separation from the law coincide." Nygren, *Commentary on Romans*, 274, agrees citing Chapter 6 and 1 Cor. 12:23; also Kümmel, *Römer 7*, 37.

[39]Dodd, 120; and John A. T. Robinson, *The Body*, (London: SCM Press, 1952; reprint Bristol, IN: Wyndam Hall Press, The Graduate Theological Foundation, 1988), 47, make reference to one's incorporation into the Church in interpreting this phrase. It seems best to regard this entire phrase with Dunn, *Romans 1-8*, 369, as a reference "to the exposition two or three paragraphs earlier (6:3-6). 'The body of Christ' is clearly Christ in his bodily crucifixion" into which we are baptized. Compare 1 Cor. 12:13; Col. 1:22; see also Heb. 10:5,10; 1 Pet. 2:24; Käsemann, 189; Morris, *The Epistle to the Romans*, 273; Nygren, *Commentary on Romans*, 274.

[40]Käsemann, 189, states, "What is done away with is not just the curse of the law. It is the Torah itself." Though he later qualifies, 190, "The Christian's freedom from the power of the Torah is proclaimed." Kümmel, *Römer 7*, 7, similarly asserts that the Law possesses only a "temporary condition" (*"zeitliche Bedingtheit"*) which is, 8, now "disposed" (*"abgetanen"*). As 3:31 and the remainder of this chapter testify, Nygren, *Commentary on Romans*, 272, properly contends, "To Paul there can be no thought of the law dying."

[41]Alford, 2:374; similarly Kümmel, *Römer 7*, 41.

Verses 5 and 6, respectively, proceed to contrast the "then" and the "now" of the believer in light of verse 4 (compare 6:17-22).[42] **"For when we[43] were in the sphere of the flesh, the passions of sins which were through the Law were operating in our members so as to bear fruit to death"** (v. 5).[44] Before Christians were put to death to the Law, we were "in the flesh." It is crucial to allow the context to determine exactly what Paul means by ἐν τῇ σαρκί since he uses σάρξ a number of times in this chapter and employs it "in a variety of ways" in his letters.[45]

In the Septuagint σάρξ normally translates בשׂר and denotes "the difference between the creating God and the creature."[46] As a result, Paul can use σάρξ in a somewhat neutral manner in order to describe the believer's life in this world and even Jesus' "fleshly" existence.[47]

---

[42]Nygren, *Commentary on Romans*, 275; Kümmel, *Römer 7*, 8; Käsemann, 191, summarizes, "Only after dominion of the Spirit . . . is the dominion of the law broken and vanquished."

[43]Paul often alternates between the first and second persons plural (for example, 6:14-16; 8:11-16; 13:11-14).

[44]Dunn, *Romans 1-8*, 365, notes how θάνατος serves as both the power ruling over man, as well as the fruit of existence "in the flesh."

[45]Morris, *The Epistle to the Romans*, 274; he summarizes that Paul uses this word 91 times to "refer to the soft constituent of the human body (1 Cor. 15:50), and thus to a human being (1 Cor. 1:29). It may mean human nature (Rom. 9:5), or this earthly life (Phil. 1:24), or human attainment (Phil. 3:3), from which it is not a long step to outward appearance (1 Cor. 1:26). But this body of flesh is weak (Rom. 6:19), and the thought of physical weakness leads on to that of moral weakness. It has this meaning here and very often in Paul."

Thus depending on what σάρξ is associated with in the context, its sense ranges from the merely physical (2 Cor. 4:11; Gal. 4:14; Col. 2:1), to human weakness (7:18; 8:3), to open opposition to God (8:8,9; Philemon 16) It is not, therefore, always "unqualifiedly evil" as Murray, 1:245, suggests or, with Herman Ridderbos, *Paul*, tr. J. De Witt (Grand Rapids: Eerdmans, 1975), 103, a "description of sin itself." Murray, 1:244,259, attempts to make a distinction between a "moral" and "physical" sense.

[46]Käsemann, 188. See Friedrich Baumgärtel, Eduard Schweizer, and Rudolf Mayer, in *TDNT*, s.v. "σάρξ," 7:98-151, especially 135. Baumgärtel, 108, notes that σάρξ translates בשׂר 145 times in the Septuagint, nearly twice as often as any other word. Schweizer summarizes, 123, that in the Old Testament "man is seen from the very first in his relation to God. As creature of God he is flesh."

[47]Rom. 1:3; 9:5; Eph. 2:15; Col. 1:22; 1 Tim. 3:16.

However, in 7:5 Paul clearly employs the phrase ἐν τῇ σαρκί to describe the Christian's past.[48] ἐν τῇ σαρκί here characterizes the time "when we were altogether under the domination of the flesh,"[49] when it was our "determining condition."[50] At that time the παθήματα τῶν ἁμαρτιῶν were active in our μέλη which were exploited for the purpose of evil.[51]

The phrase διὰ τοῦ νόμου indicates that the Law had an integral connection with the passions of sins and a life lived in the flesh. Such a statement would have shocked those Jews who viewed their performance of ἔργα τοῦ νόμου as grounds for boasting (2:17,23; 3:27-28; 9:30-10:5).

In contrast to that view of the Law's purpose and function, Paul has already noted that the Law is an active agent in the service of sin and death (2:12; 3:20; 4:15; 5:13,20). He has charged those who "relied upon the Law and boasted in God" (2:17) with misusing His Law (2:12-19; 3:27-31; 4:13-16). In fact, for Paul, his own people's relying on the Law and on circumcision in the flesh is one illustration of the existence he here describes as ἐν τῇ σαρκί (2:17-29; 7:5; 9:30-10:5; compare Phil. 3:3-4; Gal. 6:13). That life is also determined by the flesh and results in death (as in 6:21,23).

Verse 6 concludes this section with a description of the tremendous liberation from the Law which comes through the Holy Spirit. **"But now, as it is, we have been completely discharged from the Law, having died to that by which we were confined . . . "** (v.

---

[48]Murray, 1:244, points out that except for the possible exception of 6:19, "this is the first occurrence in this epistle in which the word 'flesh' is used in its full depreciatory ethical sense," as in 8:4,5,6,7,8,9,12,13; 13:14.

[49]Cranfield, 1:337, who defines this phrase as "having the basic direction of [our] lives determined and controlled by [our] fallen nature." He cites parallels in 8:4,5,12,13.

[50]Ulrich Wilckens, *Der Brief and die Römer*, Evangelisch-katholischer Kommentar, 3 vols. (Cologne: Benziger and Neukirchen-Vluyn: Neukirchener, 1978-82), 2:70, uses "*Machtphäre.*"

[51]μέλη here, as in 6:13,19; 7:23, is in itself, a neutral term. However, as Dunn, *Romans 1-8*, 364, states, "A life ruled by or lived chiefly on the level of the παθήματα is almost certain to be a tool manipulated by sin"; compare ἐπιθυμία in 1:24 and especially 7:8. While παθήματα more often has the sense of suffering and affliction in Paul (see 8:18; Murray, 1:245, n. 9), here and in Gal. 5:24 it has an even more negative sense.

6a). The νυνί moves from the past to the Christian's present (compare 3:21; 5:11). Paul declares that we were, and now stand, released from the Law because we have died to the Law (as in v. 4). This is the point of comparison with the marriage illustration in verses 2-3. The Law exercised lordship over us (v. 1) by holding us in captivity and servitude to sin and death until our own death with Christ in Baptism (6:3-4; Gal. 3:23-27).

The "actual and assured result"[52] of this death is that ". . . **we serve in the newness which comes from the Spirit**[53] **and not in the oldness which comes from the letter**" (v. 6b). Although παλαιότης occurs only here in the New Testament,[54] it is undoubtedly to be linked with ὁ παλαιὸς ἡμῶν ἄνθρωπος which was crucified with Christ in 6:6.[55] The phrase "oldness of the letter" is certainly "a reference to the law; . . . but not the law as such."[56] As Gottlob Schrenk observes, "When the reference is to γράμμα, Paul is always thinking of the legal authority which has been replaced."[57] Here Paul sets up the same contrast with πνεῦμα as in 2:29. γράμμα denotes the condemnatory power of the Law which is the only authority it has over "the old man" (6:6) who strives to live by "the letter of the Law," that is, the person

---

[52]Murray, 1:246, n. 11; purpose is implied, but the full sense is that of an actual result; see also 15:19; Phil. 1:13; Blass Debrunner, 391[2]; Cranfield, 1:339; Lenski, 454-55.

[53]πνεύματος must refer to the Holy Spirit and not the human spirit; see 5:5; 8:9-15; Gal. 3:1-14; Sanday and Headlam, 176; Cranfield, 1:339-40. For example, Alford, 2:377, states that it refers to "the Holy Spirit of God who originates and penetrates the Christian life." Thus it is difficult to consider the argument of Robinson, *The Body*, 84, who contends that the Spirit is completely absent from Romans 7; see also Franz Leenhardt, *The Epistle to the Romans*, tr. H. Knight (London: Lutterworth Press, 1961), 194. Even if this were accurate, πνεύματος has not occurred previously in Romans and one could hardly argue that the influence of the Spirit has been absent from the actions described in the previous chapters.

[54]Morris, *The Epistle to the Romans*, 275, n. 31.

[55]This is further supported by the appearance of καινότητι both here and in 6:4 and the contrast between the "then" and "now" of the believer in both passages.

[56]Dunn, *Romans 1-8*, 373; it refers specifically to the Law misunderstood in terms of works (2:27-29; 2 Cor. 3).

[57]Gottlob Schrenk, in *TDNT*, s.v. "γράμμα," 1:768; he also points out that "γράμμα is not used when [Paul] speaks of the positive and lasting significance of Scripture. This positive task is always stated in terms of γραφή."

apart from the Spirit.

Although free from the Law's lordship and condemnation, Paul includes himself in the transition to where "we" now serve God as slaves (v. 6; compare 6:15-23). Positively speaking, then, this liberation "is *not* anarchic or self-chosen freedom, but into a different kind of slavery and service—to God" (as in 6:18,22).[58] However, it is not legitimate to infer from this that the Christian is now able to refrain from transgressing against the Law completely.[59]

The first six verses of Chapter 7 describe how Christians "have been put to death to the Law through the body of Christ" (v. 4). In his discussion Paul has explicitly associated the Law with "the passions of sins" (v. 5) and he proceeds to elaborate upon that thought. In so doing, Paul can apparently

> assume a readership in Rome who were sufficiently familiar with the working of the Jewish law . . . to have experienced at least something of the effects of the law for themselves.[60]

As his use of the first person plural attests (vv. 4-6), this is also something "Paul evidently experienced," a point to be kept in mind as the chapter continues.[61]

The remainder of Romans 7 "is nearly always regarded as an excursus."[62] Yet such an evaluation fails to grasp how verses 7-25 flow

---

[58]Lenski, 455.

[59]So Kümmel, *Römer 7*, 42, "With that the question in 6:1,15, whether the Christian can or should still sin is . . . settled" (*"Damit ist die Frage 6, 1. 15, ob die Christen noch sündigen können oder sollen . . . erledigt"*). However, in Chapter 6 Paul *exhorts believers* not to remain in sin. Neither in Chapter 6 nor in this verse does he say that Christians no longer sin or that it is possible for them to refrain from sinning against the Law.

[60]Dunn, *Romans 1-8*, 372.

[61]Ibid., 373; see 8:4,14-15; 2 Cor. 3:3,18; Gal. 5:1; Phil. 3:3.

[62]Käsemann, 192. For example, Emil Brunner, *The Letter to the Romans*, tr. H. Kennedy (Philadelphia: Fortress Press, 1959), 67, states in his introduction to Romans 8, "The theme, however, is none other than that developed from the fifth chapter, with the interruption, of course, of Chapter 7." Barrett, 140, similarly calls it "a digression"; see also Bornkamm, "Sin, Law and Death," 88-89; Beker, *Paul the Apostle*, 83; H. Conzelmann, *An Outline of the Theology of the New Testament*, tr. J. Bowden, The New Testament Library (London: SCM Press, 1969), 229; C. Leslie Mitton, "Romans

from the preceding context. Verses 5 and 6, in some manner, provide the framework for the following discussion.[63] There is also no clear agreement on how to divide verses 7-25.[64] However, verse 13 is best taken as a hinge verse which concludes the thought of verses 7-12 and also marks a transition into verses 14-25.

Verses 7-13 begin with τί οὖν and, "in diatribe style," bring up a hypothetical question.[65] **"Therefore what will we say, the Law [is] sin? May it never be!"** (v. 7a). What would prompt such an incredible

---

7 Reconsidered," *Expository Times* 65 (1953-54):101; Stendahl, 211-12. Attempts to interpret these verses in one direction or the other prompt this evaluation. However, what signal would have enabled Paul's hearers to pick up on this new "digression"? It is closer to the truth to conclude with Käsemann, 210, "Paul does not grant himself the luxury of digressions."

[63]Leenhardt, 179, contends that "v. 6 foreshadows ch. 8 as v. 5 has just anticipated the sequel of ch. 7." So also Newman and Nida, 130, "Verse 5 describes the pre-Christian experience, and has its parallel in 7.7-25; verse 6 describes the present life of faith under the leadership of God's Spirit, and has its parallel in 8,1-11"; similarly Jan Lambrecht, *The Wretched "I" and Its Liberation*, Louvain Theological and Pastoral Monographs, 14 (Grand Rapids: Eerdmans, 1992), 34. Bornkamm, "Sin, Law and Death," 88, suggests that verses 7-25 describe "what 'to serve under the written code'" means" (v. 5). Bultmann, "Romans 7 and Paul's Anthropology," 41-42, similarly links 7:5 with 7:14-25; and according to Conzelmann, 229, Chapter 8 then comments on 7:6. All of these are based upon their interpretation of 7:7-25. However, Dunn, *Romans 1-8*, 358, who supports a Christian interpretation of verses 14-25, also states: "7:5 in effect traces the course of the discussion in 7:7-25: 7:5a (vv 14-25), 7:5b (vv 7-13), 7:5c (vv 10-11,13,24). Likewise 7:6 foreshadows the course of chap. 8: 7:6a (8:1-3); 7:6b (8:4ff.)."

Nygren's outline, *Commentary on Romans*, 276, stands in contrast to these: Along with 7:5, 7:7-13 describes "*What the Christian was before.*" Verses 14-25, as 7:6, depict "*What the Christian is now.*" So also Espy, 167.

[64]For example, Morris, *The Epistle to the Romans*, 276; and Wilckens, 2:74-75; divide between vv. 7-12 and 13-25. Otto Michel, *Der Brief an die Römer*, Kritischer-exegetischer Kommentar über das Neue Testament, 13th ed. (Göttingen: Vanden-hoeck and Ruprecht, 1966), 169, similarly separates 7-12, 13-17, and 18-25. However, Käsemann, 192; and Gerd Theissen, *Psychological Aspects of Pauline Theology*, tr. J. Galvin (Philadelphia: Fortress Press, 1987), 230-31; take 7-13 and 14-25. Cranfield, 1:340; and Dunn, *Romans 1-8*, 376-78; treat the entire section as one unit, though the latter divides as follows: 7-13,14-17,18-20,21-23.

[65]As also in 3:5; 4:1; 6:1; 9:14. Kümmel, *Römer 7*, 43, points out that this device is used by Paul to introduce or summarize his argument.

suggestion? Paul realizes that it represents a conclusion which could feasibly have been drawn from what he has said about the relationship between the Law and sin in 7:5, as well as from other passages (for example, 3:19-20; 4:15; 5:20; 6:14). "Paul is answering the objections to his theology that he himself has anticipated."[66]

While Paul had been using the first person plural (verses 4b-6), in verse 7 he begins to use the first person singular and employs it consistently throughout the rest of the chapter.[67] At this point it will be helpful to mention that in addition to or in place of the natural reading of the "I" as representing the author himself, in verses 7-11 it is quite typical to see Paul

> making increasingly explicit uses of the Adam narratives of Gen 2 and 3: 'I' = typical man (*homo sapiens*), אדם = *'adam* = Adam; that is, Adam is the one whose experience of sin typifies and stamps its character on everyone's experience of sin.[68]

Paul writes, "**But I would not have known sin except through the Law**" (7:7b). ἀλλά implies that in spite of Paul's emphatic denial in 7a, there is, nevertheless, a connection between the Law and sin.[69] He proceeds by offering a particular example which explains this:

---

[66]Theissen, 181.

[67]Ibid., 179, notes that Paul here uses the first person singular "for the first time after the beginning of the letter [1:13] and an isolated passage in 3:7." Leenhardt, 182, improperly attempts to drive a wedge between Paul's statements in the first person singular and the first person plural by stating, "These affirmations are mutually exclusive." Lambrecht, *The Wretched "I" and Its Liberation*, 61, similarly speaks of its "unexpected appearance."

[68]Dunn, *Romans 1-8*, 378; he evaluates this connection, 399, as "the vital clue." See Chapter 3.

[69]Kümmel, *Römer 7*, 43. concludes that ἀλλά is used to express "*eine Einschränkung*" ("a limitation") rather than "*eine Bekräftigung*" ("strengthening") of the μὴ γένοιτο. It points ahead toward and affirms what is going to be detailed in the verses to follow, that is, how sin has been able to utilize the Law; see Rudolf Schnackenburg, "Römer 7 in Zusammenhang des Römerbriefes," *Jesus und Paulus*, ed. E. Ellis and E. Grasser (Göttingen: Vandenhoeck und Ruprecht, 1975), 292. The sense is, "No, but it is true that. . . ."

"For I also had not known desire except the Law was saying, 'You shall not desire'" (7:7c).[70]

Part of what Paul says in 7:7 he has already concluded in 3:20: "For through the Law [comes] full knowledge of sin." In addition, the last phrase of verse 7 points out that the Law specifically tells the "I" that his "desires" are directed toward what is contrary to the Law. Together, οἶδα and γινώσκω describe concrete experiential involvement in sin, as well as the recognition of one's own sinfulness.[71]

With οὐκ ἐπιθυμήσεις, Paul cites a portion of the last commandment of the Decalogue (as in 13:9; from the Septuagint of Ex. 20:17; Deut. 5:21).[72] Although ἐπιθυμέω need not necessarily denote something wrong (Phil. 1:23; 1 Thess. 2:17; 1 Tim. 3:1), it normally expresses an inclination toward evil, as its use to translate this commandment indicates (see also Rom. 1:24).

The sense of ἐπιθυμέω is certainly broader than a mere reference to "sexual lust";[73] neither can it be limited to the desire to attain life through the Law.[74] The abbreviated form of Paul's citation from the Decalogue indicates that he is not referring to this commandment as one among many sins; rather, it "is chosen as [an] example for the entire Law as the alternation of νόμος and ἐντολή in 7:9 shows."[75]

---

[70]Both phrases would be contrary to fact conditionals except that no ἄν is present in either apodosis. As it stands the sentences convey that "the Law did say, therefore I did come to know."

[71]Karl Barth, *The Epistle to the Romans*, 6th ed., tr. E. Hoskyns (New York: Oxford University Press, 1933), 242.

[72]Romans 13:9 indicates that Paul has the Tenth Commandment in mind here, see below; also Dunn, *Romans 1-8*, 379; Douglas Moo, "Israel and Paul in Romans 7.7-12," *New Testament Studies* 32 (1986):123, an "unmistakable reference"; Bornkamm, 102, n. 7.

[73]As Gundry, 232, suggests. Matthew Black, *Romans*, New Century Bible (London: Oliphants, 1973), 102, responds, "*epithymia* is never purely sexual"; see 1 Cor. 10:6; also Bornkamm, "Sin, Law and Death," 102, n. 7; Espy, 169.

[74]As Bultmann, "Romans 7 and Paul's Anthropology," 45, suggests. Against this see Bornkamm, "Sin, Law and Death," 90; Käsemann, 194.

[75]Kümmel, *Römer 7*, 56, "*und dieses Gebot ist als Beispiel gewählt für das ganze Gesetz, wie der Wechsel von νόμος und ἐντολή in 7. 9 zeigt.*" Leenhardt, 185, identifies this prohibition "as the very essence of the law"; so Bornkamm, "Sin, Law and Death," 90.

Perhaps Paul has selected the Tenth Commandment in order to speak more generally "of the intention" behind every transgression as shown by his use of πᾶσαν ἐπιθυμίαν in verse 8. This is not without precedent as James 1:15 indicates.[76] All of these sins of desire can then be placed into the context of the relationship between this last commandment and the first.[77] C. K. Barrett states, "Desire means precisely the exaltation of the *ego* which we have seen to be the essence of sin."[78]

This citation from the Decalogue, as well as the fact that νόμος interchanges freely with ἐντολή in verses 7-13, is a clear indication of the sense in which Paul is using νόμος in this context. While νόμος in and of itself can refer to the entire Mosaic Torah, here it is being utilized in a narrower sense to denote those portions of the Torah which make demands upon man's conduct.[79]

Paul, in verse 7, reveals how the Law's commandments led the "I" to identify and acknowledge his own impulse toward evil. Paul proceeds to assert that the Law does even more. Although he refuses to allow any identification of the Law with sin (v. 7; also v. 12), Paul describes very graphically how sin, with the help of the commandment, awakens desires which are contrary to the Law, then provokes the "I" to enact his desires, and, finally, drives home an awareness of that transgression and its results.

---

[76]4 Maccabees 2:6 similarly states, "μὴ ἐπιθυμεῖν εἴρηκεν ἡμᾶς ὁ νόμος." See also Philo, *The Decalogue*, 142,150,173 in *Philo: VII*, tr. F. H. Colson, The Loeb Classical Library (Cambridge, MA: Cambridge University Press, 1938), 76-79,80-81,90-93; idem., *De Opificio Mundi*, 152 in *Philo: I*, tr. H. Colson and G. Whitaker (Cambridge, MA: Cambridge University Press, 1949), 120-21; "The Apocalypse of Moses" 19:3, in *The Apocrypha and Pseudepigrapha of the Old Testament*, 2:146. Bruce, *The Letter of Paul to the Romans*, 140, notes that this commandment is especially a problem for the pharisaic mind because it deals with the inner attitude and not merely outward words and actions.

[77]The connection between ἐπιθυμία and the First Commandment's prohibition against idolatry is clearly enunciated in Col. 3:5.

[78]Barrett, 141.

[79]Gutbrod, *TDNT*, 4:1070, states, "In Paul νόμος is supremely that which demands action from man." It is in this sense that one can attempt to "do" the Law (2:13,14,25; compare 10:5). The effects of these demands upon sinful man are presented in the remainder of Chapter 7.

In verse 8 Paul clarifies and expands upon the activity of verse 7:
**"But sin, seizing the opportunity, through the commandment
worked out**[80] **every desire in me"** (v. 8a). The "I" recognizes that
every sinful passion is "actually inflamed even by the Law of God. The
very law that prohibits them encourages [the "I"] to do them."[81] This is
because sin is able to use the Law's commands as a beachhead to
launch its attacks.[82]

Many parallels to this expression have been cited.[83] Yet Paul's
thought is certainly deeper than any comparable statement from
secular sources. He is dealing with the dominion and activity of sin
(for example, 6:12-16; 7:5,7). Verse 8a, as well as the similar assertion
in verse 5, must be read in light of Paul's portrayal of sin as an active
and evil power which reigns through death and completely separates
man from God (5:12-14). Additionally, in Chapter 7 Paul is discussing
the lordship of *the revealed Law* in its connection with sin

---

[80]Dunn, *Romans 1-8*, 380, identifies κατεργάζομαι as "a thematic word in ch 7."
It occurs in verses 8,13,15,17,18,20.

[81]David M. Lloyd-Jones, *Romans: An Exposition of Chapters 7:1-8:4* (Grand
Rapids: Zondervan Publishing, 1973), 80; he concludes this is so "because *we* are
impure."

[82]ἀφορμή is used in military contexts for a starting point or base of operations
from which an attack is launched. Newman and Nida, 134, point out, "In New
Testament times the word was used frequently in a metaphorical sense with the
meaning of 'opportunity (to do something).'" Its use with λαμβάνω, both actively and
passively, is common in Hellenistic Greek. Kümmel, *Römer 7*, 44, concludes that here
sin is actively seizing an "occasion" or "opportunity"; see also Cranfield 1:349-50;
BAGD, 127. Black, 103, defines it as "a kind of bridgehead into human nature for the
invading forces of Sin."

[83]Theissen states, 224, "Paul here picks up an insight that is also attested
elsewhere in antiquity." Ovid's line from *The Amores*, 3.4.17, is often cited: "*Nitimur
in vetitum semper cupimusque negata*" ("We ever strive for what is forbidden, and ever
covet what is denied"; see also 2.19.3; cited from *Ovid: Heroides and Amores*, tr. G.
Showerman, The Loeb Classical Library (New York: G. P. Putnam's Sons, 1931), 460-
61. Compare Ovid's *Metamorphoses*, 3.566 in *Ovid: Metamorphoses*, tr. F. Miller, 2
vols., The Loeb Classical Library (New York: G. P. Putnam's Sons, 1933), 1:164-65.
Within Judaism, see 4 Macc. 1:33-34. In Christian literature, Augustine states,
"Forbidden fruits are sweet" (cited from Lenski, 468). Morris, *The Epistle to the
Romans*, 280, compares this with Augustine's comments in his Confessions about the
needless stealing of pears and Mark Twain's comments about a mule! Bruce, *The
Letter of Paul to the Romans*, 140, refers to "No Smoking" signs!

and death, and its impact upon a person's relationship to God (7:1,4-6,7). As a result, his theological presuppositions defy a merely psychological explanation.

Verse 8 concludes with this terse, but striking statement: "**For without the Law**[84] **sin was dead**" (v. 8b). If one takes νεκρά in the full sense of "dead," then an application to the period prior to Genesis 3 when "sin entered the world through one man" (5:12) is likely.[85] However, prior to the fall there was not only no sin, there was also no death! It is also noteworthy that Paul uses θάνατος to refer to death in 7:5,10,13 (also the related verb in 7:6,10). The presence of νεκρά here may suggest a different nuance.

Unless Paul's reference is to the period before the fall when sin was "completely inactive,"[86] νεκρά cannot be describing a time when any "I" did not sin and was not, therefore, guilty before God.[87] Paul has used 1:18-3:20 to conclude just the opposite. "All are under sin" (3:9), "for all have sinned . . . " (3:23; compare 3:19; 5:12; Gal. 3:22).

Neither can Paul mean, as Kümmel suggests, that those who do not know the revealed commandments of the Torah are in some way not

---

[84]In light of 3:21,28; 4:6; the presence of χωρὶς νόμου is quite striking.

[85]The link with Genesis here is that before God gave the command which forced Adam and Eve to exercise their free will, there was no opportunity for sin; see Dunn, *Romans 1-8*, 381, who then cautions that "the dramatic pictorial language should not be taken too literally." For example, Leenhardt, 186, identifies the serpent as "personified sin" in 7:8 and states, "Nothing resembles a dead serpent more than a living serpent so long as it does not move!" Dunn, *Romans 1-8*, 400, himself even adds, "v 8 amounts in effect to a description of the tactics of the serpent here personified as 'sin.'"

[86]As Newman and Nida, 134; though they add, "sin is inactive, that is, powerless."

[87]Kümmel interprets it in this manner. He, *Römer 7*, 46-47, asserts, "The 'I' came into a practical relationship with sin and passion first 'through the commandment'" (*"daß das Ich zu Sünde und Begierde erst 'durch das Gesetz' in praktische Beziehung kam"*). Without this forbidding commandment, such passions "remained foreign" (*"fremd geblieben"*) to the "I." Kümmel proposes, ibid., 49, that νεκρά is used to denote the condition "where sin is not able to work the death of man" (*"wo die Sünde den Tod des Menschen nicht bewirken kann"*). He further contends, ibid., 132, "Without the law sin has no working power" (*"Ohne Gesetz hat die Sünde keine Wirkungskraft"*). Therefore, ibid., 48, "An existence of sin apart from the Law is here denied" (*"hier ein vorhandensein der Sünde ohne Gesetz geleugnet wird"*).

guilty of sin.[88] If Paul had been asked about them, he would have responded, as in 2:12-16, that no one is in reality outside of the realm of the Law. They will be judged by "the work of the Law written in their hearts, their conscience bearing witness, and their thoughts alternately accusing or else defending them" (2:15). Because of their sin, they too will perish (2:12).

Furthermore, Paul affirms that sin was in the world and active even before the Law was given through Moses (5:13). To be sure, sins committed during that period could not be charged against a person as a transgression of God's Law or make him accountable for breaking a specific *revealed* commandment (παράβασις; 4:15). However, this sin did make the person guilty before God and deserving of his condemnation (2:12,14-16). Paul affirms this by stating that *the* consequence of sin, which is death, reigned from Adam until Moses (5:14; see also 6:23).

> For the introduction of the law is not said to make death more comprehensive and more total, but only to increase the trespass (v. 20) and to make men more aware of the consequence of sin (v. 14).[89]

The coming of the Law does not, for the first time, activate sin; rather it "turns sin into transgression" of God's revealed will.[90]

What, then, is the significance of νεκρά? Paul uses it in verse 8 to describe sin as "ineffective" or "powerless" in regard to its ability to provoke transgression of the Law through its commandment.[91] Though

---

[88]Ibid., proposes, "Without the law, sin is not able to make one guilty and through that is not able to bring [him] to death" *("ohne Gesetz die Sünde den Menschen nicht schuldig machen und dadurch auch nicht zum Tode bringen konnte")*. This leads him to assert, ibid., 50, "Only when the person knows the divine command and still transgresses is the sin guilt for him" ("*nur wenn der Mensch das göttliche Gesetz kennt und doch übertritt, is die ἁμαρτία für ihn Schuld.*" Espy, 169-70, similarly states, "It is only through the Law that one becomes culpable as an individual."

[89]Andrew Bandstra, *The Law and the Elements of the World* (Grand Rapids: Eerdmans Publishing, n.d.), 137, citing 5:12-21.

[90]See Barrett, 141; Nygren, *Commentary on Romans*, 278, 279; Espy, 170.

[91]As in James 2:26 where "ἡ πίστις χωρὶς ἔργων νεκρά ἐστιν," see also v. 17; but compare Rom. 6:11. For the meaning "ineffective," see Cranfield, 1:351; Michel, 173; Dunn, *Romans 1-8*, 400. It is not that "sin is not perceptible" as *BAGD*, 535[1bβ].

sin is "already lying in ambush *and present*,"[92] sin cannot yet incite
man into open violation of God's Law as it does in verse 8a. A very
helpful parallel to this verse is 1 Corinthians 15:56 which explains the
interaction between death, sin, and the Law as follows: τὸ δὲ κέντρον
τοῦ θανάτου ἡ ἁμαρτία, ἡ δὲ δύναμις τῆς ἁμαρτίας νόμος.

The description in verses 9-10a concisely draws together the experience of the "I" throughout verses 7-11: **"And I was formerly[93]
living without the Law, but when the commandment came, sin
came to life. And I died"** (9-10a). The background of Genesis 2-3 is
said to be "all but inescapable" here,[94] yet it should also be pointed out
that Paul uses ἐγώ for the first time in Romans in 7:9. The key to
arriving at a correct understanding of verses 9-10a is a proper
interpretation of the verbs ἔζων (v. 9a), ἀνέζησεν (v. 9b), and
ἀπέθανον (v. 10). In addition, the chiastic structure of verses 8b-10a
provides an important indication of what Paul means. ἁμαρτία νεκρά
ἐγὼ ἔζων . . . ἡ ἁμαρτία ἀνέζησεν . . . ἐγὼ ἀπέθανον (vv. 8b-
10a). He does not intend for νεκρά (v. 8) to be understood in its full
literal sense, and the same is true of the other verbs in this chiasm.

Kümmel vehemently insists that ἔζων χωρὶς νόμου (v. 9a) must
be understood in a "pregnant" sense as denoting "true life" as God
intended, that is, life in its "fullest religious sense."[95] However, unless

---

[92]Käsemann, 194.

[93]Dunn, *Romans 1-8*, 382, translates ποτέ as "once upon a time" and restricts the
meaning to a time of "paradisal innocence"; similarly Stanislas Lyonnet, "L'Historie
du Salut selon le Chapitre VII de l'Epître aux Romains," *Revue Biblica* 43 (1963):130-
42. On the other extreme, Kümmel, *Römer 7*, 132-33, applies it to every condition of
life (*"ganz allgemein den Lebenszustand"*). Both of these are overly interpretive.

[94]Dunn, *Romans 1-8*, 401, concludes, "With v. 9 the reference to Adam becomes
all but inescapable. . . . For only in the case of Adam is it possible to make such a clear
distinction." For example, in Genesis Adam was created a "living being" free from sin
(2:7). Then the commandment came (2:16-17) which the serpent used (3:5) to bring sin
and death (2:17; 3:4). Espy, 169, contends that Adam and Eve were "'without the Law'
in the sense of 'without making use of it, without depending on it'" citing *BAG*,
890[2Bb or d].

[95]Kümmel, *Römer 7*, 52, *"wahren Lebens,"* and 53, *"im religiösen Vollsinn am
Leben"*; as in 1:17; 8:13; 10:5; 2 Cor. 6:9; Phil. 1:21. Ibid., 51, asserts that it cannot
mean merely "to exist" (ἤμην) and later admits, ibid., 132, how crucial this is for his
interpretation; see Bornkamm, "Sin, Law and Death," 93.

one adopts Kümmel's view that there is no sin or guilt apart from the revelation of the Law's commandment, ἔζων, in this pregnant sense, cannot refer literally to anyone other than Adam or Eve, and only to them before the Fall.

There is another alternative,[96] however, since ζάω need not be understood as designating life in the full spiritual sense. In fact, according to Pauline usage, that interpretation is unlikely.[97] It is more probable that Paul is using ζάω in "the general sense of 'alive,' 'spend one's time,'" as he utilized it already in 7:1.[98] There it hardly denoted the possession of "true life" before God. Rather, it was used to describe actual existence under the lordship of the Law. Though this life was "real," it was not so in regard to God. Bandstra concludes,

> "I was alive" apart from the law could only mean living apart from the heightened awareness of the nature of sin and its consequences.[99]

ἀνέζησεν expresses the idea "that sin, after the coming of the commandment, now exists in full working power."[100] When "I was living χωρὶς νόμου" (9a), sin was not having its utmost effect (νεκρά; v. 8). Verse 9b then speaks of a time "when I came to know about a

---

[96]One might note yet another plausible explanation which accepts Kümmel's "pregnant" sense. Perhaps Paul was actually truly living as a member of God's covenant people by virtue of his birth and circumcision which acted as a seal of the promise of God that gave life (4:11; 9:2-5; 11:1; see also Phil. 3:5). It was only when he came to view the Law as the basis of his righteous standing before God and as a reason to boast that the Law in actuality condemned him.

[97]For ζάω in Paul, see Otto Kuss, *Der Römerbrief*, 3 vols. (Regensburg: Verlag Friedrich Pustet, 1963), 2:445-46. ζάω occurs 59 times in Paul and only refers to spiritual life about nine of those times (in 1:17; 6:13; 8:13; 10:5; 2 Cor. 8:4[?]; Gal. 2:19; 3:11; 3:12; 5:25). According to Moo, 125, n. 29, the only other occurrence of this verb in the imperfect in Paul refers to "simple existence (Col. 3:7)."

[98]Bandstra, 136-37.

[99]Ibid., 137; he compares this with the statement "free in regard to righteousness" in 6:20 which similarly "cannot mean total exemption from the punitive righteousness of God (cf. 3:5)."

[100]Kümmel, *Römer 7*, 52, "*daß die Sünde sich nun, nachdem das Gebot vorhanden ist, in voller Wirkungskraft befindet.*"

commandment"[101] or when the commandment "came home to me."[102] With the "coming of the commandment" sin was able to exert its full power (ἀνέζησεν; see 5:20; 7:8) and "I died" (v. 10a).

What, then, of ἀπέθανον? Paul cannot be referring to death in a purely physical sense in verse 10a since the "I" continues to live on in verses 10-25 even after he states, "I died" (ἀπέθανον). The death in verse 10a is neither a physical death nor a spiritual death in the fullest sense, though it leans closer to the latter. In view of the parallels in verses 7 and 13, "'I died' can only mean becoming specifically aware of the penalty of sin."[103] It is death in the sense that the "I" has realized the futility of his existence under the lordship of the Law (7:1; also 3:20; 6:23a; cf., Gal. 2:19). It signifies the end of his apparent life, his assurance of life, or even the "false security" which he formerly enjoyed.[104] It is the death "of the complacent self-assurance" which comes with the full and complete knowledge of one's own sinfulness.[105] So then, as indicated by the chiasm in verses 8-10,

> The experience of death was moral and consisted in the resurgence of sin and the loss of a supposed innocence. Likewise the experience of life

---

[101] Suggested by Newman and Nida, 135; also "when I learned that I shouldn't do certain things," or, more likely, "that God said I shouldn't do certain things."

[102] As translated by James Moffatt, *A New Translation of the Bible Containing the Old and New Testaments* (New York: Harper and Brothers, 1935); compare John Calvin, *Commentary upon the Epistle of St. Paul to the Romans*, tr. C. Rosdell, ed. H. Beveridge (Edinburgh: The Calvin Translation Society, 1844), 178, "When it began truly to be understood."

[103] Bandstra, 137. Moo, 125, concludes that due to the logic of Paul's argument, "it is difficult to understand by ἀπέθανον (v. 10a) anything other than condemnation resulting from sin."

[104] The latter phrase is supported by the deception in verse 11. This "life" only binds people more hopelessly to sin's complete domination as expressed in 6:13, 16,18; see Lenski, 464,470,472. He contends that moralism and legalism increase this false security and concludes, ibid., 465, that the Pharisees are "the outstanding example" of this. This need not mean that the sense of verse 9 is reduced to "I thought I lived" as Lyonnet implies, "L'Historie du Salut selon le Chapitre VII de l'Epître aux Romains," 129-30. The "I" actually was alive (see 7:1) and presumed to be spiritually alive as well.

[105] Murray, 1:251.

must also have been moral not [merely] biological, and consisted in a false sense of personal righteousness in the absence of a genuine knowledge of sin.[106]

However, it must be pointed out that Paul's primary concern here is not to delineate a strictly temporal relationship. The main issue is not whether the Law precedes sin or follows it. Neither is Paul primarily engaged in discussing the origin of either sin (as in 5:12-21) or the Law. He is speaking about the nature of the interrelationship which exists between sin and the Law, and asserts that the Law's command serves to increase sin's activity and power (4:15; 5:20; 7:5).

The remainder of verse 10 goes together with verse 11 and is somewhat less problematic. These verses recapitulate the action of verses 9-10a and enable Paul to further elaborate upon what was already either presumed or presented. **"The commandment which was for life, this very one has been found[107] to result in death for me. For sin seizing its opportunity through the commandment deceived me and through it killed [me]"** (vv. 10b-11).

How did the Law's commandment "offer life" (10b)? It may be that this was "a self-evident opinion for a Jew"[108] which Paul himself affirms in Romans 10:5: "For Moses writes [concerning] the righteousness which is from the Law that the person who does these things will live in them."[109] On the other hand, perhaps the Law

---

[106]Milne, 14; citing Gundry, 233.

[107]Or "proven to be"; note the passive voice of εὑρίσκω which may reveal the influence of the Hebrew נמצא; Dunn, *Romans 1-8*, 383. It may also imply divine intervention in bringing home the effect of Law to the sinful "I"; see 1 Cor. 4:2; 15:15; 2 Cor. 5:3; Gal. 2:17. The nuance of "discovered," present in the disputed text of 2 Peter 3:10, is also a possible alternative.

[108]Kümmel, *Römer 7*, 53, *"wie das für den Juden eine selbstverständliche Vorstellung war."* For example, Deut. 6:24; 30:15-16; Ps. 19:7-10; Prov. 6:23; Eccl. 7:20; Ezek. 20:11; Luke 10:28. For a survey of references outside of the Old Testament, see Ephraim Urbach, *The Sages*, 2 vols. (Jerusalem: Magnes Press, 1979), 1:424-26; he cites, for example, tractate Aboth 6:7 of the Mishnah which states, "Great is the Torah, for it gives them that practice it life in this world and in the world to come"; see also Aboth 2:7; Sirach 17:11; 45:5; Baruch 3:9; 4 Ezra 14:30. Note the close verbal parallel in Psalms of Solomon 14:2: "ἐν νόμῳ ἐνετείλατο ἡμῖν εἰς ζωὴν ἡμῶν," cited from Cranfield, 1:352, n. 2.

[109]Alluding to Lev. 18:5; see Gal. 3:21 in light of verse 10.

simply holds out the plan God intends "for the life" of his people. In either case, the "I" in 7:7-11 has found out that, because of sin, the commandment which holds out the promise or the way of life had only served to accomplish his death. In stating that the Law's commandment "offers life" (εἰς ζωήν), Paul continues to exonerate the Law from blame in causing the death of the "I" (see v. 12). However, as verse 11 reveals, even this aspect of the Law was able to be diabolically manipulated by sin.

Verse 11 parallels 7:8 quite closely, but it more strongly emphasizes that death is the final product of sin (5:12; 6:21,23; 7:5). In addition, verse 11 provides the first plausible linguistic connection with Genesis. In the Septuagint of Genesis 3:13 Eve declares, "ὁ ὄφις ἠπάτησεν με."[110] There the serpent certainly deceived.[111] However, a reference to the events in the Garden is not the only possible explanation of this verse. How else has the Law been involved in a deception worked by sin?

Throughout Romans Paul indicates another manner in which sin is able to deceive through the Law's commandment. It is not that the Law "falsely" promises life or is overpowered by sin.[112] Rather, this deception occurs whenever any "I" imagines that he could secure the final verdict of "Righteous" from God by his own works of the Law and in spite of his own sin (2:17-24; 3:20,28; 4; 8:3; 9:30-10:5).

Because of the weakness of the flesh, sin is able to misuse the Law

---

[110]The verb with the prefix is used by Paul in 2 Cor. 11:3 and 1 Tim. 2:14 to describe the serpent's deception of Eve; see Leenhardt, 188. However, Kümmel, *Römer 7*, 54, points out that the prefix is not present in the Septuagint. In addition, Paul uses the verb with the prefix elsewhere (16:18; 1 Cor. 3:18; 2 Thess. 2:3) without reference to Genesis 3 (as also ἀπατάω in Eph. 5:6).

[111]In Genesis 2-3 the serpent deceived: 1) by drawing attention only to the negative portion of God's command (2:16-17; 3:1); 2) by denying the fatal punishment for disobedience (2:17 with 3:4); and 3) by using the commandment itself in order to draw forth mistrust of God's intention (3:5). See Leenhardt, 188-89; Cranfield, 1:352-53.

[112]For the former, see Bornkamm, "Sin, Law and Death," 91; countered by Espy, 162. The latter is also suggested by Bornkamm, "Sin, Law and Death," 89,90. Kümmel, *Römer 7*, 54, rejects both in stating, "The Law is spoken of as being free from all guilt, because the deception lies with sin" (*"Damit ist aber das Gesetz von aller Schuld freigesprochen, denn der Betrug liegt bei der Sünde"*).

in order to provoke "man's self-assertion."[113] Sin can use the commandment to deceive man into believing that he can adequately fulfill the Law and thereby obtain the life which the Law promises (see 9:31-10:5). Paul characterizes that approach as "a *mistaken* understanding of the law."[114] This deception, then, involves a denial of the fact that sin is in control and accomplishing death even through the Law's commandment. Although the "I" was unaware of it, the more he relied upon the Law as the way of life, the more certain the result was to be death.

The redundant δι᾽ αὐτῆς in verse 11 serves to separate the "deceiving" from the "killing." This deception persisted for a time, but the "I" now realizes that sin had actually been using God's commandment as the occasion to bring about his death! In reality, the "I" had been deceived and killed precisely through the commandment he sought to follow as the path to/for life. Sin's deception had led him only into further transgressions of the commandment.[115]

When the Law accomplishes what Paul describes in verses 7-11, "it effects . . . that which God wants done against sin and the sinner" (3:19-20).[116] "It was the divine intention with the Law that it might increase the destructive effect of sin" (4:15; 5:20).[117] But even here, where Paul details the "destructive effect" of the demanding Law, he understands

---

[113]Dunn, *Romans 1-8*, 384; he goes on to note Wilckens's "justified rebuttal of a 'too Lutheran' interpretation"; see Wilckens, 2:107-10. So Bultmann, "Romans 7 and Paul's Anthropology," 44, states, "The real intent of the law is corrupted into its opposite into actual idolatry."

[114]Dunn, *Romans 1-8*, 402; yet he concludes that this was "rendered obsolete as early as the fall." Though sin makes the obtaining of life through the Law impossible, this is not because the Law has become "obsolete" (see 3:31).

[115]An important parallel is Eph. 4:22: τὸν παλαιὸν ἄνθρωπον τὸν φθειρόμενον κατὰ τὰς ἐπιθυμίας τῆς ἀπάτης; Heb. 3:13 also speaks of the "deceitfulness of sin."

[116]Nygren, *Commentary on Romans*, 281.

[117] Kümmel, *Römer 7*, 56, "*Es war die göttliche Absicht mit dem Gesetz, daß es die verderbliche Wirkung der Sünde steigere.*" Dunn, *Romans 1-8*, 402, points out, "Paul would hardly think that [sin's misuse of the Law] had caught God unawares or altered his purposes for man."

how the law can have both a positive function and a negative function. . .
at one and the same time: negative because it is the glue which binds sin
to death; positive because it leaves the sinner no alternative to death other
than the death of Christ.[118]

Paul, in verses 12-13, arrives at the critical point in his analysis of
the Law. Verse 12 returns directly to the hypothetical question posed
in verse 7, "Is the Law sin?" The answer which follows reveals quite
definitively that "Paul is no antinomian":[119] **"So then the Law [is]
holy and the commandment [is] holy, just, and good"** (v. 12). It is
important to note that Paul was careful not to attribute any guilt to the
Law in verses 7-11. He now announces that the Law is ἅγιος,[120] an
attribute which "puts it as far away from sin as possible."[121]

In the same manner, Paul emphatically declares that ἡ ἐντολή,
which here is used synonymously with νόμος and continues to indicate
its sense in this section, is ἀγία καὶ δικαία καὶ ἀγαθή. ἐντολή might
refer to the specific commandment cited in verse 7, but, as verse 8
made clear, that commandment was chosen to typify, as well as to be
inclusive of, all of the Law's commandments. The adjectives used to
describe ἡ ἐντολή in verse 12 "are not casually chosen."[122] They serve
to point out the origin, nature, and effects of the Law. ἡ ἐντολή is holy
because its source is holy and it mandates holy conduct.[123] It is "just"
in that it does not make unfair demands but, rather, calls for the right
conduct which God exhibits and requires. Finally, its description is

---

[118]Dunn, *Romans 1-8*, 401. Furthermore, when Paul speaks of the Law in the
wider sense as the entire Torah, he can also conclude with Käsemann, 197, that "the
intention of the law was the promise of 3:21." However, one must recognize that Paul
defines νόμος in 3:21 in a wider sense to speak of the entire Torah which, along with
"the Prophets," includes the promise of the Gospel.

[119]Käsemann, 198, asserts this against Lietzmann.

[120]Compare 2:20 where Paul characterizes the Law as "the embodiment of τῆς
γνώσεως καὶ τῆς ἀληθείας." According to Murray, 1:253, the Law reflects the
purity of God and demands the same from man.

[121]Morris, *The Epistle to the Romans*, 283.

[122]Dunn, *Romans 1-8*, 402.

[123]Lev. 19:2; Murray, 1:253, concludes that it reflects the purity of God and
demands the same.

broadened out to indicate that the Law's commandment is "good." It is intended by God to be beneficial for people.[124]

Verse 13 functions as a hinge: 1) it summarizes Paul's arguments from verses 7-11; 2) τὸ ἀγαθόν picks up on the statements about the Law in verse 12, and 3) as in verse 7, Paul poses a rhetorical challenge which he proceeds to answer. **"Therefore did that which is good become for me death? May it never be!"** (13a). In light of verse 12, τὸ ἀγαθόν is to be identified with the Law's commandment and, actually, the Law itself.[125] Paul also refers to the Law's command with ἀγαθόν in verses 18 and 19, as well as with καλόν in verse 16 and τὸ καλὸν in verses 18 and 21.

Two final ἵνα clauses follow which parallel the thought and structure of verse 8 and indicate the two-fold purpose for which "I" was confronted with the Law. **"But sin, in order that it might be shown [to be] sin, [was] accomplishing death in me through that which is good, in order that sin through the commandment might become exceedingly sinful"** (13b).[126] In the first clause sin is unmasked by the Law (3:20; 7:7). It is shown to be what it truly is, "rebellion against the command of God."[127] Second, through the commandment sin becomes even more sinful (5:20; 7:8-9). Its power is enhanced and its true character is exposed. So the end product of the confrontation between "I" and the Law is only death (v. 10).[128]

---

[124]See, for example, εἰς ζωήν in verse 10; Deut. 10:12-13; Newman and Nida, 136; Murray, 1:253.

[125]Lenski, 470, defines the use of the neuter singular adjective with the article as "an equivalent of the abstract noun, . . . The context indicates what is referred to, here it is 'the law' and 'the commandment.'" The description of the Law as "that which is good" is also made in tractate Aboth 6:4 of *The Mishnah*, ed. H. Danby (Oxford: Oxford University Press, 1972), 459; see the other references cited by Strack and Billerbeck, 1:809; also Walter Grundmann, in *TDNT*, s.v. "ἀγαθός," 1:13-15; Black, 104; Newman and Nida, 136.

[126]In the last phrase κατά introduces a standard or rule of measure. Together with ὑπερβολήν it means *"to an extraordinary degree, beyond measure"* according to *BAGD*, 840; as in 1 Cor. 12:31; 2 Cor. 1:8; 4:17; Gal. 1:13; see Robertson, 609.

ἁμαρτωλός is normally a substantive (3:7; 5:8,19), but used here as an adjective according to *BAGD*, 44[1].

[127]Morris, *The Epistle to the Romans*, 289.

[128]θάνατος is present in verse 11 and twice in verse 13; the verb ἀποθνήσκω occurs in verses 10 and 11. See Dunn, *Romans 1-8*, 387; Wilckens, 2:84.

In Romans 7:7-13, two key points emerge. First, Paul clearly enunciates the "destructive effect" of the Law in arousing, exposing, and convicting sin. This is due to the fact that the encounter of the "I" with the divine commandment is no longer direct. Sin always stands in between and has fundamentally perverted the "I"'s relationships to God's commandment. This perversion is both deception and death. For it suggests that now I may grasp life, which because of sin is never any longer truly an open possibility for me."[129] Yet the blame for this rests squarely upon sin and not upon the Law.

Second, there is a recognition that the death worked by sin is what God intended to accomplish by revealing the Law's commands. God's purpose in the Law is to show sin for what it is and to demonstrate unequivocally the need for the Gospel which accomplishes that which the Law's command is unable to do (see 8:2-4). While Paul continues to enunciate the character and function of the Law in verses 14-25, his main purpose is not merely to justify or support the statements he made in 7:7-13.[130]

"For we know that the Law is Spiritual, but *I* am fleshly, sold under sin" (v. 14). In verse 14, as in 7:1, Paul draws his hearers along

---

[129]Bornkamm, "Sin, Law and Death," 92.

[130]Although Kümmel, *Römer 7*, 10, recognizes that verses 14-24 are more than a proof of 7:7-13, as suggested by Dodd, 129 ("further explanation"), he, 57, concludes that they are "first of all" (*"zunächst"*) a continuation of Paul's defense of the Law. But this need not suggest, as Kümmel, 56, intimates, that Paul's earlier statements in defense of the Law were not entirely convincing (*"nicht ganz beweisend"*).

According to Dunn, *Romans 1-8*, 406-7, Paul's specific aim as he moves ahead is two-fold: 1) He intends to counter any thought that to be under the good and holy law is not so bad after all. To base one's standing before God upon the Law is disastrously fatal. 2) Paul strives, without limiting the believer's present reality of salvation, to describe the tension which still exists due to the continued presence of sin and death in this life. As a result, ibid., 407, the "dominant feature" in verses 14-25 is an "intensified note of existential anguish and frustration." However, Dunn, ibid., 406, improperly overstates that "sin and death still have a claim" and describes the Christian as "suspended (so uncomfortably) between the death and resurrection of Christ."

Other conclusions are that verses 14-25 represent a new excursus, Hildebrecht Hommel, "Das 7. Kapitel des Römerbriefes im Licht antiker Überlieferung," *Theologia Viatorum* 8 (1961-62):102; and that "the results of 7b-11 are presented in their cosmic breadth," as Käsemann, 199; so Bornkamm, "Sin, Law and Death," 95. Bandstra, 140, states the theme as follows: "In spite of the 'I' assenting to and willing to do the good, neither the law nor the mind nor the 'I' can deliver the person from the power of sin and its consequences."

with him by assuming their agreement.[131] In so doing, he provides further evidence that his rebuke of the question posed in verse 13 was valid. Having stated the unavoidable fact that sin, through the Law's commandment, has accomplished death (v. 13), Paul proceeds to elaborate further on the blamelessness of the Law in causing that death. At the same time, he underscores why the Law is unable to overcome sin and death.[132]

With πνευματικός Paul refers, as in verse 6, to the Spirit of God.[133] Now he unmistakably associates the Spirit with the Law. This link, along with verse 12, makes it clear that Paul "will not permit any shadow to rest on the law."[134] He does not see the Law in and of itself as a negative or evil force, neither is its influence limited merely to the old age of sin and death (3:31). On the contrary, the Law is a Spirit-filled entity that is intended for life (7:10). However, due to the fallen nature of the flesh, sin has been able to utilize the Law for its own ends (vv. 8,11).

Passages such as these last three verses have led some to charge Paul with being inconsistent and even nonsensical in his appraisal of the Law.[135] At first glance verses 7-14 appear to exemplify a

---

[131]A similar construction is used in 2:2; 3:19; 8:22,28; 2 Cor. 5:1; 1 Tim. 1:8.

[132]Dunn, *Romans 1-8*, 406.

[133]Murray, 1:254; Dunn, *Romans 1-8*, 407; Black, 104. In verse 6 Paul used πνεῦμα; here he uses πνευματικός to refer to the Holy Spirit as in 1:11; 1 Cor. 2:13-15; 3:1; 10:3-4; 12:1; 15:44,46; Eph. 5:19; Col. 1:9; 3:16; compare also Matt 22:43; Mark 12:36; Acts. 1:16; 4:25; 28:25; 2 Peter 1:21. It cannot refer to a merely human spirit in Rom. 7:14 as Newman and Nida, 137, suggest, "the Law is for our spirits but I am just a body."

[134]Nygren, *Commentary on Romans*, 298, citing Heb. 7:18-19; 10:1.

[135]For example, Heikki Räisänen, *Paul and the Law*, Wissenschaftliche Untersuchungen zum Neuen Testament, no. 29 (Tübingen: J.C.B. Mohr, 1983), 11, charges that "contradictions and tensions have to be *accepted* as *constant* features of Paul's theology of the law." Later, ibid., 201, suggests Paul's view of the Law is nonsensical or "strangely ambiguous" and, 199, uses descriptions such as "oscillates" and "blurred"; see also E. P. Sanders, *Paul, the Law, and the Jewish People* (Philadelphia: Fortress Press, 1983), 77-81. Hans Hübner, *Law in Paul's Thought*, tr. J. Greig, Studies of the New Testament and Its World, ed. J. Riches, (Edinburgh: T. & T. Clark, 1984), for example, 60-65,135-36, argues Paul's view of the Law is consistent in Romans, but that it has devoloped from, and stands in contrast with, the earlier view in Galatians. For a response, see Thomas Schreiner, *The Law and Its Fulfillment* (Grand Rapids: Baker Book House, 1993). For a review of the issues, see Pate, 125-36;

contradictory attitude toward the Law on Paul's part and to justify those who criticize him. However, Paul is aware that improper conclusions could be drawn from some of his assertions about the Law and he actively and carefully opposes them. What Paul has stated previously, and makes clear in verse 13, is in no way contradictory to his definition of the Law as ἅγιος and πνευματικός (vv. 12,14). Instead, his "whole emphasis falls on the inability of the law to overcome sin and its condemnatory role is underscored."[136]

In verse 14 the Law's inability stems from the fact that, in stark contrast to this Spirit-filled Law, "*I* am composed of flesh, which is to say, I have been sold under sin" (compare 8:3). σάρκινος expresses more than a person who is "characterized by flesh and blood" by virtue of creation. It refers to the fallen, sinful "nature which I have inherited from Adam" (5:12,18).[137] This is further explained by the phrase which follows: πεπραμένος ὑπὸ τὴν ἁμαρτίαν. With the perfect passive of πιπράσκω, the picture of the slave market is reintroduced (6:16-23; 7:1).[138] This is not surprising, since "the imagery of successful surprise attack [ἀφορμη'; vv. 8,11] also naturally leads into that of slavery."[139] Here, sin is again depicted as a "personal force that takes hold of a man's life and controls it."[140]

A. J. M. Wedderburn, "Paul and the Law," *Scottish Journal of Theology* 38 (1985):613-22.

[136]Käsemann, 194-95; as becomes clear in 8:2-4.

[137]Bruce, *The Letter of Paul to the Romans*, 145.

[138]The Septuagint's phrase "ἐπράθησαν ποιῆσαι τὸ πονηρόν" is somewhat similar as used, for example, in 1 Kings 20:20,25; 2 Kings 17:17; 1 Macc. 1:15. Murray, 1:261, discusses how the first two references have led some (citing Meyer, Bengel, and Clifford; see also Lenski, 462) to conclude that the parallel to Ahab clearly indicates that the "I" is to be identified as a non-Christian. However, Murray, 1:260-61, correctly responds that in Ahab's case, he sold himself to evil before the Lord as the Hebrew Hithpael indicates (התמכר). Here the "I" has passively been sold to a power outside of himself. The two cases are not analogous. Compare also the Wisdom of Solomon 1:4: "Because wisdom will not enter a deceitful soul, nor dwell in a body enslaved to sin" ("οὐδὲ κατοικήσει ἐν σώματι καταρχέῳ ἁμαρτίας).

[139]Observed by Dunn, *Romans 1-8*, 388.

[140]Newman and Nida, 139; though Paul depicts it is as such, he does not actually consider sin to be a *personal* force.

At the same time, one cannot overlook the fact that in verse 14 "the `I' narration," so prominent in verses 7-11, is continued.[141] But now the "I" speaks for the first time in the present tense (ἐγὼ . . . εἰμί).[142] Additionally, the perfect participle (πεπραμένος) stands in contrast to the consistent use of the aorist tense in regard to the "I" in verses 7-13. It represents the condition of the "I" up to and including the present. While the transition from the consistent use of the aorist tense to the present tense here may be somewhat subtle, it is underscored by the fact that the present tense continues to be employed uniformly throughout the remainder of the chapter.[143]

It has been concluded that verse 14 depicts a situation in which the slavery of the "I" to sin is completely "unbroken."[144] This predicament would then appear to contradict *the believer's* release from slavery to sin as described by Paul both prior to and after this section.[145] As a result, it is argued that Paul cannot be speaking of his own Christian life, or of any other believer.[146] James Dunn responds by charging those who contend that verse 14 cannot be describing the

---

[141]Bandstra, 139.

[142]This transition has been the object of various interpretations. According to Nygren, *Commentary on Romans*, 285, it indicates a transition to Paul's present Christian existence. Robinson, *Wrestling with Romans*, 86, counters, "It is difficult to put the weight on it that Nygren claims." Eduard Ellwein, "Das Rätsel von Römer VII," *Kerygma und Dogma* 1 (1955):262, emphasizes that it points to an intensification (*"Steigerung"*). Karl Kertelge, "Exegetische Überlegungen zum Verständnis der paulinische Anthropologie nach Römer 7," *Zeitschrift für die neu-testamentliche Wissenschaft* 62 (1971):109, similarly concludes that in 14-25 "the I walks more strongly into the foreground" (*"tritt das Ich stärker in den Vordergrund"*). Ibid., 113, and Theissen, 228-34, then interpret this intensification as the process of becoming conscious. Dunn, *Romans 1-8*, 387, contends that it broadens out the field from "the 'once upon a time' of Adam to that of everyman in the present (εἰμί)." Käsemann, 195, similarly believes that it signals an extended focus which moves from merely the Jewish people or those under the Law in 7:7-13 to all people.

[143]The present tense occurs 34 times in verses 14-25, the only exceptions being the perfect passive participle in verse 14, the use of οἶδα in verse 18 (both of which in effect have a present sense), and the future of ῥύομαι in verse 24.

[144]Dunn, *Romans 1-8*, 406.

[145]For example, 6:14; 7:5; 8:5,8; according to Käsemann, 200, "What is being said here is already over for the Christian according to chap. 6 and chap. 8."

[146]See Chapter One; so Schweizer, *TDNT*, 7:144, applies the description in the verses to follow to Paul's pre-Christian days; as Beker, *Paul the Apostle*, 217-18.

Christian with failing to recognize the tension which is present in the Christian's life.[147] Dunn argues that Paul has outlined the believer's discontinuity with the present age in 7:1-13 and now speaks of his continuity within it.

Verse 14 does present one of the strongest arguments against viewing verses 14-25 as descriptive of a believer. In fact, if a Christian is being portrayed, one might have expected Paul to state just the opposite! "The Law belongs to the old, fleshly era and the believing 'I' is spiritual."[148] However, the contrast Paul sets up is between the Spiritual Law and the fleshly "I."[149] Whether or not one's interpretation of verse 14 is correct must be determined by the verses which follow, wherein Paul describes the "present" state of the "I" more precisely.

While verse 15 begins this description, it introduces a situation which is repeated with various nuances in the verses to follow. It is important to notice that "in each instance, the starting point is a saying on the contradiction of willing and doing."[150] Paul writes, **"For I do not approve of that which I accomplish; indeed, I do not practice that which I will, but that which I hate, this I do"** (v. 15). A crucial factor for understanding verse 15 is the sense of γινώσκω. Does Paul mean that the "I" does not know what he does, or that he fails to understand *why* he does it?[151] Both of these interpretations seem impossible. The "I" goes on to describe the very things he is and is not doing, and also indicates his own understanding of the reason why this is so (vv. 14,17,20). Neither does γινώσκω refer merely to a "knowledge" gained by experience (as in 7:7).[152] In line with the slavery motif of verse 14, Leon Morris suggests that the "I" does not know the reason or the purpose for those actions which are determined

---

[147] Dunn, *Romans 1-8*, 406, citing Rom. 6:12-23; see also Pate, 108-13.

[148] Suggested by Nygren, *Commentary on Romans*, 297-98; compare 5:20 and 8:9.

[149] It is not, as Kümmel, *Römer 7*, 59, states, "that the I stands in opposition to the πνεῦμα" (*"daß das Ich dem πνεῦμα entgegengesetzt"*).

[150] Theissen, 188.

[151] "Understand" is accepted by Kümmel, *Römer 7*, 59, *"das Nichtverständnis . . . nicht ein Nichtwissen."*

[152] Proposed by Käsemann, 202; also Dunn, *Romans 1-8*, 389.

by his enslaved flesh.[153] Cranfield properly pushes his definition further to the point of "to acknowledge" or "approve."[154]

The three words used to express "doing" in verses 15 and following are essentially synonymous.[155] Paul chooses them because their meanings overlap. In this context, however, the presence of κατεργάζομαι may be the most significant because it emphasizes the actual accomplishing, or bringing to fruition, of both good and evil (vv. 15,17,18,20). While not explicitly stated in this context, the *implied* objects of these "doing" verbs are certainly the actions which are either commanded or forbidden by the Law.[156] "The point at issue in verse 15 is . . . performance in relation to the law."[157]

The situation introduced in verse 15 virtually defies verbal explanation. The "I" here reveals that something gets in between "my willing and my doing."[158] But the "I" is never depicted as two "I"s in verses 15-25; nor do we have a schizoid, dual, or split personality in this section.[159] Rather, "it is the same 'I' each time—the 'I' 'sold under

---

[153]Morris, *The Epistle to the Romans*, 291, citing Lightfoot who translates, "I do it in blind obedience."

[154]Cranfield, 1:358-59; although he seeks a background in Greek usage, this nuance is readily appropriated to γινώσκω through the Hebrew ידע. Similarly, Lenski, 428; Bultmann, in *TDNT*, s.v. "γινώσκω," 1:697-98. Murray, 1:261, extends this to include delighting and rejoicing in something (8:9; 1 Cor. 8:3; Gal. 4:9; 2 Tim. 2:19; προγινώσκω in 11:2).

[155]Käsemann, 202, concludes that the variations "are undoubtedly rhetorical"; see also Newman and Nida, 138. Alford, 2:382, concludes that there is "no distinction between πράσσω and ποιέω here"; so also *BAGD*, 698[1]; Dunn, *Romans 1-8*, 391; Barrett, 147. Those scholars who attempt to make a subtle distinction between these verbs contend that while ποιέω is the basic word for "doing" (vv. 15,16,19,20, 21; see *BAGD*, 681[IIbe]), πράσσω indicates more of "a habitual 'doing', a practicing" (see Espy, 185, n. 62).

[156]Compare 2:13,14,25; 10:5; this is further indicated by the presence of νόμος in verses 16,22, τὸ καλόν as a reference to the Law in verses 18,21, and ἀγαθόν in verse 18 in light of verse 13.

[157]Ronald Fung, "The Impotence of the Law: Toward a Fresh Understanding of Romans 7:14-25," in *Scripture, Traditions, and Interpretation*, eds. W. Gasque and W. LaSor (Grand Rapids: Eerdmans Publishing, 1978), 43.

[158]Dunn, *Romans 1-8*, 406.

[159]Kümmel uses a variety of terms. At times he, *Römer 7*, 63, sees the "I" in terms of *"der ganze Ich."* But elsewhere he, 59, portrays this struggle in terms of two different "I"s stating, "The acting I is apparently independent of the willing I and

sin' in its fleshliness, and the 'I' as 'the inner man.'"[160] Paul does not divide or separate the "I" from "the flesh." Neither can that which is portrayed here be explained merely in terms of inner psychology[161] or moral shortcoming.[162] More profoundly, there is a "disunity" or "cleavage in the existence of *the whole man*."[163] In 7:15 we observe, for the first time, that the present slavery of the "I" mentioned in verse 14 is "a slavery under protest."[164] The "I" does what he "hates" (μισέω; v. 15)

Paul continues, "**But since I am doing that which I do not will, I agree with the Law that [it is] excellent**" (v. 16). The presence of νόμος indicates that Paul continues to discuss the effects of the Law's commandments upon the "I." However, Paul's chief interest in this verse is not to *conclude* his defense of the Law,[165] as Kümmel proposes, but to show the agreement (σύμφημι) which exists between the will of the "I" and the Law. In spite of this agreement, the sentence structure implies that what is described is actually happening. The

---

stronger than this one" (*"Das handelnde Ich is anscheinend unabhängig vom wollenden Ich und stärker als dieses"*); see also ibid., 60, *"das wollende Ich mit dem handelnden nicht identisch ist"*; and, ibid., 61 and 62, where Kümmel speaks of the "I" in a narrow and a wider sense (*"Gesamtich"*; *"in den weiteren ἐγώ-Begriff"*). Bornkamm, "Sin, Law and Death," 97, ends up with three "splits" in the "I."

[160]Dunn, *Romans 1-8*, 390.

[161]For an able attempt at a psychological interpretation, see Theissen, 222-65. While he critiques the impropriety of other psychological views, 222-28, and brings out many good points, his conclusion, 229, is that "Romans 7 depicts how [Paul's] once-unconscious conflict with the law became conscious." The latter is said to be revealed in verses 14-25.

[162]Käsemann, 200, concludes that "a purely or primarily moral interpretation of the text cannot be harmonized." Yet he wonders why "it constantly dominates exposition." Käsemann correctly understands that Paul's discussion is on a much deeper level.

[163]The former is from Lambrecht, *The Wretched "I" and Its Liberation*, 39; the latter from Schrenk, in *TDNT*, s.v. "θέλω," 3:51.

[164]Dunn, *Romans 1-8*, 389.

[165]Kümmel, *Römer 7*, 59, "and 7:16, therefore, draws out the conclusion for the defense of the Law" (*"und 7,16 zieht daraus den Schluß für die Verteidigung des Gesetzes"*). This cannot be as Paul uses νόμος seven more times in the chapter, refers to it with τὸ καλόν in verse 18, and alludes to it twice with ἀγαθόν in verses 18 and 19.

same "I" whose will (θέλω) opposes the evil and agrees with the Law, at the same time accomplishes that which is against both his will and the Law. Yet the "I" recognizes that the Law is not to blame for his own inability to live according to its commands and to refrain from what it forbids.[166] The "I" here "predicates of the law the highest quality of goodness" (καλός).[167]

With the verb σύμφημι Paul conveys an attitude toward the Law which it is difficult to conceive of him attributing to a non-believer in its literal sense. It is far more likely that Jews who "relied on the Law and boasted in God" (2:17) would display the attitude toward the Law characterized by σύμφημι, though, according to Paul, it would be improperly founded on the Law "of works" (3:27; compare 2:28-29; 9:30-32). Yet would such a "boasting" Jew ever confess to being "sold under sin" as the "I" does in 7:14?[168] Would a pharisaic mind admit that which the "I" attributes to himself at the end of the very next verse?

"But, this being the case, it is not then *I* who am accomplishing this, but sin which is dwelling in me" (v. 17). νυνί and οὐκέτι may hint back to a time when this was the case (vv. 7-13), but they more likely indicate a logical connection with the previous verse.[169]

Two assumptions which have been read into Paul's description in verses 15-17 must be rejected. First, the "I" does not attribute *all* of his actions to sin, as if he *never* did anything good but *only and always* evil.[170] Nothing in the text indicates this and, as John Murray responds,

---

[166]So ibid., 59, "Therefore the Law cannot be made responsible for the action of the I" (*"darum das Gesetz, . . . nicht für das Tun des Ich verantwortlich gemacht werden kann"*).

[167]Murray, 1:262. For the translation of καλός, see *BAGD*, 400[c], which offers, "in every respect *unobjectionable, blameless, excellent.*"

[168]As well as the statements in verses 20,23,24,25. Paul certainly strives to drive home a recognition of the just condemnation which God has pronounced upon sin to anyone and everyone who boasts before God; see 2:19-24, especially verse 23; 3:9-20.

[169]Both νυνί and οὐκέτι have a logical sense here; that is, they express what is so in light of what was said in verse 16. See 1 Cor. 13:13 and *BAGD*, 546[2a], for νυνί and, for οὐκέτι, Rom 7:20; 11:6a; 14:15; Gal. 3:18 and *BAGD*, 592[2].

[170]This is asserted by Kümmel, *Römer 7*, 62,107,133; Bultmann, "Romans 7 and Paul's Anthropology," 33-34, "According to verses 15-20 . . . the desire to do good is always destroyed by doing evil. . . . The sin . . . constantly overcomes his good intentions"; Schrenk, in *TDNT*, s.v. "θέλω," 3:50, "No true action corresponding to the

"This would be universalizing the apostle's language beyond all reasonable limits."[171] In addition, in light of 2:12-16, it is difficult to believe that Paul would conceive of any "I" whose will was *always* thwarted by his actions. "No individual indeed is so depraved that he always *does* only evil and never good."[172] If such an interpretation is pressed, it must also conclude that since we are only told about the desire of the "I" for the good in these verses, his will is *always* and only aligned with the Law. If so, could Paul possibly be speaking of an unbeliever? Paul's immediate concern in these verses is more specific.[173] He is attempting to explain how the "I" can will the good and yet repeatedly fail to accomplish it.

Second, Paul's purpose is *not* to show that the "I" is somehow completely removed from his own actions against the Law or not responsible for his failure to enact its commands.[174] In verse 17 the "I" unmistakably identifies the source which leads him to do that which his will abhors and which is counter to the good Law. It is described as ἡ οἰκοῦσα ἐν ἐμοὶ ἁμαρτία. This phrase indicates that "the fault lies once again with sin,"[175] but it does not mean the "I" is not guilty, as Kümmel asserts.[176] "To infer . . . that the I which is speaking here

---

θέλειν is achieved. The only result is something which the doer himself finds alien and abhorrent. . . . It never goes beyond readiness and purpose"; Barth, 265, "There is then no performance of *that which is good*"; Ridderbos, 127, "The discord pictured in Romans 7 consists . . . in the absolute impotence of the I to break through the barrier of sin and the flesh in any degree at all"; and Lambrecht, *The Wretched "I" and Its Liberation*, 39, who characterizes it as "a hopeless opposition."

[171]Murray, 1:273; see also the discussion below regarding παράκειμαι in verse 18b.

[172]Timo Laato, *Paul and Judaism* (Atlanta: Scholars Press, 1995), 126; though he cites a number of scholars who assert this.

[173] For his overall purpose, see Chapter Five.

[174]As attempted by Stendahl, 211-214. Barrett, 147, similarly contends that the point of verses 17-20 is that the conscience is "equally blameless with the law." This would hardly explain verse 24.

[175]Dunn, *Romans 1-8*, 407; as in verses 7-13.

[176]Kümmel, *Römer 7*, 59, asserts, "The sin, not the I, bears the guilt" (*"Die Sünde, nicht das Ich, trägt die Schuld"*). However, even though the "I" stands in opposition against sin, both sin and its guilt are not restricted merely to the flesh in these verses. Lenski, 481, points out that Paul here means that "sin dwells in me" and not merely "in

wishes to shirk responsibility would be to misunderstand the intention of the statement."[177]

What the "I" does confess is that the flesh is wholly sinful, that "I" am still fleshly, and that sin "dwells in me" (vv. 14,17). On the basis of the goodness exemplified in the Law, the only possible conclusion for the "I" to draw is that, in contrast to the Law, "I am sinful."[178] As Otto Michel puts it:

> The dwelling of sin in man denotes . . . its lasting connection with his flesh, and yet also a certain distinction from it.[179]

This "certain distinction" is most important and Paul elaborates upon it in verse 18: "**For I know that good is not dwelling in me, this is, in my flesh**" (18a). This phrase does not imply that there is a complete separation between the "I" and the flesh.[180] Verse 14 has already denied this. On the other extreme, τοῦτ᾿ἔστιν ἐν τῇ σαρκί μου does not serve as a complete identification of the "I" either.[181] In view of the fact that the "I" has just been described as willing the good and agreeing with the Law (15b,16; also 18b), this phrase is best regarded as a "necessary qualification of ἐν ἐμοί."[182] This qualifying phrase supports an identification of the "I" as a Christian. No such qualification would be necessary if Paul is speaking of an unbeliever (7:5).

---

my flesh" as in verse 18. If the "I" is a Christian, however, there is a sense in which he bears no guilt or condemnation as 8:1 declares.

[177]Theissen, 261.

[178]Murray, 1:263.

[179]Michel, in *TDNT*, s.v. "οἰκέω," 5:135. This "certain distinction" makes it difficult to believe that Paul is describing a non-Christian. This is also the case when Morris, *The Epistle to the Romans*, 293, states, "Paul is personifying sin again; it is in some sense a separate entity, even though it is within him."

[180]Kümmel, *Römer 7*, 61, contends that "in v. 18 the willing I is being separated from the total I" ("*in V. 18 von dem Gesamtich ein wollendes Ich geschieden wurde*").

[181]Bornkamm, "Sin, Law and Death," 98, claims that in this phrase, the "I" is "defined, not limited."

[182]Cranfield, 1:360; Kümmel, *Römer 7*, 61, agrees that it "can be nothing other than a delimitation of the ἐγώ" ("*Denn ἐν σαρκί μου kann nichts Anderes sein also eine Einschränkung des ἐγώ*"); so also Fung, 43, "It has a corrective or restrictive sense, qualifying *en emoi*."

Paul does not conceive of σάρξ here as man's lower self[183] or as an aspect of man which has merely been weakened.[184] Neither can his uses of σάρξ be restricted solely to the unbelieving state.[185] In this context, Käsemann appropriately defines σάρξ as "the workshop of sin."[186] σάρξ denotes "the whole fallen human nature as such"[187] together with its "unavoidable attachment and tie to this world."[188] This qualifying phrase supports an identification of the "I" as a Christian. No such qualification would be necessary if Paul is speaking of an unbeliever (7:5).

"For to will [the good] lies at hand for me, but the accomplishing of the good, no" (18b). According to Kümmel, this verse begins a new section in which Paul seeks to clarify the disparity which exists in the "I."[189] However, the Law does not drop from view. The conflict Paul has set up is between the ability of the "I" to will "the good" *commanded by the Law* and his inability to perform it. Thus *both* the excellent commands of the Law (τὸ καλόν, v. 16) *and* the disparity in the "I" are present in this verse and those which follow.

The verb θέλω, which occurs seven times in verses 15-21, is especially important for identifying the context in which this conflict is set. It should be noted θέλω is different from the word, often similarly

---

[183]Therefore Alford's distinction, 2:382-83, between *"the better ἐγώ of the ἔσω ἄνθρωπον"* or *"the self of the WILL in its higher sense"* and *"the lower ἐγώ, ἡ σάρξ μου"* or *"the lower carnal self"* is unwise. Such platonic distinctions are not operative in these verses or in Paul's theology as a whole; see Robinson, *The Body*, 11-33; Werner Kümmel, *Das Bild des Menschen*, (Leipzig: Hinrichs, 1929); reprinted in *Römer 7 und das Bild des Menschen im Neuen Testament: Zwei Studien*, Theologische Bücherei, Neues Testament Band 53 (Munich: Christian Kaiser Verlag, 1974), 178-83.

[184]As Morris, *The Epistle to the Romans*, 293, who suggests, "Flesh is not inherently sinful, but it is weak."

[185]See above on 7:5.

[186]Käsemann, 205; though the remainder of his definition (". . . the whole person in his fallenness to the world and alienation from God.") stems from his interpretation of this section. If this were so, how could it be that Paul speaks of Christians and Jesus himself as existing in the flesh? See above on Rom. 7:5.

[187]Cranfield, 1:361.

[188]Dunn, *Romans 1-8*, 391; note the distinction with σῶμα discussed below on 7:24.

[189]According to Kümmel, *Römer 7*, 10, it offers *"die Aufklärung des Zweispalts."*

translated "desire," used earlier (ἐπιθυμία/ἐπιθυμέω; 7:7,8). In contrast to Paul's use of θέλω elsewhere, Schrenk proposes that in Romans 7 it merely describes consent as "an impotent gesture."[190] Henry Alford defines θέλω in the sense of "to wish" and contends that it does not express "the *full determination* of the will."[191]

However, in verses 14-25, as well as in the context of Pauline usage in general, these definitions are too weak.[192] θέλω here represents the innate or determined will of the "I." This is indicated in two ways: First, the θέλω of the "I" in verses 14-25 is always mentioned first by Paul (vv. 15b,19,21). That which interferes with the ability of the "I" to enact his will always follows. The reason why Paul gives priority to the θέλω throughout this discussion is because it, and not the flesh or the sin "in me," represents the true, determinative identity of the "I."

Second, the θέλω in verses 14-25 is never divided. There is a disparity between willing and action, but Paul always uses θέλω to refer to that which the "I" truly desires. In this section the will of the "I" is consistently aligned with the good and opposed to the evil as they are expressed in the Law of God.

The tension and conflict depicted here are the result of something which gets in between the willing and the doing. Paul describes it as the "sin which dwells in me . . . this is, in my flesh" (vv. 17,18).[193] Yet

---

[190]Schrenk, *TDNT*, 3:50; he admits that this stands in contrast to Paul's use of θέλω elsewhere.

[191]Alford, 2:382, contends it "is not the *full determination* of the will, . . . but rather the *inclination* of the will . . . we have θέλω in the sense of to *wish*"; as in 1:13; 1 Cor. 7:7,32; 14:5; 2 Cor. 5:4; 12:20; Gal. 4:21.

[192]Lenski, 479, argues that "wish" is too weak; so also Murray, 1:262, similarly discounts "I would." Schrenk, *TDNT*, 3:50, contends that while Rom. 7:14-25 "belongs to a different context," in every other passage where Paul uses θέλω in a religious sense and together with "doing" verbs such as those present here, it *always* conveys the fact that "God effects in believers both a ready purpose and achievement." He cites 1 Cor. 7:36; 2 Cor. 8:10-11; Gal. 5:17. However, these passages do not convey what "God effects" but that which the believer desires in accordance with God's will.

[193]Nygren, *Commentary on Romans*, 290-92, notes that a tension between the believer and sin is also present in Chapters 6 and 8 and contends that the "I" must be a Christian. Dunn, *Romans 1-8*, 391, also contends that Paul places this "willing" together with a "renewed heart and enlightened mind" (see 12:2 and contrast 1:21,28; 2:5).

sin is not able to quench the determined will of the "I." Neither does Paul state or imply that sin is always able to overcome the will's ability to put itself into action. On the contrary, the sense of the verb παράκειμαι in verse 18 is not only that something is near, but that it is possible. The "I" acknowledges that to do the good is "within reach for me" or "within my grasp."[194]

Verses 19-20 further illustrate what has been said: **For I am not doing [the] good I will, but [the] evil I do not will, this I am practicing. But if *I* am doing this which I do not will, *I* am no longer accomplishing it but the sin which is dwelling in me.** There is perhaps too great a temptation to view these verses merely as "repetition."[195] Dunn suggests that "the main difference between vv. 14-17 and vv. 18-20 is that the law is not specifically mentioned in the latter."[196] It is true that for Paul sin "exercises its influence whether the law is in view or not."[197] However, in light of the unquestionable use of τὸ ἀγαθόν to refer to the Law in 7:13, the ἀγαθόν in verse 19 certainly keeps the Law in view. What stands out in these verses is that the thing willed by the "I" is now identified explicitly as the "good." Likewise, that which the "I" accomplishes against his determined will is identified as "evil" and attributed to "sin dwelling in me" (v. 20).[198]

Reference must be made to citations from non-biblical sources which have been cited as representing parallels to Paul's expressions in verses 15b, 18b and 19.[199] The most common is Ovid's statement,

---

[194]So Friedrich Büchsel, in *TDNT*, s.v. "κεῖμαι," 3:656, defines it as "to lie ready," "to lie at disposal"; similarly Sanday and Headlam, 182. This verb occurs only here and in verse 21 in the New Testament.

[195]So Cranfield, 1:361; Bandstra, 145, states that they "add very little new to the argument, except that the 'I' is distinguished further from 'my flesh' in which no good dwells."

[196]Dunn, *Romans 1-8*, 408; on 391, he points out that verse 20 compresses verses 16-17 and "the element squeezed out is the defense of the law in 16b." Similarly Kümmel, *Römer 7*, 10,59.

[197]Dunn, *Romans 1-8*, 409; as in 1:18-32; 2:12-16; 5:12-14.

[198]Murray, 1:263. While the categories may be somewhat broader here, the "I"'s knowledge of and direction toward "good" and "evil" certainly stems from the Law.

[199]For a complete survey, see Theissen, 212-19; Hommel, 106-13. In addition to those quoted here, they also cite, for example, Plato, *Republic*, 9:589a, who speaks of the opposition between the inner and outer man. Bruce, *The Letter of Paul to the Romans*, 145, cites Homer, who writes in *Epistles*, 1.8.11, "I pursue the things that

"video meliora proboque, deteriora sequor."[200] Epictetus is verbally even closer to Paul in writing, ὅ θέλει οὐ ποιεῖ καὶ ὅ μὴ θέλει ποιεῖ."[201] If these are accepted as legitimate parallels,[202] Leenhardt is correct in observing:

> We should interpret [Paul's] words in a psychological and secular sense; the inmost man is the natural man considered from the point of view of his faculties of moral judgment.[203]

However, these suggested parallels are not operating on the same level as Paul's statements in Romans 7:14-25.[204] First, they do not take cognizance of the divinely-revealed, Spirit-filled Law of God (7:1,14) which the determined will of the "I" agrees with and seeks to carry out. Second, the "I" explicitly identifies sin as that which dwells in and controls his flesh (vv. 14,17-18,20). It is the alien invader sin which actively prohibits him from doing what he wills. Finally, the

---

have done me harm; I shun the things I believe will do me good" (*"quae nocuere sequar, fugiam quae profore credo"*).

[200]"I see and approve the better course, but I follow the worse"; 7:21 of *Metamorphoses*; cited from *Ovid: Metamorphoses*, tr. F. Miller, The Loeb Classical Library, 2 vols., (New York: G. P. Putnam's Sons, 1916), 1:343.

[201]*Arrian's Discourses of Epictetus*, tr. W. Oldfather, The Loeb Classical Library, 2 vols. (New York: G. P. Putnam's Sons, 1925), 2.26.4, vol. 1, p. 432. Cranfield, 1:359, n. 3, concludes that the context renders this citation "much less relevant" to Romans 7.

[202]As by Kümmel, *Römer 7*, 134, who concludes, "They are parallels and not sources" (*"sie sind Parallelen und nicht Quellen zu Röm. 7,14ff."*). See also Sanday and Headlam, 185; Lucien Cerfaux, *The Christian in the Theology of St. Paul*, tr. Lilian Soiron (New York: Herder and Herder, 1967), 438.

[203]Leenhardt, 191.

[204]According to Black, 105, "This conflict goes much deeper in Paul than in these hellenistic writers, since it is a conflict between the ideal of obedience to the Law and the actual reality of human nature as under the pressure of an occupying power, Sin." So Bultmann, "Romans 7 and Paul's Anthropology," 37, charges, "It is impossible that in Romans 7:14ff this basic idea . . . could be abandoned in favor of the trite thought" of Ovid's statement; see also idem., *Theology of the New Testament*, 2 vols., tr. K. Grobel (New York: Charles Scribner's Sons, 1951), 1:248. Leenhardt, 193, recognizes that Ovid's statement is empty of any transcendence. In regard to Epictetus, Theissen, 219, points out "that in Paul the deception proceeds from sin, whereas in Epictetus sin is a result of deception."

"sharpness and frustration of the eschatological tension" which dominates the concluding verses of Romans 7 (vv. 24-25) are absent from these secular sources.[205] Thus the disparity in verses 14-25 "differs sharply" from the Greek world of thought.[206]

W. D. Davies contends the rabbinic teaching regarding the "Two Impulses" provides the foundation for the disparity present in verses 14-25.[207] Davies proposes that the יצר הרע is comparable to the φρόνημα τῆς σαρκός in Paul (8:6) and to what Paul describes as σάρκινος/σαρκικός (7:14).[208] The יצר הטוב is represented by πνευματικός and ψυχικός.[209] Although these terms are not consistently utilized by Paul in this manner,[210] Davies's explanation provides some valuable background and insight. For instance, the "I" acknowledges that evil inclinations (יצר הרע; see Genesis 5:6) spring forth from "the sin dwelling in me" (v. 20) and these desires are able to work "in my flesh" (7:14,18). In addition, sin's *earlier* working of "every desire in me" (7:8) is comparable.

Yet, to the "I," these desires are certainly not an "urge to self-preservation and propagation" which can be "mastered and put to good use" as the rabbinic doctrine asserts.[211] Perhaps the "I" had earlier viewed the commands of the Law in that way ("for life"; 7:10), but the outside invader, sin, had, in reality, been using the Law to "kill" (7:11).

---

[205]Dunn, *Romans 1-8*, 389. For example, Epictetus, 2.26.5, vol. 1, p. 433, finds his answer in the ψυχὴ λογικὴ. While there may be a contradiction between what a person wills and does, "as soon as anyone shows a man this, he will of his own accord abandon what he is doing."

[206]Käsemann, 201; he concludes that Paul's thought cannot be reduced merely to "the ethical conflict, which most commentators find here."

[207]W. D. Davies, *Paul and Rabbinic Judaism*, 4th ed. (Philadelphia: Fortress Press, 1980), 21-27.

[208]Ibid., 26; he cites with approval N. P. Williams, *The Ideas of the Fall and of Original Sin* (London: 1927), 150, who further asserts that "sin," "the old man," "the sinful body," "the body of this death," "the sinful passions aroused by the Law," and "the mind of the flesh" are similar expressions of the יצר הרע.

[209]Davies, 20; citing Strack and Billerbeck on 1 Cor. 3:3.

[210]See, for example, the analysis of Bruce, *The Letter of Paul to the Romans*, 143, n. 1. Paul's contrasts do not consistently match the three phases Davies, 24, identifies in Romans 7 and 8.

[211]As summarized by Davies, 20-21.

Similarly, the determined will (θέλω) of the "I" to do good can be compared with the יצר הטוב. But the "I" perceives that the source of this "good desire" is not the Law. On the contrary, its coming brought deception and death (7:11). Consequently, and in contrast with the rabbinic doctrine, the solution to the "I"'s dilemma is by no means study of and obedience to the Law.[212]

Paul draws his conclusion regarding this division between willing and action in verse 21: "**So then I find the Law for me the one who is determined to do the excellent [thing], that for me evil lies at hand.**" The language of this summarizing verse clinches the following points of interpretation. First, the repetition of ἐμοί clearly reveals that there is only one "I" who is enduring "both of these opposite experiences."[213]

Second, the verb "to lie within reach" is here associated with the doing of evil. παράκειμαι is used of the will to do good in verse 18. There it emphasizes "the *difficulty* of doing good, not that it is impossible."[214] Its presence again here indicates that the inability to do good (v. 18), as well as the failure to refrain from evil (v. 21), are not the continuous, uninterrupted state of the "I."

Third, while this verse has been interpreted as referring back to verses 7-13 or even as summarizing the entire chapter,[215] this cannot be the case. In verse 21 the "I" expresses that the determination of his will agrees with the excellent commands of the Law. When prohibited from putting his will into action by the "sin which dwells in me," the "I" is distraught, but not longer "deceived" (v. 11). The fervent will of the "I" is to fulfill the good Law, but he repeatedly fails to do so. Here a battle is going on between the determination of the will of the "I" to refrain from evil and that which makes him unable to bring that resolve to fruition. He recognizes that the reason for this inability is his sinful

---

[212]Ibid., 22; see also Pate, 104. Paul's answer to the dilemma of the "I" will be made evident in 8:1-4.

[213]Morris, *The Epistle to the Romans*, 293; though "experiences" may not be the best word.

[214]Dunn, *Romans 1-8*, 391.

[215]The text in no way justifies Bornkamm's statement, "Sin, Law and Death," 91, that "without question, v. 21 comments on the earlier statement (v. 8)." This certainly is the result of his interpretation. So also Newman and Nida, 140, conclude that "verses 21-23 are a summary of what Paul has been saying thus far in the chapter."

flesh. No struggle or conflict between will and action is present in verses 7-13. There only sin, death, and deception came through the Law's command. Here the "I" consistently expresses his "willing conformity" with the Law.[216]

At the same time, verse 21 introduces a very perplexing issue. Beginning here the sense of νόμος is disputable and the situation only gets more complex as the chapter moves toward its conclusion. Up to this point, Paul has paralleled νόμος with ἐντολή in order to indicate that he is referring to the commanding aspect of the Torah. The debated issue is whether or not he continues to do so in verses 21-25.

A number of scholars contend that in this verse νόμος refers to "a certain norm or principle" which summarizes the experience of the "I."[217] While verse 21 as a whole certainly does do that, a number of factors support the conclusion that νόμος continues to denote the Torah's command. First, the presence of εὑρίσκω here, as in verse 10, signals "that the author now notes the logical result of what precedes."[218] In verse 10 εὑρίσκω is used with ἐντολή; in verse 21 with νόμος. The parallel between these two concluding statements about the Law's effect upon the "I" indicates that νόμος continues to be employed synonymously with ἐντολή in order to designate the commands of the Law.

Second, as verse 21 draws together the experience of the "I" in verses 14-20, it "cries out for a reference to the law equivalent to that of 16b."[219] James Denney captures the essence of Paul's use by paraphrasing, "This is what I find the law—or life under the law—to come to in experience:"[220]

---

[216]Murray, 1:264.

[217]Lenski, 484; Theissen, 233, defines it "as a special instance of a 'rule,' a *nomos*, a principle." So also Bandstra, 145; Black, 107; Räisänen, *Paul and the Law*, 52, n. 45.

[218]Leenhardt, 192. According to Cranfield, 1:362, εὑρίσκω has the sense of "I prove for myself by experience"; compare the present active with the aorist passive in 7:10.

[219]Dunn, *Romans 1-8*, 392.

[220]Denney, 642; Moffatt similarly translates, 194, "So this is my experience of the Law . . ."

Verse 22 begins to explain the paradoxical situation of verse 21 and also gives the strongest evidence in favor of identifying the "I" in this section as a Christian.[221] Paul writes, "**I rejoice with the Law of God according to the inner man**" (22). The verb συνήδομαι conveys that the "I" throughout these verses not only agrees with (σύμφημι; v. 16),[222] but also "joyfully accepts" or "rejoices in"[223] the God-given Law. He strives to live his life as God wills.[224]

While Paul concedes that a Gentile unbeliever might agree that some of the commandments of God's Law were good and could possibly even perform them (v. 16; 2:14,26), Paul would not portray such a person as actually "rejoicing in the Law of God." On the other hand, one could argue that the Jew characterized earlier in Romans as relying on and "boasting in the Law" (2:17,23) could be the "I" who here rejoices in the Law of God. Against this, it should be noted that the rejoicing and boasting in the Law would be in a different sense than the "I" expresses here. That "delighting" is of one who views the Law in terms of works (ἔργα) which one *is able to do* sufficiently in

---

[221]Espy, 172; Käsemann, 207, admits that "joyful agreement with the will of God is everywhere reserved, in fact, for the pneumatic." His interpretation is this: "Here, then, reason and the inner man have the ability which is accorded to them in the Greek tradition, namely that of accepting and recognizing the divine will." Yet he must ask of his own interpretation, "How can the predicates and capacities of the redeemed person be ascribed to the unredeemed?" Bornkamm, "Sin, Law and Death," 99, explains that "even as a prisoner of sin [the 'I'] remains God's prisoner, who must almost joyously confirm God's right in his law."

[222]This is not merely a parallel expression as Kümmel, *Römer 7*, intimates, 62, by stating that verse 22 "corresponds" (*"entspricht"*) with verse 16.

[223]This is the only occurrence of this verb in the New Testament. Cranfield, 1:362, argues for translating "rejoice in" and *BAGD*, 789, gives the extended sense of "I (joyfully) agree with the law." For Käsemann, 207, it "denotes a positive agreement which is not simply forced on a person." Alford, 2:383, affirms that its sense "is a stronger expression than σύμφημι, ver. 16." Lenski, 485, cautions that it is "only a little stronger" and Dunn, *Romans 1-8*, 393, also warns against overemphasizing the "joyful agreement."

[224]Note the contrast with the attitude of the "I" toward the Law depicted in verses 7-13. In addition, Bruce, *The Letter of Paul to the Romans*, 146, concludes, "In light of 8:7-8, it is difficult to view the speaker here as other than a believer." Indeed, parallels to this thought are representative of the believer throughout Scripture; for example, Col. 3:10; compare 2 Cor. 4:16; see also Ps. 19:8; 119:14,16,24,35,47,70,77, 92.

order to obtain the verdict of "Righteous" from God.[225] This would seem to contradict the acknowledged inability of the "I" to do the Law displayed in 7:15-25.[226]

The phrase κατὰ τὸν ἔσω ἄνθρωπον is crucial for identifying this "I" who joyfully agrees with the Law of God (v. 22). According to Greek philosophy, the ἔσω ἄνθρωπος is the rational or even divine element in man which stands in contrast to his baser, animal, or earthly nature.[227] Its presence here illustrates the fact that Paul regularly employs terms which have significant backgrounds in Hellenistic philosophy. However, this does not mean that Paul adopts a Greek view of man or that he adheres to the philosophical definitions of these words.[228] The interpretation of the phrase in 7:22 must be based upon

---

[225]Paul critiques the futility of that approach to the Law in 2:17-3:21,28; 4; 9:30-10:5. As Dunn, *Romans 1-8*, 394, observes, this "law-abiding stayed on the superficial level of flesh and works (2:27-29; 3:27)." See the complete discussion in Chapter Four.

[226]Kümmel, *Römer 7*, 117, concludes, "With a Pharisee moral despair and [a] recognition of the powerlessness of the Law is unthinkable" (*"moralische Verzweiflung und Anerkennung der Kraftlosigkeit des Gesetzes bei einem Pharisäer undenkbar sind"*); see his complete discussion, 111-17. Beker, *Paul the Apostle*, 242, similarly contends that the interrelation between the Law and sin as revealed in Romans 7 "is unknown to a Pharisaic Jew." Compare Sirach 15:15, which confidently states, "If you will, you can keep the commandments, and to act faithfully is a matter of your own choice."

[227]As concluded by Joachim Jeremias, in *TDNT*, s.v. "ἄνθρωπος," 1:365; *BAGD*, 68[2ca]. Such a Platonic view readily led to the anthropological dualism of Gnosticism; see Wilckens, 2:94; also Johannes Behm, in *TDNT*, s.v. "ἔσω," 2:699, who concludes that this term derives "from a terminology of Hellenistic mysticism and Gnosticism disseminated by Platonic philosophy." Cranfield, 1:363, n. 2, cites this phrase or similar ones as used by Plato (*Republic*, 589a), and Philo (*De Congr.*, 97).

[228]Käsemann states, 208, "Now Paul undoubtedly uses the idealistic terms and motifs of the Greek tradition. This does not mean, however, that he takes over their original scope." Behm, *TDNT*, 2:699, and Lambrecht, *The Wretched "I" and Its Liberation*, 51 agree.

Paul's purpose in utilizing this terminology may be to combat incorrect anthropological definitions and to assert the proper understanding. G. B. Caird, *The Language and Imagery of the Bible* (London: Duckworth, 1980), 170-71, calls this "Polemical allegorism." Although the conception of a platonic "inner man" did find its way into Hellenistic Judaism, the Hermetic literature, and Gnosticism, Dunn, *Romans 1-8*, 394, points out that since Paul calls this same "I" fleshly (7:14), he "hardly belongs to that trajectory of thought." Kümmel, *Römer 7*, 136, agrees that Paul is not using Hellenistic definitions.

the context and the manner in which Paul employs the same or similar terminology elsewhere.

First, what does the context of verses 14-25 indicate? ὁ ἔσω ἄνθρωπος is undoubtedly to be identified with the θέλω or the "determinate will" of the ἐγώ as discussed earlier. As such it similarly denotes the "essential self"[229] of the "I" which consistently agrees with and strives to accomplish the Law of God (v. 16). Why does Paul refer to this aspect of the "I" as "the inner man"? Beyond simply a desire for variation, perhaps Paul chooses this phrase because it emphasizes a part of the "I" which is not recognized by physical sight.[230] In contrast to the visible σάρξ in which no good thing dwells (v. 18), the "inner man" is seen only "by faith."

Second, concerning Paul's use of this phrase elsewhere, ὁ ἔσω ἄνθρωπος does not occur again in Romans. However, Paul's use of ὁ ἔσω ἡμῶν [ἄνθρωπος] in 2 Corinthians 4:16 and εἰς τὸν ἔσω ἄνθρωπον in Ephesians 3:16 are undeniably restricted to Christians. These passages would seem to indicate that when Paul uses ὁ ἔσω ἄνθρωπος to denote the determinative will or the true essence of the "I" in Romans 7:22, he "evidently has in mind . . . the *inner being* of man which has been transformed by God's grace and so attempts to do God's will."[231]

In contrast to this, Paul adds, **"But I see another Law in my members waging war against the Law of my mind and taking me captive to the Law of sin which is in my members"** (v. 23). This passage is a key to understanding Paul's use of νόμος throughout this section. Here the "I" reveals that along with the Law of God in which the inner man delights, there is also "another Law" that is present "in my members." But this "Law" is not merely present. It is actively engaged in "waging war" against the "I" and "taking me captive."

---

[229]Newman and Nida, 141; see also Murray, 1:265-66, who uses such terms as "the inmost spirit," "the centre of his personality," and the "deepest and truest self."

[230]Newman and Nida, 141, refer to it as "the aspect of human personality which is not seen." Similarly Lenski, 485, "the immaterial part of man, the spirit and soul, the real ἐγώ." Compare this with Paul's use of τὸ πνεῦμα τοῦ ἀνθρώπου in 1 Cor. 2:11; see also 2 Cor. 5:7, "We live by faith, not by sight."

[231]Newman and Nida, 141; see 6:6; also Alford, 2:383; Morris, *The Epistle to the Romans*, 295.

Once again military metaphors are utilized[232] and the warfare depicted is ultimately comparable with the "having been sold under sin" in verse 14.[233]

Who or what is the assailant of the "I" in this battle? It is ἕτερον νόμον, a phrase which is certainly to be connected with "the Law of sin" later in verse 23 since both are present "in my members." Through his use of ἕτερος, Paul may indicate that he is speaking of "a law of a different kind."[234] He is then differentiating this "other law" from the "Law of God" in verses 22 and 25, as well from as "the Law of my mind" later in verse 23. If so, Paul is playing on the term νόμος in order to refer to two, four, or, even, five different "laws."[235] That is to say, his uses of νόμος in verses 21-25 are to be understood in basically two diverse senses. At times νόμος refers to the Mosaic Law. At other times it denotes a different "standard" or "rule,"[236] or, perhaps, a

---

[232]ἀντιστρατευόμενον, used only here in the New Testament, and αἰχμαλωτίζοντα are both military terms; see *BAGD*, 75 and ibid., 27. This recalls the imagery of "invasion" used previously (ἀφορμή in 7:8,11), as well as the other metaphors of warfare in the context; for example, 6:13 (ὅπλα); 6:23 (ὀψώνια); 8:7 (ἔχθρα). According to Dunn, *Romans 1-8*, 395, the predominance of these throughout this section of Romans may serve to indicate that the warfare against sin is "a continuing warfare in which his experience ('I') is typical of believers generally (6:13; 8:13)." However, for Käsemann, 207, these terms "are used to characterize human existence as the place and instrument of the conflict of the powers and which thus supports the 'transsubjective' interpretation of vv. 14-20." It is "cosmic strife."

[233]So Kümmel, *Römer 7*, 63; Dunn, *Romans 1-8*, 395-96. The two are closely connected since once the victory was won the defeated people were taken captive and sold as slaves.

[234]*BAGD*, 315[2], states that ἕτερος is used here in this sense and, therefore, strictly separates and contrasts the one νόμος from the other; Robertson, 748, states that ἕτερον denotes the idea of difference of kind; Richard C. Trench, *Synonyms of the New Testament*, ed. R. Hoerber (Grand Rapids: Baker Book House, 1989), 375-76, asserts that ἕτερος denotes a qualitative difference and negates any resemblance. It refers to "a law quite different from . . ." Newman and Nida, 140, contend that the use of νόμος here "has nothing to do with 'the law of God.'" So Murray, 1:267, concludes that this other νόμος "must be antithetical to [the Law of God] in every particular."

[235]Lenski, 468, affirms that there are "only two laws" operative here. Others have identified more. Calvin, 152, found four separate laws at work; Käsemann, 205, also refers to a "fourfold use of the term," citing Kuss, see 2:456-58. Lambrecht, *The Wretched "I" and Its Liberation*, 53, speaks of "the fivefold use of 'law.'"

[236]Alford, 2:384, similarly contends that both uses of νόμος here refer to "the standard or rule set up, which inclination follows"; so Lenski, 486, "a different law."

"principle"[237] and "authority."[238] If the latter suggestion is correct, when Paul writes, τῷ νομῷ τῆς ἁμαρτίας in verse 23, he utilizes νόμος in a metaphorical sense to describe the power exercised over the "I" by sin which has invaded his members and usurped the proper place of God's Law.

However, these metaphorical interpretations fail to take full cognizance of that fact that Paul's topic of concern throughout Romans 7 is how the Law of God and, more specifically, the commands of the Mosaic Torah affect man. In verses 5 and 8-13, Paul has vividly described how the Law's command is utilized by sin. Here again νόμος is at work in the "I."

Dunn responds to the metaphorical interpretations of νόμος by arguing that, for the following reasons, Paul uses νόμος consistently to denote the Mosaic Torah in verses 21-25. First, "All Paul's references to the law so far in the letter (3:27 not excluded) have been to the Jewish law, the Torah."[239] Dunn even asserts that this metaphorical meaning of νόμος "is unknown within the N[ew] T[estament]."[240] Positing the presence of another "law" here "fails to appreciate the sharpness of the tension in Paul's evaluation of the Torah" (3:27-31; 7:12-14).[241]

Second, the "two-sidedness" of the Law is the topic which Paul concentrates upon in verses 22-23,25 and 8:2. When Paul describes the effect of the Law upon the "I" in the aorist tense (vv. 7-11), he notes how the Law both identifies sin and then also provokes even more sin. Now, as the Law works on the "I" in verses 14-25, a "two-dimensional character" is present. Dunn defines this "as the law of God, reinforcing

---

[237]Suggested by Robertson, 796, who proposes that ἕτερον νόμον is indeterminate as to any specific law; Bruce, *The Letter of Paul to the Romans*, 146, translates, "the evil principle"; see also above on 7:21.

[238]Cranfield, 1:364, "Paul is here using the word 'law' metaphorically to denote exercised power, authority, control."

[239]Dunn, *Romans 1-8*, 393. Theissen, 257, somewhat less sharply concludes, "Even where Paul separates himself from the Old Testament law in his uses of the term *nomos*, the association with the Mosaic law is never excluded."

[240]Dunn, *Romans 1-8*, 392; though he admits, 392-93, that it has been documented in wider Greek use. Wilckens, 2:122, denies the use of νόμος in a metaphorical sense even there, but see Räisänen, *Paul and the Law*, 50-52, n. 34.

[241]Dunn, *Romans 1-8*, 409.

my desire for good; as the law used by sin, precipitating my action for evil."[242] There is not a marked distinction between the substance of the two "Laws" in 7:23. ἕτερος is rather being used like ἄλλος in order to contrast one manner in which the Law affects the "I" with "another."

Third, the phrase τῷ νόμῳ τῆς ἁμαρτίας in verses 23 and 25 "can hardly be other than the law used by sin to bring about death, as already explained in vv 11-13."[243] This corresponds with 7:5 where the Law's command is the agent of the passions of sins. It also fits in with the metaphor of captivity in verse 23 since Paul perceives that it is the commands of the Torah which have "bound" man as a prisoner (κατέχω in 7:6; Gal. 3:22-23; Rom. 11:32).[244]

Dunn's interpretation is on the right track.[245] However, two qualifications are necessary. First, his definition of νόμος as "Torah" is too broad. Paul continues to use νόμος particularly in the sense of the Torah's demand for proper conduct and undivided obedience to God, that is, in the narrow sense of its commandments. This was indicated by the consistent paralleling of ἐντολή and νόμος throughout the previous section (vv. 7-8,9-10,13). In verses 14-25 it is underscored by the repeated use of verbs "to do" which have as their implied object the fulfillment or transgression of the Law's commands.[246] Paul's understanding of ὁ νόμος in this sense throughout Romans 7 underlies an important conclusion which Paul will state with greater clarity in 8:3. In 7:15-20 the powerlessness of the "I" to do that which he wills and to refrain from that which he hates is attributed to sin's continued indwelling. Through this discrepancy between will and action, Paul illustrates that the Law understood in the

---

[242]Ibid.; see also Theissen, 188-89,255-57; Bo Reicke, "Paulus über das Gesetz," *Theologische Zeitschrift* 41 (1985):242-45.

[243]Dunn, *Romans 1-8*, 409.

[244]Theissen, 256, agrees that "it is impossible not to think of the Mosaic law with regard to the law that takes captive in v. 23."

[245]See Dunn, *Romans 1-8*, 407; he counters the tendency to readily allow a number of varied definitions of νόμος to alternate rapidly even within a few verses. Although this is not impossible, it is unlikely, especially since Paul is aware that "what he writes will be *heard* rather than personally read by most of the letter's recipients."

[246]The verbs ποιέω, πράσσω, and κατεργάζομαι are used 11 times in verses 15-21. See also 2:13; 10:5 quoting Lev. 18:5.

more narrow sense of its commands is unable to eradicate sin or defeat its power in man.

> The law is ineffectual as a means of grace, . . . The reason is that the law['s command even] properly understood (that is, *not* in terms of works) informs the willing but does not enable the doing.[247]

Second, Dunn's application of language such as "a two-dimensional character" to the Law of God is misleading. The holiness of the Law is *the* character of the Law and of its commandment (7:12). The Law's command does not have "two dimensions" in verses 14-25, but rather has two effects, or, as Dunn later calls it, a "double function."[248] On the one hand, for the ἐγώ who agrees with the Law (v. 16), its effect is to inform, direct, and guide his will. In fact, the "I" so delights in the Law of God (v. 22) that he identifies it internally as "the Law of my mind" (v. 23; also v. 25).

But this is not to the complete exclusion of that which the Law worked upon the "I" in verses 7-11. While the ability of sin to deceive the "I" through the Law's commandment is no longer present (v. 11), the "I" still confesses, "*I* am fleshly, sold under sin" (v. 14). The ἐγώ continues to admit that sin dwells in him (vv. 17,20) and, as in verse 5, works in his members *through the Law's command* (ἐν τοῖς μέλεσιν, vv. 5,23; compare vv. 7-8). This is ἕτερος νόμον, that is, the Law as sin is able to utilize its command to wage war against the mind of the "I" by leading him into evil and by preventing him from doing that which he wills.

The crucial point of distinction between verses 5,7-11 and verses 14-25 is that this sinful resident is now identified by and alien to the will of the "I." Furthermore, sin's ability to work in his members through the Law's command (vv. 17,20,23) is now so contradictory to how the "I," in his will, mind, and "inner man," views the Law, that he describes it as "another Law" (v. 23).

What then is τῷ νόμῳ τῆς ἁμαρτίας in verse 23? The manner in which the genitive is interpreted is crucial. It need not equate νόμος

---

[247]Dunn, *Romans 1-8*, 393.

[248]Ibid., 407; that the same Law can be understood and employed in different ways is already intimated in 7:6.

with sin,[249] a conclusion which Paul would deny as vehemently as he did in verse 7. However, in the intervening verses Paul has detailed how it is possible for sin to make use of the Law's command in order to provoke and identify sin (vv. 8,11,13). And when the Law identifies sin, *the Law also takes man captive to sin and condemns him to death* (see 7:1,5,24; 8:2; compare also 3:20; 4:15; 5:12,18,20; 6:14-15,23). Indeed, for Paul to speak in this sense "of 'the law of sin' is hardly much of a step beyond speaking of the law used by sin to deceive and kill (v 11)."[250] Yet, once again, there is a key contrast with the situation depicted in verses 7-13. In verses 14-25 there is a struggle going on between the "I" and the "Law as used by sin."

Cranfield and others counter that the explanations introduced in favor of this interpretation "are so forced as to be incredible."[251] However, that the Torah's commands can have various effects, uses, and misuses is a topic which permeates Romans.[252] It should therefore be maintained that νόμος, throughout this chapter, "is related consistently in its various meanings to the Torah"[253] in the limited sense of its commands.[254] Certainly then, there is a sense of "irony" present in Paul's use of νόμος in verses 21-25. But, as Bo Reicke concludes,

---

[249]As Kümmel, *Römer 7*, 62, does (*"Gleich-setzung"*).

[250]As Dunn, *Romans 1-8*, 395, contends is the case here and in 8:2; 6:14-15.

[251]Cranfield, 1:361-62; see also Alford, 2:383.

[252]See, for example, 2:11-3:21,27-31; 4:13-17; 7; 8:1-4; 9:30-10:5; 13:8-10. To view the Law merely in terms of works is an abuse of the Law apart from God's intention; see Barrett, 149. For Paul both effects of the Law delineated in Chapter 7 are divinely intended. The condemning aspect of the Law, as revealed in 7:7-11, is also present, for example, in 3:20; 4:15; 5:20. The manner in which a believer looks at the Law and properly strives to fulfill its commandments is noted in 13:8-10.

[253]Wilckens, 2:90, "*Daß νόμος in seinen verschiedenen Bedeutungsgehalten durchweg auf die Tora bezogen ist.*" So also Eduard Lohse, "ὁ νόμος τοῦ πνεύματος τῆς ζωῆς: Exegetische Anmerkungen zu Röm 8,2," in *Neues Testament und christliche Existenz*, eds. H. Betz and L. Schottroff (Tübingen: J. C. B. Mohr, 1973), 285-86.

[254]Kümmel, *Römer 7*, 61, regards this as a "false presupposition" (*"falschen Voraussetzungen"*) since νόμος does not always refer to the Mosaic Law (citing 7:23 and 8:2) and because Paul's defense of the Law has retreated into the background beginning in verse 17. While Paul's "defense" of the Law may have retreated, the Law certainly has not.

The qualitative genitive forms in these sentences do not express the essence of the Law, but the context in which it is working at the moment. Paul means in [all of these] cases the same divine Law.[255]

The presence of the term νοῦς in verse 23 is another word which is heavily utilized and significant in the world of Greek anthropological dualism.[256] F. F. Bruce proposes that Paul adopts a philosophical definition of νοῦς in this context in order to refer to "the mind responsive to the voice of conscience."[257] However, the phrase τῷ νόμῳ τοῦ νοῦς in verse 23 is further defined two verses later when the "I" declares, "I serve [the] Law of God with [the] mind" (νοΐ; v. 25). As a result, the τῷ νόμῳ τοῦ νοῦς in verse 23 cannot be weakened merely to the "voice of conscience" or taken as an expression of some "moral ideal."[258] Rather, as Kümmel points out, "Here the νοῦς has the ability to agree with the Law of God."[259] In addition, the term νοῦς must be identified with and further defined by the phrase ὁ ἔσω ἄνθρωπος, which is said to joyfully agree with the Law of God (v. 22), and with θέλω as used in verse 16 and throughout this section.[260]

---

[255]Reicke, 243, *"Die qualitative Genitivformen drücken in diesen Sätzen nicht das Wesen des Gesetzes aus, sondern den Kontext, in dem es jeweils wirkt. Paulus meinte in beiden Fällen dasselbe göttliche Gesetz."*

[256]Its use likely indicates Paul's acquaintance with Greek philosophical thought. For its philosophical use, see J. Behm, in *TDNT*, s.v. "νοῦς," 954-58. He concludes, 954, that it refers to "the organ of knowledge" in which "the theoretical relation (of thinking and perceiving) comes to the fore" and may be equated with "reason" or "spirit" (πνεῦμα).

[257]Bruce, *The Letter of Paul to the Romans*, 148.

[258]T. W. Manson, "Romans," in *Peake's Commentary on the Bible*, ed. by M. Black (New York: Thomas Nelson and Sons, 1963), 946.

[259]Kümmel, *Römer 7*, 136, *"dieser νοῦς hat hier die Fähigkeit, dem Gesetze Gottes zuzustimmen."*

[260]Paul Althaus, *Paulus und Luther über Menschen*, Studien der Luther-Akademie, 14 (Gütersloh: "Der Rufer" Evangelische Verlag, 1938), 35, concedes that Paul does not elsewhere describe the mind of unbelievers in this manner. If the "I" here is identified as an unbeliever, this is now the third word or phrase which must be interpreted in a sense that is different from the manner in which Paul utilizes them elsewhere. This is recognized by Käsemann, 206-7.

"I am a distressed/miserable man; who will rescue me from this body of death?" (v. 24). According to Kümmel, the "I" is here lamenting "that he desires a helper from outside, but knows no helper."[261] Many commentators join Denney in professing, "These words are not those of the Apostle's heart as he writes."[262] On the other hand, this same verse has convinced others that it is impossible to believe that the "I" is anyone other than Paul himself.[263] For example, Morris comments, "The language of this verse is impossibly theatrical if used of someone other than the speaker."[264]

The issue hinges partially upon one's definition of ταλαίπωρος. It need not depict the "I" in a state of hopeless despair.[265] Rather, in this context ταλαίπωρος portrays the "I" as "distressed"[266] because his actions do not correspond to his will (θέλω; vv. 15-23). It characterizes the state of a man who is being incessantly "pulled in two directions."[267] This cry, then, is the lament of an afflicted "I" who is yearning for deliverance from the frustrating battle between his will and the "sin which dwells in me" (vv. 17,20). In verses 14-23 Paul has depicted this tense battle in the sharpest possible terms, in part by making reference only to the failures of the "I" to enact his will. As a result, this outcry is hardly unexpected.

---

[261]Kümmel, *Römer 7*, 64, *"das eine Hilfe von außen ersehnt, aber keinen Helfer kennt."* Ibid., 98, describes this verse as "the despairing question concerning the Redeemer" (*"die verzweifelte Frage nach dem Erlöser"*).

[262]Denney, 643; similarly also Kümmel, *Römer 7*, 98, Leenhardt, 195. Denney, 643, continues, "They are the words which he knows are wrung from the heart of the man who realizes in himself the state just described. . . . not the cry of the Christian Paul."

[263]See Cranfield, 1:345; Beker, *Paul the Apostle*, 240; Robinson, *Wrestling with Romans*, 82, who believes it is "too heartfelt" to be otherwise; Maurice Goguel, *The Birth of Christianity*, tr. H. Snape (New York: Macmillan, 1954), 231-32, who concludes that verse 24 "cannot possibly be an abstract argument but is the echo of the personal experience of an anguished soul."

[264]Morris, *The Epistle to the Romans*, 296.

[265]Against Bornkamm, "Sin, Law and Death," 101; Kümmel *Römer 7*, 64,98. Neither is Barrett, 151, correct in interpreting it as the recognition of the "I" that "the last hope of mankind, religion, has proved to be a broken reed."

[266]*BAGD*, 803; also suggesting "miserable, wretched."

[267]Dunn, *Romans 1-8*, 396; in the latter half of this verse, the "I" is also being pulled ahead (compare 1 Cor. 15:54).

Of what does this longed for deliverance consist? In verse 24 the "I" cries out for rescue from τὸ σῶμα τοῦ θανάτου τούτου. The demonstrative pronoun is best read with the entire phrase ("this body of death")[268] and indicates that this description can be interpreted along the lines of τὸ σῶμα τῆς ἁμαρτίας in 6:6, the phrase ἐν τοῖς μέλεσίν μου which occurs twice in verse 23, and τῇ σαρκί in the following verse (7:25; see also 6:12; 7:18,23; 8:10,11,13,25). But this cry does not refer to a longing for physical death. The solution, for Paul, is not an escape from the body, but, rather, the redemption of it (8:11,23; 1 Cor. 15). This is indicated by Paul's use of σῶμα in verse 24 which "can cross the boundary of the ages, whereas σάρξ belongs firmly to this present age" (see 1 Cor. 15:44-50; 2 Cor. 4:7-5:5).[269]

Neither is the "I" here yearning for deliverance from "the lordship of sin."[270] Verses 14-23 have hardly depicted the total enslavement of the "I" to sin. On the contrary, Paul has portrayed the "will," the "inner man," and the "mind" of the "I" as engaged in a battle *against* the sin at work in his members. It is this condition from which the "I" cries out. He longs for a deliverance from the body in which sin can all too readily work, even through the Law, as described in verses 14-23 and 25b. The "I" calls out for rescue from the "fleshly, sold under sin" condition which leads to endless contradiction, warfare, and struggle between his will and the "sin dwelling in me."

---

[268]θανάτου, by Semitic influence, is an attributive adjective in the genitive case (a genitive of quality or a possessive genitive) as Robertson, 497, evaluates it. τούτου then defines the entire phrase since, according to Blass and Debrunner, 165, "such genitives never have a pronoun or some other modifier"; so Barrett, 151. Lenski, 488-89, points out that demonstrative pronouns are used to modify an entire phrase elsewhere (Ezek. 5:17; 6:7,8,12; Acts 5:20; 13:26), as are other pronouns (Ps. 41:10 and Obad. 7 in the Septuagint; Matt. 19:28; 26:38; Col. 1:20,22; Phil. 3:21; Heb. 1:3).

[269]Dunn, *Romans 1-8*, 391, points out this distinction, while also recognizing that the "range of meanings" between these words may overlap; see also Robinson, *The Body*, 31-32.

[270]Kümmel, *Römer 7*, 64. While he, 65, correctly sees verse 24 as a cry for release from the condition described in 14-23, he improperly characterizes that condition, 64, as "slavery to sin" (*"Sündenknechtschaft"*) and "the lordship of *sin*" (*die Sündenherrschaft"*).

While Hellenistic parallels may again be cited,[271] Paul is speaking
of an eschatological or theological tension, not an anthropological one
(2 Cor. 4:16-5:4).[272] The presence of the eschatologically nuanced
ῥύομαι,[273] as well as its future tense, indicate that this "rescue," or at
least its final fulfillment, is still in the future. Yet there is no hesitation
regarding the certainty of this deliverance as the following verse
reveals.[274] Neither does τίς "necessarily imply ignorance of the
deliverer" as Kümmel contends.[275] This is proven by the Septuagint's

---

[271]Bornkamm, "Sin, Law, and Death," 99, states that Paul "speaks in Platonic or
Gnostic fashion." Edgar Smith, "The Form and Religious Background of Romans VII
24-25a," *Novum Testamentum* 13 (1971):128-29 points to parallels from the Hermetic
literature, *Kore Kosmou*, par. 34-37, and the "Hellenistic-Jewish novel 'Joseph and
Aseneth' (6:1-8)." Leenhardt, 193, points to *Corpus Hermeticum* 1:15,18,21; 13:7,
where the outer man is described as a prison house in which the inner man grows.
Dunn, *Romans 1-8*, 396, contends that this quote from Epictetus, 1.3.3-6, vol. 1, pp.
24-27, is closer to the two-sidedness present here: ". . . inasmuch as these two elements
were commingled in our begetting, on the one hand the body, which we have in
common with the brutes, and, on the other, reason and intelligence, which we have in
common with the gods, some of us incline toward the former relationship, which is
unblessed by fortune and is mortal, and only a few toward that which is divine and
blessed. . . . 'For what am I? A miserable paltry man, [τί γὰρ εἰμί; ταλαίπωρον
ἀνθρωπάριον]' say they, and 'Lo, my wretched, paltry flesh.' Wretched indeed, but
you have also something better than your paltry flesh. Why then abandon that and
cleave to this?" Bruce, *The Letter of Paul to the Romans*, 147, begins by stating, "One
can find no lack of verbal parallels to this exclamation in classical literature and
elsewhere," citing specifically, 147, n. 2, Cicero, Philo, and Marcus Aurelius. But he
properly concludes this issue by affirming, "Paul is no platonist or Stoic."

[272]Dunn, *Romans 1-8*, 396, contends that the negative side of this eschatological
tension is set forth in 4 Ezra 7:62-69, 116-26.

[273]Wilhelm Kasch, in *TDNT*, s.v. "ῥύομαι," 6:1003, notes that ῥύομαι often has
an eschatological connotation; see 11:26; 1 Thess. 1:10; 2 Tim. 4:18; also Matt. 6:13;
Luke 11:4. Laato, 120, refers to 11:26 and 1 Thess. 1:10 and concludes, "In both
verses it is without doubt a matter of the parousia of Christ."

[274]Compare 8:23; 5:9-10; 6:8; 11:26. Robert Banks, "Romans 7.25a: An
Eschatological Thanksgiving?" *Australian Biblical Review* 26 (1979):39, likens it to
the future reference of the present participle διδόντι in 1 Cor. 15:57.

[275]Kümmel, *Römer 7*, 64,98; also Fung, 38.

use of τίς in Psalm 13:7 and 52:7, as well as by the reply which immediately follows.[276]

Verse 25a responds immediately to this apparently unsolvable dilemma with the terse statement: "**Thanks to God through Jesus Christ our Lord**" (compare 6:17,23). This doxology right after the question of verse 24 makes it difficult to understand how the preceding is the "doubting question" of one who "knows no helper."[277] For here is the helper, Ἰησοῦ Χριστοῦ τοῦ κυρίου ἡμῶν. In addition, Kümmel's conclusion that this response is "brief and indecisive" is hardly valid,[278] especially considering the presence of the "full soteriological name" with the *first* person plural.[279] Neither is there any textual support for "supposing a change of speaker between verse 24 . . . and verse 25a."[280]

Does this thanksgiving refer to a deliverance already possessed or the certain hope of a future rescue? The absence of any verb would normally indicate the present tense and perhaps the "I" is giving thanks for what he has already or just received.[281] If taken in this sense, these words have been touted as the conversion of the "I" and the marked achievement of his deliverance from the situation described in the preceding verses.[282] However, this interpretation is difficult to square

---

[276]Michel, 180; and Cranfield, 1:366, n. 3, point to these Psalm verses where a question similar to the one in 7:24 is followed, as in verse 25a, by a confident statement of hope in God's deliverance.

[277]Against Kümmel's assertion, *Römer 7*, 64,98. He concludes, 66, that verse 25b proves "that v. 25a had, of course, given no answer to v. 24" (*"daß V. 25a ja keine Antwort auf V. 24 gegeben hatte"*). Though he also admits, 65, that the person writing "already knows the answer" (*"schon eine Antwort weiß"*) as 8:2 reveals. Black, 107, similarly concludes, "This verse does not really supply an answer."

[278]Kümmel, *Römer 7*, 69, calls it "short and indecisive" (*"kurz und unbestimmt"*).

[279]Lenski, 490, points out the "full soteriological name."

[280]As Fung, 45, suggests.

[281]Paul gives thanks for what he has already received in Christ in 6:17 (compare 2 Cor. 2:14; 9:15). See Banks, 37.

[282]Denney, 643, states, "The exclamation of thanksgiving shows that the longed-for deliverance has actually been achieved." Manson, 946, also speaks of it as the deliverance which "comes through Christ by incorporation into his body." Leenhardt, 195, qualifies this interpretation by adding that the answer here is "brief and inadequate. Doubtless ch . 8 will add to this reply."

with the latter half of verse 25 which continues by offering a summary of the entire section.

On the other hand, there is nothing here to indicate that the "I" speaks specifically or exclusively of a deliverance already accomplished. As indicated by the future tense of ῥύομαι in verse 24, the "I" may be expressing "certainty that God will in the future deliver him."[283] The very close parallel of 1 Corinthians 15:57[284] indicates that the "I" here longs for the final fulfillment of his being united with "Jesus Christ our Lord" also in his bodily resurrection.[285] Verse 24, then, is not a call for conversion, but for the final deliverance "presumably at and/or by means of [Christ's] Parousia" (compare 11:26; 1 Cor. 15:42-57; 1 Thess. 1:10).[286] The future aspect of this doxology acknowledges that the "I" continues to exist within the tensions described in verses 14-23, though he is by no means uncertain regarding their resolution. This adequately explains the latter portion of verse 25 where the "I" "returns from his brief, but intense, anticipation of his future deliverance . . . to the realities of the present, continuing situation."[287] This same pattern occurs in 1 Corinthians 15:57-58.

ἄρα οὖν brings us to a "logical summary of what Paul has been saying."[288] It is a statement of "calm realism" and "a sober, but fitting conclusion" to verses 14-25a.[289] In a fashion comparable to verse 23,

---

[283]Cranfield, 1:369; then the cry of verse 24 could hardly have expressed complete despair. Murray, 1:269, refers to verse 25a as the "triumphant assurance of ultimate deliverance."

[284]Manson, 946, calls 1 Cor. 15:51-57 "the best commentary on Rom. 7:24." See Banks analysis, 35-36; ibid., 37, points out that the similarity of the context surrounding these "two passages is striking. In both we find the idea of 'sin' gaining 'power' through the 'law' leading to 'death' of the 'body'."

[285]Notice, for example, how σῶμα, and not the σάρξ which is unable to enter the new age, is used in 7:24; see Banks, 40. Compare 6:5; 8:11,17,21,23, which describe when and how this will occur; see also Phil. 3:21; 2 Cor. 5:4.

[286]Dunn, *Romans 1-8*, 411; this is the completion of the good work already begun (Phil. 1:6).

[287]Banks, 40.

[288]Morris, *The Epistle to the Romans*, 297; compare 5:18; Dunn, *Romans 1-8*, 397; Alford, 2:385.

[289]Dunn, *Romans 1-8*, 411; though he says that it concludes "the exposition of vv 7-25." Kümmel, *Römer 7*, 67, recognizes that this statement is a "hint back upon [or

the "I" announces, "**So then *I* myself in [my] mind am enslaved to [the] Law of God, but, on the other hand, in the flesh, [I am enslaved to the] Law of sin.**" One must take note that, as it stands, verse 25b is an "embarrassment to those who see in v. 24 the cry of an unconverted man" who, in verse 25a, has received deliverance from the situation depicted in verses 13-24.[290] As a result, numerous attempts have been made to alter the order of the text or, at least, its indication "that the triumphant thanksgiving in the early part of the verse does not itself bring an end to the conflict delineated."[291] Yet there is no textual evidence whatsoever to cite in support of these.

In verse 25b Paul concludes his description of this distraught "I" in an antithesis which draws together the terms used in the preceding context. This situation is exhibited most vividly in "I myself." This αὐτὸς ἐγώ adds further support to the view that we have here one and the same "I" who is "equally the 'I' of the mind and the 'I' of the flesh.'"[292] In addition, based upon Pauline usage, it is extremely unlikely that this emphatic form denotes anyone other than the author, that is, Paul himself.[293] If the "I" is not interpreted as reflecting "Paul's personal confession," then we are, once again, compelled to accept a definition of terminology opposed to Paul's normal usage and unparalleled elsewhere in his letters.[294]

---

recapitulation of] 14-24" (*"Rückverweis auf 14-24"*); Barrett, 151, "an apt summary of the paragraph"; Lenski, 491.

[290]Cranfield, 1:345; though he adds, "or of a Christian living on a low level of Christian life."

[291]The quotation is from Murray, 1:270; those who propose altering the order of the verses, despite the lack of any textual support, are cited in Chapter 1. Dodd, 132, responds, "We cannot avoid trusting our own judgment against their evidence."

[292]Dunn, *Romans 1-8*, 411.

[293]According to Blass and Debrunner, 147[281], "In αὐτὸς ἐγώ . . . Paul certainly applies the words to himself," though they speculate parenthetically "gloss and/or misplaced?" Kümmel, *Römer 7*, 67, asserts that this phrase can mean nothing other than *"ich selbst."* Dunn, *Romans 1-8*, 397, concludes that, in accordance with normal usages, "the αὐτός intensifies and emphasizes the ἐγώ "; citing *BAGD*, 122[1a]; see also Murray, 1:270-71; Banks, 41.

[294]If these verses are applied to a non-Christian, that is, not to Paul as he writes, this would be the fourth time this has been necessary in verses 14-25. See the discussion of θέλω, the phrase τὸν ἔσω ἄνθρωπον, and νοῦς above.

On the one hand, the "I" declares, αὐτὸς ἐγὼ τῷ μὲν νοΐ δουλεύω νόμῳ θεοῦ. It is difficult even to consider that Paul would use this phrase to represent a nonbeliever. What it describes is characteristic of the Christian who has been bound to the Law of God by the Holy Spirit and now willingly endeavors to be a slave of it. Paul has previously spoken of enslavement to God[295] in terms which indicate that this slavery is completely different in its essence and its results from slavery to sin (6:19-22; 7:5-6).[296] However, at the same time, the same "I" continues to be enslaved τῇ σαρκὶ νόμῳ ἁμαρτίας. As the text stands, it would seem to indicate that until the final fulfillment of the longed-for deliverance arrives (v. 24), the "I" exists "on both sides of the warfare and servitude."[297] Though he is certain of the outcome (v. 25a), the struggle between the θέλω of the "I" and the sin which dwells in him lasts as long as he is τῇ σαρκί.

Verse 25b clearly reveals that in this battle, the Law hits the "I" in two ways. Primarily now, as reflected in the will of the "I" to serve the Law, ὁ νόμος is that which determines and directs his "will," his "mind," and his "inner man." At the same time, however, sin continues to work in the "sold under sin" flesh (v. 14). There sin, "through that which is good" (v. 13), is able to effect what it exclusively accomplished in verses 7-13. Sin, "through the commandment" (v. 13), continues to identify sin "in my members" (v. 23), to provoke sin "in my flesh" (v. 18) and to bring about death (v. 13) *in the limited sense* of making this a "body of death" (v. 24).

Paul's purpose in Romans 7 will be discussed in detail in Chapter Five of this work. Here, however, it should be pointed out that Kümmel's influential interpretation of verses 14-25 is based again and again on two considerations. First, the "I" is said to be completely enslaved to sin.[298] Second, he is said to know of no Helper or

---

[295]Compare 6:16,18,19,22; 7:6,22; 8:4; 13:8-10. In the latter two passages, the Christian is both said, and then exhorted, to fulfill the Law. See also how Paul portrays himself as a slave (δοῦλος) of Christ Jesus (1:1; Phil. 1:1).

[296]Perhaps Paul picks up on the Old Testament use of עבד here; see Karl Rengstorf, in *TDNT*, s.v. "δοῦλος, 2:265-69.

[297] Dunn, *Romans 1-8*, 398; see also Pate, 112-13.

[298]Kümmel, *Römer 7*, 98,103,107,136-37. The "I" is overpowered (*"Über-manntwerden,"* 103) and a slave of sin (*"Sündensklave,"* 107,136).

Redeemer;[299] "he is helplessly subjected to sin and is without a Savior."[300]

Neither of these conclusions is supported by the text. First, the "I" is sold under sin" in his fleshliness (v. 14) and sin still dwells in his flesh (vv. 17,20). His will, however, is not sold under sin. Rather, it desires the good which the Law commands and hates evil (vv. 15b-16). The "determined will" of the "I," along with his "inner man" (v. 22) and "mind" (vv. 23,25), are fiercely engaged in the battle against sin and distraught at their inability to live in accordance with the good Law. Second, the "I" knows his Redeemer as verse 25a clearly indicates with Ἰησοῦ Χριστοῦ τοῦ κυρίου ἡμῶν.

Romans 8

The relationship between Chapter 7 and the initial verses of Romans 8 is crucial. Verse 1 marks a transition from 7:25. This, however, is not as strong or abrupt as many interpreters imply.[301] ἄρα νῦν (8:1) certainly indicates a pause, but how sharp is this "chapter" break? ἄρα by itself, or together with νῦν as here, need not signal "a fresh exposition" completely independent of what was just stated.[302] On the contrary, Paul normally uses ἄρα together with οὖν to indicate that what follows is a *direct conclusion* based upon that which immediately precedes.[303] Together they signal that there is an *intimate*

---

[299]Ibid., 98, 103,107,136-37. The "I" "knows no saving" (*"keine Rettung weiß,"* 107) and utters "the hopeless question in 7:24" (*"die hilflose Frage 7, 24,"* 103); see also above on v. 24.

[300]Ibid., 98, he has framed it in a question, asking, "Can Paul confess of himself that . . . ." (*"kann Paulus von sich bekennen, daß er der Sünde hilflos unterworfen und ohne Retter ist?"*). Kümmel rejects this possibility.

[301]For example, Theissen, 183, argues, "The statements in 7:14-24 represent in content the direct opposite of the statements about Christians in 8:1ff." Kümmel, *Römer 7*, 70, contends that 8:1 introduces a new thought unconnected with that which immediately precedes it. He cites 2:1 and 5:12 for comparison, but in neither case is ἄρα used. Cranfield, 1:373, concludes, "8:1 makes excellent sense where it stands provided we recognize that it connects neither with 7.25a nor with 7.25b but with 7.6." Even Dunn, *Romans 1-8*, 415, calls it "awkward."

[302]Dunn, *Romans 1-8*, 416.

[303]Paul uses ἄρα νῦν to indicate a direct conclusion in 5:18; 7:3,25; 8:12; 9:16,18; 14:12,19.

connection between Chapter 7 and the initial verses of Romans 8. John A. T. Robinson recognizes this by interpreting 7:7-8:4 as one cohesive unit.[304] Since 8:1-4 is actually the conclusion to the matter of Romans 7, the chapter division between 7:25 and 8:1 is in many respects most unfortunate.

If the νῦν in 8:1 is temporal,[305] it could indicate the eschatological "once-for-allness" of the present Christian state.[306] But it can hardly mark the conversion of one who has already given thanks to God "through our Lord Jesus Christ" (7:25). Neither does it signal "a new period of salvation history."[307] On the other hand, νῦν could also convey a logical sense (*"as things now stand"*).[308] If so, Paul affirms that in spite of the fact that "I" continue to serve the Law of sin in the flesh (7:25), "there is now no condemnation for those in Christ Jesus" (κατάκριμα; 8:1). Paul explains why this is so in the verse which follows.

"For the Law of the Spirit of life freed you in Christ Jesus from the Law of sin and of death" (8:2). This verse represents another passage in which the sense of νόμος is contested. What are ὁ νόμος τοῦ πνεύματος τῆς ζωῆς and τοῦ νόμου τῆς ἁμαρτίας καὶ τοῦ θανάτου? Many commentators exclude any reference to the Torah from one or both phrases.[309] For example, Cranfield resorts to a metaphorical sense of ὁ νόμος τοῦ πνεύματος τῆς ζωῆς by

---

[304]Robinson, *Wrestling with Romans,* 81-95.

[305]As in 8:18,22; 11:5; 13:11.

[306]Dunn, *Romans 1-8,* 415; see 5:9,11; 6:19,21; 11:30-31; 16:26; compare the use of νυνί in 7:6.

[307]So Kümmel, *Römer 7,* 70, *"eine neuen Periode der Heilsgeschichte"*; citing 3:21. Leenhardt, 201, speaks of it as ending the "transitory dispensation of the law." The first person singular in Romans 7, together with the σε in 8:2, speak against this interpretation.

[308]*BAGD,* 545[2], offer this definition in 1 Thess. 3:8 and Acts 15:10, but do not include Rom. 8:1 under this heading.

[309]Robertson, 93, identifies 8:2 as "a typical Pauline transition, with one use of *nomos* sliding into another." The Torah is excluded from ὁ νόμος τοῦ πνεύματος τῆς ζωῆς by Sanday and Headlam, 190; Murray, 1:276; Leenhardt, 201-2; and Räisänen, *Paul and the Law,* 50, who vehemently objects to this possibility because "the Torah had been superseded in Christ" and Christ is the "termination of the law" (10:4). Ibid., 52, then concludes that 8:2 "support[s] the conclusion that Paul often speaks of the actual abolition of the Torah" (but contrast Rom. 3:31!).

defining νόμος in terms of "the Holy Spirit's presence and exercised authority and constraint."[310]

But this phrase should not be interpreted as some nebulous or unattached power. νόμος designates a codified and unchanging norm.[311] In addition, the meaning of νόμος in both phrases must be related to Paul's use of νόμος throughout Romans and, especially, in the previous chapter. As in Chapter 7, there is no need to dismiss the Torah from either phrase.[312] The association of the Law's commandment with ζωή in 7:10 and the description of ὁ νόμος as spiritual in 7:14 certainly permit the Torah to be seen in the former phrase. In regard to "the Law of sin and death" in 8:2, the Law's connection with sin (7:5,7,8,9,11,13, 23,25) and death (7:5,10,11,23-24) is a prominent focus throughout Chapter 7.

νόμος, in and of itself, refers to the Mosaic Torah. But Paul often utilizes the context, in this case the qualifying genitives, in order to narrow his focus more specifically. A significant parallel to the use of νόμος in 8:2 is Romans 3:21. In 3:21a Paul defines his initial use of νόμος more precisely by placing it together with "the prophets" (τοῦ νομου καὶ τῶν προφητῶν). This indicates that νόμος refers to the five Books of Moses.[313] Yet Paul is focusing even more specifically on the promise contained within the Torah which, along with "the Prophets," testifies to the righteousness of God which is διὰ πίστεως (3:21-22). In 8:2 ὁ νόμος together with τοῦ πνεύματος τῆς ζωῆς similarly denotes the Torah and focuses upon its promise which has

---

[310]Cranfield, 1:376; this is similar to the metaphorical sense Cranfield proposes in 7:23,25, but there it is employed in regard to νόμος depicted in a negative sense as "the Law of sin."

[311]See Johann Bengel, *Gnomon Novi Testamenti*, 4th ed. (Tübingen: Sumtibus Ludov. Frid. Fues., 1855), 564, who defines this phrase as the "gospel inscribed on the heart" ("*evangelium cordi inscriptum*"); also Professor Louis Brighton, in EN-420 "Romans," Concordia Seminary, St. Louis, MO, Fall, 1989.

[312]Recognized by Hübner, 144-46; Lohse, 284-87; Peter von der Osten-Sacken, *Römer 8 als Beispiel paulinischer Soteriologie*, Forschungen zur Religion und Literatur des Alten und Neuen Testaments, no. 112 (Göttingen: Vandenhoeck & Ruprecht, 1975), 227-30; see also the discussion above on Rom. 7:23.

[313]As in Gal. 4:21; and probably 1 Cor. 14:34; see also Matt. 5:17; 7:12; 11:13; Luke 24:27; Acts. 13:15; 28:23; compare the three-fold division of the Old Testament in Luke 24:44.

now been fulfilled in Christ (3:22,24-25; 8:3; 10:4) whose Spirit works life (8:5-6,10-11). Anticipating 8:3, Cranfield earlier defined this phrase as follows:

> God has by the ministry of His Son and the gift of His Spirit re-established [the law] in its true character and proper office as 'spiritual' and 'unto life', as 'the law of the Spirit of life' which sets us free from the tyranny of sin and death (Rom. 8.2).[314]

Here ὁ νόμος is received by faith, "rightly understood, and responded to ἐν πνεύματι."[315]

In Romans 3:21b the righteousness of God to which ὁ νόμος testifies is said to be revealed "apart from the Law" (χωρὶς νόμου). As indicated by the use of ἐξ ἔργων νόμου in 3:20, as well as 3:27-28, this phrase speaks of the Law understood in terms of works done in fulfillment of the Law's commands. Paul has unequivocally demonstrated that ὁ νόμος in that limited sense is "the Law of sin and death" (8:2; see also 3:20; 4:15; 5:20; 7:9-11,13,23-24,25).[316]

A link can also be established with Paul's use of νόμος in 3:27.[317] There Paul declares, "What then of boasting? It is excluded. Through what kind of Law (νόμου)? Of works? No, but through [the] Law of faith." In light of Paul's attack upon "boasting" before God on the basis of "works of the Law" (2:17,23; ἔργων νόμου in 3:20,28), the Law of works in 3:27 "can hardly be understood otherwise than as a reference to the Torah."[318] As Chapter 7 has demonstrated, the Torah

---

[314]C. E. B. Cranfield, "St. Paul and the Law," *Scottish Journal of Theology* 17 (1964):65; the thesis of this article is "that, for Paul, the law is not abolished by Christ." In his later commentary, Cranfield rejects this interpretation of 8:2 by adopting the view cited above.

[315]Dunn, *Romans 1-8*, 417; compare 3:27-28.

[316]In light of 7:12, Dunn, *Romans 1-8*, 419, appropriately paraphrases this phrase, "the law as manipulated by sin and death." This is especially so when the Law is viewed apart from faith and the Spirit; see 2:17-29; 9:30-10:5.

[317]Hübner, 144, states, "According to our reflections on 3.27, the genitives occurring there, 'of works' and 'of faith', define the Law in regard to the perspective of the moment from which it is regarded. From this alone one might suppose that the same is also true of 8.2"; see also G. Friedrich, "Das Gesetz des Glaubens Röm. 3, 27," *Theologische Zeitschrift* 10 (1954): 401-17; Osten-Sacken, 245-46; Lohse, 284, n. 17.

[318]Dunn, *Romans 1-8*, 186.

understood in terms of its command provides no ground for boasting but, rather, is a "Law of sin and death" (8:2). What then is διὰ νόμου πίστεως in 3:27? This is ὁ νόμος as it testifies to the righteousness of God through faith (3:21-22). Indeed, in verse 31 Paul concludes that διὰ τῆς πίστεως "we establish νόμον" (3:31).[319] That is to say, the Law is established through faith in Christ whom Paul later calls the "goal" of the Law (τέλος νόμου; 10:4). By his Spirit the veil which sees the Law in terms of works is removed and ὁ νόμος points toward its own fulfillment as ὁ νόμος τοῦ πνεύματος τῆς ζωῆς (8:2; 2 Cor. 3:16-17).

In 8:2 Paul employs the second person singular to speak of the Christian who has been freed from the Law which convicted "you" as a sinner and pronounced the death sentence upon "you."[320] As in Chapter 6, Paul is careful to say that this is not yet the complete freedom from sin and death which he anticipates in 8:21-23. Rather, it is liberation "from the Law of sin and of death" (8:2b); it is freedom from the condemnation (8:1) which the Law pronounces when its commands are not carried out.[321]

---

[319]Räisänen, *Paul and the Law*, 51, objects because this interpretation ascribes "a very active role" to ὁ νόμος in both 3:27 and 8:2. Dunn, *Romans 1-8*, 187, responds that the διά in 3:27 "has the same force as in the nearly synonymous phrase διὰ πίστεως in 3:22,25,31." In addition, it is no more active than the νόμος which testifies in 3:21.

[320]Blass and Debrunner, 281, read the variant με (A,D) and conclude that it has a representative or universal sense as does the "I" in Chapter 7. However, it is easier to see this reading arising from an attempt to harmonize this verse with the first person singular in 7:7-25. The other variant, ἡμῶν, is similarly explained by attraction from 8:4. As a result, σε (א,B), which is certainly the more difficult reading, is to be preferred; see Bruce Metzger, *A Textual Commentary on the Greek New Testament* (New York: United Bible Societies, 1971), 516. According to Cranfield, 1:377, the singular is here used by Paul to point "out the individual as representative of the group. . . . to make sure that each individual in the church in Rome realized that what was being said in this sentence was something which really applied to him personally and particularly"; see 2:1,3-5,17-27; 10:9; 11:17-24; 14:4,10,15,20-22. It is difficult to understand Kümmel's willingness, *Römer 7*, 73, to include Paul in σε after *excluding* Paul from his own use of the first person singular throughout Chapter 7.

[321]This is correctly depicted by Kümmel, *Römer 7*, 73,69, as freedom from slavery to sin (*"Sündenknechtschaft"*), from the curse of sin (*"Sündenfluch"*), and from the resulting condemnation (*"von der Verdammnis"*). However, he then concludes, ibid., 68, that the Christian is now free from the power of sin and death (*"von der*

Romans 8:3 represents the climax to Paul's analysis of the Law which began in 7:1: "For that which was impossible for the Law in that it was weakened through the flesh, God, by sending his own Son in the likeness of sinful flesh and as a sin offering (περὶ ἁμαρτίας),[322] condemned sin in the flesh."

Paul has used νόμος to characterize the Torah specifically in terms of its commands throughout Chapter 7, as well as in the final phrase of 8:2. Romans 7:1-8:3 has revealed that for Paul the Law's command is active only 1) when it is used by sin to wage war against a person by provoking and increasing sin (ἀντιστρατευόμενον in 7:23; see 7:5,7-8,17-18,20) and, then, 2) when it takes a sinner captive to death by identifying and condemning his transgression (αἰχμαλωτίζοντα in 7:23; 7:10-11,13,24).[323]

While the Law's command does passively reveal the will of God to the "I" who rejoices in the Law (7:14-25), it is "impossible" for the Law to enable anyone to fulfill its demands to the extent God requires (see 2:17-24; 3:19-20). In addition, the Law's command is "unable" actively to accomplish release from sin and death. Chapter 7 has demonstrated that the Law's command can neither remove sin nor eliminate a person's failures to enact its commands. In reality, it only serves to increase both. It is in this sense that the Law is unable. Although the Law clearly specifies what God requires, it is impossible (ἀδύνατον) for the Law's command to accomplish what it demands or to free a person from the condemnation it imposes upon one's failure to live according to it.

But it is important to notice that this failure is not attributable to the Law alone. The reason why it is impossible for the Law to effect fulfillment of God's command and to deliver the life it offers (10:5; 7:10) is because the Law is weakened διὰ τῆς σαρκός (8:3).

Sündenmacht," "Todesmacht") and that the purpose of this freeing "is the sinless life of the Christian" (". . . *ist das sündlose Leben der Christen 8,4.*").

[322]As used in the Septuagint; see Lev. 14:31; Ps. 39:7 [MT: 40:6]; Is. 53:10; see also Heb. 10:6. C. F. D. Moule, *An Idiom Book of New Testament Greek* (New York: Cambridge University Press, 1959), 63, discusses this possibility but concludes that a more general sense ("from sin") which would be inclusive of the technical term is preferable.

[323]See also 3:19-20; 11:32 in light of Gal. 3:22; Gal. 3:10; see the discussion of the argument of Galatians in Chapter 5.

Here Paul's critique of the Law comes full circle. If not for the sinful flesh, the "holy" Law and the "holy, just, and good" commandment would present no problem (7:12). The Law would reveal the truth and the knowledge of God to those who could follow it (2:20). There would be no sin or death to overcome. But sin has entered the world and spread to all people (5:12). As a result, "I am fleshly, sold under sin . . . Sin dwells in me . . . this is, in my flesh" (7:14,17,18). In this situation the Law's command can declare but not effect. Thus "the inadequacy of the law lies not in itself but in the conditions in which it has to operate."[324] It is "on account of the flesh" (8:3).

But God has dealt decisively with sin, death, and the Law's condemnation by sacrificing his own Son as *the* promised sin-offering (8:3b). Verses 2-3 then have a chiastic structure. The Law's command is unable on account of the flesh and, therefore, results in sin and death (vv. 2b-3a). But God condemned this "sin in the flesh" in his Son who became both flesh and sin (1:3; 9:5; 2 Cor. 5:21), and suffered the curse of the Law, which is death, on the cross (Gal. 3:13). Those "in Christ Jesus" are set free from the Law's condemnation by the now fulfilled "Law of the Spirit of life" (vv. 2a,3b).

God's purpose in this was that "the just requirement of the Law might be fulfilled in us" (8:4a). Drawing from verse 3, 8:4 speaks of how τὸ δικαίωμα τοῦ νόμου was fulfilled for us through Christ's life and how our failures to keep the Law's command were erased by his death (as in 10:4). This verse proceeds to describe those "in Christ Jesus" (8:1) as ones in whom the Law's requirement is fulfilled. They "walk not according to the flesh but according to the Spirit" (v. 4b) who has enabled them to serve the Law willingly (7:6; compare 7:16,22).

In verses 5-8 Paul sets up a contrast between the mind of the flesh and the mind of the Spirit. This is stated in terms of their respective results, either death or life and peace (v. 6; see 7:4). The mind of the flesh is at enmity with God precisely because it cannot subject itself to the Law of God (v. 7). The fact that the flesh is unable to submit itself to God's Law and thereby to please him (v. 8) is reflected throughout Chapter 7 (7:5,14,17-18,20,25) and underscores the interpretation of 8:3 adopted above.

---

[324]Dunn, *Romans 1-8*, 419; see also Wilckens, 2:124.

Verse 9 introduces the second person plural. "However, *you* are not in the flesh but in the Spirit since the Spirit of God dwells in you" (v. 9a). As indicated by εἴπερ, ἐν σαρκί does not imply that the believer no longer lives in a fleshly body. Rather, the Christian's life is no longer determined by the sinful flesh as depicted in 7:5 (ἐν τῇ σαρκί). Since the presence of the Spirit is the "necessary qualification" which marks the believer (v. 9b; compare 7:18), both aspects of the statement in verse 10 can be applied to the Christian and only to the Christian. It can only be said that "τὸ σῶμα is dead on account of sin" (as in 7:24; compare 6:6,11) *and* that "the Spirit is alive through righteousness" if Christ is in you (v. 10).

As in Chapter 6 (vv. 5,8), Paul depicts our likeness with Christ in regard to his resurrection in the future tense (ζῳοποιήσει; v. 11). Verse 11 looks ahead to the final fulfillment of the hoped-for deliverance in a manner which is similar to 7:24. Yet the presence of the Spirit is the guarantee that God will make your mortal bodies alive through that same Spirit (v. 11).

Upon this basis Paul moves to exhortation (as in 6:12). In 8:12 he reminds the ἀδελφοί that they are no longer obligated to the flesh as they were when sin and death fearfully enslaved them (v. 15). But Paul reckons with the possibility that they might allow themselves to be enslaved to fear once again (πάλιν; v. 15). Therefore he encourages the "brothers" to continue to put the deeds of the flesh to death (θανατόω; v. 13). This is an ongoing process which is led by the Spirit who identifies himself with our spirit[325] and thereby guarantees our adoption as God's children and our place as heirs (vv. 16-17). However, so long as we are in this world, sufferings remain and Paul continues to hold off "the glory that is to be revealed" (v. 18) until the day when we and "creation itself also will be set free" (v. 21; compare 8:2).[326]

---

[325]τῷ πνεύματι ἡμῶν in 8:16 can be identified with the "will," "the inner man," and the "mind" of the "I" in Chapter 7.

[326]The future, ἐλευθερωθήσεται, contrasts with the aorist tense of the same verb in 8:2. Dunn, *Romans 1-8*, 418, concludes, "The sense of being taken prisoner (7:23) *and* of being liberated (8:2) are both part of the believer's experience in Paul's perception—still imprisoned as a man of flesh by sin and death, yet at one and the same time already liberated 'in Christ Jesus.'"

In describing the futility (μάταιος) to which creation has been subjected against its will, as well as its "anxious longing" for deliverance (ἀποκαραδοκία; v. 20), Paul places all of the universe in a situation comparable to that of the "I" in 7:14-25. While eagerly expecting the revealing of the sons of God (v. 19), creation groans and suffers (v. 22). ἡ κτίσις yearns "to be set free from its slavery to corruption" (ἀπὸ τῆς δουλείας τῆς φθορᾶς; v. 21).

Similarly, Paul says, *"We ourselves groan* within ourselves, waiting eagerly for adoption as sons, the redemption of our body" (v. 23). This tension, which is also reminiscent of the frustration which evoked the lament in 7:24, leads Paul to this conclusion: "For we were saved for this hope, but hope that is seen is not hope" (8:24). As Christians we have been saved (v. 24) and, although we do not yet visibly see that for which we eagerly hope, we do now have the "first fruits" (ἀπαρχή; v. 23) of the Spirit who helps us to battle our "weakness" (ἀσθένεια; v. 26).

It is difficult to see how this presents a totally different context than 7:14-25[327] or how Hans Conzelmann can conclude that "the redeemed man no longer cries for redemption from the body of death" (8:23; see also v. 11).[328] True, explicit mention of the Holy Spirit's activity within the "I" is withheld in Romans 7:14-25.[329] But this need not exclude the possibility of identifying the "I" in those verses as a Christian.[330]

The contrast between Chapters 7 and 8 is that in the midst of the frustration, weakness, futility, and groaning exhibited throughout 7:14-

---

[327]As Bornkamm, "Sin, Law and Death," 101; Robinson, *Wrestling with Romans,* 87. Leenhardt, 182, concludes that the two chapters are not opposites, but "the tone is totally different."

[328]Conzelmann, 230.

[329]Yet one might question how the "I" in Romans 7:14-25 could identify the Law as Spiritual (v. 14), agree with (v. 16), rejoice in (v. 22), and even serve the Law of God (v. 25) without the Spirit's presence. Above all, how could a person without the Spirit utter the doxology of 7:25a? Perhaps the absence of any direct mention to the Spirit's activity in the "I" in 7:14-25 serves to set forth the confrontation between the "I" and the "Spiritual Law" (7:14) in its sharpest terms.

[330]Banks, 41, points out that there is no mention of the Holy Spirit elsewhere in extensive passages where Paul clearly addresses the Christian life (2 Cor. 4-5; Phil. 3; Col. 2-3). This need not exclude the Spirit's presence.

8:25, the presence of the Spirit is explicitly announced in Chapter 8. There Paul seeks to demonstrate that the present situation is no cause for doubt or despair. This is because the Holy Spirit, and *decisively not the Law's command* (8:3), is the Helper who provides the intercession we so badly need (8:26-27) and who is the decisive guarantor of the future (8:16-17,22-23).

This launches Paul into the climactic portion of all of Romans (8:29-39). He affirms that since God "did not spare his own Son, but delivered Him up for us all" (v. 32), we are God's elect (v. 33), chosen before creation, justified (v. 30), and free from any condemnation (v. 33-34). Paul is so certain of this that even when he has the future glory-to-be-revealed in mind (vv. 17-18,21), he can speak of it in the aorist tense (ἐδόξασεν; v. 30). Nothing can separate us "from the love of God which is in Christ Jesus our Lord" (v. 39; cf. 7:25).

Romans 9-16

In Romans 9-11 Paul describes the effect of the δικαιοσύνη τοῦ θεοῦ upon the Jewish people. Though there is not much material directly relevant to Chapter 7 here, two things should be noted. First, the failure of Israel to attain the Law of righteousness is attributed to the fact that they pursued it "by works" (ἐξ ἔργων; 9:32). Their zeal for God is without proper knowledge (ἐπίγνωσιν; 10:2). 9:30-10:5 has been referred to often in this chapter because it offers a significant insight into Paul's evaluation of the Law.

Second, it is noteworthy that three times in these chapters (9-11) Paul uses emphatic forms of the first person singular similar to those in 7:7-25. He speaks of himself by employing αὐτὸς ἐγώ (9:3), ἐγὼ . . . εἰμί (11:1), and εἰμι ἐγώ (11:13). It is not seriously disputed that Paul refers to himself in all three instances. On the other hand, one should not overlook the fact that Paul also uses ἐγώ in a "rhetorical" sense in 11:19. He clearly indicates this by introducing his statement with ἐρεῖς οὖν. An analysis of Paul's various uses of the first person singular will be a prominent aspect in the remainder of this study.

In Romans 12:1-15:7 Paul is quite heavily involved in ethical issues. Kümmel contends that these later chapters are "only loosely connected with the first part" of Romans.[331] As a result, he concludes that "we need only examine Chapters 1-11" in order to interpret Romans 7 properly.[332] Kümmel's limitation is unwarranted.[333] While 12:1 does begin a new section, the influence of what Paul has already stated in this letter cannot be completely severed from its concluding chapters.

The first two verses of Chapter 12 clearly indicate that the Christian life, which exists "through God's mercies," remains an intense struggle. Paul urges his fellow believers to resist the temptation to be conformed to this world (v. 2). After his discussion of spiritual gifts (12:3-8), Paul's exhortations against being haughty (v. 16), repaying evil with evil (v. 17), and taking revenge into one's own hands (vv. 19-20) are summed up in verse 21: "Do not be conquered by the evil, but conquer the evil with the good." All of these admonitions reckon with the fact that what they denounce are, in fact, real possibilities. The "doing" of evil is an ever present reality for these Christians who must strive to resist being conquered (νικάω) and completely enslaved once again (as in 6:17-18,20; 7:5,7-11).[334]

In the next section, wherein Paul speaks of the Christian's responsibilities to government (13:1-7), he again urges his readers to do good and abstain from evil (vv. 3-4). The verses which follow (vv. 8-10) reveal that the Law is that which guides and directs the believer toward good and away from evil. Here ὁ νόμος freely interchanges with ἐντολή (v. 9; as in 7:7-12). This, as well as the citation of a number of the commandments from the Decalogue in verse 9,[335] indicates that in 13:8-10 νόμος is again to be understood in terms of

---

[331]Kümmel, *Römer 7*, 27; the topic here is *"mit dem ersten Teil nur lose zusammenhängen."*

[332]Ibid., *"brauchen wir nur Kap. 1-11 zu betrachten."*

[333]Cranfield, 1:346, n. 6, evaluates Kümmel's conclusion as evidence "of a blind spot in the author's theological thinking serious enough to have bedeviled a good deal of the discussion in what is in many respects a valuable and informative book."

[334]Here there is no longer total enslavement. But, rather than the signalling the end of a battle, the presence of the Spirit has marked the beginning of a struggle which persists within the believer. The situation of the "I" in 7:14-25 seems comparable.

[335]Paul undoubtedly uses οὐκ ἐπιθυμήσεις as a summation for the last commandment of the Decalogue here. This weighs heavily in favor of interpreting the expression in 7:7 in the same manner.

the Torah's commandments. As such Paul summarizes the Law in the command to "love your neighbor as yourself" (v. 9; Lev. 19:18). This "doing" "is the fulfillment of the Law" (πλήρωμα; v. 10; see also v. 8). These verses emphasize the continuing relevance of the Law's commands as a guide for believers. They reveal what "the good, pleasing and perfect will of God" is (12:2; compare 2:18-20). But Paul does not say or imply that believers are able to fulfill the Law perfectly (see 8:3).

On the contrary, the remainder of Chapter 13 urges the readers to abstain from a number of base vices (v. 13) since the day of salvation "is nearer to us than when we believed" (v. 11). Verse 14 implores, "Put on the Lord Jesus Christ, and do not make provision for the desires of the flesh" (τῆς σαρκὸς πρόνοιαν μὴ ποιεῖσθε εἰς ἐπιθυμίας).[336] What prompts this exhortation? Is it necessary because sin persists in its attempts "to work out every desire" in these Christians even through the Law's command (πᾶσαν ἐπιθυμίαν in 7:8; ἐπιθυμίαν 13:14)? Could it be that they must continue to battle their σάρξ which remains "sold under sin" (7:14)?

As Paul deals with those who are "weak in the faith" (14:1-15:8), he engages issues which are not sinful in and of themselves.[337] After rejoicing in the spread of the Gospel to the Gentiles in 15:8-13, Paul describes his own ministry and travel plans (vv. 14-33). He makes his transition between these two sections by describing his own personal confidence in the Roman Christians with the emphatic αὐτὸς ἐγώ (v. 14; compare 7:25). In the final chapter (16), Paul extends personal greetings to a large number of Christians in Rome.

This chapter has endeavored to state the semantic sense or content of what Paul writes in Romans 7 by examining the text of that chapter within its context. Conclusions regarding the controversial issues involved in Romans 7 will be made in the chapters to follow. Chapters

---

[336]Literally to give *"forethought"* or *"foresight"* to something; see Acts 24:2; *BAGD*, 708-9[2].

[337]He discusses the eating of meat which was either ceremonially unclean or offered to idols (14:1-4 in light of 1 Cor. 8-10) and the observance of Old Testament festival days (14:5-6; Col. 2:16-18; Gal. 4:10).

Three and Four will concentrate upon the identity and spiritual condition of the "I" in Romans 7:7-25. Then, in Chapter Five, we will draw conclusions about the purpose and function of Romans 7.

Chapter Three

Paul's Use of the First Person Singular:
The Referent Question

Now that the sense of what Paul writes in Romans 7 has been stated, we focus more specifically on the "I" in verses 7-25. Who is the "I?" How does Paul intend the numerous first person singular forms he uses in Romans 7:7-25 to be identified and understood? What purpose do they serve? What is a proper interpretation of Paul's use of the "I" in Romans 7?

Before attempting to answer these questions, it should be pointed out that two vital, but separate, aspects are involved in them. The first is the question of referent.[1] Paul uses ἐγώ, as well as the other first person singular forms, in Romans 7:7-25 to speak of an "I,"[2] but who does Paul intend his readers to identify as this "I"? Who is Paul writing about or referring to by using these various forms in the first person singular? In short, who is the *referent* of the "I"?

After the identity of the "I" has been established, a second factor involved in Paul's use of the first person singular can be approached. This is the field of *pragmatics* which seeks to determine the impact which an author aims to have upon his readers by using a particular

---

[1]The person generally credited with first making a distinction between sense/meaning and referent is Gottlob Frege; see *Translations from the Philosophical Writings of Gottlob Frege*, eds. and trs. P. Geach and M. Black (Oxford: Basil Blackwell, 1952), especially 56-78 which comprises an essay first published in 1892 entitled, "On Sense and Reference." The following is an example of the distinction between sense and referent: One may speak of "Pluto" and of "the last planet in our solar system." While both statements express a different sense/meaning, they are readily understood as referring to the same celestial body. However, what if another planet is discovered beyond Pluto? While the sense conveyed by the two phrases would still "mean" the same thing as before, the referent of the second would change.

[2]This is the field of semantics which was utilized in Chapter Two. There it was determined that the ἐγώ in Romans 7 denotes an "I," that is, a whole person, and not merely some component of inner psychology.

expression.[3] Specifically in Romans 7, this involves asking how Paul intends his statements of and about the "I" to function. What does Paul seek to accomplish through his consistent and extensive use of the first person singular in verses 7-25?

In interpreting Romans 7 one may not omit either of these factors. Both the referent and the function of the "I" must be considered. At the same time, although both aspects are integrally related, they must be clearly distinguished. Much of the confusion surrounding the "I" of Romans 7, as illustrated in Chapter One, stems from a failure to distinguish referent from function. For example, when the "I" is identified as Paul, Israel, or Adam, and then also identified with the experience of other people, one has made a significant jump from the text itself. A number of different referents have been combined in an effort to apply what Paul is saying and to explain his purpose.

In addition, it is only proper methodologically to deal with the pragmatic issue of function once the referent questions have been resolved. Thus the problem of the referent of the "I" in Romans 7:7-25 should be addressed first. Once the "I" has been identified, one can move on to the second aspect which concerns itself with the intended function of the first person singular in those verses. This has not always been the case. When Werner Kümmel approaches Romans 7 as

---

[3]Kevin Vanhoozer, in "The Semantics of Biblical Literature," Chapter 2 in *Hermeneutics, Authority, and Canon*, eds. D. Carson and J. Woodbridge (Grand Rapids: Academie Books, 1986), 86, defines this pragmatic aspect as "what we bring about or achieve *by* saying something, such as convincing, persuading." James Voelz, "Biblical Hermeneutics: Where are We Now? Where are We Going?" in *Light for Our World*, ed. J. Klotz (St. Louis: Concordia Seminary, 1989), 239, states, "According to the speech-act theory, language has not only a 'locutionary force' (= the meaning of the words), but also an 'illocutionary force', often defined as 'what the words *count as*.'" Ibid., 254, n. 28, further identifies the "per locutionary force" as the actual effect which the words have upon the reader. This may or may not coincide with what the speaker/author intends. Vanhoozer and Voelz both make reference to work in speech-act theory by John L. Austin, *How to Do Things with Words*, 2nd ed. (Cambridge: Harvard University Press, 1975) and by John R. Searle, *Speech Acts* (London: Cambridge University Press, 1969).

As an example of pragmatics, one might think of parents telling their young child who is preoccupied in a toy store, "We are leaving now." The statement is intended to "count as" something more than a sharing of information. Its function is something like, "It is time to go and if you do not want to be left alone in the store, come along now!"

an objective defense of the Law, he has begun with a pragmatic aspect.[4] He then ends up advocating a rhetorical interpretation of the *"I"* which virtually eliminates the issue of referent from consideration entirely. The *"I"* has become *"no one or every one."*[5]

The goal of this chapter is to consider the first of these two aspects, that of referent. Who is the *"I"* in Romans 7:7-25? The identity of the *"I"* will be determined by comparing the sense/content of what Paul says about the *"I"* in Romans 7:7-25, as determined in Chapter Two, with the sense/content of what he says elsewhere about the various referents which have been proposed. However, due to the disputed issues involved in Romans 7, an attempt to identify the referent of the *"I"* also and inevitably leads to a question of *when* these verses are to be applied to that specific referent. Behind this question lies the debate over the spiritual state of the *"I,"* particularly in verses 14-25. These *"referent"* issues are addressed here in Chapters Three and Four. Only then will the last chapter move on to examine the function or purpose which Paul's use of the first person singular in Romans 7 is intended to serve.

The Referent of the "I" in Romans 7:7-11

With whom is the *"I"* to be identified in Romans 7:7-25? A survey of this issue was conducted in Chapter One. [The reader may refer back to Chapter One for more details and additional adherents of the following interpretations.] That overview revealed the issue of referent is a problem particularly prominent in verses 7-11. Only in these earlier verses do we have scholars specifically identifying a number of different referents. This is generally because many of them have concluded that it is *"a mistake to treat the passage autobiographically*

---

[4]Werner Kümmel, *Römer 7 und die Bekehrung des Paulus* (Leipzig: Hinrichs, 1929); reprinted in *Römer 7 und das Bild des Menschen: Zwei Studien*, Theologische Bücherei, Neues Testament Band 53 (Munich: Christian Kaiser Verlag, 1974), 9,10,11,56. [Hereafter, this study is denoted *Römer 7.*]

[5]Ibid., 132, *"niemand oder jedermann ist Subjekt."*

and to look for matching stages in Paul's own experience."[6] The crucial importance of identifying the referent in verses 7-11 is underscored by the fact that the conclusions which are reached about the "I" in verses 14-25 are in large part determined by how the "I" is identified in these earlier verses. For example, of the four reasons Kümmel gives for the identity of the "I" he establishes in verses 14-25, two are directly dependent upon verses 7-11.[7] As a result, a consideration of the question of referent can, at least initially, focus upon verses 7-11.

To whom, then, does the "I" there refer? The following referents have been proposed.

The People of Israel

Douglas Moo contends that the "I" in Romans 7:7-11 represents the "redemptive-historical experience of Israel with the law."[8] Paul is speaking in the name of the nation of Israel and, particularly in verses 9-10, describing their experience at Mount Sinai.[9]

Moo supports this by pointing out that in Romans 7 Paul is defending the Mosaic Law which was "Israel's peculiar possession."[10] Moo then extends his definition of the "I" to include Paul who is, at least in a secondary sense, also the referent. Why is this so? Moo argues that the first person singular in verses 7-11 represents Israel as a *"collective body"*[11] and that Paul is a member of Israel. Therefore, Paul can identify "himself, in a 'corporate' sense, with the experiences of his own people."[12]

---

[6]James Dunn, *Romans 1-8*, Word Biblical Commentary, vol. 38a, eds. R. Martin, D. Hubbard, and G. Barker (Dallas: Word Books, 1988), 382. Kümmel, *Römer 7*, 78, contends that if this is attempted, an identification of the time in Paul's life in which these experiences should be placed is left up to the "fantasy of the scholar" (*"Phantasie der Forscher"*); see Chapter One.

[7]Kümmel, *Römer 7*, 117; these are cited in Chapter One.

[8]Douglas Moo, "Israel and Paul in Romans 7:7-12," *New Testament Studies* 32 (1986):123; see also Chapter One.

[9]Ibid., 122-35, especially 129-30.

[10]Ibid., 123.

[11]Ibid., 128.

[12]Ibid., 129; compare Richard Longenecker, *Paul* (New York: Harper and Row,

By this criterion, Paul, along with all the other members of Israel, past, present, and future, can also be the referent of the *"I."* In a similar but somewhat broader fashion, Ethelbert Stauffer proposes that the *"I"* in verses 7-11 is following the steps of mankind from Paradise through Moses.[13]

Evaluation

1. First, there is a practical consideration. Nothing in the text indicates that the various forms in the first person singular are to be taken in anything other than their literal sense. Neither is there any textual support for interpreting the *"I"* in a collective or corporate manner. As Kümmel responds to the identification of the *"I"* as the Jewish people, *"Nothing stands written in the text concerning these things."*[14]

2. This interpretation applies 7:8b to the era before the Law was given at Sinai. In that period, it is said, sin was *"dead"* or *"ineffective"* (νεκρά of 7:8). This contradicts Paul's description of the time between Adam and Moses in Romans 5:12-14. He hardly depicts it as one in which sin was in any way dormant. Just the opposite, sin reigned!

3. The situation described in verses 7-11 does not at all match the characterization which Paul makes of Israel elsewhere in this letter. Those who *"bear the name Jew"* (2:17) are pictured as standing in judgment on the sins of others (2:1-16,21-24), while relying on

---

1964), 92, who advocates the presence of this same concept in Romans 7:7-11, but then applies it to Adam. For support, Moo, 129, points to parallels from the Old Testament prophets who used the first person singular to *"narrate with intense subjective language the horrors which have befallen the city and the people"* (Jer. 10:19-22; Mic. 7:7-10; Lam. 1:9-22; 2:20-22) citing U. Luz, *Das Geschichtverständnis des Paulus*, BEVT, 49 (Munich: Christian Kaiser, 1968), 159, n. 87.

[13]*Theological Dictionary of the New Testament*, 10 vols., ed. G. Kittel and G. Friedrich, tr. and ed. by G. Bromiley (Grand Rapids: Eerdmans Publishing, 1973), s.v. ἐγώ, by Ethelbert Stauffer, 2:358-62, contends that the giving of the Law provokes the crisis of Chapter 7 which is not resolved until the coming of Christ depicted in Chapter 8.

[14]Kümmel, *Römer 7*, 85, *"daß von all diesen Dingen nichts im Texte steht"*; see also 80,84,87.

circumcision and their observance of the Law as the basis for boasting before God (2:17-29).

Specifically in regard to the Law, the members of Israel are exhibiting an attitude of complacency and self-righteousness (Romans 2; 9:30-10:5). According to Paul, Israel views the Law as the ground of their boast (2:23) and as the means for attaining righteousness (9:31-32; 10:3). They in no way "regarded the law as impossible to fulfill in principle or as a spur to sin."[15] That the Law could be involved with sin (7:7-8) and even used as a means of deception and death (7:10-11) would similarly have been regarded as blasphemous.

Paul responds by charging the people of Israel with improperly judging others and with being complacent/misguided about their observance of the Law (2:1-4,13,21-24). As a result, they fail to recognize their own transgression of the Law and the unavoidable consequences of that sin, God's wrath and judgment (1:18; 2:5-16; 3:9-20).

All of this stands in sharp contrast to the deep and personal awareness of sin exhibited by the "I" in 7:7-11. The "I" perceives that it is not possible to attain righteousness by the Law's commandment. Rather, the "I" acknowledges that sin has been able to use God's Law to identify sin, to provoke sin, to deceive, and to kill (7:7-11).

4. In light of 2:12-16, Paul does not restrict the recognition and provocation which sin is able to work through the Law's commandment to the Jewish people, that is, to those who know the revealed Torah.[16] In addition, Moo's contention that "the temporal limitation of the *torah* is a key element in Paul's theology" is refuted by Paul himself (2:20; 3:31; 7:12; 13:8-10).[17] Once the Law had been revealed, Paul refuses to allow any limitations to be placed upon its scope or its duration.

---

[15]Ernst Käsemann, *Commentary on Romans*, tr. and ed. G. Bromiley (Grand Rapids: Eerdmans Publishing, 1980), 192-93.

[16]As Moo, 123, concludes in stressing that the Mosaic Law is "Israel's peculiar possession," and, 124, "a special gift to Israel." He attempts to deal with 2:14-16, 26-27, but cannot adequately explain them. According to R. C. H. Lenski, *The Interpretation of St. Paul's Epistle to the Romans*, Commentaries on the New Testament (Minneapolis: Augsburg Publishing House, 1961), 462, this factor alone makes the identification of the "I" as Israel "untenable."

[17]Moo, 124.

5. If Israel is accepted as the referent in verses 7-11, the difficulties this identification presents if one tries to maintain it in verses 14-25 are virtually insurmountable. Kümmel illustrates this as follows:

> But then in 7:14ff., the I is divided into two parts: the willing `I' represents the behavior of the ideal Jew, but the action of the evil ['I'] that of the sinful Jew. . . . No reader could determine that here a totality is introduced in the midst of his discussion and then . . . this same totality is again separated into groups.[18]

As a result, those who support this interpretation generally do not even attempt to apply it consistently throughout the remainder of the chapter.

Adam and in Him All Mankind

According to this interpretation, Paul's terms in 7:7-11, and especially his use of the "I," are to be "defined according to the context of Genesis 1-3."[19] Adam, who has already been introduced in 5:12-21, now speaks through the ἐγώ.[20] Those who support this identification contend that the references to life and death in verses 8b-10a can be applied in their theological sense to Adam alone. Ernst Käsemann concludes, "There is nothing in the passage which does not fit Adam, and everything fits Adam alone."[21] It is then proposed that Paul's purpose is to present the inescapable fact that "every person

---

[18]Kümmel, *Römer 7*, 85, *"Dann wird aber in 7,14ff. das Ich in 2 Teile geteilt: das Wollen ist das Verhalten des idealen Juden, das Tun des Bösen aber das des sündigen Juden. . . . Kein Leser konnte merken, daß hier eine Gesamtheit als redend eingeführt wird und dann in dieser Gesamtheit wieder Gruppen unterschieden werden."*

[19]John Espy, "Paul's Robust Conscience Re-Examined," *New Testament Studies* 31 (1985):169; see Chapter One. Even Dunn, *Romans 1-8*, 404, who supports the Christian interpretation of 7:14-25 can conclude, "It was clear enough in vv. 7-13 that the 'I' was Adam, not Paul himself as such."

[20]Günther Bornkamm, "Sin, Law and Death," in *Early Christian Experience*, The New Testament Library, tr. P. Hammer (London: SCM Press, 1969), 93.

[21]Käsemann, 196; though he adds, 200, that these verses depict a general truth applicable to all those "under the shadow of Adam." See also Stanislas Lyonnet, "L 'Historie du salut selon le chapitre vii de l 'Epître aux Romains," *Revue Biblica* 43 (1963):130-42.

after Adam is entangled in the fate of the protoplast. . . . Before Christ Adam is continually repeated. "[22] The referent, initially identified as Adam, is again extended or combined with other referents.

Evaluation

It is possible that Paul had Genesis 1-3 in mind as he wrote these verses.[23] However, those who push all the details of the text in an effort to prove that the referent of the *"I"* can be Adam alone soon find that all the details do not match.

1. As with the previous interpretation, there is nothing indicated in the text which explicitly directs the hearer or reader to understand the *"I"* as Adam. For example, in Genesis 2-3 we find specific references not only to Adam, but to Eve, the serpent, the fruit, the tree, and so on. In Romans 7:7-11 Paul neither mentions nor even alludes to any of these. As a result, Gerd Theissen appropriately asks, "Is Adam speaking? But who in the Roman community would have understood that?"[24]

2. Another serious objection to identifying the referent as Adam is the fact that the Torah was not given until the time of Moses (5:13-14).[25] That the Mosaic Torah is indeed Paul's topic of discussion here is clearly indicated by his citation of a portion of the tenth commandment at the end of verse 7. It seems improbable that Paul would choose the experience of Adam in order to demonstrate the workings of the Mosaic Law's commandment or to serve as proof for his assertion that the revealed Law of God is not sin (7:7,12-13).

---

[22]Käsemann, 197.

[23]C. E. B. Cranfield, *A Critical and Exegetical Commentary on the Epistle to the Romans*, 2 vols., The International Critical Commentary, vol. 32, 6th ed. (Edinburgh: T. & T. Clark, 1975, 1979), 1:350, states, "Paul no doubt has the narrative of Genesis 3 in mind. In fact, these verses are best understood as exposition of the Genesis narrative."

[24]Gerd Theissen, *Psychological Aspects of Pauline Theology*, tr. G. Galvin (Philadelphia: Fortress Press, 1987), 251; Kümmel, *Römer 7*, 87, argues that it is not implied (*"angedeuten"*) in any sort of way; see also Moo, 132, n. 25.

[25]This is pointed about by Moo, 125, who believes that "this restriction effectively rules out the (purely) Adamic view." Kümmel, *Römer 7*, 87, similarly concludes that it makes this interpretation "impossible" (*"unmöglich"*).

3. In response to the previous objection, it is argued that there are references in Jewish sources which describe the Torah as existing even before creation.[26] The command of Genesis 2:17 is also viewed as an expression of the Torah's commandments,[27] one of which was broken in Adam's sin.[28] The wrong desire or lust of Romans 7:7 is then

---

[26]See, for example, *Midrash Rabbah: Genesis*, tr. H. Freedman and M. Simon (London: Soncino Press, 1939), 8:2, p. 56, which refers to the Torah as that "which preceded the creation of the world by two thousand years"; also *Neophyti 1: Genesis*, tr. and ed. Alejandro Diez Macho, English tr. M. McNamara and M. Maher (Consejo Superior De Investigaciones Cientificas, 1968), on Gen. 2:15, p. 501, which states that the Lord caused Adam "to dwell in the garden of Eden so that he do service according to the Law and keep its commandments." See also Dunn, *Romans 1-8*, 379; Theissen, 203-4.

[27]According to Jewish tradition, Adam received a portion of the Law with the commandment which he was given (Gen. 2:17). For example, *Midrash Rabbah: Genesis*, 24:5, p. 202, states, "R. Judah said: It was fitting that the Torah should have been given through Adam"; also ibid., 16:5-6; *Midrash Rabbah: Deuteronomy*, 24:5, tr. H. Freedman and M. Simon (London: Soncino Press, 1939), 54, discusses how the one verse of Scripture (2:17) indicates that six commandments were given to Adam; these are also detailed in Tractate Sanhedrin 56b, *The Babylonian Talmud: Seder Nezikin*, tr. I. Epstein (London: Soncino Press, 1935), 382-83, which concludes that Gen. 2:17 refers to the observance of social laws, blasphemy, idolatry, bloodshed, adultery, and robbery. See also Lyonnet, "'Tu Ne Convoiteras Pas' (Rom. vii 7)," in Neotestamentica et Patristica, Novum Testamentum Supplements, vol. 6 (Leiden: E. J. Brill, 1962), 160-65; idem, "L'Historie du salut selon le chapitre vii de l'Epître aux Romains," 140-47; Longenecker, *Paul*, 94-95; Käsemann, 196; George F. Moore, *Judaism in the First Centuries of the Christian Era*, 2 vols. (New York: Schocken Books, 1927,1930), 1:274; Hermann Strack and Paul Billerbeck, *Kommentar zum Neuen Testament: Aus Talmud und Midrash*, 6 vols (Munich: C. H. Beck, 1954), 3:37. Dunn, *Romans 1-8*, 379, cautions that "the oldest form of this teaching may well be as early as Paul."

[28]For example, "The Fourth Book of Ezra" 7:11, in *The Old Testament Pseudepigrapha*, 2 vols., tr. B. Metzger, ed. J. Charlesworth (Garden City, NY: Doubleday & Company, 1983), 2:537, records these words of the Lord concerning Israel: "For I made the world for their sake, and when Adam transgressed my statutes, what had been made was judged." This connection is supported by reference to Genesis 3:5-6 where the desire or lust is to be like God, and the tree is also said to be desirous, see Lyonnet, "'Tu Ne Convoiteras Pas' (Rom. vii 7)," 161; Cranfield, 1:350-51. However, the same word for coveting is not used in the Septuagint of Gen. 3:6 which reads: "When the woman saw that the tree was good for food and pleasing (ἀρεστόν) for the eyes to see and it was desirable (ὡραῖον) to make wise, then she took its fruit and ate. And she also gave to her husband with her and he ate."

interpreted as the root of all sin, even of the sin in Eden.[29]

One may legitimately infer that in some sense "Adam was breaking 'the law' of God."[30] However, the sharp difference between the commandment of Genesis 2:17 and the one Paul cites in Romans 7:7 would have made the proposed connection between the "I" and the experience of Adam difficult to recognize. Attempts at equating the commandment against coveting in Romans 7:7 with the prohibition against eating and touching in Genesis (2:16-17; 3:3) overlook the fact that the respective commands are markedly different.[31] It should also be noted that

> Paul, in contrast to the rabbinic tendency to consider the law eternal, attributes great significance to its secondary and historical character.[32]

4. In the Genesis narrative, the temptation to sin comes from outside of man. Adam was personally innocent and without the knowledge of sin which the serpent was trying to bring into the world (Rom. 5:12). In Romans 7:7-11 sin is depicted in terms "of inner

---

[29] "The Apocalypse of Moses" 19:3, in *The Apocrypha and Pseudepigrapha of the Old Testament*, 2 vols., ed. R. Charles, tr. L. Wells (Oxford: At the Clarendon Press, 1913), 2:146, records Eve's lament that the serpent "went and poured upon the fruit the poison of his wickedness, which is lust, the root and beginning of every sin." Tractate Shabbath 145b-46a, *The Babylonian Talmud: Seder Mo'ed*, tr. I. Epstein (London: Soncino Press, 1938), 738, states, "For when the serpent came upon Eve he injected a lust into her." See also Robert Gundry, "The Moral Frustration of Paul Before His Conversion," in *Pauline Studies*, ed. D. Hagner and M. Harris (Exeter, England: The Paternoster Press, 1980), 241, n. 10. Lyonnet, "'Tu Ne Convoiteras Pas' (Rom. vii 7)," 161, points out that Targum Neofiti at Gen. 3:6 uses חמד whose Hebrew equivalent is used to translate ἐπιθυμέω elsewhere in the Septuagint; see *Neophyti 1*, 13.

[30] Dunn, *Romans 1-8*, 400; see Rom. 5:14.

[31] Kümmel, *Römer 7*, 86-87. Moo, 131, points out that no one has furnished evidence that "Jews ever interpreted the Paradise commandment as a prohibition of 'coveting'." In addition, ἐπιθυμέω and its cognates are not present in the Septuagint of Gen. 1-3. The commands in Genesis are οὐ φάγεσθε (2:17) and μὴ ἅψησθε (3:3) compared with οὐκ ἐπιθυμήσεις in Rom. 7:7.

[32] Theissen, 203, n. 3; in support of this assertion, see, for example, Rom. 5:20; Gal. 3:17.

processes."[33] Sin is working every desire ἐν ἐμοί through the commandment (v. 8).

5. The one proposed textual link between Genesis 1-3 and Romans 7 is the verb "to deceive" (ἠπάτησεν in Gen. 3:13; ἐξηπάτησεν in Rom. 7:11). In Genesis 3:13 it refers to the deception of Eve by the serpent. Thus when Paul makes an indisputable reference to that event in 1 Timothy 2:13-14, his point is that Eve was deceived and *not* Adam.[34] If Adam is the "I" in Romans 7:7-11, this would, at the very least, represent Paul drawing diverse conclusions from the same text.

6. This interpretation contends that Romans 7:7-11 is an account of Adam's fall into sin which can then be applied to all mankind as Paul himself does in Romans 5. Even aside from the identification of more than one referent, there are problems involved in the jump from identifying the "I" as Adam to making the referent inclusive of all people. It overlooks Paul's point in Romans 5 which is that "Adam was a unique man with only one historical counterpart and that is Jesus Christ."[35] Paul also indicates that Adam's sin was in a way unlike the sin of others (5:12,14). How can it be then that he is describing all people by using the "I" for Adam in 7:7-11?

7. The consistent application of this interpretation in verses 14-25 is problematic. As a result, when the "I" is identified as Adam in verses 7-11, this referent is usually abandoned in the verses which follow.[36]

In view of these difficulties and the fact that there is only one plausible textual reference to the fall narrative (see above, point 5), it seems advisable not to "press the connection with Genesis too hard."[37]

---

[33]Theissen, 203. He, 206-9, attempts to explain this and concludes, 206, that Paul may be "interiorizing the Fall."

[34]"And Adam was not deceived (οὐκ ἠπατήθη), but the woman, having been deceived (ἐξαπατηθεῖσα), fell into transgression" (1 Tim. 2:14).

[35]Douglas Milne, "Romans 7:7-12, Paul's Pre-Conversion Experience," *The Reformed Theological Review* 43 (1984):11. He claims "the doctrine that everyman is the Adam of his own soul was Jewish not Pauline," citing 2 Baruch 54:19. However, this must not be allowed to weaken Rom. 5:12.

[36]As noted by Kümmel, *Römer 7*, 87.

[37]Leon Morris, *The Epistle to the Romans* (Grand Rapids: Eerdmans Publishing, 1988), 283; so F. F. Bruce, *The Letter of Paul to the Romans*, rev. ed., The Tyndale New Testament Commentaries, vol. 6 (Grand Rapids: Eerdmans Publishing, 1963), 142; Lenski, 467.

A Rhetorical Expression of Man in General under the Law

Kümmel proposes that Paul "uses the first person for a portrayal of general human experiences."[38] Paul, as elsewhere, intends the "I" to be understood as a rhetorical device which does not describe the actual experiences of the speaker or author.[39] Kümmel's rhetorical interpretation stems from his conclusion that the text of Romans 7:7-11 will not allow the "I" to be identified as any of the other suggested referents.[40] Since it is impossible for the referent to be Paul, Adam, or Israel, the "I" must be a figure of speech used by Paul to make his presentation of a general truth more lively. Since what the "I" states is not actually true of anyone in particular, Theissen terms Kümmel's referent "a fictive 'I'."[41]

The exegetical bases for Kümmel's conclusion have been presented in Chapters One and Two. They may be summarized as follows:

1. "Without Law or commandment, the subject would have remained without personal sin and passion."[42]
2. Sin is unable to assert its power without the Law, "that is, it cannot bring people under the dominion of death."[43] It is νεκρά (v. 8).
3. It was only "with the coming of the commandment [that] sin acquired its power."[44]

---

[38]Kümmel, *Römer 7*, 89; see above, Chapter One. In Käsemann's words, 195, the "I" describes "mankind under the law, or specifically the pious Jew" in verses 7-13.

[39]As F. Blass and A. Debrunner, *A Greek Grammar of the New Testament*, tr. and rev. R. Funk (Chicago: The University Press, 1961), 147[281] state, the "I" is used "in order to illustrate something universal in a vivid manner by reference to a single individual." Longenecker, *Paul*, 90, similarly contends, "The indefinite 'one' (*tis*) could as easily have been used in all these cases; though with considerable loss to the power and graphic character of the passage."

[40]Kümmel, *Römer 7*, 84,87; see above, Chapter One.

[41]Theissen, 191. Longenecker, *Paul*, 89, also refers to it as a "clearly gnomic and general" use of the first person singular.

[42]Kümmel, *Römer 7*, 75, *"ohne Gesetz bzw. Gebot das Subjekt ohne persönliche Sünde und Begierde belieben wäre."*

[43]Ibid., 76, *"d.h. den Menschen unter die Todesgewalt bringen kann."*

[44]Ibid., *"mit dem Kommen des Gebotes die Sünde ihre Kraft erlangte."*

4. Most significantly, the ἔζων of 7:9 must be taken in a pregnant sense denoting full spiritual life. The text speaks only of the *"true life"* and then the death of the *"I."*[45]

5. "The 'experiences' of an I, therefore, were used by Paul in order to present, on behalf of the Law, the relationship between sin and the Law."[46] Such an objective apology for the Law would not have been possible if Paul had been merely describing the experiences of his own life.

These factors, along with the continued expressions made by the *"I"* in verses 14-25, lead Kümmel to conclude that Paul is not describing his own actual possession or consciousness of life and death.[47] Rather, Paul employs the first person singular in order to speak from a Christian vantage point of unredeemed man in his objective relation to God.

Kümmel supports his interpretation by contending that Paul uses the first person singular in a number of other passages without intending himself, or anyone else in particular, as the referent. He also cites examples from Greek and Jewish literature, which are admittedly sparse, in order to demonstrate the presence of a rhetorical *"I"* in the milieu surrounding Paul.[48]

Rudolf Bultmann follows upon and expands Kümmel's approach in concluding that Paul here transcends the realm of individual consciousness and directs us toward the actual existential condition of man, that is, his trans-subjective reality.[49] Bultmann's interpretation is

---

[45]Ibid, 80, *"von seinem wahren Leben und Tod redet."* See also 78-79 where he quotes with approval Hans Lietzmann, *An die Römer*, 3rd. ed., Handbuch zum Neuen Testament, no. 8 (Tübingen, 1928), 27, "Paul cannot . . . say of himself he had 'lived' in the actual sense of the word before his conversion (ποτέ)" [*"Paulus kann nicht . . . von sich aussagen, er habe vor seiner Bekehrung (ποτέ) 'gelebt' im eigentlichen Sinne des Wortes"*].

[46]Kümmel, *Römer 7*, 76, *"Die 'Erlebnisse' eines Ich werden also von Paulus benützt, um das Verhältnis von Sünde und Gesetz zugunsten des Gesetzes darzustellen."*

[47]Ibid., 124; Käsemann, 196.

[48]Kümmel, *Römer 7*, 126; Theissen, 192, responds, "Ancient rhetoric had little interest in the use of 'I' as a stylistic device."

[49]Rudolf Bultmann, "Romans 7 and Paul's Anthropology," in *The Old and New Man in the Letters of Paul*, tr. K. Crim (Richmond, VA: John Knox Press, 1967), 45.

dependent upon identifying the ἐπιθυμία in verses 7-13 as "the desire for realizing one's true nature [which] is contained in the desire to assert oneself, although disguised and distorted."[50] This enables Bultmann to conclude that Paul's purpose is to illustrate this fact: "It is precisely man's desire to achieve this true nature which causes him to lose it. This is the deception sin practices on us (v. 11)."[51]

Evaluation

1. Once again, it should be pointed out that nothing in the text indicates that the interpretation of the "I" is to be taken in anything other than its literal sense.[52] As a result, if Paul intended this more general or rhetorical meaning, one must wonder "how much of such deeper ramifications would have been apparent to the bulk of Paul's Roman addressees."[53]

2. Kümmel's analysis requires and then presents a situation in which the "I," representing mankind in general, actually and already was in possession of life in its fullest sense before the Law came. Kümmel even concludes, "Without the Law sin has no working power; therefore the person, when he has no Law, is in a living relationship to God."[54] Paul will in no way allow that assessment of the spiritual state of any person without the Mosaic Law to stand (1:18-32; 2:12-16). Neither will he permit any such characterization of the era before the Law was revealed (Rom. 5:12-21). Paul contends that sin and death entered the world and spread to all through Adam (5:12). As a result, all people, with or without the Mosaic Law, have sinned (3:9,23). His proof of this is that all people, both before and after the Law was revealed, are placed under the reign of death (5:14; 6:23).

3. From a theological perspective, if Paul's argument is what Kümmel suggests, it makes little sense. In Kümmel's schema, man

---

[50]Ibid.

[51]Ibid.

[52]Kümmel himself makes this objection against the previous two interpretations, *Römer 7*, 85,87, yet he does not seriously consider this point against his own interpretation.

[53]Dunn, *Romans 1-8*, 372.

[54]Kümmel, *Römer 7*, 132, *"Ohne Gesetz hat die Sünde keine Wirkungskraft; darum ist der Mensch, wenn er kein Gesetz hat, in lebendiger Beziehung zu Gott."*

possessed "true life" without the Law. However, the giving of the Law changed that. If Paul's overall purpose here is to defend the Law as not being in any way "opposed to God,"[55] one must ask Kümmel why God would have introduced the Law at all. Why would God disturb the true life which the "I," representing man in general, possessed? Why would God alter a situation in which sin was unable to accomplish the death of the "I"? In view of the horrendous and fatal effects which the Law's commandment has upon the "I" in 7:7-11, would God have revealed the Law merely so "that sin, through the commandment, would be proven as truly opposed to God?"[56]

In Paul's mind this was hardly God's intention. The Law was not given by God to give sin its power or to effect the death of people who already possessed the true life which God intended them to have. Rather, it was sent to evoke a complete recognition of the sin which was already present in man (3:20; 7:7) and then to increase the working of sin (5:20; 7:8) to the point where the death it accomplishes might be unavoidably driven home to the sinner (4:15; 6:23; 7:7-10).

4. Are verses 7-11 an *objective* description of man under the Law from a Christian viewpoint? The "I" in 7:7-11 exhibits a deep, personal awareness of his own sin. The "I" recognizes the Law's involvement in his sin and the consequences of it. However, when one examines the general descriptions of unbelievers elsewhere in Romans, just the opposite is the case. From Paul's objective, Christian viewpoint, he depicts Gentiles outside of Christ as being consumed by idolatry and immorality (1:18-32).

From that same vantage point, unbelieving Jews under the Law are portrayed as standing in judgment on the wickedness of others, while remaining seemingly oblivious to their own sin (2:1-3:8). They are exhibiting an attitude of complacency and self-righteousness in regard to the Law (2:17-29; 9:30-10:10).

These passages provide us with Paul's objective characterization of unrepentant man under the Law, but his descriptions in them do not agree at all with the picture of the "I" in Romans 7:7-11. The fact that they sharply contradict each other makes it difficult to believe that

---

[55]Ibid., 76, *"so ist das Gesetz . . . nicht widergöttlich."*

[56]As Kümmel, ibid., states, *"daß die Sünde durch das Gesetz als wahrhaft widergöttlich erwiesen werde."*

Paul is using the "I" to make an objective appraisal of man in general under the Law.[57] In addition, the argument that the description in 7:7-11 is possible only from a Christian perspective, ends up concluding that "the knowledge of sin that is said to come through the Law in actual fact then comes through the Gospel."[58]

5. A final objection questions the validity of the rhetorical inter-pretation as a whole and especially Kümmel's contention that the "I" contains no personal reference whatsoever to Paul himself. From a grammatical perspective one must ask whether Paul regularly or ever uses the first person singular in a manner which excludes himself as the primary referent. This question prompts a detailed examination of Paul's use of the first person singular in his letters.

Along with Romans 7 verses 7a, 9, 14-24, and 25b, Kümmel cites the following examples of Paul's use of a rhetorical "I": Romans 3:5,7; 1 Corinthians 6:12,15; 10:29-30; 11:31-32; 13:1-3,11-12; 14:11,14-15; Galatians 2:18.[59] He contends that the first person singular in these passages parallels the use of the "I" in Romans 7. Are these passages, in fact, analogous to and supportive of his interpretation?

Totally aside from the issue of referent, a number of factors seriously weaken the similarity of Kümmel's suggested parallels. Theissen conducts an investigation of the eleven passages cited by Kümmel in regard to their sentence structure, tense, and use of an "explicit ego."[60] Four of the parallels occur in interrogative sentences (Rom. 3:7; 1 Cor. 6:15; 1 Cor. 10:29b,30). Four more have a con-ditional sentence structure (1 Cor. 11:31-32; 14:11,14-15; Gal. 2:18). Thus only three of the suggested parallels occur in declarative

---

[57]As held by Rudolf Bultmann, *Theology of the New Testament*, 2 vols., tr. K. Grobel (New York: Charles Scribner's Sons, 1951), 1:247; Hans Conzelmann, *An Outline of the Theology of the New Testament*, The New Testament Library, tr. J. Bowden (London: SCM Press, 1969), 163; and Käsemann, 192.

[58]Milne, 13.

[59]Kümmel, *Römer 7*, 121, lists these and, 121-23, proceeds to discuss them very briefly. All are appropriate to his case except for 1 Cor. 11:31-32 where the forms are all in the plural.

[60]Theissen, 191-200; however, he alters Kümmel's citation of Rom. 3:5 to 3:8. Verse 8 is cited by Kümmel as an example of the cohortative use of the first person plural in a rhetorical manner.

sentences as are present in Romans 7:7-25.[61] These are 1 Corinthians 6:12; 13:1-3,11-12. According to the criterion of tense, only one out of all of the passages cited by Kümmel, 1 Corinthians 13:11-12, utilizes the past tense as Paul does in reference to the *"I"* in Romans 7:9.[62] But since there is no *"explicit ego"* in 1 Corinthians 13:11-12, Theissen concludes that Galatians 2:19, a passage not even referred to by Kümmel, is *"the sole formally convincing parallel to Rom. 7:9."*[63]

Specifically in regard to the question of referent, an examination of Paul's use of the first person singular pronoun, ἐγώ, is especially relevant. Paul not only uses the first person singular throughout Romans 7:7-25, he also underscores it by utilizing the repetitive ἐγώ twice in verses 7-11 (vv. 9,10) and five or six additional times in verses 14-25 (vv. 14,17,20 [probably twice], 24,25). Kümmel contends that Paul uses the emphatic first person singular pronoun in these verses without specific reference to himself. Theissen counters, "The *ego* is unquestionably personal," not only in Romans 7, but "almost everywhere."[64] Is Theissen's conclusion correct or does Paul use ἐγώ, in Romans 7 and elsewhere, as Kümmel claims?

Paul's use of ἐγώ throughout Romans provides an interesting study. Outside of Chapter 7, ἐγώ occurs 12 times. Four of these are in Old Testament quotations where the referent of the ἐγώ is the one who is speaking. Three times this is the Lord (10:19; 12:19; 14:11) and once it is Elijah (11:3). In 16:22 Tertius, Paul's amanuensis, uses ἐγώ in reference to himself as he sends his personal greetings to the Roman Christians. In each of these instances, the referent of the ἐγώ, though *"fictive"* with reference to Paul himself, is clearly identified as the one speaking or writing.

---

[61]Conditional sentences are found in reference to the *"I"* of Romans 7 only in verses 7b, 16, and 20.

[62]Theissen, 195, concludes that this is *"of decisive significance."*

[63]Ibid., 199; he then cites, 199-200, 18 passages in Paul's writings where the first person plural occurs in declarative statements in the past tense with an emphatic pronoun where Paul is unquestionably included among the referents (1 Cor. 2:3; 3:1,6; 4:15b; 5:3; 9:15; 11:23; 15:10; 2 Cor. 2:10 [twice]; 12:13,16; Gal. 1:12; 6:14; Phil. 4:11; 1 Thess.2:18; 3:5; Philemon 13).

[64]Ibid., 200; he finally adds, "Without the contradiction to Philippians 3, . . . and the nonbiographical statement in Rom. 7:9, probably no one would ever have come up with the idea of considering the 'I' fictive." See the discussion of Phil. 3:4-6 below.

Romans 11:19 displays a rhetorical use of an ἐγώ which is clearly not applicable to Paul. "Therefore you will say, 'The cultivated branches were broken off in order that *I* (ἐγώ) might be grafted in'" (11:19). The manner in which Paul introduces this statement indicates the rhetorical nature of this ἐγώ and the context in Romans 11 clearly points out who the intended referent is (vv. 13,17-18). He utilizes it in order to put forth the hypothetical assertion of an individual Gentile.

While Kümmel does not make mention of 11:19, he does cite Romans 3:7 as an example of a rhetorically fictive "I." Even though Paul does not make it as evident as in 11:19, this should be accepted as such. The fact that Paul is engaged in a dialogue is the factor which explains his use of a rhetorical ἐγώ.[65] Paul is responding to hypothetical (3:7), as well as actual (3:8), objections to his teaching. In verse 7 he himself poses a potential challenge: "But if the truth of God increased by my lies (ἐν τῷ ἐμῷ ψεύσματι), why am *I* (κἀγώ) still being judged as a sinner?" (3:7). This objection charges that if man's sinfulness is merely "a foil to set off the righteousness of God,"[66] God would be unjust in punishing people for their sins. Paul counters that God will rightly judge the world (3:5-6) and that his κρίμα is just (3:8).

Romans 3:7 vindicates Kümmel's view that Paul can use a rhetorical "I" in a hypothetical or fictive manner. The referent of this "I" is not Paul or any specific person. But Paul does not use the ἐγώ without any referent whatsoever. Even though the referent is, at least at this point, imaginary, Paul has a referent in mind. His statement anticipates a potential objector who might draw this false conclusion from Paul's argument. As in 11:19, he is not using the ἐγώ simply to speak of "no one or everyone."[67]

Is the ἐγώ of 3:7 parallel with the manner in which Paul uses the

---

[65]For a study of this, see Stanley Stowers, *The Diatribe and Paul's Letter to the Romans*, Society of Biblical Literature Dissertation Series, no. 57 (Chico, CA: Scholars Press, 1981). While offering a number of valuable insights, he does not deal with 3:1-8 or Romans 7 at any length.

[66]William Sanday and Arthur Headlam, *A Critical and Exegetical Commentary on the Epistle to the Romans*, The International Critical Commentary, vol. 32 (New York: Charles Scribner's Sons, 1902), 69.

[67]Kümmel, *Römer 7*, 132, *"niemand oder jederman"*; compare also Longenecker, 90, who asserts τις *"could as easily have been used."*

"I" in Romans 7? A number of factors speak against this conclusion. First, the conditional sentence structure of 3:7 indicates the hypothetical nature of the objection being raised and the rhetorical intent of the ἐγώ. This is contrasted by the numerous declarative statements made by the "I" throughout 7:7-25 (all except vv. 7b,16,20). In regard to Paul's rhetorical use of ἐγώ both in 3:7 and 11:19, Moo concludes,

> The inherently 'unreal' nature of these constructions is so different from the narrative and confessional style of Romans 7 that it is hardly fair to compare them.[68]

In addition, the sustained argument of Romans 7 contrasts with the single occurrence of ἐγώ in 3:7. Finally, Kümmel properly recognizes that Paul, as in Chapter 3, is engaged in a dialogue style of argument in Romans 7. However, the partner he draws into the dialogue in Chapter 7 is not at all the "I." It is the questioning "we" in verse 7 and the affirming "we" in verse 14 (see also the question in v. 13).

Aside from the above instances, the other five times an ἐγώ is present in Romans, Paul utilizes it in order to make an emphatic, personal reference to himself.

> For I wish that *I* myself (αὐτὸς ἐγὼ) were cursed [away] from Christ in behalf of my brothers, my kinsmen according to [the] flesh (9:3).

> I say, then, has God rejected his people? May it never be! For indeed *I* am (ἐγὼ. . . . εἰμί) an Israelite, of the seed of Abraham, of the tribe of Benjamin (11:1).

> But I am speaking to you Gentiles; therefore inasmuch as I am (εἰμι ἐγὼ) an apostle to the Gentiles, I glorify my ministry (11:13).

> And I have been persuaded, my brothers, even *I* myself (αὐτὸς ἐγὼ) concerning you, that you are full of goodness (15:14).

> Greet Prisca and Aquila, my fellow-workers in Christ Jesus, who risked their own necks in behalf of my life, for whom not only I (ἐγὼ μόνος) give thanks but also all the churches of the Gentiles (16:3-4).

The presence of αὐτός together with ἐγώ in 9:3 and 15:14 recalls 7:25. It is difficult to comprehend how words which served Paul as an

---

[68]Moo, 129.

emphatic and personal reference to himself in 9:3 and 15:14 could, without some explicit indication, be otherwise in 7:25.[69]

Paul uses ἐγώ 84 times in his other letters.[70] In 77 of these instances, Paul is speaking of himself. In the other seven occurrences, the referent of the ἐγώ is certainly not Paul. But these do not support the general or purely rhetorical use advocated by Kümmel. In each case, the referent is unmistakably identified.

In 2 Corinthians 6:17, the ἐγώ occurs in an Old Testament citation where the referent is the Lord who is speaking. The six other occurrences are in 1 Corinthians where Paul uses ἐγώ in order to present the statements which members of the Corinthian factions are, at least in effect, making. Paul explicitly introduces these as the actual or implied statements of others. In 1:12 he writes, "But I say this, that each one of you is saying, '*I* am of Paul,' and 'I of Apollos,' and 'I of Cephas,' and 'I of Christ.'" Each one of these uses the emphatic ἐγώ. In 3:4 Paul repeats the first two of these assertions, again using ἐγώ and again explicitly introducing them as the statements of others.[71] The "I" is not Paul, but he clearly indicates who the referent is.

The only passages cited by Kümmel in support of his interpretation of Romans 7 where Paul uses ἐγώ are 1 Corinthians 6:12 and 10:29-30. In 6:12 he writes, "All things are lawful for me, but all things are not beneficial; all things are lawful for me but *I* (ἐγὼ) will not be put under authority by anything." Since nothing in the content or context of this verse indicates otherwise, Paul cannot be excluded as the referent of the "I" in this verse. On the contrary, both factors support identifying the "I" as the Apostle. It is the same Paul, for whom all

---

[69]It is interesting to notice that outside of Romans, Paul uses αὐτός in the nominative case for emphasis to refer to himself five additional times (1 Cor. 9:20,27; 2 Cor. 10:1; 12:13; Phil. 2:24). In two of these instances, ἐγώ is also present for double emphasis (2 Cor. 10:1; 12:13).

Paul uses αὐτός in the nominative 29 times altogether. Frequently it denotes God, as is exclusively the case in the Thessalonian correspondence (1 Thess. 3:11; 4:16; 5:23; 2 Thess. 2:16; 3:16).

[70]See *Concordance to the Novum Testamentum Graece*, 3rd ed., ed. by the Institute for New Testament Textual Research and the Computer Center of Münster University with the collaboration of H. Bachmann and W. Slaby (New York: Walter De Gruyter, 1987), 12*.

[71]"For when someone says, '*I* am of Paul,' and another, 'I of Apollos,' are you not [mere] men?" (1 Cor. 3:4).

things are lawful including the consumption of meat offered to idols (6:12; 9:1,19; 10:23), who later asks, "If *I* (ἐγώ) partake with thanks, why am I being blasphemed concerning that for which *I* (ἐγώ) give thanks?" (10:30). The manner in which Paul intends both occurrences of ἐγώ to function may be broader than as statements of his own apostolic convictions. But they are at least that. Paul, the founder of the Corinthian congregation (1 Cor. 4:15; 9:1-2), intends himself to be identified as the referent of the "I" in these verses.

In conclusion, when Paul uses the emphatic first person singular pronoun, ἐγώ, he always has a specific referent in mind. In addition, unless he indicates otherwise in the context, and usually unmistakably so, the referent is himself.[72] It would seem that in Romans 7 (vv. 9,10,14,17,20,24,25) a particular referent of the ἐγώ is also intended, and since there are no indications to the contrary, the "I" would appear to be Paul himself.

When the first person singular pronoun is present outside of the nominative case in Paul's letters, the outcome is even more consistent. This is illustrated by the following:

1. ἐμοῦ is present seven times in Romans and 15 additional times in Paul's other letters. Except for the Old Testament quotation in Romans 11:27 where ἐμοῦ denotes the Lord who is speaking, these are all used by Paul in reference to himself.

2. μου occurs 37 times in Romans. Four of these are in 7:7-25. Throughout Romans, μου occurs in the Old Testament quotations seven times, referring to God six times and Elijah once. Elsewhere the referent is Paul. Outside of Romans, μου is used by Paul 97 times. Three of these refer to God in Old Testament quotations. In the remainder, the μου is used by Paul to speak of himself.

3. ἐμοί is present nine times in Romans. Apart from the two Old Testament citations in which the ἐμοί is God, all seven others are in 7:7-25! ἐμοί is present 37 other times in the Pauline corpus where the referent is always Paul.

---

[72]The lone possible exception is Romans 3:7. So C. H. Dodd, *The Epistle of Paul to the Romans*, The Moffatt New Testament Commentary (London: Fontana Books, 1959), 107, concludes, "It will in fact be found on examination that Paul rarely, if ever, says 'I' unless he is really speaking of himself personally, even if he means to generalize from the particular instance"; see also Theissen, 199.

4. μοι occurs nine times in Romans, three of these in 7:7-25. μοι is present 49 times in Paul's other letters. Of these, only once is the referent other than Paul. In 2 Corinthians 6:18 God is the referent within an Old Testament quotation.

5. ἐμέ is used in three of its four occurrences in Romans as a referent to God in Old Testament quotations. Elsewhere in the Pauline corpus, all 14 occurrences denote Paul himself.

6. με is present six times in Romans, half of them in 7:7-25. Of the three other times, only once is the referent other than Paul. This is in 9:20 where με occurs in an Old Testament quotation in which the clay of a potter is personified. In the 38 other times με is used in the Pauline corpus, Paul is always the referent.

Paul also uses the first person singular as the subject of numerous verbs without an emphatic ἐγώ. It is not possible to detail all of these. Yet particular attention should be given to those instances which Kümmel identifies as rhetorical, thereby contending that Paul himself is not the referent. Of the passages Kümmel cites, 1 Corinthians 13 provides the occurrences which are most directly parallel to Romans 7. Paul writes,

> If I speak with the tongues of men and of angels, but I do not have love, I have become a brass sounding [gong] or a clashing cymbal. And if I have [the gift of] prophecy and know all mysteries and all knowledge and if I have all faith so as to move mountains, but I do not have love, I am nothing. And if I divide all my possessions and if I hand over my body in order that I might boast, but I do not have love, I gain nothing (vv. 1-2).
>
> When I was a child, I spoke as a child, I thought like a child, I reasoned as a child; when I became a man, I put aside the things of a child. For now we see through a mirror in an indistinct image, but then face to face. Now I know in part, but then I will know fully just as I am also fully known (vv. 11-12).

The suggestion that the referent of the "I" here is not Paul arises out of the universal nature and scope of these verses.[73] But those considerations introduce the pragmatic issue of the intended purpose or

---

[73]Kümmel, *Römer 7*, 122-23; compare Jan Lambrecht, *The Wretched "I" and Its Liberation*, Louvain Theological and Pastoral Monographs, 14 (Grand Rapids: Eerdmans, 1992), 80-81.

function of the *"I"* in 1 Corinthians 13. What Paul intends for the *"I"* to *"count as"* is a valid question to pursue. However, *one cannot thereby legitimately bypass the issue of referent.* Can Paul be the referent here? There is nothing in the text of these verses or in their context which would exclude Paul from being the referent of the *"I"* or which would indicate otherwise. On the contrary, the universal character of this section supports identifying Paul himself as the referent.

The situation is similar in the other passages cited by Kümmel where an *"I"* is the subject of the verb. Paul poses a question to himself in 1 Corinthians 6:15 and then soundly rejects the suggestion.[74] In 1 Corinthians 14 Paul discusses speaking in tongues. Paul uses himself as the referent in a number of conditional statements (vv. 11,14) and then declares his own resolution to this phenomenon in the context of public worship: "I will pray with the Spirit and I will also pray with the mind; I will sing with the Spirit and I will also sing with the mind" (1 Cor. 14:15). Again, Paul may intend his discussion to function as much more, but he couches his statements in the first person singular. The *"I"* is clearly Paul, the one who can thank God that "I speak in tongues more than you all" (1 Cor. 14:18).

Each one of these uses of the first person singular as the subject of various verbs indicates that in the vast majority of cases, Paul is to be identified as the *"I."* His use is consistent with the manner in which he employs the other first person singular forms. Unless Paul indicates otherwise in the context,[75] he intends himself as the referent.

Although not directly related to the use of the first person singular in Romans 7, Paul is able to speak of himself in two other ways in his letters. First, he often makes use of the first person plural. Kümmel cites a number of passages which illustrate a cohortative or questioning use of the first person plural in none of which, he contends, would Paul's "own person in any way come into consideration" (Rom. 3:8b; 6:1,15; 13:12,13; 14:13; 1 Cor. 10:8,9,22; 2 Cor. 7:1; Gal. 5:25-26; 1

---

[74] "Therefore after taking the members of Christ will I make them members of a prostitute? May it never be!" (1 Cor. 6:15b).

[75] An interesting example where Paul does indicate another referent is 1 Cor. 12:15-16 where he uses εἰμί four times, but explicitly introduces the speaker as an imaginary foot or ear. Compare the "eye" in verse 21; also 1 Cor. 1:14; 3:4.

Thess. 5:6,8-10).[76] Kümmel argues that these passages should also be taken in a rhetorically "fictive" sense. This is made most clear by Romans 13:12-13 where "the demand for conversion is without doubt not to be related to Paul."[77] However, those verses are by no means a call to conversion. They are directed toward Christians who are urged to abstain from evil works. Does not Paul need the same encouragement? Finally, Leander Keck points out that Paul discloses various things about himself in a variety of ways which do not utilize the first person form at all.[78] While both of these methods of personal revelation provide fertile soil for further study, due to the prominence of first person singular forms in Romans 7:7-25, they need not be examined extensively here.

This survey of Paul's use of first person singular forms brings the validity of Kümmel's rhetorically fictive interpretation of the "I" in Romans 7 into serious doubt. In the vast majority of the passages where Paul uses the first person singular, he himself is the referent. As a rule, if Paul does not intend himself as the referent of the "I," he explicitly indicates this to his readers and makes evident who the referent is. This is the case in his Old Testament citations and in some of the other passages discussed above (Rom. 3:7; 11:19; 1 Cor. 1:12; 3:4). No such signal is present in the text of Romans 7. Nothing suggests that the referent is anything or anyone other than Paul.

In every other passage, including those cited by Kümmel as representing Paul's use of a rhetorical ἐγώ, Paul intends himself as the referent of the "I." Whether in statements or in questions hypothetically proposed, the text always allows and even indicates that the "I" is to be understood as Paul. In some passages Paul may use the first person singular and intend a broader or more general final application, but this certainly does not exclude Paul himself as the referent of the "I." In none of these passages is it impossible for the

---

[76]Kümmel, *Römer 7*, 121, *"seine eigene Person ernstlich mit in Betracht käme."*

[77]Ibid., *"ist zweifellos die Bekehrungsmahnung nicht auf Paulus mitbezogen."*

[78]Leander Keck, "Images of Paul in the New Testament," *Interpretation* 43 (1989):343-44, terms this *"Paul disclosed"* and contrasts it with Paul's statements of *"deliberate self-projection."*

"I" to be Paul speaking of himself. When Kümmel argues that the "I" in Romans 7:7-11 cannot be Paul, his interpretation is left without parallel.

Kümmel's interpretation of Romans 7, in effect, "argues both that the 'I' does not denote Paul's personal experience but that it does denote the experience of everyman–everyman, except Paul!"[79] Paul has spoken of what is true of "man in general" previously in Romans (for example, 1:18-32; 3:19-20,23; 5:12-19) and, at times, understood himself as being included in these portrayals.[80] Through the first person plural in 7:5 (ἡμῶν), Paul includes himself in his description of a former existence "in the flesh." As Paul proceeds in verses 7-11, it is unwarranted to lessen his involvement to the point where his consistent use of the first person singular is now viewed merely as a tool utilized for dramatic effect. To do so is to "depersonalize the language and destroy the foremost quality of the passage stylistically considered."[81] Finally, when the sustained nature of the argument and the repeated and extensive use of various first person singular forms in Romans 7:7-25 are considered, there is no section in Paul in any way comparable to the manner in which Kümmel identifies the "I" of Romans 7.

Paul's usage, therefore, seriously damages even the conceivability of Kümmel's interpretation. It seems clear that in verses 7-11 "Paul does not speak of an arbitrary 'I,' but of an experience bound to his person."[82] Is that one person, then, Paul himself?

---

[79]James Dunn, "Rom. 7,14-25 in the Theology of Paul," *Theologische Zeitschrift* 31 (1975):260; he characterizes this as a "rather convoluted process of reasoning."

[80]He would certainly have included himself in 3:19-20,23 and 5:12-19. He also could see his own past in his description of Judaism in 2:1-29.

[81]Milne, 12; if such an approach is adopted, Milne argues, "The problem is then to explain how a general 'I' is capable of making such deeply personal and subjective expressions about sin and the law. One suspects that theoretical constructions are being imposed on the passage from outside instead of allowing the literal style of the writing itself to determine the lines of the exegesis."

[82]Otto Michel, *Der Brief an die Römer*, Kritischer-exegetischer Kommentar über das Neue Testament, 13th ed. (Göttingen: Vandenhoeck and Ruprecht, 1966), 170, "*P[au]l[u]s spricht nicht von einem beliebigen 'Ich', sondern von einer an seine Person gebundenen Erfahrung.*"

Paul's Personal Experience

This is *"the natural way"* to understand the first person singular in 7:7-11,[83] and *"most commentators admit that prima facie the words of Romans 7 read like autobiography."*[84] The *"existential character"* of these verses is also pointed to as being indicative of this.[85] However, a number of serious objections have been leveled against this interpretation.

Evaluation

1. The major problematic issue in identifying Paul as the referent of the *"I"* is determining an adequate period in Paul's life into which the experiences described in verses 7-11 may be placed. If the consistent use of the aorist tense in this section points to a *"definite moment"* in the past,[86] of what event does Paul speak? Can these verses be understood as describing a particular time in Paul's life?

"A favourite answer . . . has been to say that Paul here is recording his first discovery of sinfulness when as an adolescent lad he lost the innocence of childhood."[87] Paul had been living *"without the Law"*

---

[83]J. I. Packer, "The 'Wretched Man' of Romans 7," in *Studia Evangelica*, vol. 2, ed. F. Cross (Berlin: Akademie-Verlag, 1964), 622.

[84]Milne, 12; see also Kümmel, *Römer 7*, 90,124; C. K. Barrett, *A Commentary on the Epistle to the Romans*, Black's New Testament Commentaries (London: Adam and Charles Black, 1962), 143; Dodd, 123.

[85]Dunn, *Romans 1-8*, 382 and 401, contends that the portrayal is *"too sharp"* to be a presentation of a general experience. So also Dodd, 125-26; Karl Kertelge, "Exegetische Überlegungen zum Verständnis der paulinischen Anthropologie nach Römer 7," *Zeitschrift für die neutestamentliche Wissenschaft* 62 (1971):107-8; Dunn, "Rom. 7,14-25 in the Theology of Paul," 260-61; Milne, 12; John Robinson, *Wrestling with Romans* (Philadelphia: The Westminster Press, 1979), 82; J. Christiaan Beker, *Paul the Apostle* (Philadelphia: Fortress Press, 1980), 240-43; Theissen, 190-208; Alan Segal, "Romans 7 and Jewish Dietary Law," *Studies in Religion* 15 (1986):362.

[86]Käsemann, 195; so also Bornkamm, "Sin, Law and Death," 97; Gundry, 236.

[87]Milne, 13. For example, Bruce, *The Letter of Paul to the Romans*, 139-40; Adolf Deissmann, *St. Paul*, tr. L. Strachan (New York: Hodder & Stoughton, 1922), 93-94; Oskar Holtzmann, *Das Neue Testament nach dem Stuttgart griechischen Text übersetzt und eklärt* (Geißen, 1926), refers to the *"Unschuldsparadies seiner Kindheit"*; the latter is cited from Kümmel, *Römer 7*, 77. Philo, *Quis Rerum Divinarum Heres*, 294,

(7:9a) during his happy childhood, but then the Law's commandment came (v. 9b).[88] Verses 9-10 have then been interpreted as depicting the adolescent Paul's first conscious awareness of the Law and/or the day when he became a *"son of the commandment"* at his *bar mitzvah*. In either case, Paul *"became aware of the precepts and prohibitions of the Law. . . . and imperious desires for forbidden things forced themselves into his mind"* (7:7-8).[89] According to Robert Gundry, the ἐπιθυμία Paul has in mind are predominantly sexual (as in 1:24).[90]

This avenue of interpretation falters in attempting to explain how Paul was ever literally alive *"apart from the Law"* or before *"the coming of the commandment"* (7:9).[91] Even if something resembling the *bar mitzvah* was practiced already in Paul's day,[92] that event would not have confronted him with the demands of the Law for the first time.[93] It is quite evident that *for Paul* circumcision is what places one

---

does state, "The infant from the day of its birth for the first seven years, that is through the age of childhood, possesses only the simplest elements of soul, a soul which closely resembles smooth wax and has not yet received any impression of good or evil"; cited from *Philo*, tr. F. Colson and G. Whitaker, 10 vols., The Loeb Classical Library (New York: G. P. Putnam's Sons, 1932), 4:435.

[88]Aboth, 5.21, quotes Rabbi Judah ben Tema who states, "At five years old [one is fit] for the Scriptures, at ten years for the Mishnah, at thirteen for [the fulfilling of] the commandments, at fifteen for the Talmud, . . . "; cited from *The Mishnah*, ed. H. Danby (Oxford: Oxford University Press, 1972), 458.

[89]Dodd, 128.

[90]Gundry, 232-33; see also 1 Thess. 4:5; W. D. Davies, *Paul and Rabbinic Judaism*, 4th ed. (Philadelphia: Fortress Press, 1980), 21-22.

[91]Kümmel, *Römer 7*, 79; however, his objection springs from his insistence on the pregnant sense of *"to live."* He states, "The term ἔζων is very difficult to understand as a description of the childhood of Paul" (*"der Terminus ἔζων als Beschreibung der Kindheit des Paulus sehr schwer verständlich ist"*). The greater difficulty stems from discerning how Paul was ever *"apart from the Law."*

[92]This is unlikely, at least as the rite is presently understood. According to Kümmel, *Römer 7*, 82, "But the institution of the *bar-mitzvah* is itself a creation of the Middle Ages" (*"Die bar-mizwah-Institution selber aber ist eine Schöpfung des Mittelalters"*). He points out that the term occurs only once in the entire Talmud (Baba mezia 961) and there it refers to the adult slave of a Jew; see *The Babylonian Talmud: Seder Nezikin*, tr. and ed. I. Epstein (London: Soncino Press, 1935), 556.

[93]For example, Paul describes Timothy as one who knew the Scripture "from infancy" (ἀπὸ βρέφους 2 Tim. 3:15). This is further supported by two references from Philo's *De Legatione ad Gaium*. In 115 he states, "For he [Gaius] looked with disfavour on the Jews alone because they alone opposed him on principle, trained as

directly under obligation to the Law (Gal. 5:3; Phil. 3:5).[94] As a result, any *literal application* of Romans 7:9 to a period in Paul's life after circumcision when he was *"alive"* apart from the Law or without obligation to it is most improbable. It is also extremely tenuous to assert that Paul believed in the sinlessness of children or held that God would look upon their sin with any less severity (see, for example, Romans 3:19-20,23; 5:12; Galatians 3:22).[95] Moreover, restricting the ἐπιθυμία to sexual lust goes against Paul's own citation of the last commandment of the Decalogue in 7:7 which enables him to make the widest application possible (πᾶσαν ἐπιθυμίαν in v. 8).[96]

All of this speculation points to the fact that any association of these verses with Paul's childhood or adolescence must be based upon purely hypothetical grounds. Paul nowhere refers "to his youth as a time of special significance for his religious development"[97] in the same manner as depicted in Romans 7:7-11. Neither does Paul even

---

they were we may say even from the cradle, . . . of the sacred laws and unwritten customs." In 210 Philo describes the Jewish nation as "holding that the laws are oracles vouchsafed by God and having been trained in this doctrine from their earliest years, they carry the likenesses of the commandments enshrined in their souls." Cited from *Philo*, tr. F. Colson, 10 vols., The Loeb Classical Library (Cambridge, MA: Harvard University Press, 1962), 10:56-57,108-9. Theissen, 251, n. 52, refers to an inscription from a Jewish gravestone in Rome which describes a child (νήπιος) as a "lover of the law" (φιλόνομος see also 203, n. 4, where he cites G. Horsley, *euremata*, n. 60). See also Josephus, *Against Apion*, in *The Works of Josephus*, tr. William Whitson, rev. ed. (Peabody, MA: Hendrickson Publishers, 1987), 2.178, p. 805; Cranfield, 1:343; Strack and Billerbeck, 2:144-47; Leenhardt, 187. Kümmel, *Römer 7*, 83, agrees, "So the child is never apart from the Law" (*"So ist . . . das Kind niemals* χωρὶς νόμου).

[94]Dunn, *Romans 1-8*, 401.

[95]Kümmel, *Römer 7*, 81; he cites Alfred Juncker, *Die Ethik des Apostels Paulus*, 50, as contending that God would look upon their sin *"with very much milder eyes"* (*"mit sehr viel milderen Augen"*). The contention of Milne, 14, that "the idea of childhood innocence has more in common with Western romanticism than with actual reality" is certainly more in line with Paul's perspective.

[96]If Paul's intention was to speak of sexual sin, one would have to ask why he did not simply quote the Sixth Commandment with an application similar to that made by Jesus (Matt. 5:27-28)?

[97]Milne, 14. As a result, the theory that Rom. 7:7-11 reflects an adolescent transgression has no textual foundation. Kummel's opinion, *Römer 7*, 78, that this must be determined by the *"fantasy of the scholar"* (*"Phantasie der Forscher"*) has some warrant!

allude to a period when sin ran rampant over him as implied by this line of interpretation. On the contrary, when Paul speaks of his birth and upbringing, he refers to them in an unimpeachable manner (Acts 26:4-5). Paul stresses that he was born an Israelite, descended from Abraham, and of the tribe of Benjamin (Rom. 11:1; 2 Cor. 11:22; Phil. 3:5). He was circumcised on the eighth day according to the Law (Phil 3:5). Though born in Tarsus, he later arrived in Jerusalem where he was trained as a Pharisee by Gamaliel himself (Acts 22:3). He then excelled in living in accordance with "the Law of our fathers" (Acts 22:3; Gal. 1:13-14). Finally, the text of Romans 7 itself gives no indication that verses 7-11 offer a description which should be restricted or applied exclusively to Paul's young life.[98]

Is it possible that verses 7-11 refer to Paul's adult life as a Pharisee? At first glance, this seems even less possible. Many scholars reject any application of Romans 7:7-11 to Paul's life as a Pharisee by concluding that such an interpretation stands in sharp contradiction to passages such as Galatians 1:13-14 and Philippians 3:4-6.[99] A brief survey of what Paul tells us about his life in this period will be helpful before responding to this objection.

When Paul speaks of his adult life before his conversion, he emphasizes that "according to the strictest sect of our religion, I lived [as] a Pharisee" (Acts 26:5; also 23:6). He even points out, "I was advancing in Judaism beyond many contemporaries among my people, being extremely zealous (ζηλωτής) for the traditions of my fathers" (Gal. 1:14). As a result of his "zeal," Paul recalls, "*I* myself thought that it was necessary to do many things in opposition to the name of Jesus of Nazareth" (Acts 26:9). He violently and intensely persecuted Jesus' followers, beating and imprisoning them (Acts 22:4,19; 1 Cor. 15:9; Gal. 1:13; 1 Tim. 1:13). Since Paul was intent on destroying this sect (Gal. 1:13), he states, "I persecuted this Way unto death" (Acts 22:4).

---

[98]According to Lenski, 465, the "time of false security extended far beyond Paul's childhood."

[99]It is also said to contradict the general pharisaic view of the Law. See, for example, Kümmel, *Römer 7*, 109-17; Robinson, *Wrestling with Romans*, 83; Krister Stendahl, "The Apostle Paul and the Introspective Conscience of the West," *Harvard Theological Review* 56 (1963):200-1; and the others cited in Chapter One. For responses, see Theissen, 234-35,237; Cranfield, 1:344.

What do Paul's letters reveal to us about what he believed to be his status before God at this time? He characterizes all of the above as comprising a basis upon which he could have confidence before God. He writes,

> If some other person thinks [he has reason] to be confident in the flesh, I [have] more: circumcised on the eighth day, of the nation of Israel, of the tribe of Benjamin, a Hebrew of Hebrews; according to the Law, a Pharisee; according to zeal (ζῆλος), persecuting the church; according to righteousness which [is] in the Law, being blameless. (Phil. 3:4b-6)[100]

At that time Paul based his confident stance before God on his zeal for God's Law (compare 10:2).[101] He characterizes himself as being ζηλωτής ("extremely zealous") both for God (Acts 22:3b) and for "the traditions of my fathers" (Gal. 1:14; Acts 22:3a). As the ultimate mark of his zeal, Paul points to his persecution of the church (Phil. 3:6; Acts 22:3).

The description in Romans 7:7-11 does stand in sharp contrast with the appraisal Paul made of his own life in relation to God and the Law when he was a Pharisee. At that time Paul quite obviously did not view the Law as either "a heavy and uncomfortable burden" or an entity that was actually provoking sin and involved in deceiving him.[102]

---

[100]The translation of *The Holy Bible: The New International Version* (New York: International Bible Society, 1978), is somewhat interpretive of the phrase "κατὰ δικαιοσύνην τὴν ἐν νόμῳ" in verse 6. Yet its translation, "legalistic righteousness," is supported by the contrast Paul later draws between the righteousness of faith and "my own righteousness which is from the Law" in verse 9. Other statements by Paul clearly indicate that a righteousness derived from the Law was really no righteousness before God at all because of sin (Rom. 3:20; Gal. 2:16). Gal. 2:21 decisively concludes, "For if righteousness [was] through the law, then Christ died for no purpose."

[101]This fits well with the description he makes of unbelieving Israel in Rom. 10:2: "For I bear witness to them that they have a zeal (ζῆλον) for God, but not according to full knowledge" (ἐπίγνωσιν).

[102]Anders Nygren, *Commentary on Romans*, tr. C. Rasmussen (Philadelphia: Muhlenberg Press, 1949), 282. Leenhardt, 187 states, "Among the rabbis the law is presented as an efficacious help in the struggle against the 'tendency to evil' which exists prior to the knowledge of the law and prevails until the law enables one to combat it."

Is this objection then insurmountable? Are the statements in Romans 7:7-11 and in these other passages irreconcilable? The answer is *"No."* The solution to this problem, however, must be drawn from a recognition of two factors. First, in Romans 7 Paul is writing from a Christian perspective and, second, he is applying the description in 7:5 to his own pre-Christian life. Romans 7:5 provides the basic outline for verses 7-11. There Paul portrays his life when its inevitable outcome was the *"bearing of fruit to death"* (7:5 with vv. 10-11).[103] This is because his life lived *"in the flesh"* was one in which *"the passions of sins which were through the Law* were operating in [his] members*"* (7:5 with vv. 7-8).

A recognition of the interrelationship between the Law and sin as described by Paul in Romans 7:7-11 draws a sharp dividing line in Paul's own life.[104] These verses reveal an insight into the Law and its effects which Paul only perceived after his encounter with the Risen Christ on the road to Damascus.[105] It was only after reflecting upon the impact of Jesus' appearance to him that Paul realized that the Law could be used as a tool of sin and that his earlier estimation of the Law's function and purpose in his own life had, in fact, been sin's deception (7:11).[106]

This is supported by what Paul tells us about his life as a Pharisee when he writes from a Christian perspective. In Galatians 1 he implies that what he had in fact been accomplishing while he *"was advancing in Judaism beyond many contemporaries among my people"* (1:14) was not attaining a righteous standing before God. Rather, he was trying *"to please men"* (1:10). As he looks back upon his previous zeal

---

[103]Recognized by Kümmel, *Römer 7*, 45-46; John Murray, *The Epistle to the Romans*, 2 vols. (Grand Rapids: Eerdmans Publishing, 1965), 1:255.

[104]As a result, Kümmel's full title, *Römer 7 und die Bekehrung des Paulus* (*"Romans 7 and the Conversion of Paul"*) makes an important connection. However, he chose this title because, according to his interpretation of Romans 7, that chapter can no longer be utilized as a text for interpreting the events or effects of Paul's conversion.

[105]As Espy states, 175, *"Full consciousness of sin came only on the Damascus road."*

[106]Nygren, *Commentary on Romans*, 282, refers this to the time *"when, on the Damascus road, [Paul] came to see that the law was a false way of salvation."* Milne, 14, contends, *"The very vividness and poignancy of the language used would suggest a moment of religious crisis in the apostle's life"*; see also Murray, 1:255.

for God and the Law, exhibited most emphatically in his persecution of "the Way" sect, Paul now realizes that he had in reality been "a blasphemer (βλάσφημον; the most heinous of sins)[107] and a persecutor and a violent person" (1 Tim. 1:13). Certainly Paul's description of himself as the foremost (πρῶτος) of sinners is based upon those actions (1 Tim. 1:15-16). At that time, he later admits, "I acted ignorantly in unbelief" (ἀπιστία; 1 Tim. 1:13).

Even in his zeal for God and the Law, Paul acted "ignorantly in unbelief." How was this possible? Romans 7:7-11 provides the vital clue. Paul's description here is perhaps unique. However, these other passages offer support for identifying the "I" there with Paul's own experience prior to his conversion.[108] Romans 7:7-11 provides a glimpse into how Paul re-evaluates his earlier zeal for the Law, the zeal which had provided the basis for his confident standing before God (Phil. 3:4). In these verses, which expound Romans 7:5, *Paul is looking back from his Christian perspective and describing what was in reality happening prior to his conversion.* He declares that the good and holy Law brought forth sinful desires and even led to his "death" (vv. 5,8,10). Paul confesses that at that time he was deceived by sin precisely through the Law's commandment (7:11,8). Paul, the Pharisee, thought his zealous actions in behalf of the Law made him righteous and blameless before God (Gal. 1:14; Phil. 3:5-6). He was, in fact, a blasphemer (1 Tim. 1:13). His zeal for God was without the true knowledge of God and apart from the righteousness God gives by faith (see Rom. 9:31-32; 10:2-3). He was in a state of unbelief (1 Tim 1:13).

When did this deception end? The answer to this question is found in the series of events usually grouped together under the label of "Paul's Conversion." How does Paul describe these experiences? Paul speaks in the first person singular of the historical events which comprised the dramatic turning point in his life twice in Acts and briefly in 1 Corinthians (Acts 22:6-16; 26:12-18; 1 Cor. 15:8; see also Acts 9:3-19). It is noteworthy that when Paul narrates his own account of these events, he utilizes an "I"-style argument similar to what we

---

[107]See, for example, Lev. 24:10-23; 2 Chron. 32:16; Is. 65:7. Paul recalls that he was also guilty of trying to make the followers of Jesus blaspheme as well. "And as I punished them often in all the synagogues, I tried to force them to blaspheme" (Acts 26:11).

[108]So Käsemann, 192, contends.

have in Romans 7. A detailed examination of these parallel accounts is not possible here,[109] but two relevant points should be stressed.[110]

First, when the Risen Lord Jesus appears to him on the road to Damascus, Paul recounts that Jesus immediately revealed the deception sin had worked in him through the Law. In his supposed zeal for God and the Law, Paul had not been persecuting merely Jesus' followers; he had been persecuting the Lord himself! "I fell to the ground and heard a voice saying to me, 'Saul! Saul! Why are you persecuting me?'" (Acts 22:7; compare 9:4; 26:14.)

Second, Paul does not narrowly limit his "conversion" to the events which took place on the Damascus road. In fact, the events which followed three days later in Damascus are more descriptive of how Paul speaks of conversion. Paul recounts that "a certain Ananias, a man [who was] devout according to the Law, as witnessed by all the Jews living there" (Acts 22:12), reluctantly came to him at Jesus' command (Acts. 9:10-17). Ananias told Paul that his purpose in coming was that "you might see again and be filled with the Holy Spirit" (Acts 9:17). Paul remembers how Ananias then asked, "And now what are you waiting for? Get up, be baptized and wash away your sins, calling on his name" (Acts 22:16).

Paul offers his theological reflection upon these events in a number of passages. Paul speaks of them as the time when God, who "set me apart" from birth, "called me by His grace" (Gal. 1:15; compare Is. 49:1). In addition, Paul makes numerous references to the Damascus road as the place of his calling or appointment as an apostle of Jesus Christ (Rom. 1:1; 1 Cor. 9:1; Gal. 1:16; 1 Tim. 1:12; 2 Tim. 1:11).

Another aspect of Paul's theological reflection upon the events which occurred on the road to Damascus is presented Romans 7:7-11. If one wanted to suggest a time when Paul first arrived at his

---

[109]For a detailed examination, see especially Seyoon Kim, *The Origin of Paul's Gospel*, Wissenschaftliche Untersuchungen zum Neuen Testament 2, Reihe 4 (Tübingen: J. C. B. Mohr, 1981); Gerhard Lohfink, *The Conversion of St. Paul*, tr. and ed. B. Malina, Herald Scriptural Library (Chicago: Franciscan Herald Press, 1976); and Heikki Räisänen, "Paul's Conversion and the Development of His View of the Law," *New Testament Studies* 33 (1987):404-19.

[110]In addition, it is important to note that Paul's recollection of Jesus' appearance on the road and the events which followed in Damascus detail not only his conversion, but also include the appointment of Paul as "a minister and a witness" (Acts 26:16; see also 9:15; 26:17-18).

reappraisal of the Law and its effects expressed in Romans 7:7-11, the three days of blindness after Christ's awesome appearance to Paul could be pointed to most specifically (Acts 9:8-19a).[111] Perhaps it was in those intervening days that Paul "suddenly saw how completely mistaken he had been about the Law."[112] However, as his letters reflect, this event was permanently etched in Paul's memory. He continued to wrestle with its impact upon him during the years immediately following (Gal. 1:17-18) and for the rest of his life.[113]

The contrast between passages such as Philippians 3:4-6 and Romans 7:7-11 is then answered from the point of perspective.[114] These two diverse sets of passages portray the drastic difference between Paul's two appraisals of his own life under the lordship of the Law (Rom. 7:1). In Philippians 3:4b-6 Paul reveals his previous understanding of the Law and what he thought his place before God on the basis of the Law had been. In this sense, those verses have a "restricted application."[115]

---

[111]Lenski, 466. Moo, 126, counters that the accounts of Paul's conversion do not "suggest such a struggle." However, a re-evaluation of the Law certainly had to have occurred! What is recorded about the appearance of Jesus to Paul on the Damascus road reflects that this was mostly a "Law event" for Paul. James Fraser, *The Scripture Doctrine of Sanctification* (Edinburgh: R. Ogle, 1830), 192, concludes "that any special comfort to him was referred to the time when Ananias in Damascus was sent to him." It is only with the coming of Ananias three days later that Paul hears the message of sins forgiven, receives that forgiveness and the Holy Spirit through Baptism, and experiences the return of his physical sight (Acts 9:10-19a; 22:12-16).

[112]David Lloyd-Jones, *Romans: An Exposition of Chapters 7.1-8.4* (Grand Rapids: Zondervan Publishing House, 1973), 174; he continues, "He saw its spiritual character, he understood the meaning of coveting . . . that period is sufficient to account for all we have been looking at."

[113]For examples of Paul's concentration upon the events of the Damascus road, see 1 Cor. 9:1; 15:8-10; Gal. 1:13-17; 1 Tim. 1:12-16; also Acts 22:6-21; 26:11-18.

[114]One might note the contrast between passages such as Rom. 2:17-23 and 7:7-11, as well. The other attempts to explain this contrast are less convincing.

[115]Milne, 15. He points out that verses 7-11 do not provide a complete guide to the outward events of Paul's conversion, neither are they able to fully describe the "inner" or spiritual aspects of his conversion. Paul's description here is sufficient for his purpose which will be discussed in Chapter Five of this work. Milne, 15, recognizes that "for the same reason Paul omits from his summary of his change of life from Judaism to Christianity any mention of Ananias who yet played a key role in the actual course of events between the Damascus Road and the reception of Paul into. . . the Church (Acts 9:10ff)."

But

> what Paul conceals in Philippians 3—namely, how he sees his pre-Christian period in the light of the 'knowledge of Jesus Christ' (Phil. 3:8) —is precisely what he develops in Romans 7.[116]

Philippians 3, on the other hand, proceeds to detail the manner in which Paul, as a Christian, now views those things on which he formerly relied. While he once put confidence in his own flesh, in his zeal for God, and in his observance of the Law, Paul now writes, "But whatever things were profit for me, on account of Christ I regard these things as loss" (Phil. 3:7). Of those things he had previously valued so highly because of what he believed they warranted for him *coram Deo*, he now declares,

> I regard them as dung in order that I might gain Christ and be found in him, not having my own righteousness which is from the Law, but that which is through faith in Christ, the righteousness which is from God on the basis of faith. (Phil. 3:8b-9)

What period in Paul's life is described in Romans 7:7-11? As indicated by the predominance of verbs in the past tense, Paul writes from a Christian perspective about "his own experience of the Law and sin . . . prior to his conversion to faith in Jesus Christ."[117] There is no need to attempt a precise determination of a single occasion when this interaction between the Law and sin occurred or to restrict the events here depicted in that manner.[118] Paul's choice of the aorist tense "concentrates attention upon the act itself" denoted by each verb.[119]

---

[116]Theissen, 242.

[117]Milne, 14; who inserts "as an adult." There is no particular need even for that limitation except perhaps in regard to the deception of 7:11. Milne, 17, n. 2, cites the following for support: "the younger Augustin, Calvin, Fraser, Deissman, Glover, Kennedy, Garvie, Hodge, Shedd, Brown, Stewart, Lenski, Sabatier, Hausrath, Holtzmann, Wernle, Stevens, Hendricksen, Murray, Fairbairn, Nygren."

[118]As Lenski observes, 466, "Such time fixing is unwarranted."

[119]James Voelz, "The Language of the New Testament," in *Aufstieg und Niedergang der römischen Welt*, Principat, vol. 25[2], eds. H. Temporini and W. Haase (New York: Walter De Gruyter, 1984), 967; the aorist is "non-connective or neutral." In contrast, the present tense is "essentially connective: a speaker or writer using it

Verses 7-11 then offer us "an authentic transcript of Paul's own experience during the period which culminated in his vision on the road to Damascus."[120]

When one recognizes that these verses reflect "an issue which, in the most proper sense, is the problem of [Paul's] own life,"[121] it becomes perfectly understandable for him to make his presentation in the first person singular. Indeed, one would almost expect it. These verses are a deeply personal and reflective account which strikes at the very heart of Paul's existence prior to his conversion. As Paul looks back and tries to describe his previous relationship with God's Law, he now perceives what sin had led him to believe about it. Now he recognizes what had actually been happening and how he had been deceived through God's own commandment (v. 11). What Paul means in 7:9-10 may be paraphrased as follows:

> I was alive, that is, I possessed physical life and thought I possessed spiritual life. However, I was actually living a "fleshly" existence under the lordship of the Law, the end of which was death (7:1,5). I was being deceived by sin into a mistaken apprehension of the purpose and function of the Law's commandment. When my full understanding of sin and the Law came, when I realized the actual effect of God's Law upon me as a sinful man, "I died" (ἐγὼ ἀπέθανον; 10a).[122]

Paul's statement about himself "living formerly without the Law" (v. 9a) should not be taken as representing his possession of the true life God intended; neither does it necessarily express that he was living without any connection to the Law whatsoever.[123] Certainly Paul's awareness of the Law's coming to him increased at various times throughout his life. This occurred as he was instructed in the Law as a circumcised child, if and when he experienced some type of *bar mitzvah* ceremony, and while he was trained as a Pharisee. However, it was the encounter on the Damascus road which led Paul to realize that

---

connects the verbal action to the person doing the acting."

[120]Dodd, 126; however, he states this in regard to the entirety of Romans 7:7-25.

[121]Nygren, *Commentary on Romans*, 279.

[122]In this manner these verses coincide with Paul's earlier statements, for example 3:19-20; 4:15; 5:12; 6:23; compare also Gal. 2:20-21 and 3:22-24.

[123]See the discussion of these verses in Chapter Two.

even during his pharisaic life he was deceived by sin into living a life *without the full knowledge and awareness of what the Law actually says* (3:20; 4:15; 5:20; see especially 10:2).

In a similar manner, the death brought on by the coming of the commandment (9b-10a) is not the end of true spiritual life but a *recognition* that the only fruit which is produced by a life lived under the lordship of the Law is death (vv. 1,5). It is the death which recognizes that, because of sin, the Law's commandment has only been able to produce even more sin (vv. 7-8). It is the death which results from a recognition of sin's diabolical and deceptive misuse of the Law in continuing to hold out the Law as a means of life for a sinner (vv. 10-11). It is the death which realizes that there is no way in which man on his own can escape the just condemnation of God's Law. In Paul's specific case it was the death which "killed forever the proud Pharisee thanking God that he was not as other men and sure of his merits before God."[124] The Law has now done its divinely intended work upon Paul (3:19-20). *The notion that "I" am able to utilize the Law's command as a means to life has "died."*

Outside of Romans 7, the passage in which Paul *most clearly parallels the events depicted here is Galatians 2:19*: "For through the Law *I* died to the Law in order that I might live to God."[125] What Paul says of himself there matches the thematic statements of Romans 7:5-6. In addition, the events Paul describes in the first half of the verse (ἐγὼ γὰρ διὰ νόμου νόμῳ ἀπέθανον) fit the "I"'s experience with the Law in verses 7-11 very well both in vocabulary and in content.

2. Another objection to identifying the statements of the "I" in Romans 7:7-11 with Paul's own experience is the charge that this interpretation limits the application which can be drawn from these verses. Kümmel, for example, questions whether Paul's personal

---

[124]Morris, *The Epistle to the Romans*, 282. This is the death of which Paul here speaks. It is not the saving death of 6:2-4; cf. Luke 18:9-14.

[125]Donald Guthrie, *Galatians*, The New Century Bible (London: Oliphants Publishing, 1969), 93, concludes that Paul saw his being crucified with Christ in Gal. 2:20 as dying to the Law in the sense that "he ceased to live in that world in which the law was dominant (i.e., in Judaism). This dying had, in fact, come about by his experience under the law (cf. especially Rom. 7 as a commentary on this statement)." Note that Gal. 2:17-20 also heavily employs the first person singular.

experiences can really serve as an objective defense of God's Law.[126] This is a valid objection to the interpretation adopted here when the question of the referent of the "I" in Romans 7 is the only question addressed. It is a valid objection when the pragmatic function which Paul intends these verses to serve is overlooked. While the issues of purpose and function will be addressed more fully in Chapter Five, a number of points regarding the "I" as depicted in verses 7-11 should be noted.

First, the insights Paul here reveals about the working of the Law are not presented as the long-sought solution to his own unique, inner, psychological struggles. Verses 7-11 are taken this way by J. Christiaan Beker, for example, who asks, "How could the Christophany have been so traumatic and so radical in its consequences unless it lit up and answered a hidden quest in his soul?"[127] This approach disregards the fact that Paul nowhere suggests that such an inner turmoil or "quest" was present in his life when he was a Pharisee. On the contrary, he displayed confidence and even boasting before both God and men (Gal. 1:10,13-14; Phil. 3:4-6).

Second, while the death Paul here describes did lay him out flat and open him up to accept Baptism and forgiveness in the name of Jesus (Acts 9:17-19a), he does not view this "death" as conversion itself[128] or as some sort of transitional stage that is one step closer to

---

[126]So Kümmel, *Römer 7*, 84,90; so also Moo, 126, charges that this interpretation "applies Paul's ostensibly objective, descriptive language to the realm of subjective consciousness."

[127]Beker, *Paul the Apostle*, 237; compare Theissen, 235-36; John Gager, "Some Notes on Paul's Conversion," *New Testament Studies* 27 (1981):697-704.

[128]Romans 7:7-11 can be understood in a *similar*, though not equivalent, manner to the way in which Paul describes the events of conversion. He speaks of conversion in two paradoxical ways, as the death of a former existence lived to sin and as a new life which has arisen out of former "deadness." For example, it is a coming to life from the dead in 4:17(?); 6:4; 11:15; 2 Cor. 3:6; Eph. 2:1-6; 5:14; Col. 2:13. Against this, Moo, 128, charges that Paul "never uses life/death *in that order* in a theological contrast." Yet Paul does portray conversion as a death repeatedly in the previous chapter of Romans, for example, 6:2,3,5,8. This is the death of a life lived to sin. In this very context Paul refers to conversion as the death of a life lived to and under the Law (7:1,4,6). Paul ties both aspects together in 6:11: "Even so consider yourselves dead to sin but alive to God in Christ Jesus." See Milne, 14; Dunn, "Rom. 7,14-25 in the Theology of Paul," 261. However, Paul does *not* here speak of the death which occurs in conversion. Only the Gospel can bring that death. The death he speaks of

God or one rung above a state of ignorance. Neither do these verses depict a psychological progression by which Paul became more acceptable to God than when he, in his former self-righteousness, rejected Jesus as the Messiah and persecuted his followers.[129]

Who, then, is the *"I"* in Romans 7:7-11? Paul himself is the referent. These verses considered in the context of Paul's life and letters have "given the decisive answer to the question, Who am I? I am the one deceived and killed by sin" which worked through the Law's commandment.[130] The *"I"* is Paul, a man who formerly took great pride in his observance of the Law. But the *"I"* is also the Paul who, by the dramatic intervention of Jesus Christ in his life, has come to recognize the damnable effect of the statement *"that the Law exercises lordship over a man as long as he lives"* (7:1; compare 3:19-20). "After his conversion he must have realized clearly that he himself has been that Jew under the law, a Jew without Christ."[131] Why Paul describes his personal experience in Romans 7:7-11 will be discussed more fully in Chapter Five.

The Referent of the "I" in Romans 7:14-25

The manner in which the *"I"* is identified in verses 7-11 has had varying degrees of impact upon how the *"I"* is interpreted in verses 14-25. Those scholars who support identifying the *"I"* in verses 7-11 with Adam or Israel make too light of the connection between the two sections. In fact, this is one of the greatest weaknesses in proposing Adam or Israel as the referent in verses 7-11. Kümmel is more methodologically correct in drawing his conclusions about the *"I"* in verses 14-25 in large part because of the interpretation he advances in

---

here can certainly be worked by God through his Word, but it is not the death which gives life.

[129]So, for example, Milne, 16, "Paul here describes the spiritual transition of the Christian from ignorance to repentance and faith." Lenski, 464, similarly speaks of three stages. Murray entitles his treatment of 7:7-13 "Transitional Experience" and states, 1:255, that these verses represent "the preparatory and transitional phase of his spiritual pilgrimage."

[130]Bornkamm, "Sin, Law and Death," 95.

[131]Lambrecht, *The Wretched "I" and Its Liberation*, 85.

verses 7-11.[132] On that basis, however, he dismisses the entire issue of referent from his interpretation of verses 14-25 as well.

Since nothing in the text of the intervening verses indicates otherwise, it is almost inconceivable that the identity of the "I" in verses 14-25 could be anyone other than who it is in verses 7-11.[133] The "I," in all probability, has the same referent in both sections. The "I" in verses 7-11 has been identified as Paul. Barring any insurmountable difficulties, it should be assumed that the referent of the first person singular forms in the verses which follow is also Paul.

The disputed issue which has always surrounded verses 14-25 is not so much whether the referent of the "I" is Paul or not. Instead, the unresolved question concerns "when." When could what the "I" says be true of Paul? An answer to this question is dependent upon a determination of the spiritual state of the "I" in Romans 7:14-25. Is it possible for the "I" to be Paul before his conversion to Christianity? Is it possible for the "I" to refer to Paul after his conversion? Are both options permissible or is neither allowable? Each of these questions has been answered in the affirmative by some scholars and soundly rejected by others. The dispute remains.

Can this issue be resolved? Since Paul continues to speak in the first person singular in verses 14-25, this question should be considered initially in the light of what Paul says about himself in the first person singular elsewhere. Does the situation of the "I" in Romans 7:14-25 fit among the statements Paul makes about himself either before or after his conversion?

The introduction and consistent use of the present tense in Romans 7:14-25 would seem to imply that these verses describe Paul's state as he writes; that is, they represent Paul as a Christian. The greater burden of proof, therefore, lies with those who advocate another interpretation. The chief argument against the present Christian interpretation is the contention that what the "I" states could not be a description of Paul's Christian life. Is it possible that Paul is using the present tense to throw himself back into the situation he was in before his conversion? Is he

---

[132]Kümmel, *Römer 7*, 117. Of the four reasons he gives for rejecting an identification of the "I" with Paul in verses 14-25, two are directly dependent upon verses 7-11; cited above in Chapter One.

[133]Espy, 173, enunciates the "rather obvious point that the `I' is the same as the `I' of vv. 7-12." See also Kümmel, *Römer 7*, 110.

using the first person singular in a dramatic or vivid manner in order to describe his life as it was then?

Paul before His Conversion

A number of the passages in which Paul refers to the appraisal he made of himself in relation to the Law prior to his conversion have already been discussed. How do these compare with what the *"I"* says in verses 14-25?

First, Paul recounts that prior to the events on the road to Damascus, he took great pride in his fleshly lineage and upbringing; he put confidence before God in his flesh (Acts. 22:3; 26:4-5; Phil. 3:4-5). The picture Paul paints of himself before his conversion is not that of a man who would admit that sin *"is dwelling in me. For I know that nothing good is dwelling in me, this is, in my flesh"* (7:17b-18). He did not view himself in the same manner as the *"I"* who confesses, *"I am fleshly sold under sin"* (7:14), and who yearns for deliverance from *"this body of death"* (7:24).

Second, Paul, like the *"I"* in verses 14-25, viewed the Law of God and its commandments as representing the highest good (Acts 22:3; 26:5; Gal. 1:13-14; Phil. 3:6; Rom. 7:12-13,16,18). As a Pharisee, however, Paul did not view the Law of God as an entity which could actually be used to work sin and death in his members (7:17,20,23). Neither would he have allowed the Law to be spoken of as the *"Law of sin"* (7:23,25). On the contrary, he derived a righteousness from the Law which, to his way of thinking, made him blameless (Phil. 3:6; compare Rom. 9:30-10:5).

Third, both before and after conversion Paul zealously desired to do good and to abstain from evil as instructed by the Law. Prior to his conversion, the method Paul chose to that end was living in accordance with the strict rules of the Pharisees (Acts. 26:5; 23:6) and *"the traditions of my fathers"* (Gal. 1:14; Acts 22:3). Paul thought he was able to accomplish what the Law required, at least to a degree that sufficiently surpassed the achievements of others (Gal. 1:14). Paul's conception of himself as blameless *"according to the righteousness which is in the Law"* was based upon his ability to fulfill the commandments of the Law (Phil. 3:6).[134] In contrast, the "I" in Romans 7:14-25 laments his inability to do the good required by the Law and to refrain from the evil it prohibits (7:18-19,21).

Can the "I" in Romans 7:14-25, then, be identified with Paul's pre-Christian life? As illustrated below, Paul uses many of the same terms employed by the "I" in Romans 7:14-25 when he speaks of his life as a Pharisee. However, these terms are not evaluated in the same way. Before Paul's encounter on the road to Damascus, the *Law* had one determining effect upon him. Paul zealously *agreed* with the Law and *delighted* in living according to its *commandments* (Acts 22:3; 26:5; compare Rom. 7:16,22). He had progressed far beyond his contemporaries in Judaism and thought he was able to *do* the Law adequately (Gal. 1:13-14; Phil. 3:4b-6). The Law enabled Paul to put confidence in his *flesh*. According to the "I," however, the *flesh* is no basis for confidence (7:14) because sin resides "in my flesh" (7:18). Though the "I" *rejoices* in the *Law's command* (7:16,22), he also acknowledges that the same Law places him under captivity to sin and pronounces a sentence of death upon his body (7:23-24).

Is it possible that the "I" represents Paul's *Christian perspective* on his previous life? According to the interpretation of Romans 7:7-11 advanced above, it was at the point of his personal confrontation with Jesus that Paul came to realize that what he thought to be the basis of his righteousness, his own ability to fulfill the Law (Phil. 3:9), was, in fact, a deception (7:11). When Jesus appeared to him on the road to Damascus, the true nature of that deception and the involvement of the Law in it became apparent. Paul thought that the Law served him as an accessible means of life. In reality, in his life apart from faith (1 Tim. 1:13), the Law only served to kill him (7:10-11). At that specific point in time, the "I" saw the Law only as an entity which was used by sin to kill him. Then there was no agreement with the Law, no rejoicing in it (7:16,22).

In neither of these situations does Paul exhibit the view toward God's Law which we find in Romans 7:14-25. There the Law has a *double effect* upon the "I." The "I" heartily agrees with the Law's commandment which directs him toward the good and away from evil

---

[134]Those who contend that verses 14-25 depict a situation in which the "I" only does evil and can never do any good certainly cannot apply these verses to Paul's pre-conversion life!

(7:16,18-19,21). Yet the *"I"* also acknowledges that the Law identifies his own inability to do what the Law's commandment requires because of the sin which dwells in his own flesh (7:14,17-20). Paul's characterization of himself before his conversion, whether from a pre- or post-conversion perspective, is not at all the same as the picture of the *"I"* in Romans 7:14-25. These verses cannot serve as Paul's description of his own pre-Christian life or his view of it after his experience on the Damascus road.[135]

Paul after His Conversion

Is it possible for the *"I"* in Romans 7:14-25 to represent Paul's life after conversion, or does what Paul tells about his Christian life elsewhere exclude that interpretation? A more extensive survey of Paul's use of the first person singular in reference to his own Christian life is the proper starting point for attempting to answer this question.

Paul speaks of his life after conversion in the first person singular in a wide variety of areas. While not all of these can be discussed thoroughly here, we do receive quite a substantial picture of Paul's view of his own Christian existence. This survey approaches these passages with the question, "Does Romans 7:14-25 fit within this picture?"

The effects of Paul's conversion and calling were immediate. Years later he recounts,

> I was not disobedient to the vision, but first to those in Damascus and [then] Jerusalem, [and] throughout all the region of Judea and to the Gentiles, I announced that they should repent and turn to God, doing works worthy of repentance (Acts 26:20; compare 9:20).

Thereafter Paul dedicated his life to "proving that this [Jesus] is the Messiah" (Acts 9:22). He did this first to and among his own people.[136] But after the continued hostility toward and rejection of the

---

[135]Kümmel, *Römer 7*, 111-17, comes to the same conclusion on this point, though he argues more on the basis of general studies of Pharisaism and less from Paul's own words.

[136]See, for example, Acts 13:5,14-50, especially vv. 14 and 43; 14:1; 17:1-3,10-12; 18:1-4; 26:23; 1 Cor. 9:20. Note that his calling as recorded in Acts 9:15 is to bear

Gospel by many Jews, Paul turned more and more to the Gentiles with the message of salvation (Acts 13:46-48; 19:8-9; 28:17-28).

One factor often overlooked is that after his conversion Paul continues to describe himself as an Israelite or Jew (Rom. 9:3; 11:1,14; 2 Cor. 11:22).[137] Though he is no longer "under the Law" (ὑπὸ νόμον; 1 Cor. 9:20), Paul maintains his connection with the Law. He is not ἄνομος (1 Cor. 9:21). In fact, Paul even speaks to the Jewish council years after his conversion in the present tense declaring, "Men, brothers, *I* am a Pharisee, a son of Pharisees" (Acts 23:6). Paul can still challenge those who place their confidence in the flesh by asserting, "If some other person thinks [he has reason] to be confident in the flesh, I [have] more" (Phil. 3:4). Although Paul no longer describes himself as an adherent to "the traditions of my fathers" (Gal. 1:14; compare Acts 22:3),[138] he still goes up to Jerusalem to worship at the temple (Acts 24:11). He continues to profess,

> I serve the God of the fathers, believing in all things which are in accordance with the Law and which have been written in the Prophets (Acts 24:14).

In proclaiming the Gospel of Jesus both to Jews and Gentiles, Paul contends that he stands in direct continuity with the believers and Scriptures of the Old Testament (Acts 26:22-23; 2 Tim. 1:3; 2:8).

In numerous passages Paul emphasizes the distinctness of his Christian life. His authoritative proclamation of the Gospel is based upon his direct calling as an apostle by Jesus Christ (1 Cor. 16:10;

Jesus' name "before [the] Gentiles and kings and [the] sons of Israel."

[137]It is significant that Paul sees himself, as well as the other Jews who have believed in Christ (Rom. 16:7,11; Col. 4:11), to be the demonstration that "even at the present time there is a remnant according to the election of grace" (Rom. 11:5).

[138]This phrase may well refer to the Oral Law of Judaism which was added to supplement and authoritatively interpret the Old Testament. For its source, see Tractate Aboth 1:1 in *The Mishnah*, 446. Danby, xii, contends, "The Mishnah marks the passage to Judaism as definitely as the New Testament marks the passage to Christianity." Paul's earlier adherence to these "traditions of the fathers" (Acts. 22:3; Gal. 1:14) and the later omission of any reference to them may imply his recognition that adherence to the Oral Law was a wrong and tragic turn Judaism had taken. For a brief discussion of this, see Horace Hummel, *The Word Becoming Flesh* (St. Louis: Concordia Publishing House, 1979), 612-17.

Rom. 1:1; 1 Cor. 1:17; Gal. 1:10; Eph. 3:7; 1 Tim. 1:12; 2 Tim. 1:11; Tit. 1:3). Paul even points out the manner in which his ministry is distinct from the other apostles: *"I am an apostle of [the] Gentiles"* (Rom. 11:13; see also 15:16,20; Eph. 3:20; Col. 1:25; 1 Tim. 2:7). Paul describes his apostolic mission as a sacred obligation (Rom. 15:16; 1 Cor. 9:16-18).

Paul relates that his apostolic ministry entailed a great deal of strenuous labor and the endurance of much suffering, including imprisonment, at the hands of both Jews and Gentiles.[139] Yet Paul also views his apostleship as a high privilege and a great honor, writing, "I thank the one who has empowered me, Christ Jesus our Lord, because he considered me faithful, placing me into ministry" (1 Tim. 1:12). In the face of challenges, Paul staunchly defends his apostleship (1 Cor. 9:1; 2 Cor. 11:5,23; 12:22).[140] Paul's apostolic authority gives him boldness and confidence (Rom. 15:15; 2 Cor. 10:1-2).

As a result, Paul asserts that he could *"boast somewhat freely"* about the authority he had from the Lord and about his conduct as an apostle (2 Cor. 10:8; 11:17-31). He boasts that he did not make use of all of his rights as an apostle (1 Cor. 9:15). He discreetly boasts of the visions and revelations he received from the Lord (2 Cor. 12:1-6). Thus Paul concludes, *"Indeed, if I do determine to boast, I will not be foolish, for I will be speaking the truth"* (2 Cor. 12:6).

Yet above all of his reasons for boasting, Paul tells us, *"Very gladly, therefore, I will rather boast in my weaknesses"* (2 Cor. 12:9; see v. 5). He does so because his weaknesses continually point out the necessity of his reliance upon Christ. In regard to boasting he finally concludes, *"May it never be that I boast except in the cross of our Lord Jesus Christ, through which the world has been crucified to me, and I to the world"* (Gal. 6:14).

---

[139]He details these very graphically in 2 Corinthians 11:23-27; see also Acts 26:69; Gal. 5:11; 6:17; Eph. 3:1; Phil. 1:7, 12-13; Col. 1:24,29; 4:3; 1 Tim. 1:8; 2 Tim. 2:9; 3:10-12; Philemon 9,13.

[140]Paul's apostleship was often challenged, or at least questioned, as was especially true at Corinth (1 Cor. 4; 2 Cor. 10-12; see also Gal. 1-2). Some of these challenges may have arisen against Paul because he, unlike the other apostles, was not a μάρτυς of Jesus' earthly ministry (Acts 13:31). Paul's references to his calling by Jesus personally served to defend his apostleship and, more importantly, to authenticate the Gospel of which he says, "I was appointed a herald and an apostle and a teacher" (2 Tim. 1:11).

Because of his faith in Christ crucified, Paul maintains that he is free, free from trying to please men (Gal. 1:10) and free from the ceremonial regulations of the Old Testament (Gal. 5:11; Rom. 14:14). He even adds, "All things are permissible for me" (1 Cor. 6:12; see also 9:1). Yet Paul's freedom is for a purpose.

> For although I am free from all people, I enslave myself to all in order that I might gain the more. . . . And I do all things for the sake of the Gospel, in order that I might be a fellow-sharer of it (1 Cor. 9:19,23; compare vv. 20-22; cf., Rom. 6:18,19,22; 7:6).

In apparent contrast with the "I" of Romans 7:14-25, Paul expresses that he is blameless in a number of passages. First, he is without fault in regard to the performance of his apostolic duties and his relationship with the congregations he has founded and served (2 Tim. 1:3).[141] In this context, the basis for his blamelessness is revealed by the following statement:

> *You* know how, from the first days after which I entered Asia, I was with you all the time, serving the Lord as a slave with all humility and tears and trials which happened to me through the plots of the Jews, as I did not shrink away from declaring to you any of the things profitable [for you] and from teaching you publicly and from house to house, testifying to Jews and Greeks of the repentance toward God and faith in our Lord Jesus. . . . Therefore, I testify to you on this very day that I am pure from [innocent of] the blood of all (Acts 20:19-21,26; see vv. 34-35).[142]

Second, Paul also proclaims his innocence in regard to religious, civil, and political laws. In his defense before Festus Paul contends, "I have committed no offense either against the Law of the Jews or against the temple or against Caesar" (Acts 25:8; see also v. 10; 28:17).

---

[141]For Paul's descriptions of his personal relationship with various congregations, see, for example, Rom. 1:9; 1 Cor. 4:15; 14:15,18-19; 15:31; 2 Cor. 10:8; 11:2,28; Phil. 1:7-8,24; 4:10-12; Col. 2:5; 4:3; 1 Thess. 2:18; 2 Tim. 2:10; Philemon 7,19-20. He also speaks in the first person plural of the blameless conduct of his missionary team (1 Thess. 2:10; 2 Cor. 1:12).

[142]Paul's conclusion here is based upon the prophetic characterization of the Watchman (Ezek. 2:16-27; 33:7-9).

As a result of his unimpeachable conduct, Paul can call upon his fellow Christians to imitate him.[143] As the spiritual father of the Corinthian believers, Paul writes, "I urge you, therefore, be imitators of me" (1 Cor. 4:15-16; see also Phil. 3:17). Paul points out the underlying reason for this in exhorting, "Be imitators of me, just as I am of Christ" (1 Cor. 11:1).[144]

All of these statements by Paul concerning his blamelessness or innocence are in the context of what he has faithfully handed on from God or what God has accomplished in and through him both as a result of his call to faith in Jesus Christ and his call to be an apostle. In these areas of *public conduct*, Paul declares himself innocent. But does he make similar claims in regard to his standing before God? In words to the Corinthians Paul describes his own innocence with this important qualification:

> But it matters very little to me that I am examined by you or by a human court; indeed, I do not even examine myself. For I am aware of nothing against myself, but I have not in this been justified/acquitted (δεδικαίωμαι), the one who examines me is the Lord (1 Cor. 4:3-4).[145]

While Paul boasts of his innocence before people and in his relationship with the congregations he founded, he indicates that his innocence before God does not lie within himself, nor is it based upon his own conduct or awareness. Just as his acceptance of Jesus as the

---

[143]Paul does place some limitations on this, however. In regard to his unmarried status, he advises, "I wish that all men were even as I am. But each one has his own gift from God" (1 Cor. 7:7).

[144]D. M. Stanley, "'Become Imitators of Me': The Pauline Conception of Apostolic Tradition," *Biblica* 40 (1959):859-77, proposes that the imitation of Christ is the underlying force behind all of Paul's calls for Christian to imitate him.

[145]Kümmel, *Römer 7*, 103, cites this passages in support of his contention that Paul "himself was cognizant of no individual sin, at least he has said nothing concerning it. But then to construe Rom. 7:14ff. as a present confession of Paul is excluded" (*"sich keiner einzelnen Sünde bewußt war, zum mindesten nichts davon gesagt hat. Dann aber ist es ausgeschlossen, Röm. 7, 14ff. als Gegenwartsbekenntnis des Paulus aufzufassen"*). While 1 Cor. 4:3-4 would seem to vindicate the first portion of Kümmel's statement, his conclusion is based upon the further assertion, ibid., 101, "that [Paul] was totally free from fleshly conduct" (*"daß er ganz frei geworden sei vom fleischlichen Wandel"*). The discussion which follows disputes the validity of that contention, as well as Kümmel's conclusion concerning Romans 7:14-25.

Messiah was not based upon his own efforts, but came in spite of his unbelief, blasphemy and violent conduct (1 Tim. 1:13,16), so also his continued stance within that relationship is based on faith in Jesus. Why is this so?

Even after his conversion and his calling to be an apostle, Paul reveals that he must continually struggle with and against his own flesh. He does this in a number of different ways. To begin with, Paul often mentions his own personal weaknesses and the frailties of his flesh. He brings these up especially in the context of his boasting. Paul confesses to the Corinthians, *"I came to you in weakness and in fear and in much trembling"* (1 Cor. 2:3; see also Gal. 4:14). He later discloses the source of more weakness:

> Who is weak and I am not weak? Who is made to stumble and *I* do not burn? If I must boast, I will boast of the things pertaining to my weakness (2 Cor. 11:29-30).

In 2 Corinthians 12 Paul reports that because of the great revelations he received, *"A thorn in the flesh was given to me, a messenger of Satan in order to beat me so that I would not exalt myself"* (2 Cor. 12:7). The precise nature of this *"thorn"* or *"stake"* (σκόλοψ) in Paul's flesh is a matter of great debate.[146] The key point for the present discussion is that it resided in Paul's flesh and did so on a continuing basis during his Christian life. The fact that Paul calls it *"a messenger of Satan"* (ἄγγελος σατανᾶ) is sufficient for an appraisal of his own view of its source and effect. In one of his most revealing passages, Paul proceeds to depict how his own weaknesses served to strengthen his dependence upon the Gospel. When Paul asked God three times to remove this thorn in the flesh,

> He said to me, "My grace is sufficient for you, for [my] power is made perfect in weakness." Therefore I will boast all the more gladly in my weaknesses, in order that the power of Christ may dwell upon me.

---

[146]See, for example, Neil Smith, "Thorn that Stayed: An Exposition of 2 Corinthians 12:7-9," *Interpretation* 13 (1959):409-16; Terence Mullins, "Paul's Thorn in the Flesh," *Journal of Biblical Literature* 76 (1957):299-303; William Alexander, "St. Paul's Infirmity," *Expository Times* 15 (1903-4):469-73, 545-48; William Ramsay, *St. Paul: The Traveler and the Roman Citizen* (Grand Rapids: Baker Book House, 1960), 94-97.

Therefore I am pleased in weaknesses, in insults, in hardships, in persecutions and distresses on behalf of Christ. For when I am weak, then I am strong (2 Cor. 12:9-10).

In his letters Paul also reveals some of his personal anguish. Because of the rejection of the Gospel by so many Jews, Paul laments, "I have great sorrow and unceasing anguish in my heart" (Rom. 9:2). His distress is more commonly related to his ministry. It is because "the pressure [of] the daily concern for all the churches is on me" (2 Cor. 11:28; see also vv. 29-30; 1 Thess. 3:5). For example, to the Corinthians he states, "For I wrote to you out of much affliction and anguish of heart and with many tears" (2 Cor. 2:4).

Whether or not one can place the previous references into the category of "sin" is debatable. Nevertheless, they are indicative of the continuing weaknesses and frailties of Paul's own flesh. Yet Paul's letters more clearly portray his own ongoing struggles with sin in his flesh in two additional ways.

First, Paul characterizes his daily life as consisting of an enduring battle *against his own flesh*.[147] He speaks of it this way: "I beat my body and lead it into slavery, lest somehow after I have preached to others, I myself might be disqualified" (1 Cor. 9:27). Paul indicates that this struggle is not over. He has not yet reached perfection.

Not that I already received [this] or have already been made perfect, but I press on if indeed I might take hold of that for which I was also taken hold of by Christ Jesus (Phil. 3:12).

Second, as Paul looks at himself in the presence of God's holiness, he describes not only his past, but also his continuing Christian life in the present tense as follows: "The saying is faithful and worthy of full acceptance, 'Christ Jesus came into the world to save sinners, of whom *I* am (εἰμι ἐγώ) the foremost'" (1 Tim. 1:15).

It is important to note that Paul's continuing struggles in this life do not alter his assurance in the Gospel. They do not shake his confidence before God through Christ or his certainty concerning his

---

[147]In 2 Cor. 4:11 Paul speaks of his missionary team in the first person plural and describes how the life of Jesus is revealed "in our mortal flesh" (ἐν τῇ θνητῇ σαρκὶ ἡμῶν); compare Rom. 7:24.

eternal fate. Paul is personally convinced that nothing can separate him
from the love of God in Christ Jesus (Rom. 8:38-39). In the context of
his present sufferings he writes, "But I am not ashamed, for I know
whom I have believed and I am convinced that he is able to guard what
I have entrusted to him for that day" (2 Tim. 1:12). Paul even portrays
this confident attitude in the face of his own imprisonment and death:

> For I know that this will turn out for my salvation through your prayers
> and the provision of the Spirit of Jesus Christ, according to my eager
> expectation and hope, I will not be ashamed in anything, but with all
> boldness, as always even now Christ will be exalted in my body whether
> through life or through death. For to me, to live is Christ and to die is gain
> (Phil. 1:19-20,22).

In regard to his death, Paul describes it as a sacrificial offering
(Phil. 2:17; 2 Tim. 4:6). The closing words of 2 Timothy beautifully
summarize Paul's attitude toward his imminent death: "The Lord will
rescue me from every evil work and will bring me safely into his
heavenly kingdom; to whom be glory for ever and ever. Amen" (2
Tim. 4:18).[148] In words which serve as a fitting conclusion to his life,
Paul states with great assurance, "I have fought the good fight, I have
finished the race, I have kept the faith" (2 Tim. 4:7). His faith in Jesus
Christ is clearly wherein his innocence and confidence lie *coram Deo*.

In conclusion, it can be admitted that Romans 7:14-25 is unique.
Paul nowhere else speaks directly of himself with the same terms and
in the same manner as the "I" speaks there.[149] As a result, when the
complete picture of Paul's references to his own Christian life is taken
into consideration, the question of whether Romans 7:14-25 fits within
that picture is not answered as decisively as one would like. In some
passages Paul declares that as a Christian he is innocent or blameless
in a manner which would seem to exclude what is confessed by the "I"
there. Yet the statements in which Paul speaks of himself as being
without fault must be interpreted in a manner appropriate to their
context. For example, is he referring to his blamelessness before

---

[148]The presence of ῥύσεται με here recalls the wording of Rom. 7:24. There is a
manner in which a Christian still cries out for deliverance.

[149]But see, for example, his use of σῶμα instead of σάρξ in 1 Cor. 9:27.

people on the basis of the public performance of his apostolic duties, or is he speaking of his innocence before God? A determination of this is somewhat problematic since, from the outset of his Christian life, Paul describes his calling by God's grace together with his calling to be an apostle (as in Gal. 1:15-16). The two cannot be completely separated. They can, however, be distinguished. If Paul is speaking *coram Deo*, what is the basis of his innocence? It is no longer his own zeal or ability to fulfill the Law as was the case prior to his conversion. It is his faith in Jesus Christ.

On the other hand, nothing Paul writes about himself prohibits Romans 7:14-25 from being descriptive of himself as a Christian. While there are no explicit parallels, a number of the passages cited above point toward this conclusion. Perhaps Romans 7:14-25 provides the starkest portrayal of the Apostle Paul's inner struggles to fulfill the Law. Could those verses represent his most intimate disclosure of the continuing presence of sin in his own flesh when it is viewed in the presence of the holiness of both God and the Law? This interpretation has not been excluded by what Paul says about himself as a Christian elsewhere.

A more definitive resolution to the question of the spiritual state of the *"I"* in Romans 7:14-25 can be obtained by examining the broader statements Paul makes about the spiritual state of unbelievers and about the Christian life throughout his letters. These can be legitimately applied to Paul's own life as he himself reveals in this statement:

> But for this reason I was shown mercy, in order that in me, the foremost [of sinners], Christ Jesus might demonstrate [his] unlimited patience as an example (ὑποτύπωσιν) to those who are about/destined to believe on him for eternal life (1 Tim. 1:16).

As Romans 7:5 and 7-11 reveal, Paul will not allow the events of his own spiritual life before conversion to stand in opposition to his teachings about other unbelievers. Neither did Paul believe there was any contradiction between his own life after conversion and the lives of other Christians. On the contrary, Paul viewed his own experience as an example (ὑποτύπωσις) for other believers. This is, indeed, fortunate. It enables us to gather evidence concerning the spiritual state of the "I" in Romans 7:14-25 from Paul's more general descriptions of unbelievers and of Christians.

It is not here proposed that the life of any or every Christian, either before or after conversion, can be made rigidly paradigmatic for the life of Paul or *vice versa*. For example, Paul himself stresses his unique calling and mission to be the apostle to the Gentiles. As a result, his descriptions of his apostolic calling, ministry, and authority are not applicable to all other Christians. However, light can be shed upon Paul's life before conversion by examining the manner in which he describes other nonbelievers. In similar fashion, the various ways in which Paul depicts the sanctified life of Christians in general enable us to look more fully into Paul's own Christian life.

This chapter has identified the referent of the "I" in Romans 7 as Paul and placed the description of verses 7-11 within Paul's pre-conversion experience. The following chapter will examine the question of the spiritual state of the "I" in verses 14-25 within a wider frame of reference, Paul's overall view of the unbeliever and of the Christian. This will enable us to determine Paul's spiritual condition in those verses with greater assurance and conviction. Once the precise referent of the "I" throughout Romans 7 has been identified, an evaluation of Paul's purpose there can be made.

Chapter Four

Christian or Non-Christian "I" in Romans 7:14-25?

Introduction

Scholars have come to diverse conclusions regarding the spiritual state of the "I" in Romans 7:14-25. [See Chapter One for a summary of the various arguments surrounding this issue.] Is the "I" a non-Christian? If so, Paul attributes to an unbeliever the ability to acknowledge the Law is Spirit-filled and to agree with, even rejoice in, the Law of God in his "inner man" (7:14,16,22). If this is true, Paul believes that it is possible for the mind of an unbeliever consistently to will the good required by the Law (7:16,18,21,23,25) *and* to give thanks to God "through Jesus Christ our Lord" (7:25).

On the other hand, is it possible that the "I" is a Christian who nevertheless admits to being fleshly and sold under sin (7:14)? Is the "I" a believer in Christ who is unable to do the good stipulated by God's Law and led to do that which he hates by the sin still dwelling within (7:15,16,17,20)?

The fact that the debate over this question persists is one indication of its problematic nature. Each of these diverse interpretations can cite evidence in favor of its position, but is apparently unable to respond convincingly to the serious objections raised against it. Is there a solution to this impasse?[1]

---

[1] In view of the apparent difficulties with either of these positions, a third alternative has arisen. Is the "I" representative of either a non-Christian or a "lapsed" Christian who is not living up to the potential of his faith (as suggested above, see Chapter One)? The serious problems with this interpretation have been noted above and it will not be discussed at length here. The most damaging point against it is the sharp contrast which Paul incessantly draws between believers and unbelievers. For Paul the spiritual state of a person is certainly an "either/or" situation. Paul makes this clear in passages such as Romans 6:16-23; 7:4-6; 8:5-9; 2 Cor. 5:17-18, and so forth. Ernst Käsemann, *Commentary on Romans*, tr. and ed. G. Bromiley (Grand Rapids: Eerdmans Publishing, 1980), 204, points out, "Only when the arguments of 1:18-3:20, 5:12ff., and 6:3ff. are forgotten can one postulate a middle state between the fallen person and the saved person." James Dunn, "Rom. 7,14-25 in the Theology of Paul,"

The study of the sense or meaning of the text of Romans 7:14-25 in Chapter Two identified the fundamental characteristic of the "I" there portrayed. Paul is illustrating the disparity in the "I" between his willing what the Law says and his inability to accomplish that which he wills. This tension "between intention and performance"[2] may be illustrated as follows:[3]

Will	*Action*
(14) For we know that the Law is Spiritual,	but *I* am fleshly, having been sold under sin.
(15) For I do not approve	of that which I accomplish; indeed, I do not practice
that which I will, but that which I hate,	this I do.
	(16) But since I am doing
that which I do not will, I agree with the Law that [it is] excellent.	
	(17) But, this being the case, it is not then *I* who am accomplishing this, but sin which is dwelling in me.

Theologische Zeitschrift 9 (1975):269, affirms that for Paul there is no "middle path between these alternatives." In addition, the strongest arguments against both the Christian and the non-Christian identification of the "I" in 7:14-25 are negative ones. These contend that the "I" cannot be a believer or an unbeliever for certain reasons. This alternative interpretation, by positing that the "I" could be either a Christian or non-Christian, is left to face the objections weighed against both.

[2]Anders Nygren, *Commentary on Romans*, tr. C. Rasmussen (Philadelphia: Muhlenberg Press, 1949), 293.

[3]Here I am indebted to Paul Raabe, professor at Concordia Seminary, St. Louis, MO, who provided the basis for this analysis.

Will	**Action**
	(18) For I know that good is not dwelling in me, this is, in my flesh.
For to will [the good] lies at hand for me,	but the accomplishing of the good, no.
	(19) For I am not doing but [the] evil this I am practicing.
[the] good I will, I do not will,	
	(20) But if *I* am doing this
which I do not will, *I* am no longer accomplishing it	but the sin which is dwelling in me.
(21) So then I find the Law for for me the one determining to do the excellent [thing],	
	that for me evil lies at hand.
(22) I rejoice with the Law of God according to the inner man.	
	(23) But I see another Law in my members waging war against
the Law of my mind	and taking me captive to the Law of sin which is in my members.

(24) I am a distressed/miserable man; who will rescue me from this body of death? (25) Thanks to God through Jesus Christ our Lord.

Will	*Action*
So then *I* myself in [my] mind am enslaved to [the] Law of God,	but, on the other hand, in the flesh, [I am enslaved to the] Law of sin.

Is it possible for Paul to conceive of this disparity being present in an unbeliever, and/or is this contradiction between will and action characteristic of the believer?

This chapter seeks to address the question of the spiritual condition of the "I" in Romans 7:14-25 by comparing the sense/content of Paul's words about the "I" with the sense/content of other statements he makes about believers and unbelievers in Romans and then elsewhere.[4] It is here proposed that the issue of the spiritual state of the "I" in verses 14-25 and, thereby, also the specific referent of the "I," can be

---

[4]The attempt to support one's interpretation of Romans 7 by appealing to Paul's theology as a whole has been alluded to occasionally and a passage or two has been cited. For example, Nygren, *Commentary on Romans*, 289, points out that a non-Christian interpretation "flagrantly violates Paul's own thought." J. I. Packer, "The 'Wretched Man' of Romans 7," in *Studia Evangelica*, vol. 2, ed. F. Cross (Berlin: Akademie-Verlag, 1964), 625, concludes that "elsewhere Paul consistently denies the existence of any such affinity" with the Law of God in unbelievers. Yet he cites only "Eph. 2,3; 4,17ff." John Murray, *The Epistle to the Romans*, 2 vols. (Grand Rapids: Eerdmans Publishing, 1959,1965), 1:257, is properly disappointed that "modern expositors have dealt so inadequately with these considerations." The few exceptions include James Fraser, *The Scripture Doctrine of Sanctification* (Edinburgh: R. Ogle, 1830), 220-306, which is entitled, "A Dissertation concerning the General Scope and Purpose of the latter context of Chapter vii. 14-25." Fraser, however, generally extends his survey beyond the bounds of Paul's letters. See also Dunn, "Rom. 7,14-25 in the Theology of Paul," especially 264-73; David Wenham, "The Christian Life: A Life of Tension?: A Consideration of the Nature of Christian Experience in Paul," in *Pauline Studies*, eds. D. Hagner and M. Harris (Exeter, England: The Paternoster Press, 1980), 228-45; and Werner Kümmel, *Römer 7 und die Bekehrung des Paulus* (Leipzig: Hinrichs, 1929); reprinted in *Römer 7 und das Bild des Menschen im Neuen Testament: Zwei Studien*, Theologische Bücherei, Neues Testament Band 53 (München: Christian Kaiser Verlag, 1974), 134-38, who is aware of some of the difficulties his interpretation presents when viewed in the context of Paul's theology [Hereafter, *Römer 7*]; so also Paul Althaus, *Paulus und Luther über den Menschen*, Studien der Luther-Akademie, 14 (Gütersloh: "Der Rufer" Evangelische Verlag, 1938), 32-38.

satisfactorily resolved by considering it in the context of the entirety of Paul's theology as expressed in his letters and his statements in Acts.[5]

The following study is, then, divided into two parts. First, it compares the "I" portrayed in Romans 7:14-25 with the manner in which Paul depicts unbelievers and asks, "Are the two descriptions compatible?" The second portion of this chapter follows the same procedure, but focuses upon the "I" in light of Paul's characterizations of the Christian and asks, "Are these two pictures capable of accommodating one another?"

This survey is by no means meant to be a complete analysis of Paul's anthropology,[6] his view of the unbeliever,[7] the Christian life,[8]

---

[5]Those epistles accepted as genuine here are the letters which the Christian church has historically recognized as *homologoumena*. In seeking a solution to this debate by examining Paul's other epistles and his statements in Acts, one is faced with the question of whether Paul's theology is consistent or not. This vital issue is currently being addressed, for example, by J. Christiaan Beker, "Paul's Theology: Consistent or Inconsistent," *New Testament Studies* 34 (1988): 364-77; idem., "Paul the Theologian: Major Motifs in Pauline Theology," *Interpretation* 43 (1989):352-65; and Richard Longenecker, "On the Concept of Development in Pauline Thought," in *Perspectives in Evangelical Theology*, Papers from the Thirtieth Annual Meeting of the Evangelical Theological Society, eds. K. Kantzer and S. Gundry (Grand Rapids: Baker Book House, 1979), 195-207. Longenecker, 206, correctly concludes that one should allow for a "development of conceptualization and expression as brought about by God's Spirit" in Paul's letters. Paul expresses himself in various forms. He employs different language and utilizes new metaphors. However, ibid., contends that there is "continuity with an unchanging foundational core of revelation and conviction." This is especially true in regard to the question under consideration here.

[6]See, for example, the studies of Werner Kümmel, *Das Bild des Menschen im Neuen Testament* (Zürich: Zwingli-Verlag, 1948); reprinted in *Römer 7 und das Bild des Menschen im Neuen Testament: Zwei Studien*, Theologische Bücherei, Neues Testament Band 53 (München: Christian Kaiser Verlag, 1974), 178-98; William Nelson, "Pauline Anthropology," *Interpretation* 14 (1960):14-27; John Robinson, *The Body*, Graduate Theological Foundation (Bristol, IN: Wyndham Hall Press, 1988).

[7]See, for example, Rudolf Bultmann, *Theology of the New Testament*, 2 vols., tr. K. Grobel (New York: Charles Scribner's Sons, 1951), 1:190-269; Olaf Moe, *The Apostle Paul*, 2 vols. (Minneapolis: Augsburg Publishing House, 1954), 2:108-25; Herman Ridderbos, *Paul*, tr. J. De Witt (Grand Rapids: Eerdmans Publishing, 1975), 91-158.

[8]See, for example, Günther Bornkamm, "Baptism and New Life in Paul (Romans 6)," in *Early Christian Experience*, The New Testament Library, tr. P. Hammer (London: SCM Press, 1969), 71-86; Bultmann, *Theology of the New Testament*, 1:270-352; Moe, 2:307-57; Ridderbos, 205-326.

Christian ethics,[9] and so forth. Rather, it more narrowly aims to investigate the content of Paul's words in order to assess the spiritual state of the "I" in Romans 7:14-25.

Paul's Portrayal of Unbelievers and the "I" in Romans 7:14-25

In Romans 1:18-32 Paul describes Gentile non-believers as being able to perceive of God's existence by virtue of the things he has created (1:19-20). But Paul does not say that Gentiles are able to know or agree with God's revealed Law. On the contrary, he charges them with suppressing the knowledge about God which is available to them (1:23, 25,28). Far from having a mind which desires the good, Paul characterizes Gentile unbelievers as being "futile in their thinking" and having "senseless hearts" which have become even more darkened (1:21). As a result, Paul declares three times that God "gave them over" (παρέδωκεν) "in the desires of their hearts to impurity" (v. 24), to dishonorable passions (v.26), and "to a useless mind" (εἰς ἀδόκιμον νοῦν; v. 28). Paul describes Gentile unbelievers as "haters of God" (θεοστυγεῖς; v. 30); they are "foolish, faithless, heartless, ruthless" (v. 31). He concludes this section by describing the attitude of these unbelievers toward those acts committed against God's will: "They not only do them but approve of those who practice them" (1:32).

This description is in no way congruous with the "I" in Romans 7:14-25. Far from agreeing with the Law of God, the unbelieving Gentiles have a "useless mind" (ἀδόκιμον νοῦν; 1:28) which constantly and willingly opposes God, and also gives approval when what they know of God's will for right and wrong conduct is violated. There is no division between willing good and doing evil in 1:18-32. The Gentiles are portrayed as having "a senseless heart" (ἡ ἀσύνετος

---

[9]See the excellent overview of William Dennison, "Indicative and Imperative: The Basic Structure of Pauline Ethics," *Calvin Theological Journal* 14 (1979):55-78; also J. F. Bottorff, "The Relation of Justification and Ethics in Pauline Epistles," *Scottish Journal of Theology* 26 (1973):421-30; Rudolf Bultmann, "The Problem of Ethics in the Writings of Paul," in *The Old and New Man in the Letters of Paul*, tr. K. Crim (Richmond, VA: John Knox Press, 1967), 7-32; Victor Furnish, *Theology and Ethics in Paul* (Nashville: Abingdon Press, 1968); idem., *The Moral Teaching of Paul*, 2nd rev. ed. (Nashville: Abingdon Press, 1985); Ridderbos, 253-58.

αὐτῶν καρδία; 1:21)[10] which "has been filled with all wickedness" (v. 29; see vv. 29-31).

In Romans 2 Paul directs his attention toward those who judge others. He charges them with "being disobedient to the truth" (2:8). Those who condemn others have "unrepentant hearts" because they fail to recognize their own sinfulness (2:5). In 2:12-16 Paul points out that this accusation applies even to those who do not know the revealed Torah. The fact that those "without the Law" (2:12) are able to do some of "the things of the Law" (2:14) is evidence that "the work of the Law is written in their hearts" and on their "conscience" (2:15). Paul asserts that their hearts and consciences will turn to accuse them on the day of judgment when they will perish (2:12).

In 2:17 it becomes evident that Paul is speaking primarily of Jews who know the revealed Torah but are without the righteousness of faith. They are charged more specifically with failing to acknowledge their own transgressions of the Law (2:23). While being quick to admonish others on the basis of the Law, they fail to instruct themselves about their own disobedience (2:21-24). In addition, their view of circumcision is merely physical and their approach to the Law is bereft of the Spirit (2:28-29; contrast 7:6,14). As a result, their possession of the revealed Law, while potentially of great value (3:2), has become a means of deception used by sin to cloud their own sinfulness from them (2:24; 3:9-18; compare 7:7-11). This also stands in sharp contrast to the "I" of 7:14-25 who openly admits his own sinfulness (vv. 14,17-18,20), as well as his continuing inability to live according to the Law's commands.

Paul turns to discuss the effects and functions of the Law at length in Chapter 7. The attitude toward the Law depicted by the "I" in Romans 7:14-25 is utterly different from that of any unbeliever in Romans 1:18-3:20. Unlike the Gentile of 1:18-32, the "I" in 7:14-25 acknowledges the Law of God as good (7:16), joyfully agrees with what it says (7:22), and strives to accomplish that which it commands

---

[10]Bornkamm, "Faith and Reason in Paul's Epistles," *New Testament Studies* 4 (1957-58):95, notes, "Paul's terminology with reference to man shows such peculiarities as the replacement of the Greek concept νοῦς with the biblical word καρδία." This phrase is one example which portrays the Old Testament background of Paul's anthropology.

(7:15,18-19,21). Ernst Käsemann, however, contends that the situation characterized by σύμφημι τῷ νόμῳ (7:16) *"is present* among the Gentiles only in the shadow of 2:14ff."[11] Yet James Dunn rejects the possibility of including unbelieving Gentiles in the identity of the "I" because

> even if Paul does not exclude the possibility of an inward willing matching an outward doing on the part of the Gentiles (2:12-29), the point of Paul's gospel is precisely that it is only by the power of Christ's risen life that this possibility can be translated into full reality. The gospel . . . enables an obedience to the law from the heart.[12]

Furthermore, a Law-based recognition of one's own sinfulness is absent from the "moralist" of 2:1-16 and the Jew who relies on the Law and boasts in God (2:18-29). Yet this is the very thing which the "I" in 7:14-25 openly confesses of himself, albeit in a qualified manner (7:14,17-18,20). The "I" laments that he is unable to accomplish what the Law requires and to refrain from what it forbids. Even though he rejoices with the Law of God "according to the inner man" (7:22), he is distressed because he recognizes that that same Law convicts him of sin. Due to the sin which dwells in his members, he confesses that his body is a "body of death"(7:23-24).

As Paul continues in Chapters 5-8, he makes a number of descriptions of the pre-faith life of those who have now come to receive the righteousness of God. At that time, he says, we were "helpless" (5:6), "enemies" of God (5:10), "enslaved to sin" (6:6), and under the dominion of sin and death (5:17,21; 6:16-17,20). Then sin was able to use even the Law of God to arouse sinful passions leading to death (7:5; compare 7:13). Romans 8 describes those who do not have the Spirit of Christ (8:9) as ones who live "according to the flesh" (κατὰ σάρκα; 8:5). They set their minds on the things of the flesh and their end is death (8:6,13). Paul concludes,

---

[11]Käsemann, 203. He identifies the "I" in these verses with all people, and especially "the pious."

[12]James Dunn, *Romans 1-8*, Word Biblical Commentary, vol. 38a, eds. R. Martin, D. Hubbard, and G. Barker (Dallas: Word Books, 1988), 394; see 6:15-18; 7:6.

For the mind of the flesh (τὸ φρόνημα τῆς σαρκός) is hostile to God; it does not subject itself (οὐχ ὑποτάσσεται) to the Law of God, indeed, it is not able [to do so] (8:7).

How does the picture of unbelievers in Romans 5-8 compare with the "I" in 7:14-25? At first glance they appear similar. The "I" confesses, "I am fleshly, sold under sin" (7:14). However, as the "I" proceeds, this statement is clarified. The "necessary qualification"[13] of this "sold under sin" condition is that it is restricted to the "sin which dwells in me, . . . this is, in my flesh" (7:17-18; compare v. 25). Sin is at work "in my members" (7:23) and that makes the body of the "I" a body of death (7:24). Sin continues to have its domain in 7:14-25, but it is limited to sin's presence in the flesh, its activity in the "I"'s members, and its opposition to his will and mind.

In contrast, the will, the inner man, and the mind of the "I" are exhibiting traits which are clearly not characteristic of a mind which is set on the flesh (8:6). Far from being enslaved to sin (6:6), controlled by sinful passions (7:5), at enmity with God (5:10), and hostile to his Law (8:7), the "I" in 7:16 agrees with the Law of God and his inner man "rejoices" in it (7:22). His νοῦς willingly enslaves itself to God's most excellent Law and intends to live according to it (7:16,18,23,25). This clearly is not the same condition as that of the unbeliever portrayed by Paul in the context surrounding 7:14-25.

When Paul discusses the specific situation of the Jewish people in Romans 9-11, he points out that they have stumbled (προσκόπτω; 9:32-33). Their zeal for God was not in accordance with accurate knowledge (ἐπίγνωσις, 10:2; compare 3:20). As a result, they attempted to pursue a righteousness by works of the Law (ἐξ ἔργων; 9:32). In "seeking to establish their own righteousness, they did not submit to God's righteousness" which comes through faith (10:3,6).

This, again, stands in sharp contrast to the view of the Law which is present in the "I" in 7:14-25 and makes it difficult to comprehend how Paul could be using the first person singular there to depict a pious Jew.[14] Even though the "I" in 7:14-25, like Israel in 9:30-10:5,

---

[13]C. E. B. Cranfield, *A Critical and Exegetical Commentary on the Epistle to the Romans*, The International Critical Commentary, vol. 32, 6th ed. (Edinburgh: T. & T. Clark, 1975,1979), 1:360.

[14]As maintained, for example, by Käsemann, 202-3. Kümmel, *Römer 7*, 111-17,

has zeal for God and his Law (10:2), the "I" in Chapter 7 understands that the Law is not a means to righteousness for him. The Law continues to identify sin by pointing out the good which the "I" fails to do and by condemning the evil he accomplishes (7:15-20). The Law continues to provoke sin in my "members" (7:23; also vv. 8,13) and to enslave his flesh to sin (7:25; also v. 14). Even though the "I" agrees with the Law and wills to accomplish it, he has no doubt about the futility of pursuing "a Law of righteousness" (9:31). The "I" realizes the Law continues to condemn the "sin which dwells in me" (7:20). He recognizes that seeking to establish his own righteousness "by works" (9:32) of the Law is an impossibility. The "I" in 7:14-25, therefore, does not reflect the attitude toward the Law which Paul attributes to Israel in Romans 9:30-10:5.

In conclusion, the statements made by the "I" in Romans 7:14-25 cannot be equated with the picture Paul paints of unbelievers throughout Romans. This is especially evident in regard to the attitude toward the Law which the "I" exhibits. The unbelieving Gentiles do not agree with the Law and their will is not determined to live according to it. Those Jews who boast in the Law apart from the righteousness which comes by faith fail to recognize that the Law continues to place them under, and even lead them into, sin because their flesh is enslaved to sin.

Rudolf Bultmann and others attempt to evade this conclusion by contending that what Paul reveals in Romans 7:14-25 is a predicament which the unbelieving "I" does not recognize as his own. They propose that Paul's rhetorical "I" offers us an objective description of man under the Law from the viewpoint of Christian faith. However, an objective characterization of unbelievers based upon the Law and from the vantage point of Christian faith is precisely what Paul is giving throughout much of Romans.[15] The objective description he gives outside of 7:14-25 excludes the interpretation that the "I" there is an unbeliever.

---

recognizes that the "I" cannot be a pharisaic Jew or even Paul the Pharisee. The "I" is certainly not a "relying upon the Law" Jew as depicted by Paul in 2:17-25.

[15]Dunn, *Romans 1-8*, 394, states: "The illogicality of arguing that the passage here expresses with Christian hindsight the existential anguish of the pious Jew—which as a pious Jew [Paul] did not actually experience and which as a Christian he still does not experience!—is usually not appreciated."

As we turn to examine Paul's portrayal of unbelievers elsewhere, the conclusion we have reached becomes even more evident. Paul expresses his convictions quite consistently throughout his letters when he speaks about 1) the mind of unbelievers, 2) the motivation for and quality of their deeds, and 3) their spiritual status before God.

First, Paul speaks of the mind of unbelievers and the mental reasoning of Christians *prior to* faith's coming in a number of passages. What he says in them corresponds with, and further clarifies, his statements in Romans. Paul declares that "the god of this age has blinded the minds of the unbelieving" (ἐτύφλωσεν τὰ νοήματα τῶν ἀπίστων; 2 Cor. 4:4). The unbeliever's cognitive powers stand in opposition to God and to his will as revealed in the Law. Those who belong to this crooked and perverse generation (Phil. 2:15) are enemies of the cross with "minds set on earthly things" (οἱ τὰ ἐπίγεια φρονοῦντες; Phil. 3:19). Before coming to faith, Gentile Christians "were once alienated and hostile in understanding (ἐχθροὺς τῇ διανοίᾳ), doing evil deeds" (Col. 1:21). In writing to Titus, Paul characterizes unbelievers in this manner:

> To the pure ones all things are pure, but to those who have been corrupted and are without faith nothing is pure, but both the mind and the conscience (ὁ νοῦς καὶ ἡ συνείδησις) of them have been corrupted. They profess to know God, but with [their] works, they are denying [him]; they are detestable and disobedient and unfit for any good deed (1:15-16).

When Paul speaks of the mind of those Jews who only know the Law apart from faith and the Spirit, he says that they read the Law as a "written code" which kills (2 Cor. 3:6).[16] Because of the deception worked by sin through the Law, "their minds were hardened" (ἐπωρώθη τὰ νοήματα αὐτῶν; 2 Cor. 3:14). "To this day whenever Moses is read a veil lies over their hearts" (2 Cor. 3:15).

Paul speaks of those who have fallen away from or rejected the faith in a comparable manner. He describes false teachers as men who have been rejected concerning the faith and with "minds having been corrupted" (κατεφθαρμένοι τὸν νοῦν; 2 Tim. 3:8; see also 1 Tim. 6:5; Tit. 3:11). Those who have rejected and now oppose the Gospel

---

[16]Romans 9:30-10:5 explains why this is so; see also 7:7-11.

are in "the snare of the devil, having been captured by him to do the will of that one" (θέλημα; 2 Tim. 2:26).

These passages make it clear that for Paul all those who do not have the Spirit of God, or who have rejected the Spirit, have a mind united with the sinful flesh which stands in complete opposition to God.[17] Any such person is unable to know God in a relational way (ידע) or to comprehend the things of God.

> But a natural (ψυχικός) man does not receive the things of the Spirit of God, for they are foolishness to him, and he is not able to understand them because they are spiritually discerned (πνευματικῶς ἀνακρίνεται; 1 Cor. 2:14).

The implications of 1 Corinthians 2:14 for identifying the "I" in Romans 7:14-25 are far greater than merely parading the "I"'s recognition of the Law as Spiritual (7:14; but see 2:29; 7:6). In Romans 7 the "I" not only acknowledges that fact, he also joyfully agrees with the good Law (7:22). As a result, the determined desire of his will is to accomplish what the Spiritual Law commands and to strive to abstain from the evil it forbids (7:15-20). The "I" serves the Law of God with his mind (7:25) and even identifies the Law of God as "the Law of my mind" (τῷ νόμῳ τοῦ νοός μου; 7:23). It is impossible to equate the statements made about the Law by the "I" in Romans 7:14-25 with the way in which Paul depicts the mind and attitudes of unbelievers toward the Law.

Second, Paul not only views the cognitive powers of unbelievers as ignorant of and hostile to God, he contends that their fallen mind exhibits itself in actions which follow the dictates of their sinful flesh and further separate them from God. In a number of places Paul lists those deeds which dominate the will of unbelievers and which characterized the existence of Christians before faith came (1 Cor. 6:9-11; Gal. 5:19-21; Eph. 5:5; Col. 3:5-7; 1 Thess. 4:5; 2 Tim. 3:2-5). The

---

[17]Althaus, *Paulus und Luther über den Menschen*, 35, advances a non-Christian interpretation of the "I" in Rom. 7:14-25, but admits, "It is true that Paul has not elsewhere in his epistles spoken in this way about [the unbeliever's] νοῦς 'reason.' It is rather true that a whole series of passages show that νοῦς, or 'the heart,' is drawn into man's ruin ("*Es ist wahr: von dem νοῦς, der 'Vernunft', hat Paulus sonst in seinen Briefen nicht so geredet. Vielmehr zeigt eine ganze Reihe von Stellen, daß auch der νοῦς oder das 'Herz' in das Verderben des Menschen mit hineingezogen ist*").

acts which Paul enumerates are explicitly contrary to the Law of God.[18] Paul describes these as the passions, deeds, and works of the flesh which, in effect, prohibit one from entering the Kingdom of God.

Paul contends that the Law's commands are laid down "for the lawless and rebellious, for the ungodly and sinners, for the unholy and profane" (1 Tim. 1:9). God's Law was intended to identify sin as sin against God (Gal. 3:19; Rom. 3:20; 7:7) and then to restrain sin (1 Tim. 1:9). Yet in Romans Paul concedes that the Law has been misused by sin not only to provoke further sin (4:15; 5:20; 7:7-10), but also to deceive sinners into attempting to obtain a righteousness before God by keeping the works of the Law (Rom. 7:11; 9:30-10:5). Paul rebukes the latter approach to the Law in Galatians by stating, "Now that no one is justified before God by the Law is evident" (Gal. 3:11; see Ps. 142:2).[19] Paul demonstrates why this is so from the Law itself. He cites Deuteronomy 27:26 which pronounces a curse upon "everyone who does not abide by all things written in the Book of the Law, to do them" (Gal. 3:10).

The conduct of unbelievers in relation to God's Law also stands in contrast to that of the "I" in Romans 7:14-25. Unlike those unbelievers whose will and actions are devoted to carrying out the desires of the flesh, the will of the "I" is willingly enslaved to God's most excellent Law (7:16,25). He hates his own deeds which transgress against both his will and the Law (7:15). Unlike those who attempt to use the Law as a means to righteousness, the "I" recognizes that he does not and cannot perform all the good things required by the Law because of the sin which dwells in his flesh (7:15-21).

Finally, how does Paul's evaluation of the spiritual status of unbelievers compare with his portrayal of the "I" in Romans 7:14-25? Paul's letters provide a number of statements which convey his appraisal of the spiritual life of any person whose mind is separated from God's Spirit and whose deeds are united with the sinful flesh in

---

[18]For example, in 1 Cor. 6:9-11, Paul lists the following deeds which are prohibited by the commandments noted parenthetically: the immoral (6th), idolaters (1st), adulterers (6th), homosexuals (6th), thieves (7th), greedy (9th and 10th), drunkards (5th?), revilers (4th and 8th), robbers (7th).

[19]See also Gal. 2:16; 3:10,21-22; 6:13-14; compare Rom. 3:19-20. Paul's argument in Galatians will be crucial for an understanding of Paul's purpose in Romans 7; see the Excursus in Chapter Five below.

opposition to God's Law. According to Paul, the lives and activities of those outside of faith and apart from God's Spirit are dominated by their own flesh which subjects them to sin and death.

Paul depicts the former life of Gentile believers as an existence which was outside of the covenant and alienated from Christ (Eph. 2:11-12). As Gentiles they lived in darkness as "sons of disobedience" (Eph. 5:6,8; see also Col. 5:6). In view of this, Paul then exhorts them as Christians by pointing to the total depravity of the mind, deeds, and spiritual condition of those Gentiles who remain outside of Christ:

> Therefore, this I say and testify in the Lord, that you no longer live just as the Gentiles live in the futility of their mind (ἐν ματαιότητι τοῦ νοὸς αὐτῶν); they have been darkened in their understanding (τῇ διανοίᾳ), alienated from the life of God because of the ignorance (ἄγνοιαν) which is in them, on account of the hardness of their heart; such ones, having become callous, gave themselves up to unrestrained living for the working of all impurity in greediness (Eph. 4:17-19).

The complete alienation of these Gentiles from God can hardly be equated with the statements of the "I" in Romans 7:14-25. Not only does such a comparison fail to account for the will of the "I" which desires to live according to God's Law, it also overlooks the struggle which is there taking place between the θέλω and the σάρξ. In Romans 7 the will of the "I," his mind, and inner man are aligned with God's Law and engaged in fighting against the sin which continues to dwell in his own flesh. The "I" knows all too well that sin still has a foothold in his members and he is frustrated by his inability to eradicate it. Paul does not portray the will of unbelievers as being capable of rejoicing in God's Law or as engaged in a struggle against their flesh.

For Paul there is no inner conflict taking place in those without the Spirit. Before the Gentile Christians whom Paul addresses in Ephesians belonged to Christ, there was no agreement with God's Law that was being overpowered by the sinful flesh (Rom. 7:15-20). Instead, there was total and complete slavery to the passions of the flesh and to sin. Paul does not place unbelievers into categories which indicate that some can attain a higher level in relation to God than others.[20] In fact, he refuses to allow any "germ of good in human

---

[20]Ridderbos, 129, suggests, and then dismisses, the supposition "that in Romans 7:14ff. Paul is no longer speaking simply of the 'ordinary' non-Christian, but of the

nature, [any] genuine desire to do what is right."[21] Werner Kümmel concludes,

> As a matter of fact, it is clear that Paul knows of no human inner life related to God but only the complete man, who is σάρξ, σῶμα, ψυχή etc., and stands completely against God.[22]

According to Paul, prior to the time God "made us alive" (συνεζωοποίησεν) together with Christ, "we were dead through our trespasses" (Eph. 2:5; so also Col. 2:13).[23] He has described this existence quite definitively in the preceding verses:

> And you being dead in your transgressions and sins, in which you formerly walked according to the age of this world, according to the ruler of the power of the air, the spirit which is now working in the sons of disobedience; among whom *we* also formerly lived in the desires of our flesh doing the will of the flesh and the thoughts (ποιοῦντες τὰ θελήματα τῆς σαρκὸς καὶ τῶν διανοιῶν), and we were by nature children of wrath as also the rest (Eph. 2:1-3).

Paul tells these Gentile Christians that previously they were undisturbed in their spiritual death. At that time "the will of the flesh and the thoughts" of the mind were united (2:3). This condition is in no way congruous with the disparity present within the "I" of Romans

---

one who stands 'on the highest plane attainable by pre-Christian man'"; citing W. Gutbrod, *Die Paulinische Anthropologie* (1938), 53.

[21]As asserted by William Sanday and Arthur Headlam, *A Critical and Exegetical Commentary on the Epistle to the Romans*, The International Critical Commentary, vol. 32 (New York: Charles Scribner's Sons, 1902), 181. However, something similar to this is necessary for all those who would interpret the "I" of Rom. 7:14-25 as an unbeliever. For example, see also C. K. Barrett, *A Commentary on the Epistle to the Romans*, Black's New Testament Commentaries (London: Adam and Charles Black, 1962), 150-51.

[22]Kümmel, *Das Bild des Menschen*, 183, "*daß Paulus in der Tat kein Gott vewandtes menschliches Innenleben kennt, sondern nur den ganzen Menschen,* der σάρξ, σῶμα, ψυχή , *ist und als ganzer Gott gegenüber steht.*"

[23]Note the sense of νεκρούς here corresponds to that adopted above in Chapter Two for Rom. 7:8. Here these unbelievers were in some sense alive, yet spiritually and in their relationship to God they were dead. So also sin, before the Law came, was in a sense alive, yet in its ability to provoke and effect transgression of God's Law it was νεκρά.

7:14-25. The "I" there cannot be a Gentile unbeliever.

Paul then adds that "*we* also formerly lived" among these Gentiles by following the "desires of our flesh" (Eph. 2:3). It is certainly significant that Paul switches to the first person plural in verse 3. It signals that he will not allow one to restrict the application of passages such as Ephesians 2:1-3 to those unbelievers who do not know the revealed Law of God. In Romans 2:1-3:20 Paul demonstrated that "Jews and Gentiles are all under sin. . . . for all sinned" (Rom. 3:9,23a). So also in Galatians 3:22 he declares, "The Scriptures locked up all things under sin." In 1 Corinthians Paul concludes, "Thus no flesh can boast before God" (ἐνώπιον τοῦ θεοῦ; 1:29a). Apart from the righteousness of God which is received through faith, all are ultimately in the same condemned position before God.

As a result, those Jews who delighted in the Law as a means to gain or maintain their righteousness before God cannot be identified with the "I" portrayed by Paul in Romans 7:14-25. Paul charges those Jews with failing to recognize their own sin and characterizes them as being deceived by sin's perversion of the Law (Gal. 2:15-16,21; 3:10-24; also Rom. 2:1,21-24; 7:11; 9:30-10:5).

However, the "I" in Romans 7:14-25 is far from being deluded into attempting to obtain a proper standing before God by his own works of the Law. He repeatedly recognizes his own sin and is frustrated by his inability to accomplish what the Law requires. Paul has eliminated the possibility of anyone being able to rely on the Law in order to boast before God (as in Rom. 2:17; see 3:19-20; 1 Cor. 2:19; Gal. 2:1). It is only by believing in the forgiveness of sins proclaimed in Jesus Christ that anyone is justified "from all [the] things from which you were not able to be justified by the Law of Moses" (Acts 13:38).

So, then, an unbelieving Gentile, a Jew who knows the Law apart from faith, and a former Christian who has fallen away or lapsed from the faith into unbelief or false doctrine are all placed in the same condition. For Paul they all, in both mind and action, stand under the complete bondage he describes in Titus 3:

> For we ourselves were once foolish, disobedient, being deceived, being enslaved to various desires and pleasures (δουλεύοντες ἐπιθυμίαις καὶ ἡδοναῖς ποικίλαις; 3:3a; compare Gal. 3:23; 4:3,8).

Admittedly, Romans 7:14-25 also depicts a slavery to sin in the flesh.

But this slavery is restricted to the sin which dwells in the flesh of the "I" and works "in my members" (7:23; also vv. 17-18,20). This "sold under sin" condition is both regretted and protested by his will, mind, and inner man.

These passages have shown that, for Paul, before faith came there was no recognition of or battle against "the Law of sin which is in my members" (Rom. 7:23). Apart from faith there can be no true joyful agreement with the Law of God (Rom. 7:22). It is only when one is made alive with Christ that a battle is inaugurated between the fleshly desires of the body and the now Spirit-renewed mind. Is this the battle present in Romans 7:14-25? For Paul, the complete slavery to sin and the domination of death is only disturbed by the presence of the Spirit of God.

> Rom 7:14-25, if understood of the non-Christian, represents not just (in Kümmel's terms) a 'formal deviation' or 'relative departure' from Paul's view of the natural man as found elsewhere, but a radical difference, a direct contradiction.[24]

It can, therefore, be concluded that the "I" in those verses is not an unbeliever. The disparity in the "I" is not compatible with Paul's portrayal of either Jews or Gentiles outside of faith.

Paul's Description of the Christian Life and the "I" in Romans 7:14-25

Can Paul be describing the life of the Christian in Romans 7:14-25, or is such an interpretation excluded by Paul's view of the life inaugurated by faith? Does the state of the "I" there stand in contradiction to what Paul says of the believer's life elsewhere? A number of the arguments against interpreting the "I" as a believer were presented in Chapter One. However, a number of the exegetical bases for these conclusions were refuted in Chapter Two. This study now turns to examine this question from the perspective of Paul's understanding of

---

[24]Ronald Fung, "The Impotence of the Law: Toward a Fresh Understanding of Romans 7:14-25," in *Scripture, Tradition, and Interpretation*, eds. W. Gasque and W. LaSor (Grand Rapids: Eerdmans Publishing, 1978), 35-36; he affirms this, 36, in spite of "the overwhelming support [the non-Christian interpretation] currently enjoys."

the Christian life as he expresses it in Romans and then throughout his letters and in Acts.

In Romans, when Paul finally discusses how the "righteousness of God" is received, he declares that it comes "freely by his grace through the redemption which is in Christ Jesus. . . . For we maintain that a man is justified by faith apart from works of [the] Law" (3:24,28). What part does the Law play in a person being justified? Paul's decisive answer is, "None" (χωρὶς νόμου; 3:21; see also 3:20,27,28; 4:6). Christ's death has paid the once-for-all ransom price (ἀπολύτρωσις; 3:24).[25] How does a person who is righteous through faith maintain that righteousness? Already here Paul hints at the answer to the dilemma of the "I" in 7:14-25. It is because Jesus is also the ἱλαστήριον (3:25).[26] His blood is held forth as the "mercy seat" which continuously covers the sins of believers of all time (3:25-26; compare 8:34).

Abraham was not accounted righteous by his work but by his faith (4:5,11). So also the promise to his descendants did not come through the Law but through faith (4:13). The reason for this is "in order that the promise might be guaranteed to all [his] descendants" (4:16).

Those who follow in the footsteps of Abraham (4:12) are also justified through faith and by that faith have peace with God and continued access to his grace (5:1-2). Paul also states that the one who believes has been acquitted of sin, is now reconciled to God, and possesses true life (5:10,18). One who has been declared righteous by faith in Jesus Christ has, therefore, been freed from *slavery* to sin and death by the One who has overcome that which Adam brought into the world (5:12-21). None of this, including the maintaining of this state of peace with God and access to him, is based upon the Law. It is only

---

[25]On this term, see Leon Morris, *The Apostolic Preaching of the Cross* (London: Tyndale Press, 1955); reprint ed. (Grand Rapids: Eerdmans Publishing, 1956), 29-59, especially 41-42; and David Hill, *Greek Words and Hebrew Meanings*, Society for New Testament Studies Monograph Series, no. 5 (Cambridge: At the University Press, 1967), 49-81.

[26]On this term, see Morris, *The Apostolic Preaching of the Cross*, 167-74; idem., "The Meaning of ἱλαστήριον in Romans 3.25," *New Testament Studies* 2 (1955-56):33-43. ἱλαστήριον is used to translate the כפרת or "mercy seat" of the tabernacle and temple 21 of the 27 times it is used in the Septuagint. It is also used for the lip of the altar of burnt offering and, in both cases, denotes a place where atonement for sin was granted *on a recurring basis*.

certain through faith in the promise (4:16).

Even though the believer's existence is no longer determined by the consequences of Adam's sin, Paul affirms that the believer remains a fleshly descendant of the first Adam through whom sin and death were brought into the world (5:12).

> The new has not yet wholly swallowed up the old, there is still a significant degree of continuity between man's state prior to faith and his state under faith.[27]

As a result, Paul places the final fulfillment of this hope into the future (5:2b-5). There is yet a day ahead when we "will be saved" (5:9,10). Then "we will also be united with him in a resurrection like his" (6:5).

Until then, shall we continue to sin (6:1)? Some of the statements which Paul makes in Romans 6 seem to stand in contradiction to the state of the "I" in Romans 7:14-25. Paul declares that as Christians our "old self" has been crucified with Christ (6:6) and we have been "freed from sin" (6:18,22). This can hardly be the same state as that of the "I" who confesses, "I am fleshly, having been sold under sin" (7:14). Or is it?

Does Paul mean that the Christian is totally free from sin and from all its enticements?[28] If so, the question of 6:1 merely requires a simplistic answer and the exhortation in verses 12-19 is unnecessary. But the manner in which Paul does respond indicates that

> it should not be inferred from [such statements] that there is no more sin for the believer; certainly sin still seeks to enslave, but its *dominion* is absolutely excluded for the believer.[29]

---

[27]Dunn, "Rom. 7,14-25 in the Theology of Paul," 271; see also C. Marvin Pate, *The End of the Age Has Come* (Grand Rapids: Zondervan Publishing), 111; Nelson, 19, who cites this statement of Otto Piper, *The Christian Interpretation of Sex*, (New York, 1941), 16: "The two periods overlap to a certain extent; the Old 'Aeon' has not yet been fully annihilated, and the New 'Aeon' has not yet reached its consummation."

[28]This seems to be what Kümmel, *Römer 7*, 75, implies when he defines a Christian as one who is "no longer under the Law, also he no longer lives in sin" ("*nicht mehr unter dem Gesetz, auch nicht mehr in der Sünde leben*"). Paul would agree that a Christian is no longer under the dominion of sin or the Law; however, he does not state that it is possible for Christians to live without sinning.

[29]Bottorff, 428.

As pointed out previously, for Paul it is a matter of reigning and dominion.[30] Before faith, sin and death reigned over all people (5:12,14,17,21). Now that the Christian has died with Christ, his old self has been crucified "so that we might no longer be enslaved to sin" (6:6). The Christian is now freed from sin's power to reign in death (5:21; 6:11, 17,20; as is also the force of 6:18,22).

Therefore, what Paul means is that the true identity of the Christian, the "inner man" as seen by faith together with that which determines his will and governs his mind, is free from the domination of sin. Sin no longer rules over a Christian. As a result, his existence is no longer *determined by the flesh* (6:19; 7:5) and even "death no longer exercises lordship over him" (6:9). Believers have been set free from slavery to sin (6:17,18,20,22) and Paul assures them that the end of the Christian life is eternal life (6:22).

But this does not mean that believers cease to exist in the flesh, that sin no longer plays a role in the Christian's life, or that the prospect of death is eliminated.[31] On the contrary, Paul acknowledges that Christians continue to live in "mortal bodies" (ἐν τῷ θνητῷ σώματι; 6:12) where sin continues to work. Paul speaks of "the weakness of the flesh" (τὴν ἀσθένειαν τῇ σαρκός; 6:19) and urges believers not to allow their members (τὰ μέλη ὑμῶν) to be used as slaves of sin. Rather, "present your members as slaves to righteousness for sanctification" (6:19).

Paul does not say believers are totally free from sin. Instead, the believer "has been and remains justified from sin" through faith in

---

[30]See above, Chapter Two. Some of the antitheses which Paul sets up throughout Romans 5-8 are death reigning/life reigning (5:18); condemnation/life (5:18); sin reigning/grace reigning in righteousness (5:21); old self/new life of the Spirit (6:6; 7:6); slaves of sin/slaves of righteousness (6:17-22); in the flesh/in Christ (7:5; 8:1). Bottorff, 428, properly concludes that these point to "the new situation that the believer enters which may be characterized as the new dominion. . . . The actualization that the Holy Spirit accomplishes on the basis of Christ's resurrection is the ever-present breaking of the power of sin so that one is not lorded over by sin but stands under the domination of grace (cf. Rom. 6:14)"; cf. Pate, 99-121.

[31]As Robert Banks, "Romans 7.25a: An Eschatological Thanksgiving?" *Australian Biblical Review* 26 (1979):40, states, "For although in this whole section, Romans 5-8, logically, chronologically and theologically absolute distinctions exist between sin and righteousness, law and grace, flesh and spirit, death and life, *empirically* sin, law, flesh and death still affect the Christian in his ongoing life"; cf. Pate, 108-16.

Jesus Christ (perfect passive of δικαίοω; 6:7). As God reckons/considers the ungodly to be righteous (4:5), so Paul urges believers to consider themselves (λογίζομαι) dead to sin and to combat sin's attempt to reign once again (6:11-12).

> Paul does not teach that conversion-initiation brings a complete ending of or release from the flesh, or an immediate and lasting victory over the power of sin (as might have been deduced from a shallow reading of 6:1-11 or 7:1-6). On the contrary, it is spiritual warfare which is the sign of life.[32]

Paul recognizes that the believer is now engaged in a conflict against that which once possessed him completely. His battle is against sin, which no longer reigns, but which strives to do so once again by utilizing the fleshly "members" of the believer as instruments of wickedness (6:13). Paul warns Christians that if they yield themselves "as slaves" to the *dominion* of the flesh, sin, and death, they are in the same condemned position before God as they were before "being justified freely by his grace" (3:24; 6:16). Therefore, he urges resistance and warfare against sin. This is just what we see in 7:14-25.

At the same time, Paul sharply contrasts the role sin and death used to play when they dominated and reigned with the current effect they are able to have upon the believer. Sin's role is limited. It no longer reigns. Yet, sin keeps working in the members of the believer in an effort to regain domination. Death also once reigned totally and completely. Now death's power is limited to its ability to make this body a mortal one (6:12; cf. 8:11).

But what about the role the holy and Spiritual Law (7:12,14) plays before and then during the Christian life? This is the question which prompts Romans 7. The Law was given in order for people to recognize their sin (3:20; 7:7). Its commands brought God's wrath (4:15) and served to increase transgressions (5:20; 7:8,13). Sin was even able to deceive and kill through the Law (7:10-11). The Law, like sin and death, used to exercise lordship over the Christian (7:1,6). But no longer! "You were put to death to the Law through the body of Christ" (7:4). What, if any, role does God's Law now play? This question is the one which engages Paul in 7:14-25.

---

[32]Dunn, *Romans 1-8*, 412; see also Barrett, 146.

The "I" as a believer acknowledges the Law as spiritual (7:14). He agrees with and even rejoices in the Law of God and identifies it as "the Law of my mind" (7:23; see also vv. 16,22,25). The will of the "I" is positively aligned with the Law and consistently strives to accomplish the good mandated by the Law and to refrain from the evil it forbids (7:15-21,25). For Paul, only the believer is free from the Law's lordship and enabled to serve it willingly (7:4,6).

However, the Law, together with sin and death, continues to have a negative effect upon the "I" because of his flesh (7:14,18). Even though the "I" wills to accomplish the good as directed by the Law, evil lies close at hand (7:21). In fact, sin still "dwells in me, . . . this is, in my flesh" (7:17-18,20). It is in this limited, "fleshly" sphere that the "I" remains sold under sin (7:14).

In 7:14-25, then, Paul displays the Law's double effect upon the believer. Although it no longer reigns, the Law continues to identify the evil which the "I" does and hates, and to point out the good he fails to accomplish. The Law, like sin, continues to work "in my members" making this fleshly body a body of death (7:23-24). The "I" recognizes that he cannot eradicate sin's ability to work in his flesh. As a result, the Law of God remains a Law of sin which identifies, provokes, and announces God's condemnation on sin. So the "I" cries out for deliverance from "this body of death" (7:24) while knowing full-well whence this deliverance comes, "our Lord Jesus Christ" (7:25). For those in him, there is no condemnation. The sin offering has been made; the Law's requirement has been fulfilled (8:3-4).

Understood in this way, the argument of Romans 7, including the portrayal of the "I" in verses 7-25, fits squarely within the scheme Paul has developed thus far in Romans 5-7.[33] Paul first points out that sin, death, and the Law used to rule/reign before faith. Second, he describes how their *dominion* has ended and declares believers are now free from God's wrath (Chapter 5), sin's *reign* (Chapter 6), and the Law's *condemnation* (Chapter 7). Third, in each chapter Paul details the continued, but limited, negative effect of sin, death, and the Law upon the believer.

---

[33]See Nygren, *Commentary on Romans*, 295-96. Nelson, 19, concludes, "In Romans 7:14-25 Paul's experience of inner conflict is a good illustration of the Christian's double situation due to his participation in two aeons."

Chapter 8 continues, but also concludes, this discussion by pointing to the Spirit of God. It is the Spirit who directs the mind of the believer (8:5-6) and who battles together with the Christian against the inroads sin attempts to make into his life through the flesh (8:12-17). It is the Spirit who intercedes and pleads for the believer (8:25-26) and whose testimony guarantees that believers are truly heirs of God who can await with confidence "the glory to be revealed" to them (8:17-18). They are also free from *eternal* death (8:38-39).

Until then, Paul comforts believers with the assurance that both Jesus and his Spirit continue to intercede for them before the Father (8:26,34). Why is this intercession necessary? It is because the "sold under sin" flesh continues to wage war against, and at times even captivates, the believer whose "body is dead on account of sin" (8:10; 7:23). As in 7:14-25, the Spirit-renewed mind of the believer is set against the desires of the flesh (8:5-6). As in 7:14-25, the believer recognizes that his fleshly body is dead "because of sin" (8:10) and he groans inwardly while awaiting the redemption of his mortal body (8:23; compare 7:23-24). Since this is the case, Paul both announces and exhorts, "We are not debtors to the flesh to live according to the flesh" (8:12; as in 7:5). At the same time, the Spirit-renewed believer is alive because of righteousness (8:10) and his mind is directed toward life and peace (8:6).

Although Paul does not use the same word for "mind" in 8:6 (φρόνημα) as in 7:14-25 (νοῦς; vv. 21,23,25), the subject of his discussion is clearly the same. In both sections the "mind" is renewed by the Spirit and is determined to live according to God's will and the Spirit's leading.[34] In both instances the "inner man" is distraught by sin's presence in his flesh and his own existence in a mortal body (7:21,24; 8:10). He is crying out (7:24) and groaning inwardly (8:23) for the day of its redemption when all creation will be restored. It is only then that "the one who raised Jesus Christ from the dead will also

---

[34]Dunn, *Romans 1-8*, 388, properly argues that Paul can envision only a Christian serving God's Law as the "I" does in 7:14-25 and as Paul portrays the Christian doing in Chapter 8. Gerd Theissen, *Psychological Aspects of Pauline Theology*, tr. J. Galvin (Philadelphia: Fortress Press, 1987), 233, recognizes this as the fundamental difference between 7:7-11 and the verses to follow. See also Ulrich Wilckens, *Der Brief an die Römer*, 3 vols., Evangelisch-Katholischer Kommentar, Band 6, eds. J. Blank, R. Schnackenburg, and U. Wilckens (Zürich: Benziger Verlag and Neukirchen-Vluyn: Neukirchener Verlag, 1980), 2:85, n. 344.

make your mortal bodies alive" (8:11). Until that day, the flesh no longer dominates or determines the existence of the believer. But it still proves to be an unavoidable obstacle because of sin's ability to work through it. For Paul, the solution to this dilemma is *not* the Law's command (7:14-8:3a), but the work of Jesus Christ and the presence of his Spirit (8:3b-39).

In view of these similarities, it is difficult to comprehend how such a deep wedge could have been driven between Romans 7:25 and 8:1. The difference between the two sections is not at all the spiritual condition of the subject. Rather, in 7:14-25 the believer is viewed from the perspective of his struggle to live in accordance with the Law. In Chapter 8 we see the same believer from the perspective of the assistance provided by the Holy Spirit who has already guaranteed the outcome of the believer's struggle in this world against sin and the flesh.   C. E. B. Cranfield concludes,

> It is possible to do justice to the text of Paul . . . only if we resolutely hold Chapters 7 and 8 together, in spite of the obvious tension between them, and see in them not two successive stages but two different aspects, two contemporaneous realities, of the Christian life, both of which continue so long as the Christian is in the flesh.[35]

Although they provide less material that is directly pertinent,[36] Romans 9-16 are by no means irrelevant to the topic under consideration here.[37] As Paul turns to address practical and ethical issues in Chapters 12-13, his statements in Chapters 5-8 clearly serve as the integral basis. Paul begins Romans 12 by urging Christians to yield their bodies to God (12:1; as in 6:19). They are only able to do so

---

[35]Cranfield, 1:356; see also Pate, 108-16.

[36]A few points from the chapters which will not be discussed extensively may be noted. In 10:4 Paul asserts that "Christ is the end of the Law for righteousness to every one who believes." In 14:9 Paul concludes that Christ has died and risen again in order that he, and not sin, death, or the Law, might exercise lordship (κυριεύω) over all and especially over those who belong to him. In 15:14 Paul reveals that his addressees are not borderline or "lapsing" believers. On the contrary, he writes, "And I have been persuaded, my brothers, even I myself, concerning you that you yourselves are indeed full of goodness, having been filled with all knowledge, and being able to admonish one another."

[37]As Kümmel, *Römer 7*, 27, claims regarding Chapters 12-16.

because, like the "I" in Romans 7:14-25, they have been inwardly transformed by the renewal of their mind (νοῦς; 12:2; also 7:21,23,25). Even though sin is an ever present reality in their flesh which will repeatedly hinder them, Paul urges these Christians to live in accordance with God's good, holy, and acceptable will (12:2) as it is revealed to them in the Law (2:20; 7:12; 13:8-10).

Paul's exhortations throughout Chapters 12-13 are prompted by his recognition that sin is still able to work in the fleshly members of these believers, even through the Law. So he urges, "Put on the Lord Jesus Christ, and make no provision for the desires of the flesh" (13:14). This verse makes the clearest application of the situation portrayed in Romans 7:14-25, and it is one made to Christians. Their flesh is "sold under sin" (7:14). As a result, they must give no forethought to its desires which are readily manipulated by sin and directed toward evil. They are to struggle against the sinful flesh as the "I" does in 7:14-25.

But notice that Paul does not direct these Christians to their own "renewed minds" for a solution to this dilemma. Neither does he point them to the Law's command which they are striving to fulfill (13:8-10). Rather, they are to "put on the Lord Jesus Christ" (13:14). Why? Because while the Law does inform their will, it also continues to identify them as sinners in the flesh. Therefore Paul directs them to look in faith toward the Lord Jesus Christ, to clothe themselves with his righteousness, and to rely upon the Spirit whom he gives.

Within the context of the letter to the Romans, the "I" of 7:14-25 can be understood as depicting one valid aspect of the life of a believer who has been justified by faith and who still lives in this world in the flesh. While the "I" in 7:14-25 remains a sinner, the crucial difference between Paul's "blanket condemnation" of all people in 1:18-3:20 and the discussion in Chapter 7 is the intervention of the sacrificial death of Jesus Christ (3:21-26), a death in which the "I" has participated by Baptism (6:3-6; 7:4,6).

In Paul's other letters he makes numerous statements about the Christian life. The vast number of references Paul makes to the believer's life renders a complete survey impossible. The purpose here is to conduct a brief sketch of Paul's view of the Christian life specifically with the issues surrounding the "I" of Romans 7:14-25 in view. This survey asks whether or not the statements of the "I" can be placed within the Christian life as Paul portrays it elsewhere.

Though some Pauline passages present a challenge to identifying the "I" in Romans 7:14-25 as a Christian, none of them excludes it.[38] On the other hand, a number of passages support and confirm the conclusions made above. In Romans 7:14-25, Paul is utilizing warfare imagery to describe the on-going battle of the Christian life. This fits a *Christus Victor* motif which recognizes that,

> In the Christ-event, the decisive battle was fought and the gifts of the Age to Come were bestowed. Therefore, the final victory is assured. But the enemy did not disappear immediately; there are still battles to be fought. Yet it is only a matter of time until the final *coup de grace* (= the parousia/second coming).[39]

As a result, the passages most relevant to Paul's discussion in Romans 7:14-25 are those which utilize similar imagery and/or the same motif.

In his letters, Paul's conception of the Christian life begins with the believer's stance *coram Deo*.[40] "For the one who commends himself, that one is not approved, but the one whom the Lord

---

[38]This "challenge" is often due to Paul's use of antinomous models to describe the believer's existence. For descriptions of the different models in the New Testament, see James Voelz, *What Does This Mean?* (St. Louis: Concordia Publishing House, 1995) 252-56. Voelz identifies these three biblical motifs: 1) the "*Christus Victor* motif" which is prominent in the Synoptic Gospels and often utilizes battle imagery (as Rom. 7:14-25); 2) "the essential Pauline 'in Christ' (ἐν Χριστῷ) viewpoint (2 Cor. 5:17; Rom. 8:39; 2 Cor. 1:20)"; and 3) the hidden reality motif common in Johannine literature (note also 2 Cor. 5:7; Col. 3:4). The presence of these antinomous models in Paul's thought is also recognized by E. P. Sanders, *Paul and Palestinian Judaism* (Philadelphia: Fortress Press, 1977) who distinguishes, 495, between Paul's use of "forensic" and "participatory" categories. He concludes, 502-8, that while the two may overlap, the latter contains "the real bite of his theology." The participatory "in Christ" model, for example, is utilized almost exclusively when Paul discusses ethical issues; see ibid., 439-40. Identifying which of theses different "categories" or "models" is being utilized by Paul in a particular section is very helpful for interpretation. One should resist the temptation to synthesize all of Paul's expressions by coalescing these various models. The tensions which exist between them should be allowed to stand.

[39]Voelz, *What Does This Mean?*, 252; cf. Pate, 71-121.

[40]Kümmel, *Das Bild des Menschen*, 179, states, "Thus Paul also, like Jesus, sees the person exclusively as a being standing over against God" ("*Auch Paulus sieht also wie Jesus den Menschen ausschliesslich als Gott gegenüberstehendes Wesen*"); see also 196-97. This is further indicated by Col. 1:22; and 1 Thess. 3:13 as cited below. The same applies to unbelievers as well.

commends" (2 Cor. 10:18). A repeated emphasis is that it is God who has saved the believer through the Gospel Paul proclaims. This "good news" is God's redemption of the world through the suffering, death, and resurrection of Jesus Christ.[41] The Gospel Paul preaches not only announces, but also delivers, the forgiveness of sins which is received by the believer wholly and only through faith.[42]

The Christian's holiness or sanctification also comes from God and is based upon the Gospel of Jesus Christ. This was ingrained in Paul by Christ himself. In his defense before King Agrippa, Paul relates Jesus' commissioning words to him:

> *I* am sending you to open their eyes, so that they may turn from darkness to light and from the power of Satan to God, so that they may receive the forgiveness of sins and an inheritance among those who have been sanctified by faith in me (Acts 26:17b-18).

So Paul announces, "God reconciled you in the body of [Jesus'] flesh through death to present you holy and without blemish and without accusation before him" (Col. 1:22; see also Eph. 5:25-27; Tit. 2:14). It is Jesus who strengthens the hearts of believers so that they will be "blameless in holiness before our God and Father" (1 Thess. 3:13). It is God's efficacious will which effects sanctification (1 Thess. 4:3). It is God who has called you "in holiness" (1 Thess. 4:7). This is Paul's prayer for the Thessalonians:

> And may the God of peace himself sanctify you entirely, and may your spirit, soul and body be kept complete, blameless at the coming of our Lord Jesus Christ (1 Thess. 5:23).

Paul even identifies Jesus Christ as our "righteousness, holiness (ἁγιασμός) and redemption" (1 Cor. 1:30). All of this shows that the holiness which Paul ascribes to the believer comes from outside of oneself. It is not based upon one's holy conduct, but accomplished by

---

[41] 1 Cor. 1:18,21; 15:2; 2 Cor. 4:6; 13:4; Gal. 1:4; Eph. 1:5,13; 2:5-9,13,19; Col. 1:12-13; 2:6,10-13; 3:1; 1 Thess. 5:9; 2 Tim. 1:9-10; Tit. 3:4-5.

[42] 1 Cor. 4:7 asks, "What do you have that you did not receive?" See also Acts 13:38-39; 16:31; 2 Cor. 9:14; Gal. 3:25

God in Jesus Christ (1 Cor. 6:11) and received through faith. The
Christian is holy because he possesses the holiness of Christ, not
because he lives a holy life in obedience to God's Law. This allows for
the possibility that the believer whom Paul describes as holy can also
be in the situation depicted in Romans 7:14-25.

Paul's understanding of the life which a Christian possesses is
succinctly summed up in Ephesians 2. It was in Christ that God made
us alive (2:5). "For by grace you have been and remain saved (perfect
passive periphrastic of σῳζω) through faith; and this is not from
yourselves, [it is] the gift of God, not from works [of the Law!]" (ἐξ
ἔργων; Eph. 2:8-9a; see Romans 3:21,28). The saving act
accomplished in Christ comes to and remains with a believer by God's
effective grace. This new life begins at the point of conversion, but
Paul does not speak of the Gospel in terms of one shot of
forgiveness.[43] The forgiveness promised in the Gospel and received by
faith covers all of the believer's life, past, present, and future, so long
as he remains in faith. Since our righteousness before God lies in
Christ, Paul can conclude that even "if we are faithless, he [Christ
Jesus] remains faithful; for he cannot deny himself" (2 Tim. 2:13). The
believer receives all of this as the gift of God διὰ πίστεως. Paul
expresses this vividly in his thanksgiving prayer for the Thessalonians,

> But *we* ought to give thanks to God always concerning you, brothers
> having been loved by the Lord, because God chose you from the
> beginning for salvation in [the] sanctification of [the] Spirit and by faith
> in the truth (2 Thess. 2:13).

This last passage reveals that the Holy Spirit has a decisive role in
the saving and sanctifying work of God.[44] Because of God's saving
action in Christ and the sanctifying work of his Spirit, Paul prays that
believers may be, and even speaks of them as, pure, blameless, and
holy (Phil. 1:10; Col. 1:22; see also Phil. 2:14-16a; Col. 4:12; 1 Tim.
5:22). Since God has made them holy, when Paul turns to exhort
Christians to live a holy life, he is in essence saying, "Be what you

---

[43] As indicated already in Rom. 3:24-25 and 8:26,34 (see Chapter Two above).

[44] See, for example, 1 Cor. 2:13; 3:16; 6:11; 12:3; 2 Cor. 1:22; 3:17; 4:13; 6:16;
Gal. 4:6; 5:16,18,25; Eph. 1:13,17-20a; 3:16-19; 4:30; 1 Thess. 1:6; 2 Thess. 2:16-17;
2 Tim. 1:7,14; Tit. 3:5.

already are."[45] This is the motivation behind Paul's ethical directives to Christians. Their holiness is not based upon their own actions but upon God's. "Be what you already are" is a proper interpretation and application of the relationship between the indicative and the imperative which forms "the basic structure of Pauline ethics."[46]

> Paul understands exhortations to be directly related to the basic soteriological conception of Christ's death and resurrection—they cannot be divided.[47]

It is evident that the Gospel underlies Paul's pleas for holy living when he writes,

---

[45]This phrase is borrowed from Martin Scharlemann, "Exodus Ethics," *Concordia Journal* 2 (1976):169.

[46]This is the title of Dennison's article which gives a historical overview of the development of the relationship between the indicative and imperative moods in Pauline studies. Ridderbos, 253, defines the relationship as follows, "What is meant is that the new life in its moral manifestation is at one time proclaimed and posited as the fruit of the redemptive work of God in Christ through the Holy Spirit—the indicative; elsewhere, however, it is put with no less force as a categorical demand—the imperative." Dennison, 57-58, points out that Paul Wernle, *Der Christ und die Sünde bei Paulus* (Freiburg i. B. und Leipzig: Akademische Verlagsbuchhandlung von J. C. B. Mohr, 1897), first formulated this concept but saw the imperative as a contradiction since sin is no longer a factor in the Christian's life. The indicative/imperative relationship was interpreted as the basis for Pauline ethics by Rudolf Bultmann, "Das Problem der Ethik bei Paulus," *Zeitschrift für die neutestamentliche Wissenschaft und die Kunde der älteren Kirche* 23 (1924):123-40; an English translation is available in *The Old and New Man in the Letters of Paul*, 7-32; see also idem., *Theology of the New Testament*, 2:332-33; Victor Furnish, *Theology and Ethics in Paul*, especially 9,207-27.
Paul uses the imperative to direct believers to be what God has already made them, that is, to exhibit the actual state of their present existence by faith. The indicative expresses what believers are in reality, not merely "in principle" as suggested by Hermann Jacoby, *Neutestamentliche Ethik* (Konigsberg i. Pr.: Verlag von Thomas und Oppermann, 1899), 316-17; cited from Dennison, 58, notes 11,13. Bornkamm, "Baptism and New Life in Paul (Romans 6)," 84, demonstrates that "all the imperatives of Paul have their basis in what has happened to us through Christ in baptism."

[47]Dennison, 69.

Therefore, *having these promises*, beloved, let us purify ourselves from every defilement of flesh and spirit, perfecting holiness in the fear of God (2 Cor. 7:1).

Therefore, just *as you received Christ Jesus the Lord*, continue to live in him, having been rooted and being built up in him, being established in the faith just as you were taught, increasing in thanksgiving (Col. 2:6-7).

This explains Paul's view of how sanctification exhibits itself in daily life. Both as it comes into and then flows from the lives of believers, it is God's doing (Phil. 1:6,10; 2:12-13; 2 Thess. 1:11; 1 Tim. 6:14). So Paul can speak of those in Christ as lacking nothing. He tells the Corinthians,

You were enriched in every way in him, in every word and in all knowledge, just as the testimony of Christ was confirmed in you, so that you are not lacking in any spiritual gift (1 Cor. 1:5-7a).[48]

In contrast to unbelievers, "the one who is spiritual appraises all things" (1 Cor. 2:15).[49] Because they are the Lord's, believers are enabled to abound "in everything, [in] faith and speech and knowledge and all eagerness" (2 Cor. 8:7).

The manner in which Paul describes Christians, as seen above, has convinced many that the "I" in Romans 7:14-25 cannot be a Christian. However, Paul nowhere asserts that the Christian only does good or that it is even possible for a believer to do so. Rather, his point in these passages is that all of the good which a Christian does springs from the forgiveness, the holiness, and the hope which God has planted within him. That is, a believer has been transformed and enlightened by God so that he desires to do "every good deed and word" (Eph. 1:17-18; 2 Thess. 2:16-17). The picture Paul paints of the Christian is comparable to the manner in which he describes the will, the mind, and the inner man of the "I" in Romans 7:14-25 who earnestly strives to do the good

---

[48]One can possibly recognize a sarcastic tone when Paul makes similar assertions in 1 Cor. 4:7-8. There he compares the Corinthians' standing with that of the apostles. However, nothing detracts from the genuineness of his statement here.

[49]See D. W. B. Robinson, "St. Paul's Spiritual Man," *The Reformed Theological Review* 36 (1977):78-83, who concludes, 83, that in this passage "Paul's 'spiritual man' is one who, his own spirit being receptive to the Spirit of God, is guided and governed by the truths of divine revelation."

as laid down in God's Law (θέλω in 7:15,18,19; νοῦς in vv. 23,25; ὁ ἔσω ἄνθρωπος in v. 22).[50]

The absence of a specific reference to the Holy Spirit in Romans 7:14-25 has also been pointed to as indicating that the "I" there cannot be a Christian. Yet in 7:6 Paul speaks of believers as those who serve the Law "in [the] newness of the Spirit" and the "I" in verse 14 acknowledges that "the Law is πνευματικός." The "I" is able to appraise the Law as spiritual, something which is impossible for unbelievers according to Paul (1 Cor. 2:15), and desires to serve it willingly. In addition, when one considers the progression of the argument in Romans 5-8 as discussed above, the reason why Paul withholds a detailed treatment of the Holy Spirit's activity in the life of the believer for Chapter 8 also becomes apparent.

Another vital factor in Paul's teaching on the Holy Spirit was prominent in Romans 8. Not only does the Spirit seal and guarantee that we are now God's children (Gal. 4:4-6; Eph. 1:5); the Spirit is also is "a down payment" or "pledge" concerning what is to come (ἀρραβών; 2 Cor. 1:22 and 5:5).[51] The Spirit is the guarantee of our inheritance as heirs which awaits us at the day of redemption when Christ returns (Gal. 4:7; Eph. 1:13; 5:18; Tit. 3:13; cf. Acts 20:32).

There is clearly, then, both a "now" and a "not yet" aspect to the present Christian life, or an overlapping between this age and the age to come.[52] For example, in Ephesians 1 Paul speaks of redemption in

---

[50]But why does Paul present only those occasions in which the "I" fails to do what his will desires in Rom. 7:14-25? A recognition of Paul's purpose in Romans 7 explains this; see Chapter Five below.

[51]On this, see especially Geerhardus Vos, "The Eschatological Aspect of the Pauline Conception of the Spirit," in *Biblical and Theological Studies* (New York: Charles Scribner's Sons, 1912), 211-259, who contends, 241, "The present Spirit is an anticipation of the future Spirit."

[52]For the key developments in this recognition, see Pate; also E. Earle Ellis, *Paul and His Recent Interpreters* (Grand Rapids: Eerdmans Publishing, 1961), 32-34. See also Albert Schweitzer, *The Mysticism of Paul the Apostle*, tr. W. Montgomery (New York: Seabury Press, 1968); idem., *Paul and His Interpreters*, tr. W. Montgomery, A Crossroad Book, (New York: Macmillan, 1950); C. H. Dodd, *The Parables of the Kingdom of God* (London: Nisbet, 1950); and Oscar Cullmann, *Christ and Time*, rev. ed. (Philadelphia: Westminster Press, 1968); idem., *Salvation in History*, tr. S. Sowers and the editorial staff of SCM Press (London: SCM Press, 1967). Dunn, "Rom. 7,14-25 in the Theology of Paul," 264-65, contends that the tension between the two "underlies the whole of Paul's soteriology."

two ways. In verse 7 he affirms that in Christ "we *have redemption* through his blood, the forgiveness of sins" (also Rom. 3:34; Col. 1:14). Yet in verse 14 the Holy Spirit "is a down payment of our inheritance *until the redemption* of those who are God's possession" (as in Rom. 8:23).[53] There is both a present life and a life to come (1 Tim. 4:8). Paul even points out that without the guaranteed promise to be fulfilled at Christ's return, believers are most pitied (1 Cor. 15:19), trapped in world that is passing away (1 Cor. 7:31), and, along with that world, destined for wrath (1 Thess. 1:10; 5:9). As a result, an element of eager anticipation permeates the Christian's life as we await Christ's return with great hope (Phil. 3:20; Col. 1:5; 1 Thess. 1:10; Tit. 1:2; 2:13). Is this not similar to the situation of the "distressed 'I'" in Romans 7:14-25 who acknowledges Christ as Lord but also cries out for a deliverance yet to come (vv. 24-25)?

In the midst of the "not yet," the Gospel gives this assurance: "God both raised the Lord and he will also raise us through his power" (1 Cor. 6:14). Though Christians are already alive before God by faith even while in this world, they await a resurrection with Christ in which they will share fully in his glory (1 Cor. 15:49-51; Col. 3:4; 2 Tim. 2:10-11). The "I" in Romans 7 similarly yearns for that day (7:24) when "the surpassing riches of his grace" are revealed (Eph. 2:7). Then, Paul says, we will bear his likeness (1 Cor. 15:49), reign with him (2 Tim. 2:12), and receive the citizenship and crown of righteousness which are stored up for us in heaven (Phil. 3:20; Col. 1:5; 2 Tim. 4:8).

Until the day of Christ's return, Christians run as in a race (1 Cor. 9:24). Although their salvation and sanctification come totally from God and are not dependent upon the actions of their present Christian life (Eph. 2:8-9), believers are depicted by Paul as progressing (1 Tim. 4:15). Their faith is growing and their love increasing (2 Thess. 1:3). They are striving for unity, maturity, and "the measure of the stature of the fullness of Christ" (Eph. 4:13; also 2 Tim. 3:17). In short, they strive to discern "what is pleasing to the Lord" and to do "good works" (Eph. 5:10; 2:10). Yet even this growth in the sanctified life is seen by

---

[53]Dunn, "Rom. 7,14-25 in the Theology of Paul," 265, n. 41, points out that this is also the case in regard to justification (compare Rom. 5:1 with Gal. 5:5) and salvation (compare Rom. 5:9-10; 13:11; 1 Thess. 5:8-10 with 1 Cor. 1:18; 15:2; 2 Cor. 2:15; Eph. 2:5,8).

Paul as the work of God. He consistently uses the passive voice to express what God is working in them. Those in the Spirit "are *being* transformed" (2 Cor. 3:18) and their "new self . . . is *being* renewed in knowledge according to the image of the One who created it" (Col. 3:10).

The Gospel according to Paul, then, declares that God has won salvation for his elect in the blood of Jesus Christ and delivered it to them through the Gospel message. He has sanctified and sealed them with the Holy Spirit. Through the Spirit God then enables believers to stand firm in faith and has guaranteed their inheritance in heaven. All this comes from God and is received through faith. The life of the believer is, by God's power, to be one of striving to live in accordance with God's holy will. But does this exclude the possibility that the "I" in Romans 7:14-25 is a Christian? In a number of ways Paul indicates that this is not the case.

Paul repeatedly emphasizes that no one, including believers, can rely on themselves for their holiness before God precisely because he understands that Christians are not yet perfect. In writing to the Corinthian congregation, Paul contends that their knowledge is not yet what it ought to be (1 Cor. 8:2). They need to excel further in spiritual gifts (1 Cor. 14:12). They are thinking as infants (1 Cor. 14:20; also 3:1-3). Yet these descriptions cannot be limited merely to the "weak" believers in Corinth. Paul also is waiting for Christ to be formed in the Galatian Christians (Gal. 4:19). All believers need "admonishing" and "teaching" (Col. 1:28). The Thessalonians' faith is not yet complete (1 Thess. 3:10) and the Philippians continue to have differences in their thinking (Phil. 3:15). So in Ephesians Paul looks ahead to the day when "we will no longer be infants, being driven by the waves and carried around by every wind of teaching in the fraud of men, in every trickery to the scheming of deceit; but speaking the truth in love, we may grow up in all things into him who is the Head, Christ" (Eph. 4:14-15).

Paul speaks of this continuing progress in the sanctified life in the following manner: "But if our outer man is decaying, the inner [man] is being renewed day by day" (2 Cor. 4:16). This is the same condition as the "inner man" of Romans 7 who joyfully agrees with God's Law and strives to live according to it (v. 22). The fact that Paul is aware that Christians have not yet reached complete maturity is also evidenced by his many prayers that God would work to accomplish this in them (Eph. 1:17-19; 3:16-19; Col. 1:9-12a,28; 2:2-3; 1 Thess. 3:10).

Why are believers not yet complete or mature in their thinking and living? On the one hand, it is because they continue to live in this present evil age (Gal. 1:4; Phil. 2:15). Although Paul urges Christians to separate themselves from the uncleanness of this world (2 Cor. 6:17-18), he does not command them to attempt to withdraw from the world (1 Cor. 5:9-11). Instead, the believer is to remain in the earthly situation he was in when God called him (1 Cor. 7:17,20). As long as the Christian is in the world, Paul sees him engaged in a constant, life-long struggle "against the powers of this dark world" (Eph. 6:12; cf. 1 Cor. 7:33; 2 Cor. 1:5-7; 2 Thess. 1:5; 3:3; 2 Tim. 3:12).

In addition to looking at the world around him to discern what is battling against the will of God, the Christian must also look at himself. There he can even more clearly see what prohibits him from reaching maturity, perfection, or completeness in this life. This is the area in which Paul speaks of Christians in a manner that most directly parallels his description of the "I" in Romans 7:14-25. As in Romans 5-8, Paul declares that the believer's existence is no longer enslaved and dominated by the flesh. Paul tells Christians that in Christ "you were also circumcised with a circumcision not made by human hands, in the putting off of the body of the flesh, in the circumcision of Christ" (Col. 2:11; see also Gal. 5:24). Yet this does not tell the whole story. The believer continues to live in the flesh (2 Cor. 10:3; Philemon 16; see also Gal. 2:20; Phil. 1:22) and must struggle against it. Why is this so?

First, Paul portrays the fleshly body as being weak and hindering even those in whom the Spirit dwells from attaining the fullness of life with God. He speaks of this lowly body (Phil. 3:21) as a jar of clay in which we are afflicted, perplexed, persecuted, and struck down (2 Cor. 4:7-11). He portrays this earthly body as a tent in which "we groan, while being burdened" (2 Cor. 5:4; also vv. 1-3).

Second, the fleshly body in which the believer lives is mortal (ἐν τῇ θνητῇ σαρκί in 2 Cor. 4:11; compare 5:4; Rom. 6:12). The believer's body remains a perishable one, "sown in dishonor, . . . sown in weakness, . . . sown a natural body" (σῶμα ψυχικόν; 1 Cor. 15:42-44). This is the same manner in which the "I" views his "body of death" in Romans 7:24. For Paul, the believer's body will remain so until "the last trumpet" (1 Cor. 15:52). Then, at the resurrection of the dead, the fleshly body will be changed by Jesus Christ himself (1 Cor. 15:51-54). Then and only then will Christ clothe this body and make it an imperishable, immortal, Spiritual body (1 Cor. 15:42-44,53-54). It is only on that day, when "death is swallowed up in victory" (1 Cor. 15:54; citing Is. 25:8), that what is mortal in the flesh will be "swallowed up by life" (2 Cor. 5:4). This is the day for which the "I" yearns in Romans 7:24. σάρξ, then, is often used by Paul even of Christians to denote the "mortal body, [the] body dominated by weakness and corruptibility."[54]

In the third place, Paul pictures the σάρξ as full of sin and actively engaged in a struggle against that which the Spirit of God wills in the believer. The desires of the sinful flesh provide a constant foe to be battled. For example, Paul reminds Christians that they were taught to put off "the old man (τὸν παλαιὸν ἄνθρωπον) which is being corrupted according to the desires of deceit" (κατὰ τὰς ἐπιθυμίας ἀπάτης, Eph. 4:22; compare Rom. 6:6). He implores the Colossians,

> Put to death, therefore, the members (τὰ μέλη) which are upon the earth, sexual immorality, impurity, passion, evil desire (ἐπιθυμίαν κακήν) and greed, which is idolatry (Col. 3:5; for τὰ μέλη, compare Rom. 7:23; 6:13).

How is the believer to fight against the desires of the flesh? Paul points out that ascetic regulations and angel worship are of no value against the "indulgence of the flesh" (πλησμονὴν τῆς σαρκός; Col. 2:23). Rather, with vocabulary reminiscent of Romans 7 and as in the transition to Romans 8, Paul directs the Galatian Christians to the power of the Spirit in them.

> For you were called for freedom, brothers; only [do] not [use] freedom for an opportunity (ἀφορμήν) in the flesh. . . . But I say, live by the Spirit and you will *not* complete the desire of the flesh (ἐπιθυμίαν σαρκός). For the flesh desires [what is] against the Spirit, and the Spirit against the flesh. For these are opposing one another, with the result that you do not do the things which you will (θέλητε; Gal. 5:13,16-17).[55]

---

[54]Ibid., 266.

[55]Fung, 37, contends that this section of Galatians "irresistibly recalls that of

These passages reveal that the desires of the flesh, *even in the Christian*, are always directed toward evil in opposition to the believer's θέλω which is led by God's Spirit. For Paul, Christians are engaged in a constant struggle against the flesh until their death or the resurrection of the dead at Christ's return (1 Cor. 15:54: 2 Cor. 5:4). As long as a believer remains in the natural, mortal, and perishable body (1 Cor. 15:42-44), the flesh and its desires will always direct him toward evil and strive to keep him from doing the good which he wills (Gal. 5:17). Although the sinful flesh cannot be completely defeated, it must be constantly opposed.

Although his purpose in the various passages we have examined may vary, the descriptions Paul makes of the Christian's life in the flesh are certainly comparable to the situation of the "I" in Romans 7:14-25.[56] This brings us close to a determination of the point Paul is making in Romans 7. Since the sinful flesh is able to make the believer do what is contrary to both God's Law and one's own will (Gal. 5:17; Rom. 7:15-16,19,21), Paul excludes the possibility that even the Christian might base any assurance before God on his own flesh. Indeed, Paul defines those who possess a circumcision which is valid before God as

> The ones who are worshipping by the Spirit of God and who are boasting in Christ Jesus and who have not put confidence in the flesh (Phil 3:3).

According to Paul the disparity between will and action, which is so characteristic of the "I" in Romans 7:14-25, is completely absent in unbelievers. Their mind or will and their flesh are united in serving themselves and doing evil. However, a conflict between the Spirit-renewed mind and the sinful flesh is an unavoidable one for believers. The mark of the Christian is the indwelling and renewal of the Holy Spirit[57] who continually renews and works within the will or inner man

---

Romans 7."

[56]For example, Kümmel, *Römer 7*, 105-6, argues that Gal. 5:17 is not a legitimate parallel to Romans 7:14-25. Paul's purpose may not be the same in both sections, so Kümmel is in a sense correct. Nevertheless, the two passages certainly illuminate each other, particularly in regard to the role of the flesh and its implications for Christian living.

[57]As recognized by Kümmel, ibid., 104.

of the believer to battle what previously reigned (Rom. 7:16,22; 2 Cor. 10:4; Gal. 5:17). This struggle is, in fact, a sign of the Spirit's presence and of the life which the Spirit brings as Paul makes clear in Romans 8.

> Spiritual conflict is the sign of life—a sign that the Spirit is having his say in the shaping of character. Since life now must be life in this body of flesh, the Spirit can be present only as paradox and conflict.[58]

In a general way, then, Paul urges Christians who are engaged in this battle to be what God has already made them. The basis of Paul's exhortations to Christians is God's saving and sanctifying action. His use of

> the imperative expresses the total redemption of the believer because it is first grounded in the indicative and, secondly, through the Spirit of God the believer is obedient by rebelling against sin.[59]

God has made the believer pure and holy in Christ. Paul then holds up the goal that the conduct of believers be worthy of the Lord Jesus and of the God who has called them.[60] The ability to do "the will of God from the soul" (ἐκ ψυχῆς; Eph. 6:6) comes only through the gift of the Spirit by whom Paul encourages Christians to

> be made new in the Spirit of your mind (τῷ πμεύματι τοῦ νοός) and to put on the new man, the one created in accordance with God in righteousness and holiness of the truth (Eph. 4:23-24).

So it is that the will, mind, and inner man of the "I" in Romans 7:14-25 desire to live in accordance with the Spirit-filled Law as it directs him away from evil and toward what is "holy, just, and good" (7:12,14).

Paul is clearly cognizant of the enduring battle of the Christian life. In this struggle the desires of the flesh are always directed toward evil

---

[58]Dunn, "Rom. 7,14-25 in the Theology of Paul," 272; he concludes, "Consequently it is this paradox and conflict which is the mark of healthy religious experience—not its absence." See also Cranfield, 1:342,359.

[59]Dennison, 73.

[60]See, for example, 2 Cor. 5:15; Eph. 4:1; 5:8; Phil. 1:27; Col. 1:10; 1 Thess. 2:12; 1 Tim. 5:22; Tit. 2:11-12.

and against the good (Gal. 5:16-17). The sinful nature continues to inhere in the flesh. It is unreformable and, in fact, "sold under sin" (Rom. 7:14). But the Spirit has renewed the mind of the believer who now strives to do "the will of God from the soul" (Eph. 6:6; Rom. 7:18,19,21) and who fights against these fleshly desires.

Paul, therefore, acknowledges that moral perfection is not the ultimate goal of the Christian life, nor is it attainable in this world.[61] He envisions that believers will stumble by falling into sin and failing to do good as they should. They will fall short in their efforts to accomplish the good laid down in God's Law and to abstain from the evil it forbids (Gal. 5:17). In other words, the frustrated outcome portrayed in Romans 7:14-25 conveys one legitimate aspect which results from the believer's desire to live according to God's will in this age.

Although the believer does not always fail, in a number of passages Paul recognizes that sin is still present and active among believers and, at times, even publicly within the church. This is especially evident in the Corinthian letters. It is not, however, a scenario exclusive to them (see Eph. 4:32; Col. 3:13). For example, in Galatians Paul discusses the implications of the following:

> But if seeking to be justified in Christ, even we ourselves are found to be sinners, is Christ then a servant of sin? May it never be! (2:17).[62]

He later warns them, "But if you keep on biting and devouring one another, watch out lest you be consumed by one another" (5:15; see also 6:1). Paul inquires of the Colossians, "Since you died with Christ from the elemental principles of this world, why, as if living in the world, do you submit yourselves [to them]?" (2:20). Among the Thessalonian believers he hears of some who are idle busybodies (2 Thess. 3:11).

In his first letter to Corinth, Paul openly and extensively deals with the presence of sin within the congregation. Yet Paul does not

---

[61]This is recognized by Kümmel, *Römer 7*, 101-2.

[62]A variety of interpretations of this verse have been made. For an overview, see Jan Lambrecht, "The Line of Thought in Gal. 2. 14b-21, *New Testament Studies* 24 (1977):484-95.

generally question the faith of these believers.[63] On the contrary, he exalts and praises it (1 Cor. 1:2-9)! But concerning their instruction in the faith and their living it out in daily life he must add,

> And *I*, brothers, was not able to speak to you as spiritual but as worldly, as infants in Christ. I gave you milk to drink, not solid food; for you were not yet able [to receive it]. But you are still now not able. *For you are still fleshly* (σαρκικοί; cf., Rom. 7:14). For since there is jealousy and quarreling among you, are you not fleshly and living according to [the ways of] man? (1 Cor. 3:1-3).[64]

Paul rebukes them for their quarrels (1 Cor. 1:11) and their tolerance of immorality and other vices within the congregation (5:1-2,9-11). He denounces the presence of legal disputes among them which are being taken before civil judges (6:1-7), and their cheating and doing wrong (6:8). He condemns their conduct in meeting together to share the Lord's Supper (11:17-34) and the teaching of those among them who deny the resurrection of the dead (15:12). In a sense Paul writes to shame them: "Come to your senses righteously and stop sinning; for certain ones have ignorance of God, I say [this] to your shame" (15:34; also 6:5). Yet he also states, "I am not writing these things to shame you, but to warn you, as dear children" (4:14).

In 2 Corinthians, these believers have turned away from some of their gross failings (2:5-17; 7). Yet Paul is still aware that they might be deceived by the sinful flesh and led astray from pure and sincere devotion to Christ (11:3). He writes,

> For I am afraid that perhaps when I come I may find you to be not what I wish . . . [there may be] strife, jealousy, outbursts of anger, factions, slanders, gossip, arrogance, disturbance (12:20b).

However, the following verse reveals the key reason why Paul is distraught. He adds,

---

[63]The only exception is the immoral and unrepentant man who should be "delivered over" to Satan (1 Cor. 5:5). In 5:13 Paul applies Deut. 13:5 to this "so-called" brother in commanding, "Remove the wicked man from among yourselves."

[64]According to Murray, 1:260, this passage proves that "ἐγὼ σάρκινός" in Rom. 7:14 can be a description of the Christian.

I am afraid that when I come again . . . I may mourn over many of those who have sinned in the past and not repented of the impurity, sexual immorality, and sensual living which they have practiced (12:21).

Paul will not spare those who have not repented (13:2).

Because of the believer's presence in this world and due to the sinful nature of his own flesh, Paul is aware that continued sin is an inescapable fact of Christian life and that sin may even rear its head publicly within the Christian congregation.

Conclusion

Paul's view of the Christian life allows Romans 7:14-25 to be understood as a presentation of the continued, but embattled, influence of the sinful flesh in the Christian's life. The disparity between will and action exemplified by these verses is present in a person "not as a result of creation (or the fall), but primarily as the result of redemption."[65]

The reality of the overlapping of the two ages manifests itself in the idea of *struggle* in the Christian life. For Paul, the proof that a person is genuinely Christian is the fact that he or she is engaged in an inner conflict.[66]

So the "I" in Romans 7:14-25 can only be representing the Spirit-renewed mind or will of a believer who strives, in accordance with God's Law, to refrain from evil and to do good.

Chapter Three concluded that the referent of the "I" in Romans 7:7-25 is Paul. On the basis of the content of the other references Paul makes to his pre-Christian life, it was determined that verses 7-11 depict the role of the Law in his life prior to his conversion from the perspective he gained after his encounter on the Damascus road. At the same time, the content of those passages indicates that the "I" in verses 14-25 is not Paul's description of himself prior to his conversion.

This chapter agrees with that conclusion. The manner in which Paul portrays the "I" in Romans 7:14-25 is also incompatible with the

---

[65]Dunn, *Romans 1-8*, 394.

[66]Pate, 103.

characterization he makes of unbelievers in Romans and throughout his letters. On the basis of Pauline theology as a whole, it is impossible to believe that he would attribute to any unbeliever, including himself, the conflict present within, and recognized by, the "I" in these verses.

An examination of the sense of those passages in which Paul speaks about his own life as a Christian pointed toward, but did not decisively prove, the conclusion that Romans 7:14-25 describes an aspect of his own Christian life. This prompted a more general analysis of Paul's view of believers. Does Romans 7:14-25 fit within that picture? When one considers Paul's view of the Christian life in this world as he expresses it elsewhere, the situation depicted in Romans 7:14-25 can be understood as existing within it. Those objections which have arisen against a Christian interpretation and have consistently been regarded as insurmountable can, in fact, be resolved. The statements of the "I," therefore, are to be understood as expressing Paul's present Christian existence, "not all of it, but just that part of it which is germane to the subject at hand."[67]

Finally, what is "the subject at hand"? What is Paul attempting to accomplish in Romans 7? What prompts him to characterize his own life before and then after conversion the way he does in verses 7-25? In Chapter Five we shall evaluate Paul's purpose in writing Romans 7.

---

[67]Packer, 626; he concludes that "the subject at hand" is "the function of the law in giving knowledge of sin." This is essentially correct but does not fully assess Paul's purpose in pointing this out. Barrett, 153, similarly recognizes that 7:14-25 "does not tell the whole story of the Christian life."

Chapter 5

Paul's Pragmatic Purpose in Romans 7

Pragmatic Issues

The second chapter of this study discussed the semantic content of what Paul writes in Romans 7. On the basis of a comparison of that content with what Paul says about himself elsewhere (Chapter Three) and with what he says about believers and unbelievers in general (Chapter Four), the referent of the "I" in verses 7-25 has been identified. That is to say, it has been determined who Paul is talking about through his use of the first person singular. While verses 7-11 depict his pre-Christian experience with the Law, the "I" in verses 14-25 presents one aspect of his present, Christian life—his repeated failures to do the good commanded by the Law and to refrain from the evil it prohibits.

With the questions about the referent of the "I" settled, this chapter moves on to consider how the content of those verses is intended to function. In so doing, it engages the "pragmatic" issues involved in Romans 7.[1] Paul is talking about himself in verses 7-25, but Paul's interest is not *just* to tell us about himself and his own experience. Paul is doing that, but he does so with a specific purpose in mind. What, then, do the statements in these verses "count as"? How does Paul intend his statements of and about the "I" to function? What point does he convey by making reference to himself? What impact does he want to have on his hearers/readers? Why does Paul use the first person singular so extensively in Romans 7? This chapter seeks to answer

---

[1]Wolfgang Schenk, *Die Philipperbriefe des Paulus* (Stuttgart: Verlag W. Kohlhammer, 1984), 19, offers this definition: "Pragmatics describes the relationship between the signs and the people as users of signs. Here the question is addressed: What is to be accomplished with what is said? What is intended?" (*"Pragmatik beschreibt die Relation zwischen den Zeichen und den Menschen als Zeichenbenutzern: R(Z, M). Hier wird auf die Frage geantwortet: Was sollte mit dem Gesagten erreicht werden? Was ist das Intendierte?"*).

these questions and, in so doing, to delineate the function and purpose of the "I" statements in Romans 7.

The very fact that these questions are raised displays a recognition of the phenomenon that the same linguistic form, in this case the first person singular, is both able and intended to perform a variety of different functions in a variety of different settings.[2] Chapter Three demonstrated that in the vast majority of cases in which Paul uses the first person singular, he is revealing some facts or information about himself. But, at the same time, he intends these personal statements to have a given effect. They are to function or "count as" something more.[3]

A number of passages in which Paul utilizes the first person singular and *explicitly states his purpose* in the immediate context demonstrate the presence of this pragmatic aspect. For a variety of reasons, Paul regularly intends the references he makes to himself to function as an *example* or *model*. In 1 Timothy 1:12-16 Paul recounts how he was shown mercy by God (vv. 12-15). But he further contends

---

[2]For example, James Voelz, "Biblical Hermeneutics: Where Are We Now? Where Are We Going?," in *Light for Our World*, ed. J. Klotz (St. Louis: Concordia Seminary, 1989), 239-40, points out, "Thus, the question 'You are going to do that again, aren't you?', given a certain setting, may 'count as' a statement expressing amazement, a question eliciting information, a musing or thinking out loud, a rebuke, and more." See also Kevin Vanhoozer, "The Semantics of Biblical Literature: Truth and Scripture's Diverse Literary Forms," chap. two in *Hermeneutics, Authority, and Canon*, eds. D. Carson and J Woodbridge (Grand Rapids: Academie Books, 1986), 85-104.

The opposite, of course, is also true. James Voelz, "Some Things Old, Some Things New: A Response to Wolfgang Schenk, *Die Philipperbriefe des Paulus*," *Semeia* 48 (1989): *Reader Perspectives on the New Testament*, 192, points out that "quite different forms may express quite the same function"; citing Anthony Thiselton, "Semantics and New Testament Interpretation," chap. four in *New Testament Interpretations*, ed. I. Howard Marshall (Grand Rapids: Eerdmans Publishing, 1977), 77.

[3]Vanhoozer, 89, stresses that proper interpretation "involves understanding not merely the meaning of the sentence but the force with which that meaning is to be taken." See also Thiselton, 76-78 and 95-98. In the latter section Thiselton discusses "transformational grammar" on the basis of the work of Noam Chomsky, *Aspects of the Theory of Syntax* (Cambridge, MA: 1965). Thiselton, 97, defines transformational grammar as an aspect of interpretation which "often seeks to make explicit elements of meaning which are implied, but not expressed, in a sentence"; see also Voelz, "Biblical Hermeneutics: Where are We Now? Where are We Going?," 240-44. This is the task being engaged in this section of this work.

that his own experience is to serve as an example (ὑποτύπωσις) of God's patience for the comfort and assurance of all other believers (v. 16).

Philippians 3 has been referred to often here. In verses 1-14 Paul refers to himself in the first person singular again and again. He gives an appraisal of his own flesh (vv. 3b-6), of the impact which the righteousness through faith in Jesus Christ has on him (vv. 7-11), and of his outlook on life as a believer (vv. 12-14) How does Paul intend these statements to function? At the end of the section he tells the Philippians, "Therefore as many as are mature, let us think this way" (3:15; see also v. 17). The "I" in these verses is intended to serve as a pattern for the Philippian believers, as they, too, strive for maturity in the faith.

1 Corinthians 11:1 reveals that Paul's statements in the preceding verses (10:29-33) are by no means rhetorical in the manner Werner Kümmel contends.[4] Rather, they reflect Paul's own conclusions regarding a topic which has engaged his attention since Chapter 8, the eating of meat offered to idols. After stating his own convictions in the concluding verses of Chapter 10, Paul indicates the reason why he does so in 11:1.[5] He exhorts, "Be imitators of me just as I also [am] of Christ." Paul's own resolution of the issue is to function as a model for the Corinthians to imitate.

In Acts 20 Paul utilizes the first person singular in order to describe the blameless manner in which he has carried out his own ministry (vv. 18-27,33-35). He then explicitly tells the "presbyters" (πρεσβυτέρους; v. 17) or "overseers" (ἐπισκόπους; v. 28) from Ephesus that his conduct is to be a pattern for them (vv. 28-32,35).

In other passages Paul explicitly reveals that he is using the first person singular in order to perform functions other than that of

---

[4]Paul is not to be excluded as the referent of the first person singular as Werner Kümmel, *Römer 7 und die Bekehrung des Paulus* (Leipzig: Hinrichs, 1929); reprinted in *Römer 7 und das Bild des Menschen im Neuen Testament: Zwei Studien*, Theologische Bücherei, Neues Testament Band 53 (Munich: Christian Kaiser Verlag, 1974), 121,122, contends by his rhetorical interpretation of this passage. [Hereafter, *Römer 7*.] On the contrary, the context and especially 11:1 demand that the "I" be Paul. See Chapter Three.

[5]Unfortunately, the chapter division between 1 Corinthians 10 and 11 clouds the close relationship between the first verse of chapter eleven and what precedes.

providing a model or example. For instance, in the opening verses of 1 Corinthians 9, Paul is talking about his freedom, his apostolic calling, and his relationship with the Corinthians (vv. 1-2). But what are these assertions intended to "count as" in this context? In verse 3 Paul reveals his purpose: "This is my *defense* (ἀπολογία) to those who are accusing me."

The first two verses of Colossians 2 offer another example. In verse one Paul refers to the "great struggles" (ἡλίκον ἀγῶνα) he is enduring on behalf of believers. Why does he mention them here? What effect does he intend for his statement to have? Paul tells his addressees in verse two. It is *"in order that your hearts might be encouraged."*

In 1 Timothy 2:5-7 Paul recounts the Gospel message and declares that he was appointed an apostle and "a teacher (διδάσκαλος) of the Gentiles in faith and truth" (v. 7). The instructions he gives and expects to be *obeyed* in the verses which follow (vv. 8-14) are clearly based upon this authoritative appointment (οὖν; v. 8).

Finally, Paul's speaks of his own imminent death in 2 Timothy 4:6-8. Since he has "kept the faith" (v. 7), Paul knows that "the crown of righteousness" awaits him in heaven (v. 8). Yet Paul affirms his own certainty regarding this in order to declare that it is *the certain outcome for "all* those who have loved [the Lord's] appearing" (v. 8).

In the passages cited above, Paul explicitly tells his readers how he intends his statements about himself to function. However, in the majority of instances in which Paul makes reference to himself, he does *not* specifically indicate the effect which he intends his "I" statements to have. Romans 7:7-25 belongs in this group. Can Paul's intention(s) in such passages be determined? What effect(s) are those assertions supposed to have?

In most of the cases in which Paul does not explicitly state his intention, his "implied" purpose can be quite readily understood. The content and context of Paul's statement usually enable the reader to perceive how his reference to himself is intended to function. At times this is virtually an explicit part of the meaning of the text itself;[6] in

---

[6] A determination of the intended function of a given text is by no means arbitrary. As Voelz, "Some Things Old, Some Things New," 162, points out, "The function of words and other textual units is **signaled** (one might add: particularly when they are special) for the reader (in a text in writing, in spoken discourse by extra-

other passages it is less directly related to meaning and must be discerned to a greater degree from the context. An examination of the pragmatic aspect involved in a number of passages where Paul refers to himself but does not specifically reveal his intention will help to answer the questions surrounding the purpose and function of the "I" in Romans 7.

Acts 23:6 provides a good example of an instance in which Paul speaks of himself and intends his statement to perform a specific function without making it verbally explicit. This is a particularly helpful example because the narrative account in Acts proceeds to tell us the immediate impact of Paul's "I" statement. In his defense before the Sanhedrin, Paul, knowing that the Jewish council was comprised of both Sadducees and Pharisees (v. 6a), declares, "Men, brothers, *I* am a Pharisee, a son of Pharisees, I am being judged concerning [the] hope and resurrection of the dead" (v. 6b).

While this statement might seem somewhat innocuous in and of itself, Luke informs us of the sharp division between the Pharisees and the Sadducees on the question of the resurrection (v. 8). Because Paul brings up the contested issue after aligning himself with one party in the dispute, he, in all probability, intends his statement to cause some sort of disruption. In fact, Paul's reference to himself leads to a near riot and the cessation of his trial before the Sanhedrin (Acts 23:7-10).

However, in dealing with most of Paul's references to himself throughout his letters, Romans 7 included, we do not have a historical account of the impact which his statements about himself had. At times this makes it quite difficult to determine Paul's unstated intention. His purpose in referring to himself remains somewhat ambiguous (for example, 1 Cor. 4:3-4). In some passages, this is because Paul intends his statements to perform multiple functions (1 Cor. 4:18-21; 2 Cor. 10:8). Elsewhere it is due to the limited amount of information we have about the relationship between Paul and his addressees. In these cases, it can be assumed that the original recipients were more accurately and immediately able to determine Paul's intention. Their personal relationship with Paul, or at least their acquaintance with

linguistic elements)." This is to be expected since, as Vanhoozer, 89, affirms, "What one *intends* . . . is not just randomly related to what the sentence *means*. . . . The speaker intends his hearer to recognize his intention *by virtue* of his sentence meaning."

others who knew him and his reputation,[7] would have made his purpose more readily apparent to them than it is to us today. But, aside from instances such as these, it is generally possible to discern Paul's purpose even when he does not explicitly reveal his intention(s). The function he wishes to perform by referring to himself is indicated by the content of the passage, by its context, and by what we do know of Paul's relationship with the addressees.

What, then, are some of the ways in which Paul intends his statements about himself to function? What impact are they supposed to have on the hearers/readers? The results of an examination of a majority of the passages in which Paul makes reference to himself, usually without stating the response he desires, are offered below. A few preliminary points should be made. First, some of the following decisions are admittedly open to question; others involve disputed matters of interpretation. In addition, it seems that Paul often has more than one purpose in mind or, more likely, he intends one effect to move his readers toward another. [This is indicated below by a parenthetical note to the letter of the other category or categories to which the statement may also be directed.] As was illustrated above, this is particularly the case when Paul uses himself as a model or example. As a result, those instances have already been separated into categories which identify the reason why Paul utilizes himself as an example.

Paul's intended function or purpose in referring to himself in the cited passages is to:

A. Explain/give information,[8] particularly about
    1. His apostleship and conduct:
        Acts 20:18-27,33-35(E); 22:3-21(C); 24:10-21(C); Rom. 1:13-17; 15:22-29(M); 1 Cor. 3:10; 9:15-23; 11:34; 15:8-11(C); 16:5-8; 2 Cor. 1:17-24(C); 2:12-13; Gal.

---

[7]This is the case in the letter to the Romans. While Paul has not yet visited Rome (Rom. 1:11-13; 15:22-25), chapter 16 makes it clear that he is personally acquainted with a substantial number of the Christians residing there and that his reputation is well known and regarded.

[8]This category is an aspect involved in many of the others since Paul's words in reference to himself nearly always convey some information intended to enlighten his readers; see, for example, Eph. 5:32.

1:18-2:14(C); Col. 1:24-29; 2 Tim. 2:11-12; Tit. 1:3;
3:12-13.

2. His own opinion on an issue:
1 Cor. 7:10,12,28,40; 2 Cor. 8:8,10(M).

3. The Christian life:
1 Cor. 9:26-27(D); 10:29-33(E); Phil. 1:18b-26(D);
3:12-14; 4:11-13(E); 2 Tim. 3:10-12(K); 2 Tim.
4:6-8(D),16-18(D).

B. Testify to the Gospel's power in his own life in order to
proclaim its message:
Acts 26:12-23(C); Rom. 8:18,39; Cor. 15:8-10; Gal.
1:13-16(C); 2:18-21; 6:14 (D); Phil. 3:7-11; 1 Tim.
1:12-16; 2 Tim. 1:12.

C. Defend
1. His apostleship:
Acts. 26:4-23(B); 1 Cor. 4:3-5(?); 9:1-6(L); 2 Cor.
1:17-24(A); 10:1-2,8; 11:1-33(L); 12:11-18(L); Gal.
6:17; Eph. 3:2-4.

2. The Gospel he preaches:
Acts 22:3-21; 24:14-16; 26:22-23; 28:17-20; 1 Cor.
11:23; 15:1-3,8-11(L); Gal. 1:10,11-24; 2:7-10; 5:11;
Col. 1:23; 1 Tim. 1:11; 2 Tim. 2:8-13.

D. Express his personal
1. Feelings about a matter:
Rom. 9:1-3; 2 Cor. 2:1-4; 7:3-9(K); Gal. 1:6(I);
4:11(I),19-20(I); 5:20(L); 1 Thess. 3:5(K).

2. Confession/revelation:
Acts 21:13; 1 Cor. 9:26-27(A); 2 Cor. 12:1-10(L); Phil.
1:18b-26(A); 2 Tim. 4:6-8(A),16-18(A).

E. Set himself forth as an example
1. Universally:
1 Cor. 13:1-3,11-12.[9]

2. To be imitated by believers:
1 Cor. 4:3-4(?),6,16; 5:12; 6:12,14,15 (hypothetical);
7:7-8; 8:13; 10:29-11:1; 14:6 (hypothetical), 11

---

[9]Compare his use of the first person plural in Gal. 4:3.

(hypothetical), 14-15,18-19; 2 Cor. 6:13; Gal. 6:14(G);
Phil. 3:3-5(I, J), 17;4:9,11-13; 1 Tim. 1:12-16(K); 2 Tim.
3:10-12(K).

F. Identify with his audience:
Acts. 22:3; 23:1,6.

G. Direct attention away from himself:
1 Cor. 1:14-17; 2:2-5; Gal. 6:14.

H. Raise awareness/appreciation:
Acts 22:21; 26:16-18; Rom. 11:13-14; 15:15-20(M);
Gal. 1:13-17(C); Eph. 3:1-4,7-9(C); Phil. 3:4-6(I, J);
1 Tim. 2:7(L).

I. Draw forth repentance:
2 Cor. 12:20-21; Gal. 1:6-9; 4:11,21; Phil. 3:4-6(H, J).

J. Warn:
Rom. 16:17; 1 Cor. 4:14,18-21; Gal. 5:2-3;
Phil. 1:17; 3:2-6(H, J); Col. 2:4-5(K).

K. Encourage/comfort believers:
Rom. 8:18,38; 15:14; 16:19; 1 Cor. 1:4; 7:29-35;
11:2(L); 2 Cor. 2:1-4; 7:3-9, 12-13,16; Gal. 4:12-14(L);
Eph. 1:15-17; 3:12,14-19; 4:14-18; Phil. 1:3-8,12-14,
27-30; 2:12-13,16-18; 4:1, 15-20; Col. 1:24; 2:1-3(J);
1 Tim. 1:12-16; 2 Tim. 1:3-5,12; 4:6-8; Philemon 4-7.

L. Obtain acceptance of and obedience to his instruction:
Rom. 11:1; 12:1,3; 14:14; 15:15; 1 Cor. 1:10; 3:1-3;
4:15; 5:3; 6:12; 7:17; 9:1-2; 10:14-15,29-33(A); 11:
2-3,17-18,34; 12:1-3,31; 14:5; 2 Cor. 2:2-11; 7:12; 10:
1-2,8; 11:1-12:9; 13:3-4,10; Gal. 4:19-20; 5:2-4(J),16;
6:17; Eph. 4:1; Phil. 1:27; 2:12-16; 3:17-18; 4:9; Col.
4:18; 1 Thess. 5:27; 2 Thess. 3:17; 1 Tim. 1:18; 2:8,9,12;
5:21; 6:13-14; 2 Tim. 1:6-7; 2:1-2; 4:1; Tit. 1:5; 3:8;
Philemon 8-15,17-22.

M. Obtain support for his missionary work (money, prayers, and
so forth):
Rom. 1:8-12; 15:16b-19,30-32; 2 Cor. 8:8,10; 9:1-5;
Eph. 6:19-20; Col. 4:3-4.

N. Commend others so that they might be received and respected:
Rom. 16:1,4, 21; 1 Cor. 4:17; 16:3-4,10-11; Eph. 6:
21-22; Phil. 2:19-24,25-30; 4:2; Col. 4:7-9.

O. Hypothetically assume the role of another:
　　Rom. 3:7; 11:19; 1 Cor. 1:12-13; 3:4; 12:15-16,21.[10]

The results of this survey illustrate that the pragmatic possibilities open to Paul when he utilizes the first person singular are almost endless.[11] Yet the categories enumerated above can be narrowed down considerably. In essence, they comprise two general purposes. These are 1) to *inform* and 2) to *exhort/command*, that is, to elicit some type of action or response.[12] Categories A, B, and D provide instances where Paul's purpose in speaking about himself is basically to provide information. Virtually all of the other categories are aimed at drawing forth a specific response from the readers (categories E, G through N).[13] An examination of these two broader categories reveals the manner in which even they are able to interchange functionally with each other.[14]

---

[10]Gerd Theissen, *Psychological Aspects of Pauline Theology*, tr. J. Galvin (Philadelphia: Fortress Press, 1987), 252-54, proposes that Paul assumes the role of others elsewhere. Theissen contends that Paul assumes the role of the servant of Isaiah 49:1 in Gal. 1:15-16, the role of an athlete who has forgotten all of what lies behind him in Phil. 3:12-14, and even the role of Christ in 1 Cor. 9:19-23. When this is the case, Paul is still the referent. What is hypothetical is the *role* he assumes. While the role of Christ can be discerned in the "I" in 1 Cor. 9:19-23, the "I" is even more clearly and, at least initially, Paul. This is similar to the occasions when Paul calls upon believers to imitate him just as he imitates Christ (1 Cor. 11:1).

[11]The frequency with which he employs the first person singular is, in part, explained by the numerous functions these statements are able to perform. Certainly the nature of the documents as personal, written correspondence also contributes to this.

[12]The only categories which do not seem to fit are C, F, and O. However, even those passages can be understood as fitting within one of these two broader categories. The passages cited previously demonstrate that when Paul uses himself as an example he often has an indirect purpose in mind. The same is the case when he defends the Gospel or his apostleship (Category C) and when he assumes the role of another (Category O). Paul's ability to accomplish his goal in this more indirect manner is further demonstrated below.

[13]The content of these categories reveals that the term "command" is, at times, too strong. What Paul aims to attain is prompted by his pastoral concern for the recipients of his letters.

[14]One might also identify a third category. This would recognize that in a number of instances Paul is not merely giving information, but also expressing his own feelings or emotions. This "affective" aspect is especially prominent in Category D (for

How does Paul accomplish his purpose of "informing" or "exhorting/commanding?" At times he does so *directly*. The initial verses of 1 Corinthians 15 and 16 illustrate how Paul, through his use of the first person singular, accomplishes both of these purposes in a direct manner. In the first four verses of Chapter 15, Paul explicitly *informs* the Corinthians that he has faithfully handed the content of the Gospel message over to them (παραδίδωμι; 15:4). In the initial verses of Chapter 16, Paul issues a direct *exhortation* (διατάσσω; 16:1) that each one of them "lay aside" (τιθέτω; 16:2) something on the first day of the week to go toward the collection for the saints so that it is ready when he arrives.

At other times Paul accomplishes his purpose in an *indirect* manner. First, Paul can give some *information* in order to give further *information* indirectly.[15] He tells the Corinthians, "All things are lawful for me, but all things are not beneficial" (1 Cor. 6:12). Paul here describes his own freedom in the Gospel and also recognizes that even though all things are permissible for him, they are not all helpful. His statement serves to convey the same information to the Corinthians. Paul affirms that they, too, are now free in Christ from all things. But not all things are beneficial for them, as Paul proceeds to describe (1 Cor. 6:13-20).

Second, Paul can use one *exhortation/command* in order to issue another *indirectly*. The concluding verses of Philemon illustrate this quite well. He directs Philemon, "At the same time also prepare (ἑτοίμαζέ) a guest room for me" (v. 22a). Whether Paul actually visits or not, his directive to Philemon to get space ready for his coming functions as an indirect exhortation which urges Philemon to receive Onesimus back as a brother in Christ.

Third, Paul often utilizes the first person singular in order to give *information* about himself that is *indirectly* intended to *exhort/command*, that is, to elicit some type of response. In 2 Corinthians 9:2 Paul relates how he has already boasted to the Macedonians about the generosity of those in Achaia in contributing to the collection for the saints in Jerusalem. This, by itself, serves as an

---

example, Rom. 9:1-3; Gal. 4:19-20). It is also important to note its presence in Rom. 7:24.

[15]For other examples, see Rom. 14:14; 1 Cor. 3:1.

exhortation for the Corinthians to give generously. Furthermore, Paul's concern that his boasting not be in vain, as well as his sending others ahead of him, are additional incentives which urge the Corinthians to make certain that things are prepared when Paul comes (2 Cor. 9:3-5).

Likewise, in Philippians 3:4-6 Paul enumerates the reasons why he could put confidence in the flesh, but then concludes that he counts all of these as loss and as dung in light of the righteousness which comes by faith in Christ (Phil. 3:7-9). In light of verses 2-3, Paul's informative statements serve to *challenge* or to *warn*. He is dissuading others from putting confidence in their flesh.

In addition to these examples,[16] nearly all of the passages cited above in "Category C" function this way. Paul defends his apostleship so that his readers will respond to him favorably and *follow his instruction*. In similar fashion, Paul's defense of the Gospel he proclaims is information indirectly intended to lead his readers to *firmly believe* its message.

This latter goal is also Paul's aim when he testifies to the Gospel's power in his own life ("Category B"). His own example serves as an *exhortation for others to believe*. For instance, after Paul's recitation of the events and effects of his conversion during his defense before King Agrippa, the king perceives that Paul's purpose is to persuade him to believe (Acts 26:2-24,28). Paul himself affirms this as his aim for "all those who hear me" (Acts 26:29).

In conclusion, this examination has demonstrated that when Paul utilizes the first person singular with himself as the referent, he conveys personal *information* to his addressees. But at the same time and usually without explicitly stating it, his statements are also intended to have (a) desired impact(s) upon his readers. Paul's use of "I" is to function or "count as" something more than personal revelation. What he says about himself through the "I" is often intended to give information beyond what is explicitly stated in the text and, more important, frequently intended to *exhort/command*, that is, to elicit some specific action or response from the recipients.

---

[16]See also Gal. 1:12; 4:20; 6:14. At times Paul's command is evident from the context, as in 1 Cor. 6:15 in light of verse 18; 10:29-31 with 11:1 (discussed above); 15:31-32 with verse 33; possibly also 1 Cor. 4:3-4 in light of verse 5.

The pragmatic function of Romans 7 has been intentionally omitted from consideration up to this point. It has been established that Paul is telling us about himself in that chapter. He is the referent of the "I." But how are the statements of and about the "I" intended to function? Do they fit into one or more of the previous categories? Is Paul giving information about himself in order to relate in an indirect manner some facts which are also true of the Roman Christians and/or others? Is Paul utilizing these statements about himself in order to effect a change in their beliefs or actions?

Paul's Purpose in Romans 7:7-11

As Paul in verses 7-11 describes his own experience with the Law prior to his conversion, he does so from the perspective he gained after his encounter on the Damascus road. But, as in the other passages discussed above, Paul's purpose is not merely to convey information about the events of his own life to his readers.[17] An extension of the "I" here to others who were or are under the lordship of the Law, which is the overall topic of Romans 7 (v. 1), is certainly intended.[18]

But these verses do *not* simply offer a description of those who are under the Law's lordship from either an objective or subjective standpoint. Instead, Paul desires that all people would arrive at the same realization he has reached, and here reveals. His general purpose, then, is to use his own example in order *to inform* his addressees in an indirect manner *about the interrelationship between the Law, sin, and death*. Viewed in this way, there is no excluding or diminishing the fact that Paul sees himself as the actual, initial, and primary referent of the "I" in verses 7-11. As Henry Alford concludes,

---

[17]So Anders Nygren, *Commentary on Romans*, tr. C. Rasmussen (Philadelphia: Muhlenberg Press, 1949), 278, concludes that this is not just a "subjective confession." C. K. Barrett, *A Commentary on the Epistle to the Romans*, Black's New Testament Commentaries (London: Adam and Charles Black, 1962), 143, points out that Paul is "at least using [the events of his own life] to bring out his point." See also Andrew Bandstra, *The Law and the Elements of the World* (Grand Rapids: Eerdmans Publishing, n.d.), 138.

[18]Nils Dahl, *Studies in Paul* (Minneapolis: Augsburg Publishing House, 1977), 93, states, "The 'I' form . . . would hardly be meaningful unless both the speaker and his audience can in some way identify with the experience of the . . . 'I'."

We must dismiss from our minds all exegesis which explains the passage of any other, in the first instance, than of Paul himself: himself indeed, as an exemplar.[19]

It is in applying the manner in which Paul is an "exemplar" that the allusions made by various commentators to the account of Adam in Genesis 3, whether actually prominent in Paul's mind or not, find their proper place. The most that can be said in this regard is that "Adam is not the *subject* of the conflict in Rom. 7:7ff. but rather its *model.*"[20] Paul, through the use of the first person singular, *starts with his own previous existence* under the Law's lordship. However, in so doing, the "I," at least by implication, confesses *not* that he himself *is* Adam, but

---

[19]Henry Alford, *The Greek New Testament*, 4 vols. (Cambridge: Deighton, Bell, and Co., 1865), 2:377. Douglas Moo, "Israel and Paul in Romans 7.7-12," *New Testament Studies* 32 (1986):129, somewhat more weakly proposes that "Paul himself must be included in any acceptable interpretation of Romans 7."

James Dunn, *Romans 1-8*, Word Biblical Commentary, vol. 38a, eds. R. Martin, D. Hubbard, and G. Barker (Dallas: Word Books, 1988), 382, concludes that the "vivid 'I' form of Jewish Psalm tradition" is comparable to and, 390, provides the "nearest parallels" with the "I" in Romans 7:7-25. He cites Ps. 69; 77; Psalms of Solomon 5; 8; and 1 QH 3; 11. For the latter two sources, see R. B. Wright, "Psalms of Solomon," in *The Old Testament Pseudepigrapha*, ed. J. Charlesworth, 2 vols. (Garden City, NY: Doubleday & Company, 1983,1985), 2:656-57,658-60; and Geza Vermes, ed. and tr., *The Dead Sea Scrolls in English*, 2nd. ed. (New York: Viking Penguin, 1975), 157-60,185-88. On the relationship with the Qumran Hymns, see particularly Herbert Braun, "Römer 7, 7-25 und das Selbstverständnis des Qumran-Frommen," *Zeitschrift für Theologie und Kirche* 56 (1959):1-18; Hans Conzelmann, *An Outline of the Theology of the New Testament*, tr. J. Bowden (London: SCM Press, 1969), 231-32; Dahl, 92-93; Ernst Käsemann, *Commentary on Romans*, tr. and ed. G. Bromiley (Grand Rapids: Eerdmans Publishing, 1980), 201-2; Richard Longenecker, *Paul* (New York: Harper and Row, 1964), 88-89; and Otto Michel, *Der Brief an die Römer*, Kritischer-exegetischer Kommentar über das Neue Testament, 13th ed. (Göttingen: Vandenhoeck and Ruprecht, 1966), 171, who conjectures that the "I" in the Qumran Hymns might be "the Teacher of Righteousness himself" (*"der Lehrer der Gerechtigkeit selbst"*). No one doubts that the "I" is the actual speaker in these passages while, at the same time, recognizing that the scope is intended to be broadened. This should also be understood in Romans 7.

[20]Theissen, 203. He bases this, 208-211, on the four motifs common to both Genesis 2-3 and Romans 7, the motifs of life, death, deceit, and the letter.

that he is a child of the one man through whom sin came into the world and spread to all people (5:12).[21] Paul, in effect, says

> I am like Adam in that I am subject to sin's misuse of the Law whose lordship over me accomplishes my death (7:1).[22] I am a son of Adam and, therefore, imprisoned by sin's entrance into the world (5:12), by my own transgression of God's commandment (7:7-8), and by the death which has resulted (vv. 9-11).

Indeed, so are all sinners when they are confronted with the full impact of the Law. This information reveals a connection which Paul would not only not deny for his readers, but clearly intends them to make.[23]

---

[21]The initial referent must be maintained. Barclay Newman and Eugene Nida, *A Translator's Handbook on Paul's Letter to the Romans*, Helps for Translators, vol. 14 (London: United Bible Societies, 1973), 134, adequately propose that Paul "begins by interpreting his own experience in the light of Genesis 3." According to Newman and Nida, 135, Paul here reveals and confesses "that Adam's experience and his own are similar: *[in that] the commandment which was meant to bring life, in my case brought death*."

[22]Theissen, 203, is perhaps not far off here in suggesting, "The I assumes the role of Adam and structures it in the light of personal experience of conflict." However, Käsemann, 195, starts at the wrong point in stating, "Adam remarkably lives on in 'my reality.'" He attempts to solve the problems here by applying the concept of the corporate personality and stresses the logical continuity between Romans 5 and 7; similarly also Moo, 128-29.

[23]If Paul is alluding to Adam, Theissen, 255, concludes that the role of Adam "served him as a way of presenting his personal conflict with the law as a general human conflict." In any event, the result is assuredly a malady common to all people, including Paul, in light of 5:12-21. So also Moo, 128, perceives that "Paul sees a basic similarity in the situations of Adam . . . and Israel confronted by the Law." Yet he fails to begin with Paul and, only then, to apply this description of Paul's experience to the situation of all other people confronted with the Law.

In the case of Paul's readers who had formerly been Gentile unbelievers and had then come to know the Law through the synagogue before conversion to Christianity, many of the difficulties involved in determining when or in what manner the "I" was alive "apart from the Law" and then experienced a coming of the commandment readily vanish (v. 9). Moo's argument, 125-28, that the "narrative sequence" of these verses refers to the coming of the Law at Sinai would then be somewhat parallel. Yet in light of 2:12-16 this cannot be pushed to its extreme, either. It was admitted that the interpretation adopted here did not take the most literal sense of χωρὶς νόμου in verses 8-9. If the literal sense is insisted upon, the meaning of this phrase could be applied literally to Paul's Gentile readers whose role Paul is at least partially adopting through

In verses 7-11, then, Paul's use of the "I" is intended to relate his experience under the Law as an example. In so doing, the first person singular functions as a creative and personal way to *inform* his addressees that all descendants of Adam are similarly affected detrimentally by God's Law.[24] However, these verses are also intended to *command* or to evoke a particular response. They are "aimed at dispelling a reader's possibly false notion concerning the law."[25]

For example, if there are those among Paul's addressees who are being deceived by sin into relying upon the Law (see 2:17-29), as he did prior to the Damascus road event (7:11; see also Gal. 1:13-14; Phil. 3:4-6), Paul's words are intended *to raise their awareness* and *to warn* them about the true effects of the Law's commands upon sinful man.[26] The "I" here is not a description of a typical or pious Jew.[27] What the "I" realizes is precisely what is absent in Paul's other portrayals of unbelieving Jews (2:21-24; 10:2). Rather, verses 7-11 express what Paul wants anyone who relies upon their performance of the Law to recognize. The intended effect of Paul's words about himself is to move such a person to the same point of despair Paul was in when confronted by the risen Jesus Christ.[28] If the reader is basing confidence upon his flesh (Phil. 3:4) and living comfortably under the lordship of the Law (Rom. 7:1), Paul reveals that such a person, like him prior to the Damascus Road experience, is in reality being deceived into thinking the Law does not kill the sinner (v. 11).

---

the "I" (note the comparable suggestions of Theissen, 252-54). However, this conclusion has been rejected here because it excludes Paul as the primary referent.

[24]Certainly the commands of the Mosaic Torah are most specifically in Paul's mind here. Whether a person has been confronted by the revealed Torah or "the work of the Law" written in the heart will determine the standard of judgment, but makes no ultimate difference (Rom. 2:12-16; 3:9,19-20).

[25]Brice Martin, "Some Reflections on the Identity of ἐγώ in Rom. 7:14-25," *Scottish Journal of Theology* 34 (1981):41; he is referring to the entirety of verses 7-25.

[26]See above, Categories H and J.

[27]As suggested by Käsemann, 195; Robert Gundry, "The Moral Frustration of Paul Before His Conversion," in *Pauline Studies*, eds. D. Hagner and M. Harris (Exeter, England: Paternoster Press, 1980), 232.

[28] See above, Category I.

On the other hand, for Paul's Christian addressees who, together with him, now realize that the identification, provocation, and condemnation of sin are one aspect of the Law's function, Paul's words serve *to warn* them about how the Law's command can be misused by sin (vv. 7-8,13). "Paul is depicting himself . . . in order to warn his fellow Christians not to fall back into the former unregenerate state."[29] If a believer begins to rely upon his observance of the Law as the basis for his life, he, too, is being deceived.

So, then, while the effect(s) may vary, Paul's words are pertinent both to believers and unbelievers. He assumes that "what he says has relevance for all men in all periods of history."[30] The purpose of Paul's description of himself in verses 7-11 is that every sinner would realize what the Law's command in fact accomplishes in him and how this affects his standing before God (Rom. 3:20; 4:15; 5:20; 7:7-8,13).

If Paul intended all along to reveal a generally applicable truth about how sin is able to misuse the Law to provoke sin, to deceive and to kill, why does he employ the first person singular at all? As concluded in Chapter Three, Paul here discusses very poignantly "the problem of his own life."[31] Yet Paul's use of the first person singular is also both creative and effective. It enables him to demonstrate, from the experience of his own life, that even a man who meticulously observes the Law in a manner so far surpassing others that he considers himself blameless according to the righteousness of the Law (e.g., Gal. 1:13-14; Phil. 3:4b-6) is, in actuality, being deceived by

---

[29]Jan Lambrecht, *The Wretched "I" and Its Liberation*, Louvain Theological & Pastoral Monographs, 14 (Grand Rapids: Eerdmans, 1992), 91; though he contends this is the purpose of the entire chapter. See Category J above.

[30] Newman and Nida, 134; however, they precede this by contending "that every other man's experience is similar to [Paul's] own." Dunn *Romans 1-8*, 383, similarly concludes, "The typicality of the experience of everyman expressed in the archetypal language of Gen 2-3 presumably therefore should be allowed to embrace a wide and diverse range of particular experiences." So also Nygren, *Commentary on Romans*, 280, states, "For what Paul says about himself is equally true of every man and of mankind as a whole." None of these is accurate. Those who try to avoid the Law or who are deceived by sin into depending upon the Law do not experience or recognize what the "I" states here. Rather, Paul's words are written to the end that all of his readers would *come to realize* that which Christ's appearance revealed to him.

[31]Nygren, *Commentary on Romans*, 279.

sin's misuse of the Law (Rom. 7:11). Paul could have made his point
here by writing

> in calm didactic fashion: 'No the law is not sin but helps make the sinner
> conscious of his sin'. . . . [But] when Paul uses himself as a *corpus* for
> dissection he lifts us above the abstract into actual life, into viewing our
> own actual life and experience.[32]

What Paul writes in Romans 7:7-11, therefore, is not intended to
be a portrayal of his personal religious crisis or of his inner
psychological development. It only becomes that when the description
in those verses is removed from the *coram Deo* level. But Kümmel
very correctly points out that the terms in these verses "must be
understood as expressions concerning the existence of the person in his
relationship to God."[33] Verses 7-11 reflect and strive to drive home a
recognition of what one's standing is *coram Deo* on the basis of the
Law and apart from Christ.[34]

Paul's Purpose in Romans 7:14-25

As demonstrated in Chapter Four, verses 14-25 do not discuss the
role of the Law in the life of an unbeliever (see 7:1,5,7-11). The "I"
here is not in the same situation as in verses 7-11. F. F. Bruce
observes,

---

[32]R. C. H. Lenski, *The Interpretation of St. Paul's Epistle to the Romans*,
Commentaries on the New Testament (Minneapolis: Augsburg Publishing House,
1961), 459-60,462.

[33]Kümmel, *Römer 7*, 124, *"muß diese Termini als Aussagen über das Sein des
Menschen in seiner Beziehung zu Gott, . . . verstehen."* See also Longenecker, *Paul*,
91.

[34]John Espy, "Paul's 'Robust Conscience' Re-examined," *New Testament Studies*
31 (1985):167, concludes that we have here "the man apart from Christ, sinning under
the Law though the Law is not at fault." Here the Law's commands have *also* worked
the recognition that one is unavoidably accountable for the wages of sin which is death
(3:20; 6:23).

> There sin assaulted the speaker by stealth and struck him down; here, he puts up an agonizing resistance, even if he cannot beat back the enemy.[35]

The deception sin worked upon Paul through the Law is ended (7:11). In contrast, the "I" in Romans 7:14-25 is fully aware of what is happening. Paul is portraying the "double effect" which the Law has upon him as a believer who is actively engaged in the struggle against his own sinful flesh.

In part, Paul utilizes his own experience as an example in order *to inform* his readers about the role and activity of the Law in the Christian life. Paul reveals that the Law of God hits the believer in two diverse ways. First and primarily, the Christian agrees with and rejoices in the Spirit-filled Law which directs his will away from evil and toward good (7:16,18,19,20, 21,22,25).

On the other hand, because believers continue to live in the sinful flesh, sin also dwells in them and fleshly desires continue to spring up (7:14,17-18,20). When this is the case, the Law is used by sin to provoke evil against the resolve of the renewed will (7:15,16,18,19,20, 21,23). Then the Law proceeds to identify sin as such and pronounces its sentence of death (7:23,24,25; 8:2b). As a result, so long as a believer remains in this body as it is, he is trapped in a mortal body (8:10). And so he cries out together with Paul, "Who will rescue me from this body of death?" (Rom. 7:24).

Although Paul affirms that believers are now free from the Law's lordship and enabled by the Spirit to serve it willingly (7:4,6), he here utilizes the experience of his own Christian life in order to point out and explain why they still cannot fulfill the Law in the flesh.[36] Even though a Christian's will rejoices in the good as revealed in the Spiritual Law (7:14,16, 22), the sin which dwells in his flesh continues to wage war against his sanctified mind (7:23). It is able to prevent the believer from doing the good he wills and continues to lead him into the evil he hates (vv. 15-21). Even his sanctified and altogether proper intention to live in accordance with the Law's command is inevitably met with futility and even despair.

---

[35]F. F. Bruce, *The Letter of Paul to the Romans*, The Tyndale New Testament Commentaries, vol. 6 (Grand Rapids: Eerdmans Publishing, 1963), 143; see also Lenski, 491; and Nygren, *Commentary on Romans*, 286.

[36]Nygren, *Commentary on Romans*, 303.

With a specific purpose in mind, verses 14-23 present *only* those repeated and inevitable instances in which sin, dwelling in the flesh, succeeds in taking the "I" captive (7:23). The fact that the sinful flesh is able to continue to enact evil and to prohibit the good required by the Law is sufficient to make Paul's point. It is not that believers engaged in this struggle are once again slaves to sin or utterly powerless against sin.[37] Rather, they, like Paul, are distraught by their inability to eradicate sin completely from the flesh. There is "a foreign element that has yet to be dislodged and expelled."[38]

There are only two ways to avoid this condition as an ever-present reality for the believer. The first is to lessen the perfect holiness required by God and, thereby, to overlook the total obedience demanded in his Law. The second is to contend with Albert Schweitzer that "believers are raised above all the limitations of the being-in-the-flesh,"[39] so that it is possible for them to refrain from sin completely. The latter position is essentially Kümmel's conclusion, when he asserts that the "Spirit, whom every Christian possesses (Rom. 8:9), enables the Christian at all times to put to death the deeds of the body."[40]

Paul, however, refuses to allow either of these alternatives to stand. He insists that the Law requires the doing of all the things which

---

[37]As argued, for example, by Rudolf Bultmann, "Romans 7 and Paul's Anthropology," in *The Old and New Man in the Letters of Paul*, tr. K Crim (Richmond, VA: John Knox Press, 1957), 38; Kümmel, *Römer 7*, 125,133,136-37; and Herman Ridderbos, *Paul*, tr. J. De Witt (Grand Rapids: Eerdmans Publishing, 1975), 127, who characterizes this as "the absolute impotence of the I to break through the barrier of sin and the flesh in any degree at all."

[38]Lenski, 480.

[39]Albert Schweitzer, *The Mysticism of Paul the Apostle*, tr. W. Montgomery, A Crossroad Book (New York: The Seabury Press, 1968), 167.

[40]Kümmel, *Römer 7*, 104, "*dieses* πνεῦμα, *das jeder Christ besitzt (Röm. 8,9)*, *ermöglicht es dem Christen jederzeit* τὰς πράξεις τοῦ σώματος θανατοῦσθαι." As a result, he, ibid., 108, wonders "'how is it to be explained that our Christianity deviates so far from the Pauline that we once more find ourselves in the form of the Pauline non-Christian?'" ("*'wie ist es zu erklären, daß unser Christentum von dem paulinischen soweit abweicht, daß wir uns im Bilde des paulinischen Nichtchristen wiederfinden?'"). Kümmel, ibid., finally must conclude "that our Christianity is indeed different from the eschatologically determined Christianity of the Pauline congregations" ("*daß unser Chistentum von dem eschatologisch bestimmten Christentum der paulinischen Gemeinden recht verschieden ist*").

are written in it (Rom. 10:5; see also Gal. 3:10-12,19-23). At the same time, the ability to accomplish these works fully is excluded for each and every person since the fall into sin (Rom. 1:18-3:20; especially 3:9,19-20,23; 5:12; cf. Gal. 2:16; 3:11). Paul recognizes that, prior to the death of the believer or Christ's return, Christians inevitably remain a part of this present age. In Romans 7:14-25 Paul acknowledges that "sin still holds sway over the world to which 'I' still belong as a man of flesh."[41] Here, the desires of the flesh are always directed toward evil in opposition to the good which God reveals in his Law (7:14,18; see Gal. 5:17).

Therefore, even though the sanctified will, mind, and inner man dominate Paul's existence as a believer, he remains "sold under sin" in so far as he is still flesh (7:14). His will determines to do the good and strives to abstain from evil in accordance with the Law. But when the "sold under sin" flesh gains the fore, Paul repreatedly does the evil which he hates and is hindered from enacting the good that his will determines to do.

> Once we admit that sin persists in the believer, the tension of 7:14-25 is inevitable and it is not the way of truth to ignore it.[42]

Romans 7:14-25, then, offers no easy excuse for sin.

> Only an excuse for sin experienced as *defeat*, as a wretched captivity and slavery to sin. Paul can and does readily conceive of believers being frequently defeated by sin (v. 23) . . . , but he cannot conceive of believers treating such defeats as a matter of little consequence.[43]

---

[41]Dunn, *Romans 1-8*, 408.

[42]John Murray, *The Epistle to the Romans*, 2 vols. (Grand Rapids: Eerdmans Publishing, 1959,1965), 1:258.

[43]Dunn, *Romans 1-8*, 412.

Indeed, the closer one gets to the holiness of God, the more glaring and frustrating one's sin becomes.[44]

Yet, Paul also intends these verses to function as more than a detailing of the role of the Law in the Christian life. His use of the "I" not only serves to inform; it also "counts as" an *exhortation/command.* It is intended to have an impact. Here, Paul aims to dispel a Christian "reader's possibly false notion concerning the Law."[45]

These verses, which express one aspect of Paul's own Christian life, are intended *to raise the awareness* or alertness of his hearers and, then, *to warn* them against basing their continued relationship with God upon the Law.[46] As he earlier inquired of those who "rely on the Law" (2:17), "You who boast in the Law, are you dishonoring God through [your] transgression of the Law?"(2:23). Paul's goal is to prohibit himself and all other believers from attempting to maintain their justified status, to any degree, upon their own Law-based striving for perfection or any supposed "moral victory."[47] This is because every Christian who stands before God from the perspective of the Law must admit with Paul, "So then *I* myself in [my] mind am enslaved to [the] Law of God, but, on the other hand, in the flesh, [I am enslaved to the] Law of sin" (Rom. 7:25b).

As with sin and death, Paul declares that the Law no longer reigns over him or other believers (7:1,6). Yet, as a Law of sin and death (7:23,25; 8:2), it continues to have a limited, negative impact. It continues to provoke and identify sin in the flesh, thereby making this fleshly body one of death (7:24). If a believer places himself under the lordship of the Law once again, he is under the reign of sin and death

---

[44]Dunn, *Romans 1-8*, 389, "It is precisely the saint who is most conscious of his own sinfulness." C. E. B. Cranfield, *A Critical and Exegetical Commentary on the Epistle to the Romans*, 2 vols., The International Critical Commentary, vol. 32, 6th ed. (Edinburgh: T. & T. Clark, 1975,1979), 1:358, contends that "the more seriously a Christian strives to live from grace . . . the more sensitive he becomes to the fact of his own sinfulness." See also C. Marvin Pate, *The End of the Age Has Come* (Grand Rapids: Zondervan Publishing, 1995), 102-4; Lenski, 439-40; Murray, 1:258; and Espy, 173-74, who argues that we do not have a weak Christian here, but a Christian at his best.

[45]Martin, 41.

[46]See Categories H and J above.

[47]Gundry, 240; also cited in Chapter One.

(7:1,5).[48] However, so long as one remains dead to the Law ἐκ πίστεως (7:4,6; see also 3:22,26,28), the Law's condemnation is no longer valid. It has already been removed by Jesus Christ (8:1,3).

The initial verses of Romans 8, then, provide the vital key to 7:14-25. Since Paul, in 8:1-4, draws his conclusions regarding what has just been illustrated, the chapter division is most unfortunate. He has demonstrated why it is impossible for the Law's command to be the basis of his life and freedom, even while he is "in Christ Jesus" (8:1). It is because of sin which continues to dwell in the flesh and to work in his members (7:14,17,18,20,23). And "the law (spiritual and good as it is) is powerless to deliver him from his bondage to indwelling sin" (ἀδύνατον; 8:3).[49]

To be sure, Paul affirms that every believer is free from the Law's condemnation of sin and its pronouncement of eternal death (8:1-2; 7:6). But a believer does not stand justified from sin (6:7) because of the Law's command or because of one's ability to fulfill the Law. Rather, he has been freed, even from that under which he continues to exist, because God, by his Spirit, has brought freedom and life by fulfilling the promise of the Torah (8:2; also 3:21; 4, especially vv. 23-25; 10:4). God accomplished this by "sending his own Son in the likeness of sinful flesh and as an offering for sin" (8:3).

In Jesus Christ, God has done what the Law *is* unable to accomplish because of our weak flesh (8:3). He has fulfilled the legal requirements laid down by God's Law in our place (8:4a). The presence of the Spirit now enables believers willingly to determine to live according to the Law (as in 7:15-25). But when they fail, the Spirit also assures them that through faith God has given them, and continues to cover them with, what Christ has accomplished in their behalf.[50]

---

[48]See Rom. 8:2 and 6:16; Paul makes this very clear in his letter to the Galatians, see the Excursus below.

[49]Ronald Fung, "The Impotence of the Law: Toward a Fresh Understanding of Romans 7:14-25," in *Scripture, Tradition and Interpretation*, eds. W. Gasque and W. LaSor (Grand Rapids: Eerdmans Publishing, 1978), 40; see also 43,45.

[50]See the discussion above in Chapter Four concerning 3:24-25 and 8:26,34. So we do not here have a picture of "the believer failing to reach final (complete) salvation" or of a liberation which "has begun, and begun decisively, but is not yet complete" as Dunn contends, *Romans 1-8*, 396, 407; see also idem., "Rom. 7,14-25 in the Theology of Paul," *Theologische Zeitschrift* 31 (1975):271.

As a result of all of this, Paul's description of himself in Romans 7:14-25 has two additional functions. His personal attestation to the fact that an ongoing struggle against the "sold under sin" flesh is an inescapable aspect of the Christian life serves both *to encourage* and *to comfort* believers who continue to live in the flesh in this world.[51] On the one hand, Paul's own express inability to fulfill the Law as he fervently desires prohibits believers from becoming complacent and "too easily satisfied with the disposition and frame of their own hearts."[52] When they examine their own lives before God's Law, as Paul does here, the Law points out when and how they continue to fall into sin by failing to accomplish the good and by doing evil. But Paul's example also urges them to strive to live in accordance with God's will as revealed in the Law with the same resolve Paul displays in verses 14-23.

On the other hand, since Paul's confidence before God is not based upon the flesh (Phil. 3:3-11), the conflict present in verses 14-25 is no cause for complete and total despair.[53] In spite of the ongoing disparity between his will and action, Paul comforts believers by giving thanks "to God through Jesus Christ our Lord" (Rom. 7:25). Because of the presence of the Spirit who inaugurated this struggle, Paul knows that he will be delivered from "this body of death" at the day of Jesus' return (Rom. 7:24). This mortal, natural, and perishable body will then be changed to be like Jesus' glorified body (Rom. 7:24; 8:10; cf. 1 Cor. 15:42-44,51-53; Phil. 3:20-21).

But even now Paul asks, "Who will bring a charge against God's elect?" (Rom. 8:33a). Even though he and other believers remain in the sinful flesh (Rom. 7:14,17-18,20), no one can. "God is the one who justifies; who is the one who condemns?" (Rom. 8:33b-34a). Even

---

[51]See above, Category L.

[52]James Fraser, *The Scripture Doctrine of Sanctification* (Edinburgh: R. Ogle, 1830), 418; he continues, "But, if with sincere and earnest desire to advance in holiness, they looked more closely into the law, as it is spiritual, and into their own hearts, they would see, to their great benefit, more of these motions of sin in them, by which they do what they would not, and are unable to do, in manner and degree, as they would."

[53]Recognized by Dunn, "Rom. 7,14-25 in the Theology of Paul," 272-73; also Pate, 102.

though the Law remains a Law of sin and death to the believer who continues to live in a mortal body (Rom. 7:23-24; 8:2,10), no one can.

Why can the Law no longer condemn the believer? It is *not* because Paul or any other believer is now able to fulfill the Law (Rom. 7:14-23). On the contrary, the Law continues to point out the believer's failure to do so. It is rather because "Christ Jesus [is] the one who died, and much more was raised, who is, indeed, at the right hand of God, who also intercedes in our behalf" (Rom. 8:34). And so those who believe in him can already now join Paul in giving thanks to the God who has given them victory over the death which the Law pronounces upon sin (Rom. 7:25a; 8:2b-3; also 1 Cor. 15:57). Already now there is "no condemnation for those in Christ Jesus" (Rom. 8:1).

The "I" is able to perform a number of functions most effectively in Romans 7:14-25. But *why does Paul choose to use that form of expression in these verses?*[54] First, it is a natural continuation of the first person singular which he employed in reference to himself in verses 7-11. [See the discussion earlier in this chapter.]

Second, and as a direct result, the first person singular serves to maintain the *coram Deo* level of Paul's discussion about the Law. This factor explains how Paul can be describing his own Christian life in what appears to many to be a very dismal manner. Paul is *not* speaking of his own *public conduct* before others, but picturing his current standing *before God* on the basis of his performance of the Law.[55] This also resolves the apparent contradiction between Romans 7:14-25 and passages such as 1 Corinthians 4:3-4.

A third aspect is related. The first person singular enables Paul to make his point unmistakably clear. How was Paul seen by others? Paul's letters reveal that when one viewed him from a human point of view, there was some weakness (for example, 1 Cor. 2:3; Gal. 4:14). But among his fellow Christians, Paul was, no doubt, the great Apostle

---

[54]Espy, especially 169-70, suggests that the singular is necessary because a person is only guilty under the Law as an individual. This is not the case. A person becomes guilty *of transgressing the revealed Law* as an individual once the Law comes. But the person is still guilty, is condemned, and perishes as an individual apart from the Law (2:12; 3:9,19-20; 5:12-21, especially vv. 12,18,19).

[55]Dahl, 93, similarly observes, "When we confess our sins before God, our self-evaluation is very different from what it normally is when we communicate with other people." He compares this with the Hymns of Qumran.

who had been chosen and visited by the risen Lord Jesus himself, who had been at the forefront as the church spread throughout Asia Minor and into Europe, and who was now finally planning to come and visit the Roman church on his way to spread the Gospel in Spain. Within and among the churches, Paul himself stresses that his conduct faithfully adhered to his calling and was above reproach.[56]

This is congruent with the manner in which Paul addresses the Roman Christians, particularly in Romans 1:1-15 and 15:14-22. Those who did not know Paul personally had certainly heard about him from those in their midst who had met Paul (Romans 16). In all likelihood these Roman Christians pictured Paul as an unconditionally determined Apostle who endeavored with all his life to spread the Gospel which had been delivered to him directly by Jesus.

Yet Romans 7 reveals that this man, this great theologian, church leader, and missionary, realizes that he dare not base his standing before God in any way upon his works of the Law. He now acknowledges that this was true prior to his conversion when the Law pointed out his sin, provoked sin, deceived him, and pronounced a sentence of death upon him (Rom. 7:7-11). But verses 14-25 disclose that Paul also knew this was true of him as a Christian.[57] He was not only inept at becoming righteous by keeping the Law's command (vv. 7-11), he could not even maintain that righteousness by his observance of the Law (vv. 14-25). To attempt to do so, would be, as he warned the Galatians years earlier, to fall from the grace of God in Jesus Christ (Gal. 5:2-4; see below). Verses 14-25 illustrate why Paul could not fulfill the Law as God required. It is because he, too, was hindered by

---

[56]See, for example, Acts 20:18-35; elsewhere Paul declares that he has been faithful to his calling (Acts 26:19); he has faithfully carried out the task given to him (2 Tim. 1:3); he has fought the good fight and preserved the faith (2 Tim. 4:6). See the complete discussion in Chapter Three above.

[57]Maurice Goguel, *The Birth of Christianity*, tr. H. Snape (New York: Macmillan, 1954), 213, argues that verses 14-25 describe Paul immediately after his conversion. On the basis of 1 Cor. 9:24-27, Bruce, *The Letter of Paul to the Romans*, 144-45, responds, "Even at the height of his apostolic career, [Paul] made it his daily business to discipline himself so as not to be disqualified in the spiritual contest" (see 1 Cor. 9:27). Dunn, *Romans 1-8*, 407, points out that the "deceived" Pharisee Paul "knew no such frustration or self-deprecation in his preconversion days"; citing Phil 3:4-6. However, as a humble believer, he is aware, as never before, of the power of sin in his own life.

sin which still resided in his flesh and was at work in his members (vv. 14,17-18,20,23). The continued presence and activity of sin rendered his body a body of death (v. 24).

Paul's use of *himself* as an example serves both to *inform* and to *warn* his readers most effectively.[58] Even the great Apostle is not able to rely on his own performance of the Law before God. They would conclude, "If this is true of Paul, how much more so of me?" No matter how far a believer might progress in the sanctified life in this world, even as far as Paul, he will always be plagued by the sinful flesh. Paul's portrayal of the ongoing and all-too-often contradictory tension between his will and his actions serves to point out that such a disparity is an unavoidable aspect of present Christian existence.[59] The resulting frustration (7:24) reflects both Paul's determination and his maturity.

Of course, this situation does not stop Paul from urging himself and others to battle the sinful flesh (6:12-13; 13:14), to offer themselves as "living sacrifices" to God (12:1), and to strive to fulfill the Law by loving one another (13:8-10). It is precisely this disparity between the believer's intention and performance which prompts Paul's exhortations. Of greater significance, however, is the fact that the solution which Paul holds out to this disparity is not the Law. The Law's command is unable (Rom. 8:3). The answer is "our Lord Jesus Christ" (7:25) who declares and already effects his verdict of "no condemnation" (8:1).

A final factor involved in Paul's choice of the first person singular is related to the topic of the excursus below. In contrast to the situation when Paul wrote Galatians, in Romans he has no crisis to address. There was not, apparently, an overt controversy among the Christians in Rome regarding the necessity of circumcision and observing the Law for salvation.[60] He knows of no specific opponents to refute openly. As a result, when Paul addresses the same issue he had earlier

---

[58]See above, Category J.

[59]See above, Category A,3.

[60]But see 14:1-15:13 and *The Romans Debate*, rev. ed., ed. Karl P. Donfried (Peabody, MA: Hendrickson Publishers, 1991), especially Francis Watson, "The Two Roman Congregations: Romans 14:1-15:13," 203-215.

dealt with in his letter to the Galatians, the role of the Law in the Christian life, he employs the first person singular.

Excursus: Confirmation from Galatians

Paul's letter to the Galatians is the best commentary on his epistle to the Romans and *vice versa*.[61] Paul's purpose in Romans 7:14-8:4 is to give a proper evaluation of the role of the Law in the Christian life. He illustrates its actual functions, effects, and limitations. If, as has been maintained here, Paul addresses an issue vital to his theology in Romans 7, one would expect it to be a point of discussion elsewhere in his letters and, particularly, in Galatians. This is, in fact, the case.[62] The situation which prompted Paul's letter to the Galatians necessitated that he discuss the issues surrounding the Law and the Christian life with even greater fervor. In Galatians Paul speaks even more directly to this topic and clearly draws forth its implications. In so doing he clarifies, amplifies, and confirms the interpretation and application of Romans 7:14-25 adopted here.

In Galatians Paul is sharply responding to his opponents who have been identified as "Jewish Christian Judaizers from Jerusalem who were forcing the Galatians to be circumcised and to keep the Law" in order to be saved (see Acts 15:1,5).[63] As he speaks to the Galatian

---

[61]Note, for example, Paul's use of Hab. 2:4 in Rom. 1:17 and Gal. 2:11; and Lev. 18:5 in Romans 10:5 and Gal. 3:12. Some other similarities will be stated in the discussion here; see also C. H. Dodd, *The Epistle to the Romans*, The Moffatt New Testament Commentary (London: Fontana Books, 1959), 23; Fung, 42; Michel, 25.

[62]The discussion to follow disproves the contention of Paul Althaus, "Zur Auslegung von Röm. 7,14ff," *Theologische Literaturzeitung* 77 (1952):479, who asserts that if Rom. 7:14-25 is applied to the Christian those verses "would be completely isolated and without analogy among all the letters of Paul" (*"wäre völlig isoliert und analogielos unter allen Paulusbriefen"*). However, even if Althaus is correct, this would not present an insurmountable objection. The fact that an interpretation of a section makes those verses unique among Paul's letters is not of itself a sufficient criterion to reject that interpretation.

[63]George Howard, *Paul: Crisis in Galatia*, Society for New Testament Studies Monograph Series, 35 (New York: Cambridge University Press, 1979), 19; see also Donald Guthrie, *New Testament Introduction*, 3rd ed. (Downers Grove, IL: Inter-Varsity Press, 1970), 466. For a complete discussion of the various theories, see Howard, 1-19.

Christians,[64] Paul scolds them: "I am astounded that you turned away so quickly from the one who called you in the grace of Christ to a different gospel" (1:6). Yet, as the letter continues, one observes that the Galatians are not so much abandoning faith in Jesus Christ as they are attempting to add something to it. At the urging and even insistence of these agitators, they are on the verge of submitting to circumcision and obedience to the Law as a necessary requirement for completing or maintaining their justified status before God (e.g., 3:3).[65]

For Paul this amounts to an abandonment of the Gospel. Paul vehemently argues that any gospel which includes obedience to the Law is really no Gospel at all. In order to prove this, he not only speaks to the issue of how one becomes righteous before God, he also addresses how one maintains this justified status. Paul's point is that reliance upon the Law, even as a means to maintain a proper standing with God, is futile and even damning (cf. Rom. 7:1-8:4).

How does one become right with God? These Christians should know

> that a man is not justified by works of the Law, but only through faith in Jesus Christ; *we* have also believed in Christ Jesus, in order that we might be justified through faith in Christ, and not by works of the Law, because by works of the Law no flesh will be justified. . . . For if righteousness [were] through the Law, then Christ died for no purpose" (Gal. 2:16,21b).

---

[64]His addressees were comprised of both Jewish and Gentile Christians as indicated by Gal. 3:28; 5:1-6; 6:12-15; Acts 13:42,48; 14:1,27.

[65]Lambrecht, "The Line of Thought in Gal. 2. 14b-21," 26, suggests "that Paul, both in Romans and Galatians, is not primarily dealing with the Lutheran (anthropological) question, 'How do I find righteousness in God's sight?' Paul is more concerned with what could be called a socio-ecclesiastical problem, 'Under what conditions can Gentiles become Christians?'" Dunn, "The New Perspective on Paul," *The John Rylands University Library Bulletin* 65 (1982-83):107-10, similarly theorizes that Paul is attacking the view that God's acknowledgment of covenantal status is bound up with and dependent upon the particular observances of circumcision and Jewish food laws. These were merely, ibid., 107, "identity markers" or "badges of covenant membership." While Lambrecht and Dunn make valid assessments of what was, perhaps, the surface issue, the manner in which Paul deals with the problem in Galatia reveals the significance of its ramifications.

In the intervening verses Paul employs the first person singular in a manner which parallels Romans 7:7-11 in content as well. Paul affirms, "For through the Law *I* died to the Law" (Gal. 2:19a; compare Rom. 7:1,4,6,10-11). Concerning that Law he asserts, "For if I again build these things which I have destroyed, I prove myself [to be] a transgressor" (2:18).

What then has "bewitched" the Galatians ("ἐβάσκανεν"; 3:1)? Though they received the Spirit by faith (3:2), Paul identifies their particular problem by asking, "Having begun by the Spirit, are you now completing yourselves by the flesh?" (3:3). If they attempt to do so, Paul charges that their faith may indeed have been in vain (3:4). Why is this so? It is because those who are under the Law are under a curse. It has been written, "Cursed [is] everyone who does not abide by all the things which have been written in the Book of the Law to do them" (3:10; citing Deut. 27:26). Since no one is able to "do" the commands of the Law as God demands within the Torah, no one can be justified by them (2:16; 3:11-12; citing Lev. 18:5; cf. Rom. 2:12-3:20; 9:30-10:5). On the contrary, the Scriptures condemn all people by locking all things up under sin (3:22; cf. Rom. 3:9,23). Because of sin the Law is unable to give life to those under the Law (3:21-23; compare Rom. 7:10; 8:3). Just the opposite, it was added "for the sake of defining transgressions" (Gal. 3:19; compare Rom. 3:20; 4:15; 5:20; 7:7-8).

But Paul declares that Christ has come and redeemed us from the curse which the Law placed upon us. He did this by becoming a curse for us on the tree of the cross (Gal. 3:13,24). Now that faith has come believers are no longer under the Law (3:25). Those who are righteous ἐκ πίστεως are, and always have been, those who receive the promise as true sons of Abraham (3:7-9,17-18).

Paul more sharply focuses his debate with the Galatian Christians who desire to stand before God on the basis of the Law by asking, "Tell me, those [of you] who wish to be under Law, do you not hear the Law?" (4:21). What is the problem with a believer who has been justified through faith in Christ wanting to be under the Law? Paul declares, "And I testify again to every man who allows himself to be circumcised that he is *obligated to do the whole Law*" (5:3; also 3:2,10). However, Paul has already excluded this as a possibility even for those who are justified and now alive before God, *including himself*! ("But if. . . *we ourselves* were also found [to be] sinners"; 2:17; also 2:16; 3:10-11; cf. Rom. 7:14-23). This is also true of the "agitators," about whom Paul concludes,

> For those who allow themselves to be circumcised *do not themselves keep the Law*, but they are determined for you to be circumcised in order that they might boast in your flesh (6:13).

It is impossible for a believer to rely upon the Law as the means to maintain or complete his righteous standing before God. This is because the Law is not ἐκ πίστεως (3:12; cf. Rom. 9:30-10:5). Rather, it demands doing, a doing which no one can accomplish to the extent the Law requires. Even the Spirit-led believer is hindered from fulfilling the Law as he is determined to do by the sinful desires of his own flesh. The Spirit and the flesh "are opposing one another, with the result that *you do not do the things which you will*" (5:17). This is precisely the point Paul demonstrates in Romans 7:14-25.

In both Romans and Galatians Paul concludes that the Law is unable to give life because of sin (Gal. 3:21; cf. Rom. 3:19-20; 7:10; 8:3). In Galatians Paul openly declares that the Law also places a curse upon those who possess righteousness through faith and who would again place themselves under the Law. To do so is to forfeit life. If any Galatian Christian submits to circumcision, he thereby obligates himself to do all that the Law commands (5:3). Paul draws out the consequences of this very sharply:

> Behold, I, Paul, am telling you that if you allow your selves to be circumcised, Christ will be of no benefit to you. . . . You have been separated from Christ, those of you who try to be justified by the Law, you have fallen away from grace. . . . You were running well; who hindered you with the result that you are not persuaded by the truth? This persuasion [is] not from the one who called you. A little leaven leavens the whole lump (5:2,4,7-9).

The "little leaven" to which Paul refers is the attempt of Christians, who have attained justification *through faith*, to draw the Law into what follows. They possess leaven by submitting to the requirement of circumcision in order to maintain their status as justified people. They possess leaven by accepting the necessity of adhering to the commands of the Law in order to retain their place among God's justified people. But Paul responds that to place oneself under circumcision and, thereby, the Law (5:2; 4:21) is to submit once again to the lordship of the Law (Rom. 7:1) and, thus, to fall from God's grace.

The pragmatic impact Paul intends his argument to have is obvious. "Do not let yourselves be ensnared to a yoke of slavery again!" (πάλιν; 5:1). Along with this stern *rebuke*, Paul *encourages* the Galatian Christians by directing them, first, to the Holy Spirit whom they have received (3:1-2). He affirms, "If you are being led by the Spirit you are not under the Law" (5:18; cf. 3:24-25; Rom. 6:14; 7:4). If the Spirit has worked faith in a person, the Law cannot effect its condemnation upon his inability to do all that the Law requires because of "the desires of the flesh" (5:16,17). Second, Paul points them to Christ. These Galatians are to *follow Paul's own example*:[66]

> But may it never be that I boast except in the cross of our Lord Jesus Christ, through whom the world has been crucified to me and I to [the] world (6:14).

Paul's use of "I" in this last passage prompts the question, "If Paul is addressing the same topic as he does in Romans 7:14-25, why did he not use the first person singular in Galatians as well?" First, Paul does do so briefly here and in 2:18-21. However, of greater significance is the fact that Paul is constrained to address an actual situation in writing to the Galatians. He is engaged in a critical argument with real-life believers whom he has brought to faith in Jesus Christ. His converts are on the verge of placing themselves under the Law's lordship and, thereby, are in danger of falling away from the Gospel. As a result, Paul employs the third person in order to rebuke his opponents and also heavily utilizes the second person to speak directly to the Galatian Christians.

---

[66]See above, Categories E and G.

Conclusion

In the third and fourth chapters of this book the *referent* of the "I" in Romans 7:7-25 was identified. This was accomplished through *semantics*, that is, by comparing the sense/content of those verses, as determined in Chapter Two, with the sense/content of the other statements Paul makes about himself, as well as his general descriptions of believers and unbelievers, throughout his letters and in Acts. Chapter Five discussed Paul's purpose in Romans 7 and demonstrated the *pragmatic* aspects involved in his use of the first person singular. We now return to the focus of Chapter Two. In light of the issues resolved in the intervening chapters, this conclusion will summarize the *semantic* content of Romans 7. What is the overall sense or meaning of Paul's discussion in Romans 7:7-25?

Paul announces and briefly describes the Gospel which he proclaims throughout his letter to the Romans in the seventeenth verse of the first chapter. This Gospel is the one in which "the righteousness of God is revealed from faith to faith" (1:17). Precisely what Paul means by the phrase ἐκ πίστεως εἰς πίστιν has been vigorously debated.[1] In any event the repetition of πίστις certainly underscores the place of faith. As Paul proceeds to elaborate upon the δικαιοσύνη θεοῦ (1:16) in this Epistle, Chapters 1-8 are properly evaluated as the primary exposition of Paul's teaching on the topic. But what is the place of Romans 7? What purpose does it serve within the entire book?

In *Paul and Palestinian Judaism*, E. P. Sanders defines the essence or function of a religion in terms of *"how getting in and staying in are understood."*[2] Sanders applies this definition to first-century Judaism

---

[1] C. E. B. Cranfield, *A Critical and Exegetical Commentary on the Epistle to the Romans*, 2 vols., The International Critical Commentary, vol. 32, 6th ed. (Edinburgh: T. & T. Clark, 1975,1979), 1:99-100, gives his usual thorough treatment of the options. He concludes, 100, that this phrase most probably has "much the same effect as the *'sola'* of *'sola fide'*." Compare the interesting use of ἐκ and εἰς in 2 Cor. 2:16.

[2] E. P. Sanders, *Paul and Palestinian Judaism* (Philadelphia: Fortress Press, 1977), 17.

which, he contends, was characterized by "covenantal nomism."[3] By this Sanders means that the predominant belief among the Jews of the time was that salvation was granted to them freely by God's election. Submitting to the commands of his Law was merely viewed as the required *response* or the means of "staying in" the covenant.[4]

Whether Sanders's analysis of first-century Judaism is correct or not is a matter of dispute.[5] But if his definition of the vital essence of a religion is appropriate, perhaps it gives an important insight not only into the phrase ἐκ πίστεως εἰς πίστιν (Rom. 1:17), but also into the structure of Romans and, especially, the place of the seventh chapter within that letter.

Paul does not speak specifically in terms of "getting into God's covenant" in Romans.[6] Rather, in somewhat broader fashion and with legal terminology, he addresses the issue of how one can and cannot become righteous before God. Paul asserts that a person is not justified before God "by works of the Law" but through faith in Jesus Christ, the One in whom God has fulfilled his promise to Abraham (3:28; see also 2:1-4:25, especially 3:22,26; 4:13-16; 9:30-10:13). What God has accomplished through the death of his Son (3:21-26) is credited (λογίζομαι) to the sinner purely, totally, and completely ἐκ πίστεως (3:28; 4:5). This is the only way that God's eschatological verdict of

---

[3]According to Sanders, 75, "Covenantal nomism is the view that one's place in God's plan is established on the basis of the covenant and that the covenant requires as the proper response of man his obedience to its commandments, while providing means of atonement for transgression." He later adds, 420, "Obedience maintains one's position in the covenant, but does not earn God's grace as such."

[4]Ibid., 141,146-47,420. He asserts, 420, that statements which "sound like" legalism are not to be taken as doctrine but as exhortations toward obedience which "maintains one's position in the covenant."

[5]See, for example, James Dunn, "The New Perspective on Paul," *The John Rylands University Library Bulletin* 65 (1982-83):95-122; Jacob Neusner, "Comparing Judaisms," *History of Religions* 18 (1978):177-91; A. J. M. Wedderburn, "Paul and the Law," *Scottish Journal of Theology* 38 (1985):613-22.

[6]In Galatians Paul speaks explicitly in terms of the covenant (3:15-18; 4:22-31, especially v. 24), but he does not do so in Romans until chapters 9-11. There he speaks in the plural of the "covenants" which belong to Israel (9:4). The only other occurrence of the term διαθήκη in Romans is in Paul's Old Testament citation in 11:27 (apparently a conflation of Jer. 31:33 and Is. 27:9). Perhaps his scant use of the term is indicative of Paul's view that the redemption accomplished through Christ has fulfilled the covenant and eliminated its nationalistic restrictions.

"Righteous" can be attained and possessed with certainty already in the present age. For Paul, "such a life is given by God, earned by Jesus Christ his Son, and activated in the Christian by the indwelling Spirit."[7]

Does Paul, in Romans, address the issue of how one "remains in" the covenant or maintains his justified status? Once again, Paul does not speak specifically in terms of maintaining one's place in the covenant. But he does deal with the topic of how the believer's justified status is either retained or forfeited. One clear example of this is in Romans 11. There Paul depicts Gentile Christians as the wild olive branches which God has grafted into his tree, Israel, by faith (vv. 17,20). Paul warns these Gentile believers that their standing is not unalterable. Although God's calling is indeed irrevocable (v. 29), they should not become arrogant over against the people of Israel (v. 18). Indeed, if God did not spare the unbelieving and disobedient branches which by nature belonged to the tree, how much less will the grafted-in Gentiles be spared if they too fall away into unbelief (ἀπιστία, v. 20; compare 23; 4:20)? Paul concludes,

> Behold, therefore, [the] kindness and severity of God; upon those who fell, severity, but upon you (σὲ), [the] kindness of God, if you remain in [his] kindness, otherwise you will also be cut-off (11:22).

In this argument Paul contends that an individual believer[8] continues or remains (ἐπιμένω) in God's gracious kindness (χρηστότης) the same way in which he becomes righteous. Verse 20 declares that a believer has been established righteous before God through faith *and retains that righteous standing* in the same way (σὺ δὲ τῇ πίστει ἔστηκας; perfect of ἵστημι; v. 20). It is ἐκ πίστεως εἰς πίστιν (1:17).

These insights support the conclusion that *Paul uses Romans 7 to exclude the possibility of anyone attempting either to become righteous or to maintain a righteous standing before God by observing the Law's*

---

[7]Jan Lambrecht, *The Wretched "I" and Its Liberation*, Louvain Theological and Pastoral Monographs, 14 (Grand Rapids: Eerdmans Publishing, 1992), 91.

[8]The second person singular form in Rom. 11:22 is interesting. It speaks to each individual believer as the first person singular in 7:7-25 is also able to do; compare also the second person singular in 8:2.

commands. All those who are under the Law's lordship (7:1) or who rely upon the Law before God (2:17) are, rather, condemned by the Law. This is because God's Law requires man's "doing" (2:13,25; 10:5 citing Lev. 18:5; see also Gal. 3:10-12, citing Deut. 27:26 and Lev. 18:5) and no one, not even one who has faith, is able to fulfill the Law to the extent God requires (Rom. 3:19-20; 7:14-25; Gal. 2:16; 3:11).

In Romans 7:7-25 Paul vividly illustrates why this is so from the experience of his own life. The Law's command had no positive role in his attainment of the δικαιοσύνη θεοῦ (vv. 7-11); neither was Paul's continued justified status a matter of first faith and then obedience to the Law (vv. 14-25). His own life exemplifies why it is "impossible" (Rom. 8:3) to use the Law as a means to earn or maintain God's favor.

Why does Paul speak to this issue while writing to the Christians in Rome? Verses 7-13 are certainly applicable to unbelieving Jews who are addressed in a rhetorical manner and characterized as relying on the Law throughout the Epistle (particularly 2:17-29, 3:9-11; 9:30-10:5). However, Paul is *not* using verses 14-25 to attack those who attempt to *gain* a righteous standing before God by obeying the Law's commands.[9] Rather, as Andrew Bandstra observes, "The Apostle was well aware of the threat of Christians returning to the bondage of the law" (7:1).[10] Franz Leenhardt similarly proposes that Paul, as in

---

[9]This is often suggested. For example, F. F. Bruce, *The Letter of Paul to the Romans*, rev. ed., The Tyndale New Testament Commentaries, vol. 6 (Grand Rapids: Eerdmans Publishing, 1963), 136-37, concludes, "In this section of Romans Paul tells us more clearly than anywhere else how he found the law so inadequate as a way to secure a righteous standing before God." According to John A. T. Robertson, *Wrestling with Romans* (Philadelphia: Westminster Press, 1979), 85, Paul's point here is that the Law is powerless to "bring life." Anders Nygren, *Commentary on Romans*, tr. C. Rasmussen (Philadelphia: Muhlenberg Press, 1949), 296-97, also argues that the Law's position in the Christian life is "essentially negative, since even the Christian cannot attain to righteousness by way of the law." For Paul the believer already has life and has already "attained to righteousness" before God. Paul is addressing what the Law effects *within one who is already righteous*. His purpose is to eliminate the possibility of even a believer being able to rely on the Law to maintain his status before God. James Dunn, "Rom. 7,14-25 in the Theology of Paul," *Theologische Zeitschrift* 31 (1975):268, n. 56, properly critiques Nygren on this point.

[10]Andrew Bandstra, *The Law and Elements of the World* (Grand Rapids: Eerdmans Publishing, n.d.), 149; Paul's earlier struggles with the Galatians is likely a factor here. Ronald Fung, "The Impotence of the Law: Toward a Fresh Understanding of Romans 7:14-25," in *Scripture, Tradition, and Interpretation*, ed. W. Gasque and W. LaSor (Grand Rapids: Eerdmans Publishing, 1978), 42,45, contends that these

Galatians, is opposing "Judaizing temptations."[11] Paul's words in verses 14-25 serve to rebuke any believer, Jew or Gentile, who tries to maintain or complete one's place in the covenant, that is, their justified status through the performance of works done in accordance with God's will as revealed in his Word.

Paul responds to that erroneous view of the believer's life particularly in Romans 7:14-25. There he endeavors to show why the Law, even though it is spiritual and holy (7:14,12), even though it informs and directs the will of the believer, can ultimately accomplish nothing *coram Deo* for fleshly man.[12] If there were Christians who believed that they maintained their justified status by living according to the Law, Paul soundly rebukes that approach. So also, if first-century Judaism did in fact contend that obedience to the Law's commands enabled one to "stay in" God's covenant,[13] Paul similarly rejects that view. Paul's crucial point in Romans 7:14-25 is that the Law cannot be relied upon as that which *maintains* the justified believer's continued righteous, pure, and holy standing before God.

Is Romans 7 then, after all, a "defense of the Law"?[14] The "I" is used by Paul in verses 7-25 to describe the actual effects which the Law's command had in relation to sin and death upon him as an unbeliever (vv. 7-11; see 1 Tim. 1:13) and, then, to portray the Law's

---

verses speak of an immature or legalistic Christian. Bruce, *The Letter of Paul to the Romans*, 143, similarly contends, "Paul may have known believers who were nevertheless living in legal bondage because they had not appreciated or appropriated the fullness of gospel freedom." The last two statements, however, imply that there is some middle ground for Paul. Paul's discussion of the same issue in Galatians excludes this.

[11]Franz Leenhardt, *The Epistle to the Romans*, tr. H. Knight (London: Lutterworth Press, 1961), 198; similarly, Matthew Black, *Commentary on Romans*, New Century Bible (London: Oliphants, 1973), 100. Leenhardt, 198, adds, "This relapse into legalism and moralism is a failing characteristic of Christians." Perhaps it is a constant temptation and an enduring tendency, but to call it a "characteristic failing" is too extreme.

[12]Robinson, *Wrestling with Romans*, 91.

[13]As Sanders contends, 17; see above.

[14]As suggested by Werner Kümmel, *Römer 7 und die Bekehrung des Paulus* (Leipzig: Hinrichs, 1929); reprinted in *Römer 7 und das Bild des Menschen im Neuen Testament: Zwei Studien,* Theologische Bücherei, Neues Testament Band 53 (Munich: Christian Kaiser Verlag, 1974), 56.

"double effect" on him as a Christian (vv. 14-25).[15] On the one hand, it is true that "above all *Hamartia* . . . is the object of Paul's attack in this chapter."[16] But the fact that an interrelationship between the Law and sin exists is what necessitates Paul's statements in defense of the Law. Certainly, then, one of Paul's major concerns in this chapter, as revealed especially by his assertions in verses 12-13, is to exonerate the Law from blame. In addition, verses 14-25 affirm that the Spiritual Law informs the believer of God's will and directs him toward the good and away from evil.

However, as the end of Romans 7 is reached, and as the initial verses of Chapter 8 make even more clear, verses 7-25 ultimately "cannot be meant as an apology for the law."[17] For while Paul defends and vindicates the Law, "at the same time, as suggested by v. 6, the Apostle wishes to demonstrate the inadequacy of the law for salvation."[18] As a result, Paul's praise of the Law in this chapter is neither unequivocal nor unlimited. Paul himself had been incited to sin, deceived, and then killed by sin through the Law's command (vv. 7-11). And even now, as a Christian, though he joyfully agrees with the Law and willingly strives to carry it out, Paul cannot do so (vv. 14-25). This is because the Law is weakened "through the flesh" (Rom. 8:3; compare 7:14).

Romans 7 reveals an aspect of Paul's theology which dare not be neglected. His main point is to illustrate why no one can, in any way, depend on their "doing" the Law either for earning (vv. 7-11) or maintaining one's righteousness before God (vv. 14-25). Through his use of the "I," Paul demonstrates precisely why he or any other person is unable to rely upon his own observance of the Law. It is because sin, which reigns in the flesh of unbelievers (6:14,17,22), is able to misuse

---

[15]See Chapter Two above. Gerd Theissen, *Psychological Aspects of Pauline Theology*, tr. J. Galvin (Philadelphia: Fortress Press, 1987), 190, states, "Both sections of the text make the point that the law leads into conflict, not in principle, but functionally."

[16]Black, 104; also Ernst Gaugler, *Der Brief an die Römer*, Prophezei, 2 vols. (Zürich: Zwingli-Verlag, 1945), 1:204-5.

[17]Ernst Käsemann, *Commentary on Romans*, tr. and ed. G. Bromiley (Grand Rapids: Eerdmans Publishing, 1980), 210.

[18]Bandstra, 134.

the Law's commandment in order to provoke sin, to deceive, and to kill (vv. 7-11,13). It is because sin, which continues to dwell in the believer's flesh and to work in his members (vv. 14,17,20), is able to prohibit him from doing the "good" the Law requires and he desires. As long as the believer remains in this world, there is that within him, namely, his flesh which, corrupted by sin, also leads one to do the evil "I hate" (vv. 14-23). Paul's own example affirms this is true even after a person has been declared justified from sin (6:7) through faith in Jesus Christ and, thereby, freed from the *lordship* of sin, death, and the Law.

As a result, the content of what the "I" speaks in Romans 7:14-25 fits squarely within Paul's view of the Christian life. If a believer, indeed, even if Paul attempts to rely upon his observance of the Law for retaining his righteous standing before God, he is subject, once again, to the Law's condemnation and to the same accusations leveled against the Jew in 2:17-24.[19] Paul is using the first person singular in order to make this point very clear to his readers: "Do not rely upon the Law for that which it is impossible for the Law to accomplish because of sin which dwells in the flesh" (see 8:3a).

At the same time, throughout his letters Paul urges believers to follow the lead of the Spirit who renews and directs their "will," "mind," and "inner man" to strive to fulfill the Law in their daily lives. [Note the presence of these terms throughout verses 14-25.] However, even after being justified through faith, believers must remain aware that their actions fail to live up to the Law's demands. Since the desires of their sinful flesh prohibit them from fulfilling all of the requirements of the Law, they cannot base their continued status as a justified believer on their obedience to the Law.

But while the Law's command is "unable" to overcome the sinful flesh,[20] the Gospel declares that *God has fulfilled the just requirement*

---

[19]See Bandstra, 144; earlier in Romans Paul has generally used the second person to draw out the tragic consequences for those Jews who are relying upon the Law (2:17-29; 3:19-20; see also vv. 1-16).

[20]According to C. Marvin Pate, *The End of the Age Has Come* (Grand Rapids: Zondervan Publishing, 1995), 104-5, this stands in sharp contrast to the views expressed at Qumran and in rabbinic doctrine, where "the antidote to the fleshly impulse is the Law."

(δικαίωμα) of the Law in Jesus Christ (8:3b-4a). The Law can no longer effect its condemnation against those who are "in" him (8:1). As a result, Paul exhorts Christians to be ever cognizant that the Gospel is what has made, and also keeps, them holy because it proclaims and continuously delivers the forgiveness and righteousness Christ has won for them (3:24-25). When they do fall away from the Spirit's leading, as the believer in this world will inevitably do, it is only the Gospel of Jesus Christ which can continue to cover them (ἰλαστήριον in 3:25) with God's grace.

In Romans 7 Paul decisively proves that his and our righteous standing before God cannot be either earned or maintained by obedience to the Law's command. Thankfully (7:25), it is not a matter of works "I" do or am able to refrain from doing. Rather, our righteousness must be and, in fact, has already been accomplished solely by God's action in Jesus Christ. Paul reveals this when he draws his conclusion regarding the Law in the initial verses of Chapter 8: "For what was impossible for the Law in that it was weakened through the flesh, God [accomplished] by sending his own Son in the likeness of sinful flesh" (8:3a). Faith in Jesus Christ alone establishes *and maintains* a righteous standing before God. "For we maintain that a person is justified by faith *apart from works of [the] Law"* (3:28). The δικαιοσύνη θεοῦ is received and retained ἐκ πίστεως εἰς πίστιν (1:16-17).

Appendix

A Survey of the Interpretations of the "I" in Romans 7 in Sources Prior to 1900

The analysis conducted in Chapter One covered the contemporary interpretations of the "I" in Romans 7:7-25. However, the introduction to this thesis noted that a division of interpretations has surrounded Romans 7 "from the earliest centuries until today."[1] For historical perspective it will be helpful to survey a number of the identifications which were made of the "I" prior to 1900.[2] These will be presented in the same format as was utilized in Chapter One.

Romans 7:7-11

Paul

As early as Origen (circa 185-245), the difficulties involved in applying Romans 7:9 to Paul's own life were recognized. Origen contends that Paul was never alive apart from the Law of Moses (*"sine lege Moysi"*).[3] Yet he is able to resolve the issue in a manner which maintains Paul as the "I." When and how was Paul living "apart from the Law" (χωρὶς νόμου 7:9)? Origen answers that Paul is not using νόμος here to refer to the Mosaic Law, but to the Law "which is

---

[1]James Dunn, "Rom. 7,14 in the Theology of Paul," in *Theologische Zeitschrift* 31 (1975):257.

[2]For a more extensive survey, see Otto Kuss, *Der Römerbrief*, 3 vols. (Regensburg: Verlag Friedrich Pustet, 1963), 2:462-85, entitled "Zur Geschichte der Auslegung von Röm 7,7-25"; Werner Kümmel, *Römer 7 und die Bekehrung des Paulus*, Leipzig: Hinrichs, 1929; reprinted in *Römer 7 und das Bild des Menschen im Neuen Testament: Zwei Studien*, Theologische Bücherei, Neues Testament Band 53 (Munich: Christian Kaiser Verlag, 1974), especially 76-97,109,119-20. [Hereafter *Römer 7.*]

[3]Origen, "Commentaria in epistolam b. Pauli ad Romanos," Latin translation by Rufinius, in *Patrologiae: Patrum Graecorum*, ed. J. P. Migne, vol. 14 (Paris: 1862), col. 1082.

written in the human heart."[4] Origen then applies this phrase to the time when "both Paul and all men are certain to have formerly lived, that is, in early childhood."[5]

Augustine (354-430) further amplifies this line of interpretation. He proposes that Paul was living apart from the Law in his earliest years ("*ab infantia*") before his rational powers took hold ("*ante rationales annos*").[6] According to Augustine, verse 9a "should be understood to mean, 'I seemed to be alive' [*vivere mihi videbar*], since before the command sin lay hidden."[7] The coming of the commandment (v. 9b) then signifies that "sin began to make itself known, and moreover I came to recognize [*cognovi*] that I was dead."[8]

In his lectures on Romans from 1515-16, Martin Luther (1483-1546) clearly identifies the "I" in Romans 7:7-11 as Paul, but extends the application of these verses to the experience of others as well. Paul "is speaking of his own person and of all the saints."[9] How does Luther then interpret this passage? In his gloss on verse 9 he writes,

> *And I was once,* just as anyone else, *alive,* not because there was no law, *apart from the Law,* apart from a knowledge of the Law and therefore also

---

[4] Ibid., col. 1080, *"illa lex, quae in hominum cordibus scripta est."*

[5] Ibid., 1082, *"Sine hac lege et Paulum et omnes homines certum est aliquando vixisse, hoc est in aetate puerili."*

[6] Augustine, "Contra duas Epistolas Pelagianorum," in *Patrologiae: Patrum Latinorum*, ed. J. P. Migne, vol. 44 (Paris: 1865), 8.14, col. 558, *"haec omnia potest videri apostolus de sua vita commemorasse praeterita, ut illud, quod ait, 'ego autem vivebam aliquando sine lege', aetatem suam primam ab infantia ante rationales annos voluerit intelligi."*

[7] Augustine, *Augustine on Romans*, text and tr. P. Landes, Society of Biblical Literature Texts and Translations, no. 23, Early Christian Literature Series, no. 6 (Chico, CA: Scholars Press, 1982), 14-15.

[8] Ibid., 15.

[9] Martin Luther, "Lectures on Romans: Glosses and Scholia" (1515-16), *Luther's Works*, American Edition, vol. 25, ed. H. Oswald, tr. W. G. Tillmanns and J. A. O. Preus (St. Louis: Concordia Publishing House, 1972), 61, in his gloss on verse 10; see also idem., "Der Brief an die Römer" (1516-17), *D. Martin Luthers Werke*, Weimar Ausgabe, Band 56, ed. F. Ficker (Weimar: Hermann Böhlhaus Nachfolger, 1938), 68, n. 2, *"loquitur in persona sua et omnium sanctorum."* It should be noted that this is "early" Luther.

without sin, *but when the commandment came,* came to be known, *sin,* which previously had been dead because it was not known, *revived.*[10]

The coming of the commandment denotes the occasion when "we recognize that we have been made subject" to the old man and to sin through the Law.[11]

The question of when the "I" in verses 7-11 refers to Paul cannot be determined precisely from Luther's commentary.[12] On the one hand, it seems that Luther understands the "I" in Romans 7 as descriptive of the Christian Paul beginning already in verse 7. After citing 7:7, Luther states,

> From this passage on to the end of the chapter the apostle is speaking in his own person and as a spiritual man and by no means merely in the person of a carnal man.[13]

Luther proceeds to detail twelve reasons which support this contention.[14] However, none of the passages he cites in that section are from verses 7-11. This points toward an alternate possibility. Did Luther view verses 7-11 as applicable to Paul prior to his conversion? In his explanation of the manner in which sin lies dead apart from the Law (v. 8), Luther cites Augustine's reference to the time when a child's reason awakens.[15] Luther says,

> The Law revives and sin begins to make its appearance when the Law

---

[10]Luther, "Lectures on Romans," 61; see also idem., "Der Brief an die Römer," 67, which speaks of the period when Paul was *"sine cognitione legis."*

[11]Luther, "Lectures on Romans," 58, note 6.

[12]Kümmel, *Römer 7,* 77, suggests that "the opinion of the Reformers" (*"die Meinung der Reformatoren"*) was that "the 'coming of the commandment' . . . signified the conversion" of Paul (*"das 'Kommen des Gebotes' . . . bezeichne die Bekehrung"*). This is not the interpretation of Luther, however. More appropriate to Luther is Kümmel's later statement, ibid., 88, which contends that the Reformers, except for Bucer and Musculus, support interpreting verses 7-25 of Paul the Christian.

[13]Luther, "Lectures on Romans," 327.

[14]Ibid., 327-36.

[15]Ibid., 337, after citing Augustine with approval; see ibid., n. 8, which refers to Augustine, "Contra Julianum," *Patrologiae: Patrum Latinorum,* ed. J. P. Migne, vol. 44 (Paris: 1865), 2.4.8, col. 679; see above.

begins to be recognized; then concupiscence which had lain quiet during infancy breaks forth and becomes manifest.[16]

This description would certainly allow placing these verses in the period prior to Paul's conversion. But Luther then finds "a still deeper meaning" in verses 7-11 and applies what they describe to those "who are children in their understanding even if they are a hundred years old."[17] Since Luther believed that the Christian's battle against the old man continues throughout his earthly life, verses 7-11 are also applicable to Paul after his conversion. According to Luther, then, these verses are descriptive of Paul *both* before *and* after his conversion.[18]

In his commentary on Romans, John Calvin (1509-64) proposes an interpretation of verses 7-11 which is similar to the one adopted here. Calvin contends that Paul begins with a "universal proposition" (vv. 7-8), but then proceeds "by his [own] example" (vv. 9-11).[19] Paul was living apart from the Law (v. 9a) when "he, being void of the Spirit . . . did please himself in the external show of righteousness."[20] Though "Paul did mount higher than the common capacity of man is able to reach,"[21] the Law finally came to him (v. 9b) as a "minister of death."[22] Then "the filthiness of [his] sin was revealed by the law."[23]

Adam

Throughout history a number of exegetes have identified the "I" in Romans 7:7-11 with the experience of Adam. Those who advocate this position generally contend that Adam's experience is also, and

---

[16]Luther, "Lectures on Romans," 337.

[17]Ibid.

[18]This is because Luther does not distinguish between the solely negative effect which the Law has upon the "I" in verses 7-11 and the "twofold servitude" of the "I" to the Law in verses 14-25. Luther, ibid., 336, does specifically identify the latter.

[19]John Calvin, *Commentary upon the Epistle of Saint Paul to the Romans*, tr. C. Rosdell, ed. H. Beveridge (Edinburgh: The Calvin Translation Society, 1844), 177.

[20]Ibid., 178.

[21]Ibid., 176.

[22]Ibid., 178.

[23]Ibid., 179.

generally, applicable to others. Methodius (died circa 311) identifies the time "without the Law" in verse 9 as the days in Paradise and then quotes Genesis 2:17 in reference to the coming of the commandment.[24] Theodore of Mopsuestia (circa 350-428) contends that through the "I" Paul is utilizing the experience of Adam as an example (ὑπόδειγμα).[25] Theodoret (circa 390-457) also identifies the "I" with Adam who received the sentence of death after sin sprang to life.[26]

The Jewish People

John Chrysostom (circa 374-407) disagrees with those who interpret the commandment in Romans 7:9b in terms of either the "natural law"[27] or the commandment given in Paradise (Gen. 2:17).[28] He asserts that νόμος must be a reference to the Mosaic Law.[29] Chrysostom then identifies the time before the Law's coming (7:9a) as the period before Moses.[30] As a result, the "I" represents the experience of the Jewish people to whom the commandment came at Mount Sinai. This interpretation is adopted by Hugo Grotius (1583-1645). He contends that the first person singular pronoun in verse 9 denotes the "people of Israel who indeed lived before the Law, namely in Egypt."[31]

---

[24]Methodius, "Ex libro de resurrectione," in *Patrologiae: Patrum Graecorum*, ed. J. P. Migne, vol. 18 (Paris: 1857), col. 297.

[25]Theodore of Mopsuestia, "Epistolam ad Romanos" (fragments), in *Patrologiae: Patrum Graecorum*, ed. J. P. Migne, vol. 66 (Paris: 1864), col. 809; see also col. 811.

[26]Theodoret, " Ἑρμηνεία τῆς πρὸς Ῥομαίους ἐπιστόλης," in *Patrologiae: Patrum Graecorum*, ed. J. P. Migne, vol. 82 (Paris: 1864), col. 117.

[27]See, for example, Origen, as discussed above.

[28]See, for example, Methodius, as discussed above.

[29]John Chrysostom, "Ἑρμηνεία τῆς πρὸς Ῥομαίου ς ἐπιστόλης ," in *Patrologiae: Patrum Graecorum*, ed. J. P. Migne, vol. 60 (Paris: 1862), col. 502.

[30]Ibid., col. 501, "πότε, εἶπε μοὶ πρὸ Μωϋσέως.

[31]Hugo Grotius, *Annotationes in Novum Testamentum*, Ed. nova. Tom. II. Erlangen: 1757, 267, *"id est genus Israeliticum, vixit et ante legem, in Aegypto scilicet"*; cited from Kümmel, *Römer 7*, 85.

A General Use of the "I"

Werner Kümmel suggests that Ambrosiaster (active circa 363-84) was the first to advocate a more general interpretation of the "I" which is similar to his own.[32] Ambrosiaster disputes that the first person singular in Romans 7:7-11 is used by Paul to refer either to the Jews or to Christians who are devoting themselves to live in accordance with the Law.[33] Specifically in regard to the last phrase in verse 7, he concludes that Paul "brings up his own person as a general case."[34] Augustine's initial interpretation of verses 7-25 is comparable.[35] He writes, "It appears to me that at this place the Apostle transfigures in himself a man placed under the Law, he is speaking of himself by [these] words from his own person."[36] Pelagius (circa 400) also advocates the view that "here in his own person [Paul] is speaking of man who receives the Law."[37] Johann Bengel (1687-1752) adopts a similar position. He contends,

> Paul often puts forth an indefinite discourse through the first person, not only for the sake of clarity, but for a general application to himself. It is so in this place.[38]

The "rhetorical" interpretation of the "I" in Romans 7:7-11 has been present throughout history. However, one should not identify this

---

[32]Kümmel, *Römer 7*, 87.

[33]Ambrosiaster, "Commentaria in XIII epistolas beati Pauli," in *Patrologiae: Patrum Latinorum*, ed. J. P. Migne, vol. 17 (Paris: 1879), cols. 112-13, on Rom. 7:5.

[34]Ibid., col. 114, *"sub sua persona quasi generalem agit causam."*

[35]*Circa* 388-97; but compare his later interpretation below.

[36]Augustine, "De Diversis Quaestionibus ad Simplicianum," in *Patrologiae: Patrum Latinorum*, ed. J. P. Migne, vol. 40 (Paris: 1887), col. 103, *"quo loco videtur mihi Apostolus transfigurasse in se hominem sub lege positum, cuius verbis e persona sua loquitur."*

[37]Pelagius, "Expositiones XIII Epistularum Pauli," in *Patrologiae Latinae Supplementum*, ed. Adelberto Hamman, vol. 1 (Paris: Éditions Garnier Frères, 1958), 1142, *"hinc in persona eius hominis loquitur, qui legem accipit."*

[38]Johann Bengel, *Gnomon Novi Testamenti*, 3rd ed. (Tubingae: Sumtibus Ludov. Frid. Fues., 1855), 560, *"Saepe Paulus indefinitum sermonem proponit per primam personam, non solum perspicuitatis gratia, sed ex perpetua applicatione ad se ipsum. Et sic hoc loco."*

completely with Kümmel's view which asserts that the "I" is totally without any connection to Paul's own experience.[39] Those who previously advocated a more general interpretation of the "I" in verses 7-11 seem to be in closer agreement with Origen who identifies the subject in these verses as "Paul and all men."[40]

Romans 7:14-25

Kümmel points out that the issue which has received the greatest amount of attention in the history of the church is not whether the "I" portrayed in verses 14-25 is Paul or not, but whether the "I" there is a regenerate or unregenerate person.[41] While the latter question has dominated the discussion of these verses, and continues to be a major point of contention, the issue of whether Paul himself is to be identified as the "I" has not been completely overlooked.

In the Name of Unregenerate Man

Origen questions whether the "I" in these verses is Paul and then suggests that Paul might be speaking of another.[42] On verse 25 Origen concludes that Paul is not, in fact, speaking "of his own person but from his apostolic authority."[43] Origen identifies the description in verses 14-25 as that of an unregenerate person and this view was adopted by "the mass of Greek Fathers," as well as by some of those in the West.[44] Among the latter, Augustine can be included, but only in

---

[39]See, for example, Kümmel, *Römer 7*, 84; also those cited above in the survey of Chapter One.

[40]Origen, col. 1082, *"Paulum et omnes homines."* See the citations from Augustine and Pelagius above.

[41]Kümmel, *Römer 7*, 76; he contends that Augustine was the first to apply these verses explicitly to Paul's own life and that Luther then championed this view.

[42]Origen, col. 1085, *"Nam Paulus qui in aliis dixit."*

[43]Ibid., col. 1089, *"jam non ex illius personae, sed ex apostolica auctoritate."*

[44]William Sanday and Arthur Headlam, *A Critical and Exegetical Commentary on the Epistle to the Romans*, The International Critical Commentary, vol. 32 (New York: Charles Scribner's Sons, 1902), 184. Kümmel, *Römer 7*, 119-20, identifies Chrysostom and Theodoret in the East, as well as Ambrosiaster, Pelagius, and Julian in the West, among those who advocate a non-Christian interpretation.

his earlier years (circa 388-97). In his "Propositions from the Epistle to the Romans," Augustine writes the following concerning verses 15-16:

> The man described here is under the Law, prior to grace; sin overcomes him when by his own strength he attempts to live righteously without the aid of God's liberating grace.[45]

A number of those who agree with Augustine's initial view have attempted to define Paul's use of the first person singular in a variety of different ways. For example, Hugo Grotius refers to the verb μετασχηματίζω in 1 Corinthians 4:6 and contends that Paul is similarly applying the description in Romans 7 to himself in a figurative manner.[46]

Paul and Other Christians

Among the Greek Fathers, only Methodius appears to have held the position that Paul is speaking of his present Christian life in verses 14-25.[47] In the West this interpretation was more common. For example, Ambrose (circa 340-97) contends,

> The Apostle himself, [as] a chosen vessel of the Lord, speaks: [cites Rom. 7:23]. But he himself was not able [to overcome] in this fight and therefore he flees to Christ saying: [cites v. 24].[48]

However, Augustine's interpretation of these verses is the one which proves most interesting. In his later writings (circa 418-19),

---

[45] Augustine, *Augustine on Romans*, 17. Ibid., 19, contends that Paul "begins to describe the man constituted under grace" in verse 25.

[46] Grotius, 267; cited from Kümmel, *Römer 7*, 120. See also the other suggestions noted and then rejected by Kümmel, ibid., 120-21.

[47] Methodius, cols 299-301; he, col. 301, compares the state of the "I" with the experience of David by citing Psalm 18:13-14 (Septuagint). Kümmel, *Römer 7*, 90, contends that Methodius was the only one of the Greek fathers to hold this position; see also Sanday and Headlam, 185.

[48] Ambrose, "De Abraham Libro Duo," in *Patrologiae: Patrum Latinorum*, ed. J. P. Migne, vol. 14 (Paris: 1882), 2.6.27, col, 490, *"ipse apostolus, vas electionis dominicae, dicit:* [cites Rom. 7:23]. *Sedare hanc pugnam ipse nequiverat, et ideo ad Christum confugit dicens:* [cites v. 24]."

Augustine explicitly repudiates his earlier position[49] and contends that verses 14-25 depict Paul's present condition. He refers to these verses as a place where Paul,

> by introducing his own person, instructs us saying, "For what I wish, this I do not perform, but what I hate, that I do," that is by concupiscence, because this [concupiscence] is also not willing to do, so that everything is perfected [only] in part.[50]

Thomas Aquinas (circa 1225-1274) refers to Augustine's two different interpretations and concludes that this, his second position, is "ever so much better."[51]

Martin Luther addresses this question specifically in response to Nicholas of "Lyra and others [who] say that the apostle is speaking regarding the person of some degraded man and not of his own person."[52] Luther contends that Paul

> is speaking of his own person and of all the saints and of the abysmal darkness of our heart, by which even the saints and the wisest men have nothing but an imperfect concept of themselves and thus of the Law.[53]

In an extensive discussion of these verses, Luther enumerates twelve points in favor of his interpretation that Paul here describes himself, as well as other Christians.[54] The "I" cannot be an unbeliever because this

---

[49]See Augustine, "Retractionum S. Augustini," Books 1 and 2, in *Patrologiae: Patrum Latinorum*, ed. J. P. Migne, vol. 32 (Paris: 1845), 1.23.1, cols. 620-21 and 2.1.1, cols. 629-30.

[50]Augustine, "De Nuptiis et Concupiscentia," Book 2, in *Patrologiae: Patrum Latinorum*, ed. J. P. Migne (Paris: 1865): 27.30, col. 431, *"et alio loco apostolus loquens velut ex suae personae introductione nos instruit dicens: 'non enim quod volo, hoc ago, sed quod odi, illud facio', id est concupisco, quia et hoc nollet facere, ut esset omni ex parte perfectus."* Kümmel, *Römer 7*, 90-94, discusses the source and significance of Augustine's change in interpretation at length. A key point is that the desire toward evil is no longer understood in terms of sexual lust and adultery but is seen as rational desire or concupiscence as in the citation here.

[51]Thomas Aquinas, *Super Epistolas S. Pauli Lectura*, ed. P. Raphaelis Cai, 13th ed., rev. (Rome: Marietti Editori, 1953), 101, *"quamvis secunda expositio melior sit."*

[52]Luther, "Lectures on Romans," 61, note 15.

[53]Ibid.

[54]See ibid., 326-36. Luther does not completely separate the two parts of a Christian

struggle against sin is "never heard of in the case of carnal man."[55] Luther concludes that the "I" must be a believer whom he defines as follows:

> The saints at the same time as they are righteous are also sinners [*quod simul Sancti, dum sunt Iusti, sunt peccatores*]; righteous because they believe in Christ, whose righteousness covers them and is imputed to them, but sinners because they do not fulfill the Law, are not without concupiscence, and are like sick men under the care of a physician.[56]

Luther also identifies one of the effects which Paul's admittance of his own sinfulness might have upon his readers.

> It is a comfort to hear that such a great apostle was involved in the same sorrows and afflictions as we are when we try to be obedient to God.[57]

Calvin similarly refutes the "common error" which proposes that all of Romans 7 describes "the nature of unregenerate man."[58] He responds that in verses 14-25 Paul is speaking of the faithful in whom the Spirit flourishes. The Apostle is illustrating "the consent of a sound [believing] mind with the righteousness of the law, because the flesh cannot hate sin."[59]

Augustine's later interpretation of the "I" as a regenerate man dominated for a number of centuries in this millennium due to the influential support it received from Aquinas and the Reformers. However, as illustrated in the first chapter of this study, the tide of

---

which battle one against the other, but rather unites them together in the "I." He, ibid., 332, concludes, "Therefore we must note that the words 'I want' and 'I hate' refer to the spiritual man or to the spirit, but 'I do' and 'I work' refer to the carnal man or to the flesh. But because the same one complete man consists of flesh and spirit, therefore he attributes to the whole man both of these opposing qualities which come from the opposing parts of him."

[55]Ibid., 335.

[56]Ibid., 336; the Latin is cited from idem., "Der Brief an die Römer," 347.

[57]Luther, "Lectures on Romans," 335; see Chapter Five of this study. In the light of statements such as this, Kümmel, *Römer 7*, 95, concludes that the reason Luther adopted his interpretation of Romans 7 was largely due to his own religious experience.

[58]Calvin, 185.

[59]Ibid., 186.

current scholarly opinion has turned toward the conclusion that Augustine's earlier position, which identified the "I" in verses 14-24 as an unbeliever, was correct. Kümmel concludes that "this interpretation, generally widespread in the case of Catholics, has become the usual [one] among Protestant exegetes."[60]

Conclusion

While one or the other interpretation of the "I" in Romans 7:7-25 has prevailed at times, this brief overview illustrates that a variety of identifications have been made, and have persisted, throughout the history of the church. Since the earliest centuries of the New Testament era, interpreters have been aware of the difficulties presented by Paul's use of the first person singular in Romans 7:7-25 and these difficulties continue to confound exegetes in our own day.

This survey also reveals that the various identifications of the "I" which are currently being advocated are not, at least in their basic form, without precedent. Each of the interpretations discussed in the first chapter of this work has its source or, at least to some degree, a background and foundation within the history of interpretation.

---

[60]Kümmel, Römer 7, 95, *"Seither ist diese Auslegung, bei den Katholiken allgemein verbreitet, auch unter den protestantischen Auslegern die übliche geworden."* With "since then" (*"seither"*), Kümmel, ibid., refers to Philipp Spener (1635-1705) who questioned whether verses 18-19 could be true of Paul and then identifies August H. Francke (1663-1727) as the one who adopted, and began to turn the tide back toward, the non-Christian interpretation of verses 14-25. Ibid., 95-96, admits that the later Augustinian position is still defended in a variety of forms, citing, for example, Paul Feine, M. R. Engel, and Theodor Zahn.

Bibliography

Romans 7 and Pauline Theology

Achtemeier, Paul J. "Some Things in Them Hard to Understand."
Interpretation 38 1984):254-67.

Alexander, William. "St. Paul's Infirmity." *Expository Times* 15
(1903-4):469-73,545-48.

Alford, Henry. *The Greek New Testament*. 4 vols. 5th edition.
Cambridge: Deighton, Dell, and Co., 1865.

Althaus, Paul. *Der Brief an die Römer*. Das Neue Testament Deutsch,
vol. 6. 10th ed. Edited by Paul Althaus and Gerhard Friedrich.
Göttingen: Vandenhoeck & Ruprecht, 1966.

_____. *Paulus und Luther über den Menschen*. Studien der Luther-
Akademie, 14. Gütersloh: "Der Rufer" Evangelische Verlag, 1938.

_____. "Zur Auslegung von Röm 7,14ff." *Theologische
Literaturzeitung* 77 (1952):cols. 475-80.

Ambrosiaster. "Commentaria in XIII epistolas beati Pauli." In
Patrologiae: Patrum Latinorum, ed. J. P. Migne, vol. 17, cols. 45-
184. Paris: 1879.

Aquinas, Thomas. *Super Epistolas S. Pauli Lectura*. Edited by P.
Raphaelis Cai. Revised 13th edition. Rome: Marietti Editori, 1953.

Arndt, William F. *The Life of Saint Paul: The Greatest Missionary*.
Concordia Teacher Training Series. St. Louis: Concordia
Publishing House, 1944.

_____. "Romans." Notes. Concordia Seminary Library, St. Louis,
MO. No date.

Augustine. *Augustine on Romans: Propositions from the Epistle to the
Romans [and] Unfinished Commentary on the Epistle to the
Romans*. Text and Translation by Paul Fredricksen Landes.
Society of Biblical Literature Texts and Translations, no. 23. Early
Christian Literature Series, no. 6. Chico, CA: Scholars Press, 1982.

Augustine. "Expositio quarumdam propositionum ex epistola ad
Romanos." In *Patrologiae: Patrum Latinorum*, ed. J. P. Migne,
vol. 35, cols. 2063-88. Paris: 1845.

Bader, Günter. "Römer 7 als Skopus einer theologischen Handlungstheorie." *Zeitschrift für Theologie und Kirche* 78 (1981):31-56.

Bandstra, Andrew. *The Law and the Elements of the World.* Grand Rapids: Eerdmans Publishing, n.d.

Banks, Robert. "Romans 7.25a: An Eschatological Thanksgiving?" *Australian Biblical Review* 26 (1979):34-42.

Barosse, Thomas. "Death and Sin in Saint Paul's Epistle to the Romans." *Catholic Biblical Quarterly* 15 (1953): 438-459.

Barrett, Charles Kingsely. *A Commentary on the Epistle to the Romans.* Black's New Testament Commentaries. Edited by Henry Chadwick. London: Adam and Charles Black, 1962.

Barth, Karl. *The Epistle to the Romans.* Translated from the Sixth Edition by Edwyn C. Hoskyns. New York: Oxford University Press, 1933.

Baur, Ferdinand C. *Paul the Apostle of Jesus Christ.* Translated by E. Zeller. 3 vols. London: Williams and Norgate, 1873.

Bear, James E. "The Epistle to the Romans." *Interpretation* 9 (1955):53-70.

Beker, Johan Christiaan. *Paul the Apostle: The Triumph of God in Life and Thought.* Philadelphia: Fortress Press, 1980.

_____. "Paul the Theologian: Major Motifs in Pauline Theology." *Interpretation* 43 (1989):352-65.

_____. "Paul's Theology: Consistent or Inconsistent." *New Testament Studies* 34 (1988):364-77.

Beld, A. van den. "Romans 7:14-25 and the Problem of 'Akrasia'." *Religious Studies* 21 (1985):495-515. Dutch in *Bildragen* 46 (1985):39-58.

Bengel, Johann Albert. *Gnomon Novi Testamenti.* 3rd ed. Tubingae: Sumtibus Ludov. Frid. Fues., 1855.

Bergmeier, Roland. "Röm 7:7-25a (8:2) der Mensch - das Gesetz - Gott - Paulus—die Exegese im Widerspruch?" *Kerygma und Dogma* 31 (1985):162-172.

Best, Ernest. "Dead in Trespasses and Sins (Eph. 2:1)." *Journal for the Study of the New Testament* 13 (1981):9-25.

_____. *The Letter of Paul to the Romans.* The Cambridge Bible Commentary. Cambridge: At the University Press, 1967.

Black, C. Clifton. "Pauline Perspectives on Death in Romans 5-8." *Journal of Biblical Literature* 103 (1984):413-433.

Black, Matthew. *Commentary on Romans*. New Century Bible. London: Oliphants Publishing, 1973.

Borchert, Gerald L. "Romans, Pastoral Counseling, and the Introspective Conscience of the West." *Review and Expositor* 83 (1986):81-92.

Bornkamm, Günther. "Baptism and New Life in Paul: Romans 6." Chap. in *Early Christian Experience*, The New Testament Library. Translated by Paul L. Hammer. London: SCM Press, 1969.

_____. "Faith and Reason in Paul's Epistles." *New Testament Studies* 4 (1957-58):93-100.

_____. *Paul: Paulus*. Translated by M. G. Stalker. New York: Harper and Row, 1971.

_____. "Sin, Law and Death: An Exegetical Study of Romans 7." Chap. in *Early Christian Experience*, The New Testament Library. Translated by Paul L. Hammer. London: SCM Press, 1969.

Bottorff, J. F. "The Relation of Justification and Ethics in the Pauline Epistles." *Scottish Journal of Theology* 26 (1973):421-30.

Branick, Vincent. "The Sinful Flesh of the Son of God (Rom. 8:3): A Key Image of Pauline Theology." *Catholic Biblical Quarterly* 47 (1985):246-262.

Braun, Herbert. "Römer 7:7-25 und das Selbstverständnis des Qumran-Frommen." *Zeitschrift für Theologische und Kirche* 56 (1959):1-18.

Brighton, Louis. Lecture Notes, "Romans." Course No. EN-420, Exegetical Department, Concordia Seminary, St. Louis, MO. Fall, 1989.

Bruce, Frederick F. *The Letter of Paul to the Romans: An Introduction and Commentary*. Revised Edition. The Tyndale New Testament Commentaries, vol. 6. Grand Rapids: Eerdmans Publishing, 1963.

_____. "Paul and the Law of Moses." *The John Rylands University Library Bulletin* 57 (1974-75):259-79.

_____. *Paul, Apostle of the Heart Set Free*. Grand Rapids: Eerdmans Publishing, 1977.

Bruce, Frederick F. "The Romans Debate - Continued." *Bulletin of the John Rylands University Library* 64 (1982):334-356.

Brunner, Emil. *The Letter to the Romans: A Commentary*. Translated by H. A. Kennedy. Philadelphia: The Westminster Press, 1959.

Buck, Charles Henry and Greer Taylor. *Saint Paul: A Study of the Development of His Thought*. New York: Charles Scribner's Sons, 1969.

Bultmann, Rudolf. "Glossen im Römerbrief." *Theologische Literaturzeitung* 72 (1947):cols. 197-99.

_____. "The Problem of Ethics in the Writings of Paul." Chap. in *The Old and New Man in the Letters of Paul*. Translated by Keith R. Crim. Richmond, VA: John Knox Press, 1967.

_____. "Romans 7 and Paul's Anthropology." Chap. in *The Old and New Man in the Letters of Paul*. Translated by Keith R. Crim. Richmond, VA: John Knox Press, 1967.

Byrne, Brendan. "Living Out the Righteousness of God: The Contribution of Rom 6:1-8:13 to an Understanding of Paul's Ethical Presuppositions." *Catholic Biblical Quarterly* 43 (1981):557-581.

Byskov, Martha. "Simul Iustus et Peccator: A Note on Romans 7:25b in Honour of Professor Ragnar Bring, On His Eightieth Birthday, 10 July 1975." *Studia Theologica* 30 (1976):75-87.

Calvin, John. *Commentary upon the Epistle of Saint Paul to the Romans*. Translated by Christopher Rosdell. Edited by Henry Beveridge. Edinburgh: The Calvin Translation Society, 1844.

Campbell, William S. "The Romans Debate." *Journal for the Study of the New Testament* 10 (1981):19-28.

Cerfaux, Lucien. *The Christian in the Theology of St. Paul*. Translated by Lilian Soiron. New York: Herder and Herder, 1967.

Chrysostom, John "Ἑρμήεία τῆς πρὸς Ῥωμαίους ἐπιστόλης." In *Patrologiae: Patrum Graecorum*, ed. J. P. Migne, vol. 60, cols. 391-682. Paris: 1862.

Clark, Gordon H. "Romans." In *The Biblical Expositor: The Living Theme of the Great Book*, ed. Carl F. H. Henry, vol. 3, 237-57. Philadelphia: A. J. Holman, 1960.

Conzelmann, Hans. *An Outline of the Theology of the New Testament*. The New Testament Library. Translated by John Bowden. London: SCM Press, 1969.

Cramer, J. A. *Catenae Graecorum Patrum in Novum Testamentum.*
  Volume 4, *Catena in Sancti Pauli Epistolam ad Romanos.* Oxonii:
  E. Typographeo Academico, 1844.
Cranfield, C. E. B. *A Critical and Exegetical Commentary on the
  Epistle to the Romans.* Two Volumes. The International Critical
  Commentary, volume 32. Sixth Edition (Entirely Rewritten).
  Edinburgh: T. & T. Clark, 1975, 1979.
_____. "St. Paul and the Law." *Scottish Journal of Theol-ogy* 17
  (1964):43-68.
Dahl, Nils. "The Doctrine of Justification: Its Social Function and
  Implications." Chapter in *Studies in Paul: Theology for the Early
  Christian Mission.* Minneapolis: Augsburg Publishing, 1977.
_____. *Studies in Paul: Theology for the Early Christian Mission.*
  Assisted by Paul Donahue. Minneapolis: Augsburg Publishing
  House, 1977.
_____. "Two Notes on Romans 5." *Studia Theologica* 5 (1951):37-
  48.
Davies, Donald M. "Free from the Law." *Interpretation* 7
  (1953):156-162.
Davies, William D. *Paul and Rabbinic Judaism: Some Rabbinic
  Elements in Pauline Theology.* 4th edition. Philadelphia: Fortress
  Press, 1980.
Deissmann, Adolf. *St. Paul: A Study in Social and Religious History.*
  Translated by Lionel R. M. Strachan. New York: Hodder and
  Stoughton, 1922.
Denney, James. "St. Paul's Epistle to the Romans." In *The Expositor's
  Greek New Testament*, ed. W. Robertson Nicoll, vol. 2, 555-725.
  Grand Rapids: Eerdmans Publishing, 1897.
Dennison, William D. "The Indicative and Imperative: The Basic
  Structure of Pauline Ethics." *Calvin Theological Journal* 14
  (1979):55-78
Derrett, J. Duncan. "Romans vii. 1-4: The Relationship with the
  Resurrected Christ." Chap. in *Law in the New Testament.* London:
  Darton, Longman & Todd, 1970.
Deuser, Hermann. "Glaubenserfahrung und Anthropologie: Röm 7:14-
  25 und Luthers Theses - 'totum genus humanum carnem esse'."
  Evangelische Theologie 39 (1979):409-431.

Dibelius, Martin, and Werner Georg Kümmel. *Paul*. Philadelphia: Westminster Press, 1953.

Dockery, David S. "Romans 7:14-25: Pauline Tension in the Christian Life." *Grace Theological Journal* 2 (1980): 239-257.

Dodd, C. H. *The Epistle of Paul to the Romans*. The Moffatt New Testament Commentary. London: Fontana Books, 1959.

Donfried, Karl P. *The Romans Debate*. Revised and Expanded Edition. Peabody, MA: Hendrickson Publishers, 1991.

Drane, John. *Paul: An Illustrated Documentary*. New York: Harper and Row, 1976.

Dunn, James D. G. "The New Perspective on Paul." *The John Rylands University Library Bulletin* 65 (1982-83):95-122.

_____. "Rom. 7,14-25 in the Theology of Paul." *Theologische Zeitschrift* 31 (1975):257-273.

_____. *Romans 1-8*. Word Biblical Commentary, vol. 38a. Edited by Ralph Martin, David Hubbard, and Glenn Barker. Dallas: Word Books, 1988.

Ellis, E. Earle. *Paul and His Recent Interpreters*. Grand Rapids: Eerdmans Publishing, 1961.

Ellwein, Eduard. "Das Rätsel vom Römer VII." *Kerygma und Dogma* 1 (1955):247-268.

Engel, M. R. *Der Kampf um Römer, Kapitel 7: Eine historisch-exegetische Studie*. Gotha: Verlagsbureau, 1902.

Espy, John M. "Paul's 'Robust Conscience' Re-Examined." *New Testament Studies* 31 (1985):161-188.

Farrar, F. W. *Life and Work of St. Paul*. New York: E. P. Dutton, 1889.

Fatum, Lone. "Die Menschliche Schwäche im Römerbrief." *Studia Theologica* 29 (1975):31-52.

Findlay, George G. *The Epistles of the Apostle Paul: A Sketch of Their Origin and Contents*. London: C. H. Kelly, n.d.

Franzmann, Martin H. *Concordia Commentary: Romans*. St. Louis: Concordia Publishing House, 1968.

Fraser, James. *The Scripture Doctrine of Sanctification: Being a Critical Explication and Paraphrase of Romans VI. VII. & VIII. 1-4*. Edinburgh: R. Ogle, 1830.

Friedrich, G. "Das Gesetz des Glaubens Röm. 3, 27." *Theologische Zeitschrift* 10 (1954):401-17.

Fung, Ronald Y. K. "The Impotence of the Laws: Toward a Fresh Understanding of Romans 7:14-25." In *Scripture, Tradition and Interpretation: Essays Presented to Everett F.Harrison*, eds. W. Ward Gasque and William S. LaSor, 34-48. Grand Rapids: Eerdmans Publishing, 1978.

Furnish, Victor Paul. *The Moral Teaching of Paul: Selected Issues*. 2nd ed. Nashville: Abingdon Press, 1985.

_____. *Theology and Ethics in Paul*. Nashville: Abingdon Press, 1968.

Gager, John. "Some Notes on Paul's Conversion." *New Testament Studies* 27 (1981):697-704.

Garvie, Alfred E. *Romans*. The Century Bible, vol. 27. London: The Caxton Publishing Company. n.d.

Gaugler, Ernst. *Der Brief an die Römer*. 2 vols. Die Prophezei Schweizerisches Bibelwerk für die Gemeinde. Zürich: Zwingli-Verlag, 1945.

Goguel, Maurice. *The Birth of Christianity*. Translated by H. C. Snape. New York: Macmillan, 1954.

Goodspeed, Edgar J. *Paul*. Philadelphia: The John C. Winston Co., 1947.

Grafe, Eduard. *Die paulinische Lehre vom Gesetz nach der vier Hauptbriefen*. Tübingen: J. C. B. Mohr, 1884.

Grant, Michael. *Saint Paul*. London: Weidenfeld and Nicolson, 1976.

Gundry, Robert H. "The Moral Frustration of Paul Before His Conversion: Sexual Lust in Romans 7:7-25." In *Pauline Studies: Essays Presented to Professor F. F. Bruce on his 70th Birthday*, eds. Donald A. Hagner and Murray J. Harris, 228-245. Exeter, England: The Paternoster Press, 1980.

Guthrie, Donald. *Galatians*. The New Century Bible. London: Oliphants Publishing, 1969.

Hall, Jerome. "Paul, the Lawyer, on Law." *The Journal of Law and Religion* 3 (1985):331-379.

Harrisville, Roy A. "Is the Coexistence of the Old and New Man Biblical?" *Lutheran Quarterly* 8 (1956):20-32.

Hodge, Charles. *Commentary on the Epistle to the Romans*. New Revised Edition. New York: A. C. Armstrong and Son, 1906.

Hommel, Hildebrecht. "Das 7. Kapitel des Römerbriefs im Licht Antiker Überlieferung." *Theologia Viatorum* 8 (1961-62):90-116.

Howard, George. *Paul: Crisis in Galatia.* Society for New Testament Studies Monograph Series, 35. New York: Cambridge University Press, 1979.

Hübner, Hans. *Law in Paul's Thought.* Translated by James C. G. Greig. Studies of the New Testament and Its World. Edited by John Riches. Edinburgh: T. & T. Clark, 1984.

Jonas, Hans. "Philosophical Meditation on the Seventh Chapter of Paul's Epistle to the Romans." In *The Future of Our Religious Past: Essays in Honour of Rudolf Bultmann,* ed. James M. Robinson, trs. Charles E. Carlston and Robert P. Scharlemann, 333-350. New York: Harper & Row, 1971.

Joest, Wilfried. "Paulus und das lutheresche 'simul justus et peccator'." *Kerygma und Dogma* 1 (1955):269-320.

Kalberg, Mark W. "Israel's History Personified: Romans 7:7-13 in Relation to Paul's Teaching on the 'Old Man'." *Trinity Journal* 7 (1986):65-74.

Käsemann, Ernst. *Commentary on Romans.* Translated and Edited by Geoffrey W. Bromiley. Grand Rapids: Eerdmans Publishing, 1980.

Keck, Leander. "Images of Paul in the New Testament." *Interpretation* 43 (1989):343-51.

Kertelge, Karl. *Der Brief an die Römer.* Geistliche Schriftlesung, vol. 6. In Cooperation with Karl Hermann Schelkle and Heinz Schürmann. Edited by Wolfgang Trilling. Düsseldorf: Patmos-Verlag, 1971.

Kertelge, Karl. "Exegetische Überlegungen zum Verständnis der paulinische Anthropologie nach Römer 7." *Zeitschrift für die neutestamentliche Wissenschaft* 62 (1971):105-114.

Keuck, Werner. "Dienst des Geistes und des Fleisches: Zur Auslegungsgeschichte und Auslegung von Rm 7,25b." *Theologische Quartalschrift* 141 (1961):257-80.

Kim, Seyoon. *The Origin of Paul's Gospel.* Wissenschaftliche Untersuchungen zum Neuen Testament 2, Reihe 4. Tübingen: J. C. B. Mohr, 1981.

Knox, John, and Gerald R. Craig, "Romans: Introduction, Exegesis and Exposition." In *The Interpreter's Bible,* gen. ed. George A. Buttrick, vol. 9, 353-668. Nashville: Cokesbury Press, 1954.

Kohlbrügge, Hermann Friedrich. *Das siebte Kapitel des Römer briefes: In ausführlicher Umschreibung.* With an introduction by Prof. D. Alfred de Quervain. Biblische Studien, no. 28. Neukirchener Verlag, 1960.

Kraeling, Emil G. *I Have Kept the Faith: The Life of the Apostle Paul.* Chicago: Rand McNally, 1965.

Kümmel, Werner Georg. *Das Bild des Menschen.* Zürich: Zwingli Verlag, 1948; reprinted in *Römer 7 und das Bild des Menschen im Neuen Testament: Zwei Studien.* Theologische Bücherei. Neues Testament Band 53. Munich: Christian Kaiser Verlag, 1974.

_____. "'Individualgeschichte' und 'Weltgeschichte' im Gal. 2,15-21." In *Christ and Spirit in the New Testament: Studies in Honour of C. F. D. Moule,* ed. Barnabas Lindars and Stephen S. Smalley, 157-73. Cambridge: At the University Press, 1973.

_____. *Römer 7 und die Bekehrung des Paulus.* Leipzig: Hinrichs, 1929; reprinted in *Römer 7 und das Bild des Menschen im Neuen Testament: Zwei Studien.* Theologische Bücherei. Neues Testament Band 53. Munich: Christian Kaiser Verlag, 1974.

Kuss, Otto. *Der Römerbrief.* 3 vols. Regensburg: Verlag Friedrich Pustet, 1963.

Laato, Timo. *Paul and Judaism: An Anthropological Approach.* Atlanta: Scholars Press, 1995.

Lambrecht, Jan. "The Line of Thought in Gal. 2:14b-21." *New Testament Studies* 24 (1977):484-95.

_____. *The Wretched "I" and Its Liberation: Paul in Romans 7 and 8.* Louvain Theological & Pastoral Monographs, 14. Grand Rapids: Eerdmans Publishing, 1992.

Leenhardt, Franz J. *The Epistle to the Romans: A Commentary.* Translated by Harold Knight. London: Lutterworth Press, 1961.

Lenski, Richard C. H. *The Interpretation of St. Paul's Epistle to the Romans.* Commentaries on the New Testament. Minneapolis: Augsburg Publishing House, 1961.

Little, Joyce A. "Paul's Use of Analogy: A Structural Analysis of Romans 7:1-6." *Catholic Biblical Quarterly* 46 (1984): 82-90.

Lloyd-Jones, David Martyn. *Romans: An Exposition of Chapters 7.1-8.4.* Grand Rapids: Zondervan Publishing House, 1973.

Lohfink, Gerhard. *The Conversion of St. Paul.* Translated and edited by Bruce Malina. Herald Scriptural Library. Chicago: Franciscan Herald Press, 1976.

Lohse, Eduard. "ὁ νόμος τοῦ πνεύματος τῆς ζωῆς: Exegetische Anmerkungen zu Röm 8,2." In *Neues Testament und christliche Existenz*, Festschrift für Herbert Braun, eds. H. Betz and L. Schottroff, 279-87. Tübingen: J. C. B. Mohr, 1973.

Longenecker, Paul. "On the Concept of Development in Pauline Thought." In *Perspectives on Evangelical Theology: Papers from the Thirtieth Annual Meeting of the Evangelical Theological Society*, eds. K. Kantzer and S. Gundry, 195-207. Grand Rapids: Baker Book House, 1979.

_____. *Paul: Apostle of Liberty.* New York: Harper and Row, 1964.

Lundgren, Sten. "Ananias and the Calling of Paul in Acts." *Studia Theologica* 25 (1971):117-22.

Luther, Martin. "Der Brief an die Römer" (1515-16). *D. Martin Luthers Werke.* Weimar Ausgabe. Band 56. Edited by F. Ficker. Weimar: Hermann Böhlhaus Nachfolger, 1838.

_____. "Lectures on Galatians" (1535). *Luther's Works.* American Edition. Volumes 26-27. Translated by Jaroslav Pelikan. St. Louis: Concordia Publishing House, 1964.

_____. "Lectures on Romans: Glosses and Scholia" (1515-16). *Luther's Works.* American Edition. Volume 25. Edited by Hilton C. Oswald. Translated by Walter G. Tillmanns and Jacob A. O. Preus. St. Louis: Concordia Publishing House, 1972.

_____. "Prefaces to the New Testament" (1546). *Luther's Works.* American Edition. Volume 35. *Word and Sacrament I.* Translated by Charles M. Jacobs. Revised and edited by E. Theodore Bachmann. Philadelphia: Muhlenberg Press, 1960.

Lyonnet, Stanislas. *Les étapes du mystère du Salut selon l'épître aux Romains.* Bibliothèque Oecuménique, 8. Paris: Les Éditions du Cerf, 1969.

_____. "L'historie du Salut selon le chapitre VII de l'epître aux Romains." *Revue Biblica* 43 (1962):117-51.

_____. "'Tu ne convoiteras pas' (Rom 7:7)." In *Neotestamentica et Patristica*, Novum Testamentum Supplements, vol. 6, 157-65. Leiden: E. J. Brill, 1962.

Maillot, Alphonse. "Notule sur Romains 7:7-8ss." *Foi Vie* 84 (1985):17-23.

Manson, T. W. "Romans." In *Peake's Commentary on the Bible*, eds. Matthew Black and Harold H. Rowley, 940-53. New York: Thomas Nelson and Sons, 1963.

Martin, Brice L. "Some Reflections on the Identity of *ego* in Rom. 7:14-25." *Scottish Journal of Theology* 34 (1981): 39-47.

Maultsby, Hubert. "Paul and the American Nomos: An Exegetical Study of Romans 7 and A Hermeneutic for Biblical Theology [Diss Abst]." *The Drew Gateway* 46 (1975-76):108-9.

McCant, Jerry. "A Wesleyan Interpretation of Romans 5-8." *Wesleyan Theological Journal* 16 (1981):68-84.

McNeile, Alan H. *St. Paul: His Life, Letters and Christian Doctrine.* Cambridge: At the University Press, 1920.

Michel, Otto. *Der Brief an die Römer.* Kritischer-exegetischer Kommentar über das Neue Testament. 13th ed. Göttingen: Vandenhoeck and Ruprecht, 1966.

Milne, Douglas J. W. "Romans 7:7-12, Paul's Pre-conversion Experience." *The Reformed Theological Review* 43 (1984):9-17.

Mitton, Charles Leslie. "Romans 7 Reconsidered." *Expository Times* 65 (1953-54):78-81,99-103,132-35.

Moe, Olaf Eduard. *The Apostle Paul.* 2 vols. Translated by L. A. Vigness. Minneapolis: Augsburg Publishing House, 1954.

Moo, Douglas J. "Israel and Paul in Romans 7.7-12." *New Testament Studies* 32 (1986):122-135.

Morris, Leon. *The Apostolic Preaching of the Cross.* London: Tyndale Press, 1955; reprint ed., Grand Rapids: Eerdmans Publishing, 1956.

_____. *The Epistle to the Romans.* Grand Rapids: Eerdmans Publishing, 1988.

_____. "The Meaning of ἱλαστήριον in Romans 3.25." *New Testament Studies* 2 (1955-56):33-43.

_____. "The Theme of Romans." In *Apostolic History and the Gospel*, eds. W. Ward Gasque and Ralph P. Martin, 249-63. Grand Rapids: Eerdmans Publishing, 1970.

Müller, F. "Zwei Marinalien im Brief des Paulus an die Römer." *Zeitschrift für die neutestamentliche Wissenschaft* 40 (1941):249-54.

Mullins, Terence. "Paul's Thorn in the Flesh." *Journal of Biblical Literature* 76 (1957):299-303.

Murray, John. *The Epistle to the Romans: The English Text with Introduction, Exposition and Notes.* 2 vols. Grand Rapids: Eerdmans Publishing, 1959,1965.

Nelson, William R. "Pauline Anthropology: Its Relation to Christ and His Church." *Interpretation* 14 (1960):14-27.

Newman, Barclay M. "Once Again - The Question of 'I' in Romans 7:7-25." *The Bible Translator* 34 (1983):124-135.

Newman, Barclay M. and Eugene A Nida. *A Translator's Handbook on Paul's Letter to the Romans.* Helps for Translators, vol. 14. London: United Bible Societies, 1973.

Nickle, Keith F. "Romans 7:7-25." *Interpretation* 33 (1979): 181-87

Nygren, Anders. *Commentary on Romans.* Translated by Carl C. Rasmussen. Philadelphia: Muhlenberg Press, 1949.
_____. "Objektives und Persönliches im Römerbrief."
Theologische Literaturzeitung 77 (1952):cols. 591-96.

O'Neill, J. C. *Paul's Letter to the Romans.* Pelican Books. Baltimore, MD: Penguin Books, 1975.

Origen. "Commentaria in epistolam b. Pauli ad Romanos." Latin translation by Rufinius. In *Patrologiae: Patrum Graecorum*, ed. J. P. Migne. vol. 14, cols. 837-1292. Paris: 1862.

Osten-Sacken, Peter von der. *Römer 8 als Beispiel paulinischer Soteriologie.* Forschungen zur Religion und Literatur des Alten und Neuen Testaments, no. 112. Göttingen: Vandenhoeck & Ruprecht, 1975.

Packer, J. I. "The 'Wretched Man' of Romans 7." In *Studia Evangelica*, ed. F. L. Cross, vol. 2, 621-27. Berlin: Akademie-Verlag, 1964.

Pate, C. Marvin. *The End of the Age Has Come: The Theology of Paul.* Grand Rapids: Zondervan Publishing, 1995.

Pelagius. "Expositiones XIII Epistularum Pauli." In *Patrologiae Latinae Supplementum*, ed. Adelberto Hamman, vol. 1, cols. 1110-374. Paris: Éditions Garnier Frères, 1958.

Philonenko, Marc. "Sur l'expression `vendu au péché' dans l'Épître aux Romains." *Revue de l'Histoire des Religions* 203 (1986):41-52.

Räisänen, Heikki. "Das 'Gesetz des Glaubens' (Röm 3:27) und das 'Gesetz des Geistes' (Röm 8:2)." *New Testament Studies* 26 (1979):101-117.

_____. *Paul and the Law*. Wissenschaftliche Untersuchungen zum Neuen Testament, no. 29. Tübingen: J. C. B. Mohr, 1983.

_____. "Paul's Conversion and the Development of His View of the Law." *New Testament Studies* 33 (1987): 404-19.

Ramsay, William M. *St. Paul: The Traveller and the Roman Citizen*. 3rd edition. London: Hodder and Stoughton, 1897; reprint Grand Rapids: Baker Book House, 1962.

Reicke, Bo. "Paulus über das Gesetz." *Theologische Zeitschrift* 41 (1985):237-57.

Ricciotti, Guiseppe. *Paul: The Apostle*. Translated by Alba I.Zizzamia. Milwaukee: Bruce Publishing, 1953.

Ridderbos, Hermann. *Paul: An Outline of His Theology*. Translated by John Richard De Witt. Grand Rapids: Eerdmans Publishing, 1975.

Riddle, Donald W. *Paul: Man of Conflict*. Nashville: Cokesbury Press, 1940.

Robinson, D. W. B. "St. Paul's `Spiritual Man.'" *The Reformed Theological Review* 36 (1977):78-83.

Robinson, John A. T. *The Body: A Study in Pauline Theology*. London: SCM Press, 1952; reprint, Bristol, IN: Wyndam Hall Press, The Graduate Theological Foundation, 1988.

_____. *Wrestling with Romans*. Philadelphia: The Westminster Press, 1979.

Sanday, William and Headlam, Arthur C. *A Critical and Exegetical Commentary on the Epistle to the Romans*. The International Critical Commentary. Volume 32. New York: Charles Scribner's Sons, 1902.

Sanders, Ephraim Paul. *Paul and Palestinian Judaism: A Comparison of Patterns of Religion*. Philadelphia: Fortress Press, 1977.

_____. *Paul, the Law, and the Jewish People*. Philadelphia: Fortress Press, 1983.

Schenk, Wolfgang. *Die Philipperbriefe des Paulus*. Stuttgart: Verlag W. Kohlhammer, 1984.

Schnackenburg, Rudolf. "Römer 7 im Zusammengang des Römer-briefes." In *Jesus und Paulus: Festschrift für Werner Georg Kümmel zum 70. Geburtstag*, eds. E. Earle Ellis and Erich Gräßer, 283-300. Göttingen: Vandenhoeck & Ruprecht, 1975.

Schoeps, Hans. *Paul: The Theology of the Apostle in the Light of Jewish Religious History*. Translated by Harold Knight. Philadelphia: Westminster Press, 1961.

Schottroff, Luise. "Die Schreckensherrschaft der Sünde und die Befreiung durch Christus nach dem Römerbrief des Paulus." *Evangelische Theologie* 39 (1979):497-510.

Schreiner, Thomas. *The Law and Its Fulfillment: A Pauline Theology of Law*. Grand Rapids: Baker Book House, 1993.

Schweitzer, Albert. *The Mysticism of Paul the Apostle*. A Crossroad Book. Translated by W. Montgomery. New York: Seabury Press, 1968.

_____. *Paul and His Interpreters*. Translated by W. Montgomery. London: Adam & Charles Black, 1912.

Segal, Alan F. "Romans 7 and Jewish Dietary Law." *Studies in Religion* 15 (1986):361-374.

Selby, Donald Joseph. *Toward the Understanding of St. Paul*. Englewood Cliffs, NY: Prentice-Hall, 1962.

Smith, Edgar. "The Form and Religious Background of Romans VII 24-25a." *Novum Testamentum* 13 (1971):127-35.

Smith, Neil. "Thorn that Stayed: An Exposition of 2 Corinthians 12:7-9." *Interpretation* 13 (1959):409-16.

Smyth, Bernard T. *Paul: Mystic and Missionary*. Maryknoll, NY: Orbis Books, 1980.

Snodgrass, Klyne. "Justification by Grace - to the Doers." *New Testament Studies* 32 (1986):72-93.

Stanley, D. M. "'Become Imitators of Me': The Pauline Conception of Apostolic Tradition." *Biblica* 40 (1959):859-77.

Stendahl, Krister. "The Apostle Paul and the Introspective Conscience of the West." *Harvard Theological Review* 56 (1963):199-215; reprinted in *Paul Among Jews and Gentiles and Other Essays*, 78-96. Philadelphia: Fortress Press, 1976.

Stewart, James S. *A Man in Christ: The Vital Elements of St. Paul's Theology*. New York: Harper and Brothers, n.d.

Stoeckhardt, Georg. "The Epistle to the Romans: A Translation of Stoeckhardt's Romerbrief." 2 vols. (Unpublished translation by Erwin W. Koehlinger). Concordia Mimeograph Company, Concordia Seminary, St. Louis, MO, 1943.

Stowers, Stanley Kent. *The Diatribe and Paul's Letter to the Romans.* Society of Biblical Literature Dissertation Series, no. 57. Chico, CA: Scholars Press, 1981.

Strelan, John G. "A Note on the Old Testament Background of Romans 7:7." *Lutheran Journal of Theology* 15 (1981): 23-25.

Theissen, Gerd. *Psychological Aspects of Pauline Theology.* Translated by John P. Galvin. Philadelphia: Fortress Press, 1987.

Theodore of Mopsuestia. "Epistolam ad Romanos" (fragments). In *Patrologiae: Patrum Graecorum*, ed. J. P. Migne. vol. 66, cols. 787-876. Paris: 1864.

Theodoret, "Ἑρμηνεία τῆς πρὸς Ῥωμαίους ἐπιστόλης." In *Patrologiae: Patrum Graecorum*, ed. J. P. Migne, vol. 82, cols. 43-226. Paris: 1864.

Trocme, Etienne. "From 'I' to 'We': Christian Life According to Romans, Chapters 7 and 8." Translated by M. Benedict. *Australian Biblical Review* 35 (1987):73-76.

Vos, Geerhardus. "The Eschatological Aspect of the Pauline Conception of the Spirit." In *Biblical and Theological Studies by Members of the Faculty of Princeton Theological Seminary*, 209-59. New York: Charles Scribner's Sons, 1912.

_____. *The Pauline Eschatology.* Grand Rapids: Eerdmans Publishing, 1961.

Weber, Reinhard. "Die Geschichte des Gesetzes und des Ich in Römer 7:7-8:4." *Neue Zeitschrift fur systematische Theologie und Religionsphilosophie* 29 (1987):147-179.

Wedderburn, A. J. M. "Paul and the Law." *Scottish Journal of Theology* 38 (1985):615-22.

Weder, Hans. "Gesetz und Sünde Gedanken zu einem qualitativen Sprung im Denken des Paulus." *New Testament Studies* 31 (1985):357-76.

Weinel, Heinrich. *St. Paul: The Man and His Work.* Theological Translation Library. Translated by G. A. Bienemann. Edited by W. D. Morrison. New York: G. P. Putnam's Sons, 1906.

Weiss, Johannes. *The History of Primitive Christianity*. 3 vols.
Completed by Rudolf Knopf. Translated and edited by Frederick
C. Grant. New York: Wilson-Erickson, 1937.

Wenham, David. "The Christian Life: A Life of Tension?" In *Pauline
Studies: Essays Presented to Professor F. F. Bruce on his 70th
Birthday*, eds. Donald A. Hagner and Murray J. Harris, 228-245.
Exeter, England: The Paternoster Press, 1980.

Westerholm, Stephen. *Israel's Law and the Church's Faith: Paul and
His Recent Interpreters*. Grand Rapids: Eerdmans Publishing,
1988.

Wilckens, Ulrich. *Der Brief an die Römer*. 3 vols. Evangelisch-
Katholischer Kommentar, Band 6. Edited by Josef Blank, Rudolf
Schnackenburg, Eduard Schweizer, and Ulrich Wilckens. Zürich:
Benziger Verlag and Neukirchen-Vluyn: Neukirchener Verlag,
1980.

Wrede, William. *Paul*. Translated by Edward Lummis. Lexington,
KY: American Theological Library Association, 1962.

Zeisler, J. A. "The Role of the Tenth Commandment in Romans 7."
Journal for the Study of the New Testament 33 (1988):41-56.

Zeller, Dieter. "Der Zusammenhang von Gesetz und Sünde im
Römerbrief: kritischer Nachvollzug der Auslegung von Ulrich
Wilckens." *Theologische Zeitschrift* 38 (1982):193-212.

Zens, Jon. "Romans 7: Released from the Law." *Search Together* 13
(1984):23ff.

_____. "'When We Were in the Flesh': Should Rom 7:7ff Shape
the Christian's Self Image." *Baptist Reformation Review* 10
(1981):13-21.

Secondary Literature

Ambrose. "De Abraham Libro Duo." In *Patrologiae: Patrum
Latinorum*, ed. J. P. Migne, vol. 14, cols. 437-524. Paris: 1882.

"The Apocalypse of Moses." In *The Apocrypha and Pseudepigrapha
of the Old Testament*, ed. R. H. Charles, tr. L. S. Wells, vol. 2, 138-
54. Oxford: At the Clarendon Press, 1913.

Augustine. "Contra duas Epistolas Pelagianorum." In *Patrologiae:
Patrum Latinorum*, ed. J. P. Migne, vol. 44, cols. 549-640. Paris:
1865.

Augustine. "Contra Julianum Pelagianum." Book 4. In *Patrologiae: Patrum Latinorum*, ed. J. P. Migne, vol. 44, cols. 641-874. Paris: 1865.

_____. "De Diversis Quaestionibus ad Simplicianum I." In *Patrologiae: Patrum Latinorum*, ed. J. P. Migne, vol. 40, cols 101-148. Paris: 1887.

_____. "De Nuptiis et Concupiscentia." Book 2. In *Patrologiae: Patrum Latinorum*, ed. J. P. Migne, vol. 44, cols 415-476. Paris: 1865.

_____. "Retractationum S. Augustini." Books 1 and 2. In *Patrologiae: Patrum Latinorum*, ed. J. P. Migne, vol. 32, cols. 619-634. Paris: 1845.

Bammel, C. P. Hammond. "Philocalia IX, Jerome, Epistle 121, and Origen's Exposition of Romans VII." *Journal of Theological Studies* 32 (1981):50-81.

Barr, James. *The Semantics of Biblical Language*. Oxford: Oxford University Press, 1961.

Bultmann, Rudolf. *Theology of the New Testament*. 2 vols. Translated by Kendrick Grobel. New York: Charles Scribner's Sons, 1951.

Caird, George B. *The Language and Imagery of the Bible*. London: Duckworth, 1980.

Conzelmann, Hans, and Andreas Lindemann. *Interpreting the New Testament: An Introduction to the Principles and Methods of N.T. Exegesis*. Translated by Siegfried S. Schatzmann. Peabody, MA: Hendrickson Publishers, 1988.

Cullmann, Oscar. *Christ and Time*. Revised edition. Philadelphia: Westminster Press, 1968.

_____. *Salvation in History*. Translated by S. Sowers and the Editorial Staff of SCM Press. London: SCM Press, 1967.

Dodd, C. H. *The Parables of the Kingdom of God*. London: Nisbet, 1950.

Epictetus. *Epictetus: The Discourses as Reported by Arrian, the Manual, and Fragments*. With a Translation by W. A. Oldfather. 2 volumes. The Loeb Classical Library. Edited by T. E. Page, E. Capps, and W. H. D. Rouse. New York: G. P. Putnam's Sons, 1925.

"The Fourth Book of Ezra: A New Translation and Introduction." In *The Old Testament Pseudepigrapha*, ed. James H. Charlesworth, tr. Bruce M. Metzger, vol. 2, 517-59. Garden City, NY: Doubleday and Company, 1983, 1985.

Frege, Gottlob. *Translations from the Philosophical Writings of Gottlob Frege*. Edited and Translated by Peter Geach and Max Black. Oxford: Basil Blackwell, 1952.

Hummel, Horace. *The Word Becoming Flesh: An Introduction to the Origin, Purpose and Meaning of the Old Testament*. St. Louis: Concordia Publishing House, 1979.

Josephus, Flavius. *The Works of Josephus*. Translated by William Whitson, Revised edition. Peabody, MA: Hendrickson Publishers, 1987.

Kümmel, Werner Georg. *Introduction to the New Testament*. Founded by Paul Feine and Johannes Behm. 14th Revised Edition. Completely Reedited. Translated by A. J. Mattill. New York: Abingdon Press, 1966.

Methodius. "Ex libro de resurrectione." In *Patrologiae: Patrum Graecorum*, ed. J. P. Migne, vol. 18, cols. 265-328. Paris: 1857.

Moore, George Foote. *Judaism in the First Centuries of the Christian Era: The Age of the Tannaim*. 2 vols. Schocken Paperbacks on Jewish Life and Religion. New York: Schocken Books, 1971.

Neophyti 1: Targum Palestinense Ms de la Biblioteca Vaticana. Volume 1: Genesis. Translated (Spanish) and Edited by Alejandro Diez Macho. English Translation by Martin McNamara and Michael Maher. Madrid: Cansejo Superior de Investigaciones Cientificas, 1968.

Ovid. *Ovid: Heroides and Amores*. With a Translation by G. Showerman. The Loeb Classical Library. Edited by T. E. Page, E. Capps, and W. H. D. Rouse. New York: G. P. Putnam's Sons, 1931.

_____. *Ovid: Metamorphoses*. With a Translation by Frank Justus Miller. 2 volumes. The Loeb Classical Library. Edited by T. E. Page, E. Capps, and W. H. D. Rouse. New York: G. P. Putnam's Sons, 1933.

Philo, Judaeus. *Philo*. 10 Volumes with 2 Supplements. With a translation by Francis Henry Colson and George Herbert Whitaker. The Loeb Classical Library. Cambridge, MA: Harvard University Press, 1929-1953.

"Psalms of Solomon: A New Translation and Introduction." In *The Old Testament Pseudepigrapha*, ed. James H. Charlesworth, tr. R. B. Wright, vol. 2, 639-70. Garden City, NY: Doubleday and Company, 1983,1985.

Scharlemann, Martin. "Exodus Ethics." *Concordia Journal* 2 (1976):165-70.

Thiselton, Anthony C. "Semantics and New Testament Interpretation." In *New Testament Interpretation: Essays on Principles and Methods*, ed. by I. Howard Marshall, 75-104. Grand Rapids: Eerdmans Publishing, 1977.

Urbach, Ephraim. *The Sages*. 2 vols. Jerusalem: Magnes Press, 1979.

Vanhoozer, Kevin J. "The Semantics of Biblical Literature: Truth and Scripture's Diverse Literary Forms." In *Hermeneutics, Authority, and Canon*, Academie Books, eds. D. A. Carson and John D. Woodbridge, 49-104. Grand Rapids: Zondervan Publishing House, 1986.

Voelz, James W. "Biblical Hermeneutics: Where Are We Now? Where Are We Going?" In *Light for Our World: Essays Commemorating the 150th Anniversary of Concordia Seminary, St. Louis, Missouri*, ed. John W. Klotz, 235-57. St. Louis: Concordia Seminary, 1989.

_____. "The Language of the New Testament." In *Aufstieg und Niedergang der Römischen Welt*, eds. Hildegard Temporini and Wolfgang Haase, vol. 2, part 25.2, 893-977. New York: Walter De Gruyter, 1984.

_____. "'Some Things Old, Some Things New': A Response to Wolfgang Schenk, *Die Philipperbriefe des Paulus*." *Semeia* 48 (1989):*Reader Perspectives on the New Testament*, 161-69.

_____. *What Does This Mean? Principles of Biblical Interpretation in the Post-Modern World*. St. Louis: Concordia Publishing House, 1995.

Whyte, Alexander. *Bible Characters: New Testament*. Grand Rapids: Zondervan Publishing House, 1952.

Reference Works

The Babylonian Talmud. Translated with notes, glossary, and indices under the editorship of Isidore Epstein. London: Soncino Press, 1934-1948.

Bauer, Walter. *A Greek-English Lexicon of the New Testament and Other Early Christian Literature.* 2nd ed. Translated by William F. Arndt and F. Wilbur Gingrich. Revised and Augmented from Walter Baur's 5th Edition, 1958, by F. W. Gingrich and Frederick Danker. Chicago: The University of Chicago Press, 1979.

Biblia Hebraica Stuttgartensia. Edited by Karl Elliger and Wilhelm Rudolph. Stuttgart: Deutsche Bibelgesellschaft, 1976-77.

Blass, F., and Debrunner, A. *A Greek Grammar of the New Testament.* Translated and Revised by Robert Funk. Chicago: The University of Chicago Press, 1961.

Charles, R. H., ed. *The Apocrypha and Pseudepigrapha of the Old Testament.* 2 vols. Oxford: At the Clarendon Press, 1913.

Charlesworth, James H., ed. *The Old Testament Pseudepigrapha.* 2 vols. Garden City, NY: Doubleday and Company, 1983, 1985.

Concordance to the Novum Testamentum Graece of Nestle-Aland, 26th Edition, and to the Greek New Testament, 3rd Edition. 3rd Edition. Edited by the Institute for New Testament Textual Research and the Computer Center of Münster University with the collaboration of H. Bachmann and W. Slaby. New York: Walter De Gruyter, 1987.

The Dead Sea Scrolls in English. Edited and translated by Geza Vermes. 2nd edition. New York: Viking Penguin, 1975.

Die Gute Nachricht: Das Neue Testament in heutigen Deutsch. Herausgegeben von den Bibelgesellschaften und Bibelwerken im eutschsprachigen Raum. Stuttgart: Deutsche Bibelgesellschaft, 1976.

Hanna, Robert. *A Grammatical Aid to the Greek New Testament.* Grand Rapids: Baker Book House, 1983.

Hill, David. *Greek Words and Hebrew Meanings.* Society for New Testament Studies Monograph Series, no. 35. New York: Cambridge University Press, 1979.

The Holy Bible: New International Version. New York: International Bible Society, 1978.

Metzger, Bruce M. on behalf of and in cooperation with the Editorial Committee of the United Bible Societies' Greek New Testament. *A Textual Commentary on the Greek New Testament.* New York: United Bible Societies, 1971.

Midrash Rabbah. 10 vols. Edited by H. Freedman and Maurice Simon. London: Soncino Press, 1939.

The Mishnah. Edited by Herbert Danby. Oxford: Oxford University Press, 1972.

Moffatt, James. *A New Translation of the Bible Containing the Old and New Testaments.* New York: Harper & Brothers, 1935.

Moule, C. F. D. *An Idiom Book of New Testament Greek.* New York: Cambridge University Press, 1959.

Moulton, J. H. *A Grammar of New Testament Greek.* Volume 1. Edinburgh: T. & T. Clark, 1908.

The New Oxford Annotated Bible With the Apocrypha: Revised Standard Version. Edited by Herbert G. May and Bruce M. Metzger. New York: Oxford University Press, 1973.

Novum Testamentum Graece. Edited by Eberhard Nestle and Kurt Aland. 26th edition. Stuttgart: Deutsche Bibelstiftung, 1979.

Rienecker, Fritz. *A Linguistic Key to the Greek New Testament.* Translated, with additions and revisions, and edited by Cleon L. Rogers. Grand Rapids: Zondervan Publishing House, 1980.

Robertson, A. T. *A Grammar of the Greek New Testament.* Nashville: Broadman Press, 1934.

Septuaginta: Id est Vetus Testamentum graece iuxta LXX interpretes. Edited by Alfred Rahlfs. 2 vols. in 1. Stuttgart: Deutsche Bibelgesellschaft, 1979.

Theological Dictionary of the New Testament. 10 vols. Edited by Gerhard Kittel and Gerhard Friedrich. Translated and edited by Geoffrey Bromiley. Grand Rapids: Eerdmans Publishing, 1973.
    S.v. "ἀγαθος," by Walter Grundmann, 1:10-17.
    S.v. "ἄνθρωπος," by Joachim Jeremias, 1:364-67.
    S.v. "γινώσκω," by Rudolf Bultmann, 1:689-714.
    S.v. "γράμμα," by Gottlob Schrenk, 1:761-69.
    S.v. "δοῦλος," by Karl Rengstorf, 2:261-79.
    S.v. "ἐγώ," by Ethelbert Stauffer, 2:356-62.
    S.v. "ἐντολή," by Gottlob Schrenk, 2:545-56.

S.v. "ἐπιθυμία, ἐπιθυμέω," by Friedrich Büchsel, 3:168-171.

S.v. "ἔσω," by Johannes Behm, 2:698-99.

S.v. "θέλω, θέλημα, θέλησις," by Gottlob Schrenk, 3:44-62.

S.v. "κεῖμαι," by Friedrich Büchsel, 3:654-56.

S.v. "μέλος," by Johannes Horst, 4:555-68.

S.v. "νόμος," by W. Gutbrod, 4:1022-85.

S.v. "νοῦς," by Johannes Behm, 4:951-60.

S.v. "οἰκέω," by Otto Michel, 5:135-36.

S.v. "παράβασις," by Johannes Schneider, 5:739-40.

S.v. "πολλοί," by Joachim Jeremias, 6:536-45.

S.v. "πράσσω," by Christian Mauer, 6:632-644.

S.v. "ῥύομαι," by Wilhelm Kasch, 6:998-1003.

S.v. "σάρξ, σαρκικός, σάρκινος," by Friedrich Baumgärtel,
    Rudolf Mayer, and Eduard Schweizer, 7:98-151.

Strack, Hermann L. and Billerbeck, Paul. *Kommentar zum Neuen
    Testament: Aus Talmud und Midrash*. 6 vols. Munich: C. H. Beck,
    1954.

Trench, Richard C. *Synonyms of the New Testament*. Edited by Robert
    G. Hoerber. Grand Rapids: Baker Book House, 1989.

Turner, Nigel. *A Grammar of New Testament Greek*. Volume 3.
    Edinburgh: T. & T. Clark, 1963.

_____. *Grammatical Insights into the New Testament*. Edinburgh:
    T. & T. Clark, 1965.

Subject Index

Scripture Index